EARTH SCIENCE AND THE NATURAL HERITAGE:

INTERACTIONS AND INTEGRATED MANAGEMENT

The Natural Heritage of Scotland

Each year since it was founded in 1992, Scottish Natural Heritage has organised or jointly organised a conference that has focused attention on a particular aspect of Scotland's natural heritage. The papers read at the conferences, after a process of refereeing and editing, have been brought together as a book. The titles already published in this series are:

1. *The Islands of Scotland: a Living Marine Heritage*
    Edited by J.M. Baxter and M.B. Usher (1994), 286pp.

2. *Heaths and Moorlands: a Cultural Landscape*
    Edited by D.B.A. Thompson, A.J. Hester and M.B. Usher (1995), 400pp.

3. *Soils, Sustainability and the Natural Heritage*
    Edited by A.G. Taylor, J.E. Gordon and M.B. Usher (1996), 316pp.

4. *Freshwater Quality: Defining the Indefinable?*
    Edited by P.J. Boon and D.L. Howell (1997), 552pp.

5. *Biodiversity in Scotland: Status, Trends and Initiatives*
    Edited by L.V. Fleming, A.C. Newton, J.A. Vickery and M.B. Usher (1997), 309pp.

6. *Land Cover Change: Scotland from the 1940s to the 1980s*
    By E.C. Mackey, M.C. Shewry and G.J. Tudor (1998), 263pp.

7. *Scotland's Living Coastline*
    Edited by J.M. Baxter, K. Duncan and S.M. Atkins (1999), 209pp.

8. *Landscape Character: Perspectives on Management and Change*
    Edited by M.B. Usher (1999), 213pp.

This is the ninth book in the series.

Earth Science and the Natural Heritage: Interactions and Integrated Management

First published in 2001 by The Stationery Office Limited
73 Lothian Road, Edinburgh, EH3 9AW

Applications for reproduction should be made in writing to
Scottish Natural Heritage, 12 Hope Terrace, Edinburgh EH9 2AS.

British Library Cataloguing in Publication Data
A catalogue record for this book is available from the British Library

ISBN 0 11 497283 4

Cover photography: Luskentyre and Taransay, Harris. (Photo copyright: P. and A. Macdonald). Background photograph (copyright: L. Gill/SNH).

PREFACE

Since its inception in 1992, Scottish Natural Heritage (SNH) has held a series of annual conferences on key aspects of Scotland's natural heritage. These have focused on: 'The Islands of Scotland: a Living Marine Heritage' (1992), 'Heaths and Moorland: Cultural Landscapes' (1993), 'Soils, Sustainability and the Natural Heritage' (1994), 'Freshwater Quality: Defining the Indefinable?' (1995), 'Biodiversity in Scotland: Status, Trends and Initiatives' (1996), 'Scotland's Living Coastline' (1997) and 'Landscape Character: Perspectives on Management and Change' (1998). Together, the proceedings from these conferences provide a collection of authoritative publications about the natural heritage of Scotland. The 1999 Conference, held appropriately at Our Dynamic Earth in Edinburgh in November of that year, addressed 'Earth Science and the Natural Heritage: Interactions and Integrated Management'. With the proximity of the new millennium, it was particularly timely to focus on the unity of the Earth's geological and biological systems and the need for greater awareness and integration of the Earth sciences in the management of the natural heritage and sustainable use of natural resources. This conference complemented an earlier conference on 'Landscape Sensitivity' held at the University of Stirling in September, 1999, under the auspices of The Royal Society of Edinburgh and in collaboration with The Royal Scottish Geographical Society, Scottish Natural Heritage and the Department of Environmental Science, University of Stirling. The proceedings of the latter conference are published in a special issue of the journal, *Catena* (Thomas and Simpson, 2001).

The need to protect our most important geological and geomorphological sites is widely recognised. However, Earth heritage conservation is about much more than site protection, and the agenda in Scotland has moved forward to involve the wider links between Earth science and the natural heritage. Rocks, landforms and soils are an integral part of our natural heritage. They have formed our distinctive landscapes and scenery. Together they provide the basis for the diversity of our natural habitats and the species they support. The actions of physical processes on our mountains, rivers, coasts and soils produce habitat changes and affect ecological processes. These physical processes also impinge on human activities through flooding, coastal erosion and soil erosion, with attendant economic and social costs. The significance of these wider links is now particularly relevant in view of current interest in sustainable use of natural resources, landscape interpretation, geotourism and integrated management. In particular, more integrated management of Scotland's landscapes and coasts is heavily predicated on a better understanding of physical processes. At another level, there is growing public interest in Earth heritage (e.g. through television programmes, media interest and the establishment of centres such as Our Dynamic Earth), combined with a recognition of the potential role of more holistic interpretation and contributions to tourism and rural development. It was therefore timely to address not only the broader links of the Earth sciences to ecosystems and landscapes, but also the practical value of the Earth sciences in land and water management, resource management, environmental education and geotourism. This conference brought all these issues together under the common focus of sustainable management of our natural heritage.

The principal themes of interactions, sustainable management and raising awareness were all explored in the Conference presentations, workshops, posters and discussions and are reported in the chapters in this book. These clearly demonstrate the importance of geology, geomorphology and soils, not only as a fundamental component of the natural heritage in their own right, but also in the underpinning of habitats and their biodiversity. Part One of the book emphasises this continuum and the role of geology in global change. Part Two highlights the links between Earth science and the natural heritage. It sets out the geological and geomorphological framework of the present landscape and examines crucial links in three sensitive environments – the coast, uplands and rivers. In Part Three, the pressures on the resource and the management responses are examined. These clearly demonstrate the relevance and value of integrated approaches that involve working with, rather than against natural processes, and provide examples of applications. Part Four addresses the importance of raising awareness of our Earth heritage and presents recent successes from Scotland and elsewhere. In Part Five, the main messages from the conference are developed as part of a forward look to the key challenges for the 21st century. Throughout the book, extended abstracts of poster presentations have been included where they relate closely to the main themes.

As with all conferences, a great many people helped both in the organisation and running of the event. We are particularly grateful to Dominic Counsell, Helen Forster, Jim Hansom, George Lees, Ed Mackey, Alan McKirdy, John McManus and Stuart Monro for advising on the programme; to Helen Forster, Jo Newman and Sylvia Conway for dealing most capably and efficiently with the administration; to the speakers for their presentations; to the referees who reviewed the papers in this book; and to Professor Michael B. Usher for his encouragement and guidance throughout. We also acknowledge the assistance of the staff at the Stationery Office in progressing the manuscript to publication.

John Gordon and Katherine Leys

May 2001

Reference

Thomas, M.F. and Simpson, I.A. (eds) 2001. *Landscape Sensitivity: Principles and Applications in Northern Cool Temperate Environments. Catena*, **42**(2-4), 81-383.

CONTENTS

List of Plates
(between pages 238 and 239)

LIST OF CONTRIBUTORS

S. Angus, Scottish Natural Heritage, 27 Ardconnel Terrace, Inverness IV2 3AE

R.V. Birnie, Macaulay Land Use Research Institute, Craigiebuckler, Aberdeen AB15 8QH

P.J. Boon, Scottish Natural Heritage, 2 Anderson Place, Edinburgh EH6 5NP

G.S. Boulton, Department of Geology and Geophysics, University of Edinburgh, Grant Institute, West Mains Road, Edinburgh EH9 3JW

V. Brazier, Scottish Natural Heritage, 2 Anderson Place, Edinburgh EH6 5NP

E.J. Brown, Centre for Quaternary Research, Department of Geography, Royal Holloway, University of London, Egham, Surrey TW20 0EX

J.E. Cavill, British Geological Survey, Murchison House, West Mains Road, Edinburgh EH9 3LA

G.S. Cordiner, Ontario Ministry of Natural Resources, 300 Water Street, Peterborough, Ontario K9J 8M5, Canada

D. Counsell, Scottish Natural Heritage, 12 Hope Terrace, Edinburgh EH9 2AS

M. Cressey, CFA Archaeology Ltd, Suite 2, Archibald Hope House, Eskmills Park, Musselburgh, East Lothian EH21 7PQ

R. Crofts, Scottish Natural Heritage, 12 Hope Terrace, Edinburgh EH9 2AS

R.J. Davidson, Ontario Ministry of Natural Resources, 300 Water Street, Peterborough, Ontario K9J 8M5, Canada

D. Davison, Dynamic Earth Enterprises Ltd, Holyrood Road, Edinburgh EH8 8AS

L. Erikstad, Norwegian Institute for Nature Research (NINA), Box 736 Sentrum, N-0105 Oslo, Norway

J. Finlay, John Finlay Associates, 7 Bellevue Terrace, Edinburgh EH7 4DT

J.Z. Fraser, Ontario Ministry of Natural Resources, 300 Water Street, Peterborough, Ontario K9J 8M5, Canada

E. Gallagher, Geological Survey of Ireland, Beggars Bush, Haddington Road, Dublin 4, Ireland

K.M. Goodenough, Scottish Natural Heritage, 2 Anderson Place, Edinburgh EH6 5NP (Present address: British Geological Survey, Murchison House, West Mains Road, Edinburgh EH9 3LA)

J.E. Gordon, Scottish Natural Heritage, 2 Anderson Place, Edinburgh EH6 5NP

I.C. Grieve, Department of Environmental Science, University of Stirling, Stirling FK9 4LA

J.D. Hansom, Coastal Research Group, Department of Geography and Topographic Science, University of Glasgow, Glasgow G12 8QQ

S. J. Harrison, Department of Environmental Science, University of Stirling, Stirling FK9 4LA

V.M. Haynes, Department of Environmental Science, University of Stirling, Stirling FK9 4LA

C. Hopkins, c/o National Museums of Scotland, Chambers Street, Edinburgh EH1 1JF

P.L. Horne, Macaulay Land Use Research Institute, Craigiebuckler, Aberdeen AB15 8QH

D. Horsfield, Scottish Natural Heritage, 2 Anderson Place, Edinburgh EH6 5NP

G. Hudson, Macaulay Land Use Research Institute, Craigiebuckler, Aberdeen AB15 8QH

H. Johnson, British Geological Survey, Murchison House, West Mains Road, Edinburgh EH9 3LA

A.H. Kirkpatrick, Department of Environmental Science, University of Stirling, Stirling FK9 4LA

P.S.G. Kor, Ontario Ministry of Natural Resources, 300 Water Street, Peterborough, Ontario K9J 8M5, Canada

P.D. Laidler, Department of Geography, University of Durham, Science Laboratories, South Road, Durham DH1 3LE

R.G. Lees, Scottish Natural Heritage, 2 Anderson Place, Edinburgh EH6 5NP

S.G. Lewis, Department of Geography, Queen Mary and Westfield College, University of London, Mile End Road, London E1 4NS

K. F. Leys, Scottish Natural Heritage, 2 Anderson Place, Edinburgh EH6 5NP

A. Lilly, Macaulay Land Use Research Institute, Craigiebuckler, Aberdeen AB15 8QH

I. Lindley, Tarmac Northern, Lingerfield, Scotton, Knaresborough, North Yorkshire HG5 2JN

M. Lipkewich, Mining Association of British Columbia Education Division, Mining House, 840 West Hastings High Street, Vancouver, Canada, VC6 1CS

D. Long, British Geological Survey, Murchison House, West Mains Road, Edinburgh EH9 3LA

C.C.J. MacFadyen, Scottish Natural Heritage, 2 Anderson Place, Edinburgh EH6 5NP

F. Mactaggart, Scottish Natural Heritage, 2 Anderson Place, Edinburgh EH6 5NP

A. Manning, Institute of Cell, Animal and Population Biology, University of Edinburgh, Ashworth Laboratories, West Mains Road, Edinburgh EH9 3JT

J. Maslen, GeoWise GIS Consultants, 38 Fowler Terrace, Edinburgh EH11 1DA

L.J. McEwen, Geography and Environmental Management Research Unit (GEMRU), Cheltenham and Gloucester College of Higher Education, Francis Close Hall, Swindon Road, Cheltenham, Gloucestershire GL50 4AZ

W. McGhee, Borders Forest Trust, Monteviot Nurseries, Ancrum, Jedburgh, Roxburghshire TD8 6TU

P.J. McKeever Geological Survey of Northern Ireland, 20 College Gardens, Belfast BT9 6BS, Ireland

A.P. McKirdy, Scottish Natural Heritage, 2 Anderson Place, Edinburgh EH6 5NP

J. McManus, School of Geography and Geosciences, University of St Andrews, St Andrews, Fife KY16 9AL

A.A. McMillan, British Geological Survey, Murchison House, West Mains Road, Edinburgh EH9 3LA

S. Miller, National Museums of Scotland, Chambers Street, Edinburgh EH1 1JF

J. Milross, Mining Association of British Columbia Education Division, Mining House, 840 West Hastings High Street, Vancouver, Canada, VC6 1CS

C. Mitchell, Scottish Natural Heritage, Battleby, Redgorton, Perth PH1 3EW

S. K. Monro, Dynamic Earth Enterprises Ltd, Holyrood Road, Edinburgh EH8 8AS

P. Price-Thomas, Department of Environmental Science, University of Stirling, Stirling FK9 4LA

G. Puri, Scottish Natural Heritage, 2 Anderson Place, Edinburgh EH6 5NP

M.F. Quinn, British Geological Survey, DTI Core Store, 376 Gilmerton Road, Edinburgh EH17 7QS

K. Salt, Department of Geography and Topographic Science, University of Glasgow, Glasgow G12 8QQ

C. Soulsby, Department of Geography and Environment, University of Aberdeen, Elphinstone Road, Aberdeen AB9 2UF

O. Stabbetorp, Norwegian Institute for Nature Research (NINA), Box 736 Sentrum, N-0105 Oslo, Norway

S.J. Stoker, British Geological Survey, DTI Core Store, 376 Gilmerton Road, Edinburgh EH17 7QS

D.B.A. Thompson, Scottish Natural Heritage, 2 Anderson Place, Edinburgh EH6 5NP

R. Threadgould, Scottish Natural Heritage, 12 Hope Terrace, Edinburgh EH9 2AS

C. Tilbrook, Scottish Natural Heritage, The Beta Centre, Innovation Park, University of Stirling, Stirling FK9 4NF

N.H. Trewin, Department of Geology and Petroleum Geology, University of Aberdeen, Meston Building, King's College, Aberdeen AB24 3UE

M.B. Usher, Scottish Natural Heritage, 2 Anderson Place, Edinburgh EH6 5NP

T. Willison, Scientific Advisors' Unit, Scottish Executive Rural Affairs Department, Pentland House, 47 Robb's Loan, Edinburgh EH14 1TY

P. Woolgar, Scottish Environment Protection Agency, Castle Business Park, Stirling FK9 4TR

FOREWORD

The eighth annual Scottish Natural Heritage conference, *Earth Science and the Natural Heritage: Interactions and Integrated Management,* was held at *Our Dynamic Earth* in Edinburgh. It was timely to examine the opportunities and challenges facing Earth heritage conservation in Scotland at the start of the new millennium. Earth heritage, which encompasses rocks, fossils, landforms and soils, is highly relevant to Scotland today. It is central to understanding Scotland's natural environment, and has also shaped many aspects of our much valued scenery and vibrant economy. The links between geology, geomorphology and landscape mean that our Earth heritage is now recognised in Government and beyond as being a valuable resource for education, enjoyment and tourism, as well as for scientific study.

Geology is a vital part of our cultural and scientific heritage. Scotland was the birthplace of modern geology, and its geologists have led the way in the development of the subject and its applications world-wide. Scotland's rocks and landforms are also a resource of national and international importance. They have contributed to the better understanding of volcanic processes, plate movements, colliding continents and mountain building, and ice-age history. Scotland's fossils have had a crucial role in studies of the evolution of the plant and animal kingdoms. Many Earth heritage sites in Scotland are therefore of great scientific importance and it is essential that such sites continue to be protected.

Rocks, landforms and soils form the basis of our natural heritage. The biodiversity 'web of life' is dependent upon the provision of suitable soils and landforms, and the active processes that form and change them. They combine to create Scotland's rich variety of nationally and internationally important habitats. By safeguarding our Earth heritage, we are helping to protect the foundations of our habitats and the species that they support, contributing to the UK Biodiversity Action Plan and securing a sustainable future for Scotland.

Reading the geological record in Scotland gives us an understanding of the origins of the modern landscape and its sensitivity to current and likely future changes. This understanding is fundamental to sustainable management approaches for land and water resources. We all need to adopt sustainable approaches and to work with, rather than against, nature and natural processes. This has important implications for planning and land management on issues such as land stability, erosion and flooding in the coastal and floodplain zones, soil erosion, sustainable use of soils and conservation management. There are exciting opportunities ahead for the development of new partnerships to deliver integrated management of our more sensitive environments in the uplands, in river basins and along the coast.

There is currently a high level of public interest in our Earth heritage. This has been fostered by a series of excellent television programmes, books and magazines, and by media attention to issues such as climate change, sea-level rise and changes in the frequency of storms and floods. All of these issues may have significant economic and social impacts, as well as effects on our natural heritage. The opening of *Our Dynamic Earth* in Edinburgh has generated significant public interest and an increased awareness of the way that our Earth changes. The challenge for the Earth heritage community is to do even more to foster awareness and to promote management in harmony with the natural processes. The different needs of varied audiences - schools, the general public, planners, decision makers and their advisors - must be recognised and addressed.

The designation of the first two proposed National Parks in Scotland, at Loch Lomond and the Trossachs and in the Cairngorms, will provide important opportunities to promote Earth heritage interpretation and to demonstrate sustainable management in practice. Developments in Earth heritage interpretation could contribute to economic development through niche marketing and promotion of geotourism. Equally, the Earth heritage can provide the foundations for holistic interpretative and educational projects that draw together geology, landscape and industrial archaeology. Local voluntary groups will have an important part to play in helping to develop local community involvement and 'ownership' of such projects.

Public interest in the Earth heritage and the increased awareness of its wider importance lead me to suggest that geology and geomorphology have finally come of age. Two hundred years after their inception in Scotland, they are achieving just recognition as subjects which are important and relevant today. The conference made a significant contribution to our knowledge in this area. I welcome the publication of this book as a means of disseminating the conference's conclusions to a wider audience.

Alasdair Morrison MSP
Deputy Minister for the
Highlands and Island and Gaelic
November 1999

PART ONE

EARTH SCIENCE AND THE NATURAL HERITAGE:
EXPLORING THE CONTINUUM

EARTH SCIENCE AND THE NATURAL HERITAGE: EXPLORING THE CONTINUUM

The unity of the environment and human interactions with Earth systems have long been acknowledged by geographers. The inextricable links between the physical and living (including human) components of the environment apply across a range of both spatial and temporal scales, as recognised by Manning (Chapter 2) and Boulton (Chapter 3). However, this unity has to a large extent been neglected by those concerned with environmental management, both at the policy and planning levels and at the design and implementation stages of intervention and mitigation schemes. In conservation, too, the Earth and biological sciences have remained to a degree apart, as reflected in the selection of separate systems of protected areas in the Nature Conservation Review and the Geological Conservation Review. Soils, arguably at the interface between physical and biological systems, have featured explicitly in neither. The three chapters in this part of the book reaffirm the unity of Earth systems and emphasise the role and contribution of the Earth sciences.

As a starting point, Gordon and Leys (Chapter 1) describe the traditional site-based approach to Earth heritage conservation. While this remains a core activity, they note three major requirements for developing a more unified approach. These form the central themes in this book: 1) wider recognition of the links between the Earth's physical and biological systems; 2) promotion of sustainable management of the environment based on the application of Earth science knowledge and understanding; and 3) raising public awareness of Earth heritage and promoting greater involvement. Addressing these requirements, to some extent in progress, forms part of a process of redefining the role and contribution of the Earth sciences in sustainable management of the natural heritage.

The first requirement, for greater recognition of the links and dependencies between habitats, species, geology, soils and geomorphological processes, forms part of 'the new synthesis' identified by Manning (Chapter 2). Both Manning (Chapter 2) and Boulton (Chapter 3) emphasise the global picture and that unifying theories have been developed which enable us to undertand the evolution of the Earth and its unique life-supporting qualities. Throughout geological time, biological and geological interactions have affected key processes on the planet. In the geological past, mass extinctions associated with global events provided the survivors with increased opportunities. However, we are now on the brink of a new mass extinction, caused by human activity rather than by planetary activity, but at the same time we are not helping the planet to support life better.

Boulton (Chapter 3) stresses the continuity of geology and geological processes through time, linking the past and present. Geology is not something that happened in the deep past. It is relevant today. Boulton also highlights the continuity between processes deep in the Earth and processes at the surface. For example, plate tectonic processes replenish mineral material that weathers to form plant nutrients, while surface water facilitates deep Earth processes. Fundamental links exist at a global scale between physical and biological processes in the oceans, on the continents, in the atmosphere and with climate change.

The second requirement is for a greater recognition of the human interactions with, and dependencies on, Earth systems and resources. Sustainable management hinges on planners, decision makers, advisors and those in other professions understanding these links and the dynamics of Earth systems, a message emphasised by Boulton (Chapter 2) and one that is reiterated throughout the book. Not only is the rate of use of many resources greater than their rate of replenishment, there are also many uncertainties about the long-term environmental effects of the disposal of waste from human activities. Significantly, human activity is now an important geological process, as well as having a major impact on other Earth systems such as climate. A major new challenge is to understand human activities as geological agents (Boulton, Chapter 3). This will require finding the means to restore areas damaged by human impacts, to mitigate future impacts and to develop strategies for sustainable use of the Earth's resources. It will involve cross-disciplinary collaboration, application of new methods and development of predictive models of future changes in Earth systems.

The geological record clearly demonstrates the inevitability of change (Boulton, Chapter 3). It reveals how Earth systems have evolved in the past and can provide a guide to the way in which they might behave in the future. The predictive value of models can be tested against geological evidence. A major challenge lies in understanding the effects of global climate and environmental change on Earth systems and developing appropriate responses and mitigation. In doing so, it is important to couple the study of geological evidence of past changes with studies of modern processes, for example in relation to rivers, flooding and land use. It is essential to understand the sensitivity of geomorphological systems and thresholds for change and as far as possible to work with natural processes. Gordon and Leys (Chapter 1) recognise progress in sustainable management of the coast and rivers, based on understanding physical processes, as well as in the application of environmental geology in planning. However, there still remains a need for better predictive environmental engineering that addresses engineering *into* the environment (Boulton, Chapter 3). As part of sustainable environmental management, there is also a need for more integrated conservation management for the benefit of habitats, species and the Earth heritage, in the area of soils management and in wider landscape approaches to conservation.

The third requirement is to raise greater awareness and understanding of the Earth heritage and Earth systems among the public and to increase their involvement. There is now a focus on doing so through an emphasis on the heritage aspect rather than the science. However, more integrated approaches are required that link Earth heritage with other components of the landscape such as scenery, land use and archaeology. There are potentially important roles for geotourism and raising awareness of Earth heritage in the urban environment.

Overall, the need to help others to understand the way the Earth works is a cornerstone of sustainable development (Manning, Chapter 2). This will involve a deeper understanding of the planet and its dynamic systems. It will also require new institutions and processes to tackle the challenges, both to improve policy and decision making processes, and to enhance public understanding of uncertainty and risk (Boulton, Chapter 3).

1 EARTH SCIENCE AND THE NATURAL HERITAGE: DEVELOPING A MORE HOLISTIC APPROACH

John E. Gordon and Katherine F. Leys

Summary

1.   The role of Earth science in conservation of the natural heritage has traditionally been focused on the assessment and protection of sites of geological and geomorphological interest. This reflected a prevailing nature conservation philosophy of site protection for scientific reasons. A major achievement of this approach has been the completion of the Geological Conservation Review, a national inventory of key Earth science sites throughout Great Britain.

2.   While site protection continues to be important, there is now a more holistic approach, embracing sustainable management of natural resources and systems. Such an approach offers new opportunities and challenges for the Earth sciences. The opportunities lie in contributing to the development of integrated, rather than sectoral, management based on an understanding of natural processes and landscape evolution. The challenges lie in being more outward looking and in demonstrating the applications and added value that Earth science can bring to integrated management.

3.   Promoting wider awareness is crucial in developing a more holistic approach. This applies equally to dissemination of current knowledge of natural processes to policy makers, planners and land managers, as well as to enhancing public understanding of the Earth heritage and the links with landscape and biodiversity.

1.1 Introduction

Scotland has a remarkably long and varied geological history. Rocks, fossils and landforms show how life itself evolved; they reveal how the climate has lurched between desert conditions and ice ages over millions of years, and they illustrate how the face of the land has changed in the past and continues to change now. The soil records the effects of climate and land use changes in the 15,000 years or so since the end of the last ice age, and it provides the medium for plant growth and habitat development. Rocks, fossils, landforms and soil comprise the 'Earth heritage' of Scotland, and they tell a fascinating story of our past. This alone makes them a valuable environmental and scientific resource worthy of conservation. Such a rationale has provided the basis for the traditional site-based approach to Earth science conservation, not only in Britain (Nature Conservancy Council, 1990; Ellis *et al.*, 1996), but also further afield, as described in the publications from a series of international conferences (e.g. Martini, 1994; O'Halloran *et al.*, 1994; Alexandrowicz, 1999; Barettino *et al.*, 1999).

In recent years, three significant developments have broadened the vision of Earth science conservation, and these form the main themes that run through this book. First, there is now much greater awareness of the wider role and significance of Earth systems as an integral part of the natural heritage and a recognition of the dependencies of habitats and species on geology, soils and geomorphological processes (e.g. Swanson *et al.*, 1988; Nichols *et al.*, 1998; Gordon *et al.*, 1998, 2001).

Second, sustainability has become a key concept in guiding our use and management of natural resources (World Commission on Environment and Development, 1983; Scottish Natural Heritage, 1993; Department of the Environment, 1994a). This applies equally to the conservation and management of features and dynamic systems of Earth science interest (e.g. Stevens *et al.*, 1994; Wilson, 1994), as well as to the wider landscapes and ecosystems of which they are an integral part. Sustainable management of natural resources also places a strong requirement on the need to understand the temporal and spatial links between physical processes and landscape sensitivity.

The third key development has been greater recognition of the need to raise public awareness (e.g. McKirdy and Threadgould, 1994; Doyle and Bennett, 1998). The Earth sciences start from a much lower level of public awareness and general interest than the natural sciences, in part reflecting a traditional emphasis on the science and an over-technical approach in communicating the key messages. However, more recent promotional work has seen a significantly greater emphasis placed on the heritage interest, also reflected in the wider use of the term 'Earth heritage conservation' rather than 'Earth science conservation'.

Earth science conservation, narrow in outlook and appeal and with a focus on sites, may be viewed as being at a threshold. There is now a wider vision that recognises the integration of Earth and biological systems (Manning, this volume; Boulton, this volume), and with that recognition, there are opportunities to secure an essential role in sustainable management of the natural heritage and natural resources, and to promote wider public understanding and appreciation. In this chapter we examine some of the traditional core values which remain at the foundation of Earth heritage conservation, as well as the recent developments. This provides the context for an outline of the new vision, opportunities and challenges which are developed in subsequent chapters.

1.2 Threats to the Earth heritage resource

Land in Scotland has to serve many, often competing, purposes. Our use of land for agriculture, forestry, mining, quarrying and building is intimately related to the nature of the underlying rocks, landforms and soils, and to climate and natural processes such as erosion and deposition. This relationship is not new - the progress of the Industrial Revolution depended on the availability and distribution of coal, oil, gas and metal ores, and these resources remain of great economic value and importance.

Much of our geological legacy is hidden beneath the land surface and is thus not accessible for study. Underlying geology can be exposed at the coast, in river gorges, cliffs, mountain crags, quarries and road and railway cuttings, and sites such as these provide an important resource for study and demonstration purposes (Ellis *et al.*, 1996). Some prime Earth heritage sites are therefore created and maintained by natural processes, and some by human activities such as quarrying. There is, nevertheless, a general feeling that rocks and landforms are stable and static (i.e. unchangeable) and are not in need of protection. However, disused quarries and cuttings have been used as convenient sites for landfill; glacial features have been destroyed for the sand and gravel they contain; and fossil bearing rocks have been excavated and specimens sold (particularly abroad, where a profitable market exists). Land development can also prevent sub-surface resources from being studied; for example the landfilling of Kirkhill Quarry in Aberdeenshire, which buried one of the most important Quaternary sites in Scotland.

Flooding and erosion are natural processes and will always happen to some extent on coastal cliffs and river banks. Erosion and flooding are generally incompatible with land use and development, and many of the human activities, property and infrastructure that occur in the coastal fringe or floodplain zone require to be protected by defences which can change the natural processes or obscure geological exposures. The series of damaging flood and erosion events experienced throughout Britain in the last decade has belatedly raised public awareness of the reality of geomorphological processes and the implications of future climate change (Plate 20). As a result, questions are being asked about the appropriateness of some land uses in vulnerable floodplains and coastal areas. Economic investments requiring the construction of coastal or river defences may now be seen to be inappropriate (through cost-benefit analysis) in terms of the geomorphological risk and public concern.

Whilst development is necessary for the continued prosperity of the country, it needs to be balanced in some cases against the loss of irreplaceable elements of our Earth heritage. The identification and protection of the most important Earth heritage sites remains a necessary component of a strategic approach to sustainable use of finite resources.

1.3 Earth Heritage conservation: statutory and voluntary approaches

The justification for Earth heritage conservation rests on two main conservation principles: 1) the duty to future generations to preserve our heritage so that it may become theirs; and 2) the direct benefits for mankind and the natural world, with natural resources underpinning every aspect of our life (Nature Conservancy Council, 1990). Whilst it is impractical to conserve every rock exposure or landform, it is essential to conserve those which make a unique contribution to Scotland's Earth heritage. In consequence, Earth heritage conservation has traditionally been based on the premise that geological exposures and landforms can be considered as discrete sites which, if their importance warrants it, may be systematically conserved (Nature Conservancy Council, 1990). This concern with a site-based approach reflects a traditional emphasis in nature conservation in Great Britain on the protection of wildlife and physical features for scientific reasons (Ratcliffe, 1977). It was also reflected in four of the six themes in a national strategy for Earth science conservation (Nature Conservancy Council, 1990).

In Britain, the systematic identification of key Earth heritage sites for protection first began over 50 years ago (e.g. Gordon, 1994). In 1977, the Nature Conservancy Council initiated a systematic review of the site coverage, designed to identify and help conserve those sites of national and international importance. This review, undertaken by several hundred scientists from higher education, government, industry and the voluntary sector, is known as the Geological Conservation Review (GCR) (Ellis *et al.*, 1996). It was completed in 1990 and is the most comprehensive review undertaken by any country. Publication of the results, written for a scientific readership, will be completed in 42 volumes by 2002.

The GCR site series is designed to reflect the range and diversity of Great Britain's Earth heritage, with each site satisfying scientific requirements for notification as a Site of Special Scientific Interest (SSSI) under the *National Parks and Access to the Countryside Act 1949* and the subsequent *Wildlife and Countryside Act 1981*, by reason of its 'geology or physiography'. Over 800 GCR sites were selected in Scotland and many have been notified as SSSIs (Gordon and MacFadyen, this volume). Notification of a site affords a measure of legal protection but does not, however, mean that there is any right of way or access to it. In consequence, the site selection process and site management have seemed 'closed', with members of the public often being unaware of interesting and important sites on their doorsteps. Scientific study and site management have been seen as 'experts talking to experts'. There have been few opportunities through the site-based system to foster a wider understanding of the subject, and there is a strong case to make better use of existing designated sites to promote and support integrated management, education and better public awareness.

Outside the SSSI network, protection of Earth heritage sites is mainly undertaken through the voluntary Regionally Important Geological/Geomorphological Sites (RIGS) network. Sites are selected on the basis of their educational, research, historical and aesthetic importance, with less formal criteria than for SSSIs. These sites reflect local uses and interests, rather than national or international interests (Nature Conservancy Council, 1990), and in Scotland are only designated with the landowner's consent. Whilst this system is also site-based, it is run by local volunteers and participation is open to all those interested in Earth heritage conservation. It is therefore more accessible than the SSSI system and widens Earth heritage conservation for greater public participation. This makes increased public access to privately owned land a possibility. National Planning Policy Guideline (NPPG) 14 *Natural Heritage* (The Scottish Office, 1999) highlights the place of RIGS within a statutory framework. As a result, many local authorities are including conservation policies for the protection of RIGS in their Local and Strategic Plans, along with other local wildlife sites.

On a wider front, there have been moves to obtain international recognition for, and promotion of, the most important Earth heritage sites. One approach has involved working through the World Heritage List (e.g. the nomination of the Cairngorms for its physical features on the UK Tentative List – Department for Culture, Media and Sport, 1999) and the UNESCO Man and the Biosphere Reserve Programme (Weighell, 1999). Under the latter programme, proposals to recognise a new type of site, 'Geoparks' (Patzak and Eder, 1998), would give wider recognition to Earth heritage conservation and allow closer links with biological and cultural interests and economic development as part of an integrated programme (e.g. Villalobos and Guirado, 1999). In Scotland, such objectives might be achieved through the planned national parks and through greater integration of Earth heritage interests in the promotion of existing National Nature Reserves. The International Union of Geological Sciences (IUGS) also has a 'Geosites' programme to encourge individual countries to undertake an inventory of important Earth science sites, comparable to the GCR (Wimbledon *et al.*, 1998). Such lists may provide a more systematic basis than at present for the recognition of internationally important sites.

1.4 Earth science and the natural heritage: recognising the links

There is now increasing recognition of the links between Earth science and the natural heritage. This is particularly apparent in freshwater, coastal and upland environments in the geomorphological underpinning of ecosystems and biodiversity (Soulsby and Boon, this volume; Hansom and Angus, this volume; Thompson *et al.*, this volume; Plates 17-19). Understanding the links is central to developing appropriate conservation management strategies in these dynamic environments, where maintaining geomorphological diversity and the range of natural processes may be as important as trying to preserve communities and species that are in transition (Nichols *et al.*, 1998). The concept of geomorphological sensitivity provides a useful starting point in this respect (Schumm, 1979; Gordon *et al.*, 2001; Soulsby and Boon, this volume).

There is also an important temporal dimension, since understanding the historical context of landscapes and ecosystems is crucial to predicting future changes across a range of spatial scales (e.g. Swanson *et al.*, 1988; Delcourt and Delcourt, 1988). Palaeoenvironmental records provide a longer-term perspective on geo-ecological processes, for example as discussed by Thompson *et al.* (this volume) in relation to the uplands. They allow contemporary processes, such as peat erosion or the decline of heather moorland, to be placed in their historical context and may show how plant communities will respond to future environmental changes (Huntley, 1991). Further, palaeoenvironmental studies may allow assessment of naturalness and fragility of ecosystems, conservation status of rare species and ecosystem responses to human activities (Birks, 1996).

Recognition of the need for greater integration of Earth science and the natural heritage is also becoming apparent in relation to habitat management. The Conservation (Natural Habitats, &c.) Regulations 1994 enacts in British law an EC directive commonly known as the 'Habitats Directive'. This gives protection to certain species of wild animals and plants which are rare, endangered or vulnerable in the EC (wild birds are protected separately under the 1979 EC Wild Birds Directive). The overall aim of the Habitats Directive is to encourage the conservation of biodiversity in Europe through a network of designated sites (known as Natura sites). Whilst the Habitats Directive does not apply to Earth heritage features, conservation management of Natura sites has had to recognise the fundamental dependency of habitats on soils, underlying geology and active processes. This has been demonstrated, for example, in the case of 'embryonic shifting dunes' (the first stage of dune development), 'dry heaths' (heath formed on siliceous podzolic soils), 'active raised bogs' (dependent on high water tables) and limestone pavements. Such dependence is also clear in species management. For example, species such as Atlantic salmon depend on the provision of adequate habitat (in the form of variable channel features such as pools, riffles and glides), which itself is a function of active processes including floods, erosion and deposition. It is becoming increasingly clear that management of sites for the benefit of habitats and species alone cannot succeed without reference to the physical setting and geomorphological processes. The lessons currently being learned in managing sites designated under the Habitats Directive and through the biodiversity process will be valuable in demonstrating the wider importance and relevance of Earth science understanding.

The widespread recognition of the value of the country outwith designated sites, particularly in relation to quality of life and landscape issues, has also prompted a more holistic approach to sustainable management of natural resources and landscapes, as in

Natural Heritage Zones in Scotland (Mitchell, this volume) and in the Landscape Areas programme in England (Duff, 1994). In a wider European context, the need for such integrated approaches to conservation of landscapes is one of the challenges identified in the Pan-European Biological and Landscape Diversity Strategy (Council of Europe, 1996). This emphasises the value of landscapes as a mosaic of cultural, natural and geological features. A further application is illustrated by the Oak Ridges Moraine strategy in Ontario, Canada (Davidson *et al.*, this volume).

1.5 Developments in sustainable management

1.5.1 Government initiatives in sustainable management

Government commitment to biodiversity has resulted in two major, UK-wide initiatives in sustainable managementent: the Local Biodiversity Action Plan (LBAP) process and Local Agenda 21 (LA21). The LBAP process is part of the UK Government's Biodiversity Action Plan, an element of its commitment to the 'The Convention on Biodiversity' signed at the 1992 Rio Summit. The Convention aims to achieve sustainability and emphasises that conservation of biodiversity needs to be at the heart of the policies which drive our economy. As all species and habitats are dependent upon one another to survive, the conservation of biodiversity needs to be tackled at all levels from international to local (hence the phrase 'think global, act local'). Inputs to local plans are usually led by local authorities in association with conservation agencies and local wildlife and voluntary conservation groups. To date, despite the fundamental relationships between Earth heritage and biodiversity, representation of Earth heritage interests within local plans, has been mixed. However, SNH has worked in partnership with RIGS Groups, the Convention of Scottish Local Authorities (COSLA), the British Geological Survey (BGS) and others to produce a guidance note to help LBAP officers identify the important links.

Sustainable development and sustainable use of Earth's resources have been drivers for the LA21 process. The sustainable use of finite Earth resources, such as coal, sand and gravel and fresh water, is fundamental to achieving the greater goal of sustainable development (Lindley *et al.*, this volume; Johnson *et al.*, this volume). Sustainable management of dynamic systems remains a challenge which is currently being tackled in different ways, as outlined below.

1.5.2 Coastal management

It is becoming more widely recognised that understanding Earth systems is essential for sustainable environmental and conservation management (e.g. Hooke, 1999; Boulton, this volume; Crofts, this volume). At the coast, this is well established in strategic approaches to shoreline management. Following developments in England (e.g. Ministry of Agriculture, Fisheries and Food, 1993; Hooke, 1998; Leafe and Collins, 1999), understanding of processes based on coastal cells and whole systems analysis now provides a sound basis for coastline management and preparation of Shoreline Management Plans, where appropriate, in Scotland (HR Wallingford, 1997; Hansom, 1999; Hansom *et al.*, 2000). The application and relevance of this type of work is demonstrated, for example, at Montrose Bay (Plate 21) and Aberdeen Bay where interruption of sediment cells through inappropriate construction of coast protection might have affected National Nature Reserves (Halcrow Crouch, 1998, 1999). Similarly, as part of the 'Focus on Firths' project, a series of studies that address understanding of coastal processes provides a basis for the development of sustainable management of Scottish estuaries (e.g. Stapleton and Pethick, 1996; Firth *et al.*, 1997). Concurrently, best practice guidance has been prepared for coastal protection, with emphasis on alternative forms, including managed retreat (e.g. Pethick and Burd, 1995; Hansom *et al.*, this volume) and beach recharge and dune re-profiling (HR Wallingford, 2000).

1.5.3 River management

SNH has been working to promote understanding of natural processes and the need for sustainable management of Scottish river systems. This approach is demonstrated in a study of sustainable methods of river engineering for Scottish gravel bed rivers (Hoey *et al.*, 1998), and has been fundamental to the success of WWF Scotland's 'Wild Rivers' project (WWF, 2000). It is now widely recognised that the best regime for river systems is a natural one (Richter *et al.*, 1996; Poff *et al.*, 1997), including the hydrological, geomorphological and biological components. Linked closely to this is an understanding of geomorphological sensitivity (Schumm, 1979; Werritty and Leys, 2001) and a move away from interventionist management (Plate 27).

Member states have recently agreed the text of the EU 'Water Framework Directive', which comprises comprehensive legislation to maintain and improve the aquatic environment in Europe. This directive is significant for conservation management since its enactment in Britain will enshrine in legislation the need to manage freshwater on a catchment scale (referred to as 'River Basin Districts'). Management will be achieved through the process of integrated catchment management (ICM), in which the physical landscape is used to define the management units (Werritty, 1995), and the inter-relationships between aspects of the landscape and land management activities are used to determine the extent of any impacts upon the riverine environment.

1.5.4 Soils

Soils form an integral part of our Earth heritage and merit greater attention than they have received in the past. Soils lie at the interface between Earth and biological systems. They perform crucial functions in maintaining above- and below- ground ecosystems, including habitats of conservation value. Pressures on soils arise from land use practices and contamination, and concerns have been expressed about the sustainable use of soil arising, for example, from intensification of agriculture, afforestation, waste disposal, acid deposition and urban expansion (Taylor, 1995; Royal Commission on Environmental Pollution, 1996; Taylor *et al.*, 1996). A holistic approach is required that recognises the multi-functionality of the soil as a basis for its sustainable management. As discussed by Puri *et al.* (this volume), such an approach should form the basis of national soil strategies currently being prepared for England and Wales and under consideration in Scotland, following the recommendations of the Royal Commission on Environmental Pollution (1996).

1.5.5 Environmental geology in planning

The value of the Earth heritage and Earth science information is widely recognised in environmental geology and land use planning through the availability of a range of information and guidance which stresses the importance of working with natural processes (e.g. Department of the Environment 1994b, 1995; McKirdy *et al.*, 1998; Thompson *et al.*, 1998; Gilvear, 1999; Hooke, 1999; McKirdy, in press). This is well illustrated by the numerous case studies in Thompson *et al.* (1998), which span a diverse range of subjects - ground instability, flooding, coastal planning, landform replication in land restoration, and Earth heritage conservation issues. Further applications are illustrated by Erikstad and Stabbetorp (this volume) in relation to impact assessments for road developments in Norway.

In the minerals sector, strategic approaches have been developed to ensure more sustainable management and conservation of landscapes with minerals resources (e.g. Kontturi and Lyytikäinen, 1985; Knight *et al.*, 1999; Scottish Natural Heritage, 2000), supported by planning policy guidelines. In addition, the minerals industry is now better informed and aware of its responsibilities and obligations to make more efficient use of non-renewable resources, to minimise impacts on the natural heritage and to ensure that restoration follows best practice (Scottish Natural Heritage, 2000; Lindley *et al.*, this volume). In many parts of the country where natural exposures are poor, quarry sites are a key resource for demonstrating geological features. It is crucial that restoration of such sites fully addresses their contribution to geodiversity and that this is recognised in the preparation of good practice guidance that integrates both geodiversity and biodiversity (cf. English Nature *et al.*, 1999).

In Scotland, there is a long history of using natural building stone based on the varied geological resource. The use of such stone not only contributes to local vernacular building and landscape character, but also the existence of many small stone quarries (McMillan, 1997) has provided a valuable resource for Earth heritage conservation. Revival of building with natural stone, promoted through the Scottish Stone Liaison Group, should provide important opportunities to raise awareness of our distinctive Earth heritage and its manifestation in the built environment, as well as local economic opportunities and a contribution to sustainable development (Hutton and Rostron, 1997).

1.6 Promoting wider awareness and involvement

Interpretation has traditionally been an integral part of Earth science conservation and was rightly recognised as a key theme in an earlier strategy (Nature Conservancy Council, 1990). However, traditional interpretation has often been based on boards or leaflets that have too frequently been written by scientists assuming too great a technical knowledge by their audience. Attitudes and approaches are now changing, with the production of much more appropriate materials (e.g. Threadgould and McKirdy, 1999), the use of other media (for example, television series such as *Earth Story*, *Walking with Dinosaurs* and *On the Rocks*, as well as several others on natural forces), the opening of 'Our Dynamic Earth' (Monro and Davidson, this volume) and initiatives such as the Rockwatch Club for children promoted by the Royal Society for Nature Conservation. Future developments are likely to see more integrated interpretation, including links with landscape history, soils, vegetation, human impacts and industrial archaeology (Larwood and Prosser, 1998). Novel approaches might include exploration of the links between Earth heritage and the arts, as demonstrated for example by Clifford (1993) and Pestrong (1994). Such approaches are not so much a new development, but rather a rediscovery of a more holistic view of science, literature, the arts and the landscape expressed, for example, in the work of Miller (1893) and Geikie (1905).

Much of the focus in the past has been on interpretation of sites and landscapes in the rural environment. However, Scotland has a remarkable diversity of geology and geomorphology that forms an equally distinctive part of many of our urban environments. The forms of our urban landscapes reflect both the rock types present and the geomorphological processes that have shaped them over millions of years. In some cases, such as Edinburgh and Stirling, distinctive volcanic landforms are a striking feature of the urban landscape (Plate 1); in others, the influence is more subtle but nevertheless apparent, for example in the drumlin landscape of Glasgow. Local geology has also strongly influenced the building stone used in many towns and cities, and the buildings themselves provide many opportunities for raising awareness of geology (McMillan *et al.*, 1999). For example, sandstones from Craigleith Quarry were used extensively in Edinburgh buildings, and although the quarry is now infilled and the site of a supermarket, interpretation panels have been erected by the Edinburgh and Borders RIGS Group. Urban geology, therefore, has a potentially significant role in helping to raise awareness of the Earth heritage (Bennett *et al.*, 1996; Doyle and Bennett, 1997, 1998), although the lessons from urban wildlife conservation point particularly to the need for local community involvement (Barker, 1996).

Geotourism is another potential growth area. As well as helping to raise awareness, it also has an economic dimension through contributing to rural development (McKirdy *et al.*, this volume). The potential is illustrated, for example, in the appeal to tourists of 'scenic wonders', show caves and unusual rock outcrops in many parts of the world. Scotland has a great diversity of distinctive landscapes and landforms that already attract many visitors for their scenic quality. Experience in Ireland (McKeever and Gallacher, this volume) shows how additional benefits might be derived from promoting geotourism. Raising awareness in this way should also help to increase support for Earth heritage conservation among a wider constituency, while at the same time, effective conservation can maintain the attraction for visitor numbers at appropriate sites (Larwood and Prosser, 1998). However, it will be crucial for Earth scientists to work with professional interpreters to ensure selection of appropriate themes, use of the best media and that the message is pitched at right level, as well as to build on best practice in other areas of interpretation (Hose, 1998; Brown, this volume).

The creation of national parks in Scotland will provide a stimulus for integrated interpretation, but much more could be made of appropriate National Nature Reserves (NNRs), SSSIs and RIGS to promote better awareness of the Earth heritage, particularly where there are opportunities to involve schools (including the often neglected primary sector) and local communities (e.g. Miller and Hopkins, this volume). The success of an innovative Canadian approach illustrates the potential benefits of partnerships between industry and schools (Milross and Lipkevich, this volume). Similarly, school-industry partnerships, such as developed between the Quarry Products Association, the National Stone Centre and the School Curriculum Industry Partnership (e.g. Quarry Products Association, 1997), have significant potential to promote Earth heritage awareness, involvement and conservation.

1.7 Conclusion

The conference explored interactions between Earth science and the natural heritage, and examined progress towards holistic management of our most precious finite resource - the

Earth. It demonstrated significant support for the wider role and opportunities for Earth heritage conservation in sustainable management of natural resources. One noteworthy aspect was the degree of cross-institutional and cross-disciplinary liaison that occurred in the preparation of the presentations and the papers published in this book. The breaking down of institutional barriers is an important step in the development of integrated management, and it is clear that the attitude and response of individuals within organisations, as well organisational culture, will be fundamental in achieving this goal. The size of the audience and the wide range of their interests and experiences indicated the increased importance and relevance of Earth heritage today.

However, while the conference participants recognised the value of the Earth heritage and the importance of Earth science information in sustainable management, there is still a significant challenge for Earth scientists to communicate more effectively (McKirdy, 2000; Boulton, this volume; Crofts, this volume). This applies at two levels: first, communication of the value of Earth science understanding and its applications to policy makers, planners and land managers; and second, enhancement of the public's understanding of their Earth heritage and the dynamic nature of Earth systems. Such improved communication is fundamental in developing the kinds of partnerships and community involvement that were envisaged as being essential to realise the opportunities identified for greater integration.

References

Alexandrowicz, Z. (ed.) 1999. Representative Geosites of Central Europe. *Polish Geological Institute Special Papers*, 2. Warsaw.

Barettino, D., Vallejo, M. and Gallego, E. (eds) 1999. *Towards the Balanced Management and Conservation of the Geological Heritage in the New Millenium.* Sociedad Geológica de España, Madrid.

Barker, G.M.A. 1996. Earth science sites in urban areas: the lessons from wildlife conservation. *In* Bennett, M.R., Doyle, P., Larwood, J.G. and Prosser, C.D. (eds) *Geology on your Doorstep. The Role of Urban Geology in Earth Heritage Conservation.* The Geological Society, London, 181-193.

Bennett, M.R., Doyle, P., Larwood, J.G. and Prosser, C.D. (eds) 1996. *Geology on your Doorstep. The Role of Urban Geology in Earth Heritage Conservation.* The Geological Society, London.

Birks, H.J.B. 1996. Contributions of Quaternary palaeoecology to nature conservation. *Journal of Vegetation Science*, **7**, 89-98.

Clifford S. 1993. Sculpture, community and the land. *In* O'Halloran, D., Green, C., Harley, M., Stanley, M. and Knill, J. (eds) *Geological and Landscape Conservation.* The Geological Society, London, 487 - 491.

Council of Europe 1996. *Pan-European Biological and Landscape Diversity Strategy.* Nature and Environment No. 74. Council of Europe Publishing, Strasbourg.

Delcourt, H.R. and Delcourt, P.A. 1988. Quaternary landscape ecology: relevant scales in space and time. *Landscape Ecology*, **2**, 23-44.

Department for Culture, Media and Sport 1999. *World Heritage Sites. The Tentative List of the United Kingdom of Great Britain and Northern Ireland.* Department for Culture, Media and Sport, London.

Department of the Environment 1994a. *Sustainable Development. The UK Strategy.* HMSO, London.

Department of the Environment 1994b. *Landsliding in Great Britain.* HMSO, London.

Department of the Environment 1995. *The Occurrence and Significance of Erosion, Deposition and Flooding in Great Britain.* HMSO, London.

Doyle, P. and Bennett, M.R. 1997. Earth-heritage conservation in the new millenium: the importance of urban geology. *Geology Today*, **13**, 29-35.

Doyle, P. and Bennett, M.R. 1998. Earth heritage conservation: past, present and future agendas. *In* Bennett, M.R. and Doyle, P. (eds) *Issues in Environmental Geology: a British Perspective.* The Geological Society, London, 41-67.

Duff, K.L. 1994. Natural areas: an holistic approach to conservation based on geology. *In* O'Halloran, D., Green, C., Harley, M., Stanley, M. and Knill, J. (eds) *Geological and Landscape Conservation.* The Geological Society, London, 121-126.

Ellis, N.V., Bowen, D.Q., Campbell, S., Knill, J.L., McKirdy, A.P., Prosser, C.D., Vincent, M.A. and Wilson, R.C.L. 1996. *An Introduction to the Geological Conservation Review.* Joint Nature Conservation Committee, Peterborough.

English Nature, Quarry Products Association and Silica & Moulding Sands Association 1999. *Biodiversity and Minerals. Extracting the Benefits for Wildlife.* Entec UK Ltd.

Firth, C.R., Collins, P.E.F. and Smith, D.E. 1997. Coastal processes and management of Scottish estuaries. IV. The Firth of Forth. *Scottish Natural Heritage Review*, No. 87.

Geikie, A. 1905. *Landscape in History and Other Essays.* Macmillan and Co., London.

Gilvear, D.J. 1999. Fluvial geomorphology and river engineering: future roles utilizing a fluvial hydrosystems framework. *Geomorphology*, **31**, 229-245.

Gordon, J.E. 1994. Conservation of geomorphology and Quaternary sites in Great Britain: an overview of site assessment. *In* Stevens, C., Gordon, J.E., Green, C.P. and Macklin, M. (eds) *Conserving our Landscape.* Proceedings of the Conference, Conserving Our Landscape: Evolving Landforms and Ice-Age Heritage, Crewe 1992. Peterborough, 11-21.

Gordon, J.E., Brazier, V., Thompson, D.B.A., and Horsfield, D. 2001. Geo-ecology and the conservation management of sensitive upland landscapes in Scotland. *Catena*, **42**, 323-332.

Gordon, J.E., Thompson, D.B.A., Haynes, V.M., MacDonald, R. and Brazier V. 1998. Environmental sensitivity and conservation management in the Cairngorm Mountains, Scotland. *Ambio*, **27**, 335-344.

Halcrow Crouch 1998. Montrose Bay Shoreline Management Study. Unpublished report to Angus Council and Glaxo Wellcome (2 vols).

Halcrow Crouch 1999. Aberdeen Bay Coastal Protection Study. Final Report. Unpublished report to Aberdeen City Council, Scottish Natural Heritage and Grampian Enterprise.

Hansom, J.D. 1999. The coastal geomorphology of Scotland: understanding sediment budgets for effective coastal management. *In* Baxter, J.M., Duncan, K., Atkins, S.M. and Lees, R.G. (eds) *Scotland's Living Coastline.* The Stationery Office, London, 34-44.

Hansom, J., Crick, M. and John, S. 2000. The potential application of Shoreline Management Planning to Scotland. *Scottish Natural Heritage Review*, No. 121.

Hoey, T. B., Smart D.W.J., Pender, G. and Metcalfe, N. (Edited by Leys, K.) 1998. Engineering methods for Scottish gravel bed rivers. *Scottish Natural Heritage Review*, No 47.

Hooke, J.M. 1998. *Coastal Defence and Earth Science Conservation.* The Geological Society, London.

Hooke, J.M. 1999. Decades of change: contributions of geomorphology to fluvial and coastal engineering and management. *Geomorphology*, **31**, 373-389.

Hose, T.A. 1998. Mountains of fire from the present to the past – or effectively communicating the wonder of geology to tourists. *Geologica Balcanica*, **28**, 77-85.

HR Wallingford 1997. Coastal cells in Scotland. *Scottish Natural Heritage Research, Survey and Monitoring Report*, No. 56.

HR Wallingford 2000. *A Guide to Managing Coastal Erosion in Beach/Dune Systems.* Scottish Natural Heritage, Perth.

Huntley, B. 1991. Historical lessons for the future. *In* Spellerberg, I.F., Goldsmith, F.B. and Morris, M.G. (eds) *Scientific Management of Temperate Communities for Conservation.* Blackwell, Oxford, 473-503.

Hutton and Rostron 1997. *A Future for Stone in Scotland.* Research Report, Historic Scotland, Technical Conservation, Research and Education Division, Edinburgh.

Knight, J., McCarron, S.G., McCabe, A.M. and Sutton, B. 1999. Sand and gravel aggregate resource management and conservation in Northern Ireland. *Journal of Environmental Management,* **56**, 195-207.

Kontturi, O. and Lyytikäinen, A. 1985. Assessment of glaciofluvial landscapes in Finland for nature conservation and other multiple use purposes. *Striae,* **22**, 41-59.

Larwood, J. and Prosser, C. 1998. Geotourism, conservation and society. *Geologica Balcanica,* **28**, 97-100.

Leafe, R. and Collins, T. 1999. Experiences and opportunities of shoreline management plans. *In* Baxter, J.M., Duncan, K., Atkins, S.M. and Lees, R.G. (eds) *Scotland's Living Coastline.* The Stationery Office, London, 63-68.

Martini, G. 1994. Actes du Premier Symposium International sur la Protection du Patrimoine Géologique. *Mémoires de la Société Géologique de France,* NS, 165.

McKirdy, A.P. 2000. Environmental geology: reaching out to a wider audience. *Scottish Journal of Geology,* **36**, 105-109.

McKirdy, A.P. in press. Environmental geology. *In* Trewin, N.H. (ed.) *Geology of Scotland.* 4th edition.

McKirdy, A.P. and Threadgould, R. 1994. Reading the landscape. *In* O'Halloran, D., Green, C., Harley, M., Stanley, M. and Knill, J. (eds) *Geological and Landscape Conservation.* The Geological Society, London, 459-462.

McKirdy, A.P., Thompson, A. and Poole, J. 1998. Dissemination of information on the earth sciences to planners and other decision-makers. *In* Bennett, M.R. and Doyle, P. (eds) *Issues in Environmental Geology: a British Perspective.* The Geological Society, London, 22-38.

McMillan, A.A. 1997. Quarries of Scotland: an illustrated guide to Scottish geology and stone working methods based on the British Geological Survey photographic archive of selected building stone quarries. *Historic Scotland Technical Advice Note,* No. 12.

McMillan, A.A., Gillanders, R.J. and Fairhurst, J.A. 1999. *Building Stones of Edinburgh.* Edinburgh Geological Society, Edinburgh.

Miller, H. Jr. 1893. Landscape geology: a plea for the study of geology by landscape-painters. *Transactions of the Edinburgh Geological Society,* **6**, 129-154.

Ministry of Agriculture, Fisheries and Food 1993. *Strategy for Flood and Coastal Defence in England and Wales.* MAFF Publications PB 1471.

Nature Conservancy Council 1990. *Earth Science Conservation in Great Britain. A Strategy.* Nature Conservancy Council, Peterborough.

Nichols, W.F., Killingbeck, K.T. and August, P.V. 1998. The influence of geomorphological heterogeneity on biodiversity. II. A landscape perspective. *Conservation Biology,* **12**, 371-379.

O'Halloran, D., Green, C., Harley, M., Stanley, M. and Knill, J. 1994. *Geological and Landscape Conservation.* The Geological Society, London.

Patzak, M. and Eder, W. 1998. 'UNESCO GEOPARK'. A new programme – a new UNESCO label. *Geologica Balcanica,* **28**, 33-35.

Pestrong, R. 1994. Geosciences and the arts. *Journal of Geological Education,* **42**, 249-257.

Pethick, J. and Burd, F. 1995. *Coastal Defence and the Environment. A Guide to Good Practice.* Ministry of Agriculture Fisheries and Food, London.

Poff, N.L., Allan, J.D., Bain, M.B., Karr, J.R., Prestegaard, K.L., Richter, B.D., Sparks, R.E. and Stromberg, J.C. 1997. The natural flow regime. A paradigm for river conservation and restoration. *BioScience,* **47**, 769-784.

Quarry Products Association 1997. *Investigating the Quarrying Industry: Sand and Gravel. Forming School and Business Partnerships.* Quarry Products Association, London.

Ratcliffe, D.A. 1977. Nature conservation: aims, methods and achievements. *Proceedings of the Royal Society of London*, **197B**, 11-29.

Richter, B.D., Baumgartner, J.V., Powell, J. and Braun, D. P. 1996. A method for assessing hydrologic alteration within ecosystems. *Conservation Biology*, **10**, 1163-1174.

Royal Commision on Environmental Pollution 1996. *Sustainable Use of Soil.* Royal Commision on Environmental Pollution, 19th Report. HMSO, London.

Schumm, S.A. 1979. Geomorphic thresholds: the concept and its applications. *Transactions of the Institute of British Geographers*, NS **4**, 485-515.

Scottish Natural Heritage 1993. *Sustainable Development and the Natural Heritage. The SNH Approach.* Scottish Natural Heritage, Perth.

Scottish Natural Heritage 2000. *Minerals and the Natural Heritage in Scotland's Midland Valley.* Scottish Natural Heritage, Perth.

Stapleton, C. and Pethick, J. 1996. Coastal processes and management of Scottish estuaries I: The Dornoch, Cromarty and Beauly/Inverness Firths. *Scottish Natural Heritage Review*, No. 50.

Stevens, C., Gordon, J.E., Green, C.P. and Macklin, M.G. (eds) 1994. *Conserving Our Landscape.* Proceedings of the Conference, Conserving Our Landscape: Evolving Landforms and Ice-Age Heritage, Crewe, 1992. Peterborough.

Swanson, F.J., Dratz, T.K., Caine, N. and Woodmansee, R.G. 1988. Landform effects on ecosystem patterns and processes. *BioScience*, **38**, 92-98.

Taylor, A. 1995. Environmental problems associated with soil in Britain: a review. *Scottish Natural Heritage Review*, No. 55.

Taylor, A.G., Gordon, J.E. and Usher, M.B. 1996. *Soils, Sustainability and the Natural Heritage.* Edinburgh, HMSO.

The Scottish Office 1999. *Natural Heritage. National Planning Policy Guideline NPPG 14.* The Scottish Office, Development Department, Edinburgh.

Thompson, A., Hine, P.D., Poole, J.S. and Greig, J.R. 1998. *Environmental Geology in Land Use Planning. A Guide to Good Practice.* Report to the Department of the Environment, Transport and the Regions by Symonds Travers Morgan, East Grinstead.

Threadgould, R. and McKirdy, A. P. 1999. Earth heritage interpretation in Scotland: the role of Scottish Natural Heritage. *In* Barettino, D., Vallejo, M. and Gallego, E. (eds) *Towards the Balanced Management and Conservation of the Geological Heritage in the New Millenium.* Sociedad Geológica de España, Madrid, 330-334.

Villalobos, M. and Guirado, J. 1999. Tourism promotion and economic use of the geological patrimony on the protected natural spaces of the sub-desertic environment in Almeria (Spain). *In* Barettino, D., Vallejo, M. and Gallego, E. (eds) 1999. *Towards the Balanced Management and Conservation of the Geological Heritage in the New Millenium.* Sociedad Geológica de España, Madrid, 425-429.

Weighell, A.J. 1999. Earth heritage conservation in the United Kingdom, the World Heritage List and UNESCO Geoparks. *In* Barettino, D., Vallejo, M. and Gallego, E. (eds) 1999. *Towards the Balanced Management and Conservation of the Geological Heritage in the New Millenium.* Sociedad Geológica de España, Madrid, 24-27.

Werritty, A. 1995. Integrated catchment management: a review and evaluation. *Scottish Natural Heritage Review*, No. 58.

Werritty, A. and Leys, K. F. 2001. The sensitivity of Scottish rivers and upland valley floors to recent environmental change. *Catena*, **42**, 251-274

Wilson, C. 1994. *Earth Heritage Conservation.* The Geological Society in association with the Open University, Milton Keynes.

Wimbledon, W.A. and others. 1998. A first attempt at a Geosites framework for Europe – an IUGS initiative to support recognition of world heritage and European geodiversity. *Geologica Balcanica*, **28**, 5-32.

World Commission on Environment and Development 1983. *Our Common Future*. Oxford University Press, Oxford.

WWF 2000. *What's good for rivers is good for people*. Project report by the Wild Rivers Demonstration and Advisory Project. WWF, Aberfeldy.

2 TOWARDS A NEW SYNTHESIS OF THE BIOLOGICAL AND EARTH SCIENCES

Aubrey Manning

Summary

1.   In spite of the age geology as a science, it is only recently that unifying theories have been developed which enable us to undertand the evolution of the planet.
2.   Modern astrophysics and space exploration have helped biologists and geologists to understand the uniqueness of Earth in the solar system.
3.   Life has affected crucial Earth processes. For example, Cyanobacteria first photosynthesised carbohydrates to produce free oxygen which precipitated out iron from seas and rivers (as seen in banded iron rock deposits).
4.   Physical processes such as volcanism and plate tectonics alter the planet and have had major effects on the course of evolution. The end result has been greater biodiversity. Mass extinctions of biological life have occurred but so far each has provided the survivors with increased opportunities.
5.   Human activities and high population numbers are causing the decline of biodiversity and the extinction of many species, whilst simultaneously destroying the ability of the planet to support life comfortably.
6.   We must use the synthesis between Earth science and biology to help others to understand the way the Earth works, and thus promote sustainable development and the survival of humanity.

2.1 Introduction: a biologist's view of the Earth

It was an honour to be asked to provide the keynote address for the conference reported in this book, which looks for a synthesis, and a celebration, of the *whole* of Scotland's natural heritage.

I am a biologist who never had the fortune to take a course in geology as a student and, until recently, had absorbed the modern transformation of the Earth sciences only as general knowledge. Having had the great opportunity of acting as 'presenter' of BBC2's *Earth Story*, I found myself playing the role of a kind of honest broker between the Earth science experts and the public - interested and wanting to be informed!

I did indeed become informed and, more significantly, enthused by the fascination of the new ideas. In the process I found that the manner in which I viewed my own biological science changed, as did the nature of some of my long-held assumptions. Perhaps then, I am in a position to act as one kind of bridging factor, although I am acutely aware that I remain without expertise in the Earth sciences. I can provide only a biologist's impressions of what has been happening.

I have been struck by just how young is so much of the new Earth science. When I was a student studying the geographical distribution of animals, we were told of Wegener's ideas on 'continental drift' but we were not expected to take them too seriously; we stuck to changes in sea level and past land bridges to explain the anomalies! I feel that until the 1960s, Earth science was rather like pre-Darwinian biology. We had a huge amount of detailed knowledge and a good understanding of some processes, but there was no unifying general theory. Now there are theories of great power and beauty which, for the first time, enable us to understand how our planet 'works'. One of the remarkable bonuses of this short history is that many of the people whose work has been crucial in the new thinking are still with us! Amongst many, to be able to *talk* to Marie Tharp, George Plafker, Dan Mackenzie and Fred Vines, is how a biologist might have felt speaking to Darwin, Wallace or Mendel!

2.2 The uniqueness of Earth

One immediate task for the biologist is to grapple with the concept of geological time - deep time. The history of life on Earth has hitherto been so much concentrated on the multicellular forms which first really show in the Cambrian. The 600 million years since the Palaeozoic seemed an infinity enough when I was studying palaeontology. We were not asked even to *contemplate* the Archaean, and anyway there were not any pre-Cambrian fossils! Now, we must all share something of John Playfair's response when he wrote so memorably after visiting Siccar Point with James Hutton, '...the mind seemed to grow giddy from looking so far into the abyss of time.' There has been time enough for processes of unimaginable slowness to have enormous effects on the Earth. The Atlantic opens up, mountain ranges rise and are worn away again.

Our generation has been fortunate in being the first to be able to see the Earth from space and to get detailed images of the Moon, Mars and other parts of the solar system. I believe this has changed for ever our perceptions of human existence. Modern astrophysics allows us to look back some 4.5 *billion* years to the origins of the solar system and recognise our Sun as a modest, second, or possibly third generation star since the Big Bang around 15 billion years back. We can recognise the uniqueness of the Earth in the solar system, the planet whose properties of size and distance from the Sun have enabled liquid water to exist at the surface for at least 3.8 billion years and thereby supported life (Figure 2.1). The so-called 'Goldilocks' metaphor contrasts us (the bowl of porridge that was 'just right') with our immediate neighbours who began along lines very much similar to our own. Venus (too hot), its water dissociated in its upper atmosphere, lost the hydrogen to space; carbon dioxide could not be fixed by rock weathering and remains in high concentration, producing a surface temperature which would melt lead. Mars (too cold) must have started with abundant liquid water like us, but is too small to have retained sufficient volcanism to recycle carbon dioxide which remains locked up in its rocks. The thin atmosphere cannot retain warmth from the Sun, and although the water is still there, it is frozen beneath a kilometre or more of permafrost. There is an excellent account of the early history of the three main rocky planets, especially as concerns their atmospheres, in Nunn (1997).

It is this recognition of Earth's unique life-supporting qualities in the solar system (*currently* unique, for it is certainly possible that life began on Mars, but has been frozen out) that engages biologists. To recognise this is not just to accept the obvious and for two reasons. First, we owe to James Lovelock the general recognition that life has not been merely a passenger on the planet; it has affected certain crucial processes throughout most

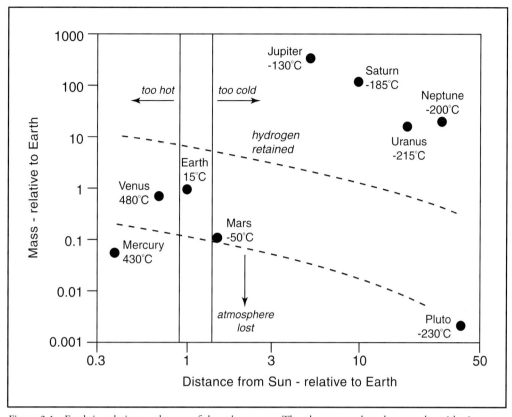

Figure 2.1. Earth in relation to the rest of the solar system. The planets are plotted on two logarithmic axes – distance from the Sun and mass – both taking the value of Earth as 1. The mean surface temperature of each is given. The two vertical lines delimit the space in which liquid water can exist; the two curving dotted lines delimit the space in which the gravitational pull of a planet will hold any kind of atmosphere. The gas giants are large enough to hold even hydrogen. Only Earth has a surface temperature and a mass which conserve liquid water and an atmosphere (from Nunn, 1998).

of Earth's history.   Second, we now realise that life began extraordinarily early at a time when, though past its most violent bombardment phase and with the Moon in place, Earth was still subject to meteor strikes and volcanism which must have led to extreme temperatures in the young oceans.   There are now abundant fossil bacteria from rocks more than 3.5 billion years old of types which suggest they were laid down in sites similar to the mid-ocean vents.   Descendants of these bacteria live there to this day and also in surface hot springs. Some of these so-called thermophiles live and reproduce at temperatures above the boiling point of water; they would have been well-adapted to cope with the conditions early in Earth's existence.

2.3 Biological and geological interactions
It is only recently that microbiologists have been able to assess the whole range of archaic bacteria which are still living in a variety of extreme habitats throughout the Earth and sometimes at depths of a kilometre or more in the crust.   Their total biomass can only be guessed at, but must be enormous.   Many of these prokaryotic organisms are anaerobes and

metabolise sulphur. No alternative was offered in the early history of life until the emergence of the group once called 'blue-green algae' now known as the Cyanobacteria. They evolved a way of photosynthesising carbohydrates, utilising light energy from the Sun, and for the first time free oxygen appeared in the shallow seas where these bacteria lived.

We have unequivocal evidence of the early history of Cyanobacteria because some live in masses which secrete calcium carbonate around themselves to form eventually a sizeable mushroom-like structure perhaps a fifth of a metre high - a stromatolite. They fossilise well and we find them from as early as 3.5 billion years ago. Over the following billion years they flourished, and this period coincides with vast sedimentary deposits of iron-rich rock - the banded irons. It seems likely that the free oxygen produced by these bacteria precipitated the iron out from the seas and rivers.

The huge areas of banded irons, in Western Australia and elsewhere, represent a turning point in the history of life and the Earth; they show for the first time the influence of life on the structure of the planet itself. Thenceforth, life has exerted a constant influence, forming part of the carbon cycle in the oceans, and on land contributing to the circulation of water and the patterns of erosion through the formation of soils. It is a unique two-way interaction.

Yet the history of life shows time and time again, that the planet is no benign partner as some have suggested who misunderstand Lovelock's Gaia hypothesis. The various physical processes which are driven by the convective cooling of the mantle have imposed huge constraints on the evolution of life and have more than once threatened its entire survival. Colossal ice sheets have periodically locked up the land and shallow seas for thousands of years; gigantic bursts of volcanic activity have occluded sunlight. Yet there have always been survivors and the diversity of life is greater now than at any time in Earth's history.

For the great majority of life's existence, organisms remained at the level of tiny single-celled prokaryotes. These anucleate cells could not grow in size until, as Margulis (1971) first suggested, they came together as a symbiotic colony within a single cell wall and enclosed their genetic material within a nucleus, to form a eukaryote cell. Beyond this, the next great achievement was the capacity for dividing cells to stay together, to specialise and differentiate and thus to become multicellular organisms - plants, animals and fungi. This is the stage which we encounter fully fledged, as it were, in the Burgess Shale and other great Cambrian sites of 500-600 million years ago.

However much we may choose to ignore them when we can, the prokaryotes are still with us in colossal abundance. Evolution is not simply replacement. At every stage, living organisms adapt to opportunities which the environment may offer. Descent with modification has enabled life to move into various habitats and adopt various means of existence. It has been able to go beyond the oceans into fresh water and then on to land, which has many advantages for both plants and animals. Nevertheless the oceans still teem with life - protists, crustaceans, echinoderms, fish, seaweeds - and all are immensely successful. Evolution has led to greater diversity but there is no sustained progress towards the ultimate success, and extinction has been commonplace.

2.4 The development of biodiversity

The best way to comprehend the development of biodiversity and the way in which it has been affected by planetary events is to record the total number of different families represented in the fossil record. Such a scale is bound to be rather arbitrary; a family is not any kind of natural 'unit', but nor is it subject to systematic error over time and so gives us a reasonable estimate of diversity. We can deal only with multicellular forms, which means beginning with the Cambrian, and since then for the most part there has been a steady increase in diversity. The emergence of new forms has more than made up for the inevitable extinctions. However, this growth has been interrupted by five clear breaks when the number of families declined rapidly. These mark five so-called 'mass extinctions' during which a significant proportion of living forms disappeared within - in geological terms - a brief period (Figure 2.2). With little doubt these extinctions were associated with major planetary events. The cause of three of the largest can be identified with fair certainty. That at the close of the Ordovician, about 450 million years ago, occurred when much of the land formed one great continent centred close to the South Pole. The land and shallow seas were enveloped in ice and life struggled. The largest extinction of all, which some estimates put at *95% of all life*, occurred at the Permian/Triassic boundary. It was at this time that a huge basalt flow took place which now centres around Noril'sk in Siberia. This flow covered 2.5 million square kilometres to a depth of 3 kilometres and such a scale is hardly paralleled before and certainly not since. The atmosphere must have been choked with dust for many years and photosynthesis almost extinguished. Third, there is the most famous extinction

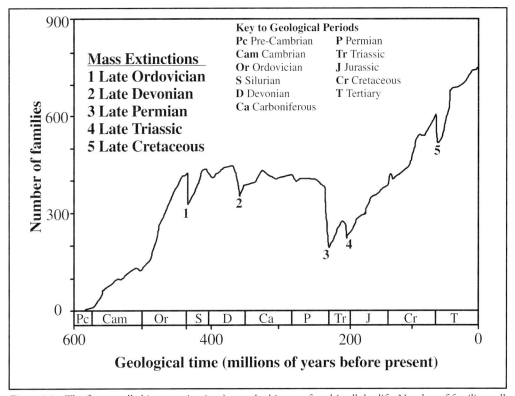

Figure 2.2. The five so-called 'mass extinctions' over the history of multi-cellular life. Number of families well represented in the marine fossil record is taken as a measure of diversity. Time runs back to the first great rise in diversity at the beginning of the Cambrian. The later extinctions will have involved terrestrial life also, but the timing of these major events was shared. (Reprinted with permission from Raup and Sepkoski, 1982. Copyright 1982 American Association for the Advancement of Science).

of all - at the close of the Cretaceous when the dinosaurs left us. This is associated with a big meteor impact in the Gulf of Mexico and with another great basalt flow, perhaps triggered by the impact, which now forms the Deccan Traps of SE India.

From all of these catastrophes, life has recovered, most dramatically so in the 250 million years since the Permo/Trias event. Taking the demise of the great reptiles in its stride, as it were, diversity has climbed steadily. We owe this in great measure to the evolution of the flowering plants and above all the insects, which now comprise three quarters of all known animals.

It is noteworthy that each of the mass extinctions of the past has provided the survivors with increased opportunities. Many ecological niches have been rendered suddenly vacant, and life, always pushing up against the edges of the possible, has been swift to take advantage. The insects, in particular, have been amazingly successful at filling vacant niches and carving out new ones. The huge and rapid radiation of the mammals and birds once the great reptiles had gone is another dramatic case. Mammals had been around as small nocturnal insectivores since the Triassic, but could not compete with reptiles in most niches until the meteor intervened.

2.5 Human threats to the Earth's well being

There is a modern postscript to this brief history of life and it carries a powerful message for us. At the moment a sixth mass extinction is in progress. This time it is not related to any planetary event, but is caused by the activities of one single species - *Homo sapiens* - which is rapidly creating a voracious monoculture of humans in which space and resources are being converted to our use at the expense of most other life forms, particularly those of any size. It is probably accelerating now with the recent exponential growth of human numbers and human technology, but it had already begun on a significant scale following the last glacial maximum (Diamond, 1992). By definition almost, the aftermath of this extinction will *not* leave the environment clear for other life.

We are not rendering the planet any better positioned to support us either. The ozone layer, whose development early in Earth's history has shielded life from damaging levels of UV radiation, is being broken open. Fossil fuel is being consumed at a high rate, and correspondingly high amounts of carbon dioxide are being put into the atmosphere. Many authorities are convinced that global warming is already detectable as a result. The overall effects on global climate are unpredictable, but the study of climate history suggests that there have sometimes been very rapid swings. The past 10,000 years, in which civilisations as we know them have developed, have been remarkably tranquil in both geological and climatic terms - no large basalt flows, no earthquakes of magnitude 10 on the Richter scale, and so on. The world is now a crowded place and such events today would be hugely damaging. Such is the nature of our planet that there is little or nothing we can do to prevent them recurring, although there are some measures we could take in the long term to ameliorate their effects. For example, I would advocate encouraging and allowing the human population to fall to 20% of its current level, but that is another story!

Having gained some understanding of Earth's dynamic nature, I find that my position as a biologist and conservationist has changed. In one sense I have to accept that, in the end, efforts at conservation may be futile. I remember expressing concerns over global warming to a distinguished glaciologist, whose response was to point out that in 20,000 years time we shall be under a kilometre of ice! Of course everything depends on the time scale. In 4 billion years or so, our Sun will have become a red giant but it remains the case that a century is an extreme human lifespan. If a week is a long time in politics, then certainly 10 years can transform political systems and our future prospects. Our task, as informed people with a concern for the natural world, is to help others to understand the way the Earth works and thus to adopt policies which will enable humanity get through the next 50 years or so. We cannot expect to do more and, employing the currently fashionable phrase, we must aim for 'sustainable development.' If we can manage this, then the following 50 years might well be easier. Common sense and enlightened self-interest would seem to go together here and suggest that we should operate using the precautionary principle, slowing down resource consumption and reducing pollution. Since climate has been unstable in the not very distant past and the situation which triggered rapid changes is not fully understood, we should interfere with the atmosphere and the seas as little as possible.

2.6 Conclusion: towards a new synthesis

It is here that 'the new synthesis' can help us, because although biology and the Earth sciences have always been connected, the new developments make a closer integration of our subjects much easier. It makes good sense to begin from an early stage to introduce the history of life and the history of the Earth together. I was much struck when I was in the field with geologists to see how they 'read' the landscape and pieced together its history from the clues in the landforms and the rocks themselves. They operated in just the same way that biologists would do in reconstructing the history of the ecosystem which occupies the landscape. Further, and just as importantly, I sensed that like field biologists they revelled in its beauty and diversity. Many chapters in this book are concerned with communicating a sense of the wonder and beauty of Scotland's physical structure to the general public in whose care ultimately it rests. The enjoyment of living organisms, which often catch the eye more easily, will be augmented by understanding and thus coming to enjoy the nature and history of the land itself.

Recently I was delighted to note that a portrait of Robert Jameson (1774-1854) which hangs on the stair in my Institute - the old zoology building - also appears on the stair of the Grant Institute of Geology and Geophysics next door. Jameson held the Chair of Natural History at Edinburgh for 50 years and at that time the professor taught zoology, geology and mineralogy; that was natural history. Plants were there too, of course, even if botany had already been taken into the medical school! Our sciences have moved on, but their attractiveness to young people has never been greater. Surely there is now a chance to make sure that education, at all levels, uses a new synthesis to bring out the full significance of our natural heritage.

References

Diamond, J. 1992. *The Rise and Fall of the Third Chimpanzee*. Penguin, London.

Margulis, L. 1971. Symbiosis and evolution. *Scientific American*, **225**(2), 48-57.

Nunn, J.F. 1998. The evolution of the atmosphere. *Proceedings of the Geologists' Association*, **109**,1-13.

Raup, D.A. and Sepkoski, J.J. 1982. Mass extinctions in the marine fossil record. *Science*, **215**, 1501-1503.

3 THE EARTH SYSTEM AND THE CHALLENGE OF GLOBAL CHANGE

Geoffrey S. Boulton

Summary

1.   There has long been a gulf in geology, between the study of old, 'hard rocks' formed as a result of dissipation of the Earth's internal energy and of young 'soft rocks' formed by Earth surface processes driven by solar energy. It is now imperative that the gulf is closed and that geology contributes to a science that treats the Earth as a holistic planetary system in which the surface and sub-surface are strongly coupled as a consequence of interactions between physical, chemical and biological processes, and which deals with planetary history as part of a spectrum of change from the 'Big Bang' to the present day.

2.   Some of the major processes of planetary evolution over this time spectrum are described. However, humanity has now become a powerful geological agent, and has had impacts on the Earth system that have the capacity to affect its evolution, such as changes in the global climate system, with potentially severe implications for humanity and the sustainability of our mode of life. Understanding the Earth system, using that understanding to mitigate damaging human impacts, and finding strategies for sustainable use of the planet's resources pose great challenges to the Earth sciences in analysing complexity, in modelling and prediction and in forging the collaborations between geologists, geophysicists, biologists, cosmologists, geomorphologists and engineers that are required for these tasks.

3.   The application of Earth science to some of the key issues of global change are assessed, particularly in relation to Scotland, including development of a sustainable energy regime, the disposal of waste, mitigating and adapting to hydrological changes, managing changes in landscape and biodiversity, and environmental engineering.

4.   The application of science to issues of public policy requires scientists to adopt some key principles, and to recognise that policy decisions are determined by social, economic, political and ethical constraints, as much as by scientific advice. The difficulty of creating policy in many science-driven issues, where uncertainty is great and impacts are perceived to be large, has arisen, to a large degree, because of the erosion of public trust in existing processes and institutions. New processes need to be forged for this task.

3.1 Traditional perspectives of the past

Geology made one of the great contributions to humanity's awareness of its place on this planet through James Hutton, a graduate of Edinburgh University, when he deduced from his observations of the rocks on the Berwickshire coast that the Earth showed "no vestige of a beginning, no prospect of an end" (Hutton, 1788). 'Deep time' had been discovered. It was one of a series of scientific insights, on a par with those of Copernicus and Darwin, which shattered humanity's belief in its own transcendent importance by demonstrating that rather than living on a young Earth, ruled by human will within days of its birth, we appeared late in its history, almost as an afterthought. Mark Twain, an instinctive geologist, captured the point with irony, when he wrote: "Man has been on the Earth 32,000 years. That it took a hundred million years to prepare the Earth for him proves that that is what it was done for. If the Eiffel Tower represents the Earth's age, and the skim of paint on the pinnacle on top represents man's share of that age, anybody could tell that that is what it was built for" (in Baender, 1973).

Concern with the old and the deep has, however, left geologists with blind spots. One is implicitly reflected in a distinction in the topics chosen in the symposium from which this book derives, between one entitled the "Geological Inheritance" of Scotland and another its "Quaternary History". It is as if 'geology' happened in the deep past and is separated by a gulf of time from the Quaternary, which is the immediate antecedent of the present. This distinction is easy to understand in areas like Scotland, where there *is* a great gulf of time between ancient rocks formed deep in the lithosphere or mantle, and which ring clearly when hit by a hammer, and the thin skin of soft, 'drift' sediments that overlie them, produced by more recent surface processes. But there is also another gulf of time implicit in the outlook, and often explicit in the philosophy, of many non-geologists, that the drama of human history has been played out against a static environmental backdrop, divorced from the violent changes of the geological past. People know that the geological past had dinosaurs, continental drift and ice ages, but in countries like Britain, not plagued by volcanic eruptions and earthquakes, it is easy to believe that a great gulf separates us from such a past. They are not views, however, that appeal to those living in areas of subsiding sedimentary basins, such as western Alaska. Here, not only is the continuity between the deep past and the recent past all too apparent, but so is the continuity between the recent past and the present reflected in the modern glaciers that are the remains of the more extensive ice sheets of the last glacial period of only 10,000 years ago, and perennial volcanic eruptions and earthquakes that are reminders that powerful and dramatic natural forces are still at work.

One of the classical distinctions that remains embedded in much modern geology is that between deep Earth processes, driven by the Earth's internal heat, and surface processes driven by energy from the Sun. In some European universities the geological curriculum still distinguishes between *Endogeology*, deep Earth processes, and *Exogeology*, surface processes. Students rarely study both. Endogeology is about the internal forces that drive up mountain chains, create volcanoes, and are best reflected in old, deep rocks such as those of the Scottish Highlands. Exogeology is about the processes driven by solar energy in the Earth's thin fluid envelope of atmosphere and oceans, including the flow of glaciers, oceans, rivers and the atmosphere.

These distinctions of time and place, although understandable, represent partial and disabling views, both for geologists and citizens. They hide more than they illuminate. Unless modern geology fully recognises the continuity between the past and present, and the holistic nature of interactions between different parts of the Earth system, it will fail to transmit some of its most important messages, fail to adapt to the changing agenda of modern science, lose the opportunity offered to science as it moves from the background to the foreground in public consciousness and fail to respond adequately to human needs.

3.2 The Earth system: a changed perspective

It is now possible to give a holistic account of the evolution of the Earth as part of the larger evolution of the Universe and the Solar System, and of the way in which the solid, mineral Earth has interacted with its fluid envelope of oceans and atmosphere and the life that they contain to create the modern planet. Understanding that evolution and the operation of the Earth system is vitally important in determining how humanity can achieve a sustainable mode of life that will ensure that nature's capital can be passed on to future generations. For it has become clear that the rate at which we are currently using many planetary resources is far greater than the rate at which nature replenishes them. These are not abstruse and distant concepts. They are important considerations for everyday practical decisions made in Scotland.

Our modern understanding of the Earth system has come from the use of:

- **new observational tools**, able to sense acoustic and electromagnetic radiation that both emanate naturally from within and beyond the Earth, and are actively emitted by devices using radiation to probe Earth and planetary interiors and pick up returning pulses;
- **new observational platforms**, such as Earth-orbiting satellites, space probes, ocean vessels and means of drilling deep into the Earth both on land and in the oceans;
- **new methods of chemical and biochemical analysis,** that permit us to infer details of the chemistry of Earth and planetary atmospheres and rock composition, both on retrieved samples and remotely by analysing radiation characteristics; and
- **new theories and powerful computers**, that permit us to simulate and understand the behaviour of these complex natural systems.

These new approaches still depend upon classical geological and biological field and laboratory observations, but also create new demands for further field observations.

The new Earth and planetary synthesis (e.g. Broecker, 1985; Brown *et al.*, 1992; Lamb and Sington, 1998) is not the work of any one conventional discipline, but of cosmologists, geophysicists, geologists and biologists pursuing a common objective. Although classical disciplines are the means by which many core concepts and skills are developed, the purpose to which they are applied should now be the broader one of understanding the planet, rather than being constrained within arbitrary disciplinary boundaries.

What have we learned about the Earth system?

3.2.1 *Formation of the planet*

It all began with a 'Big Bang' (Figure 3.1), which we calculate, from the rate at which galaxies in the universe are moving apart, occurred about 15 billion years ago. The neutrons created by the 'Big Bang' split into electrons and protons, which combined to form hydrogen and helium, the two lightest elements, which still form 99% of all the matter in the visible universe. By 12 billion years ago, gravity began to pull this cosmic matter together to form the first stars. Helium and hydrogen were compressed together in their hot dense cores and the atoms fused to create the heavier elements. As the stars exhausted their nuclear fuel, after about 11 billion years ago, they collapsed in upon themselves to create supernova explosions, dispersing their detritus through the universe, including the heavier elements formed in the stars. Our solar system began to form by gravitational attraction of

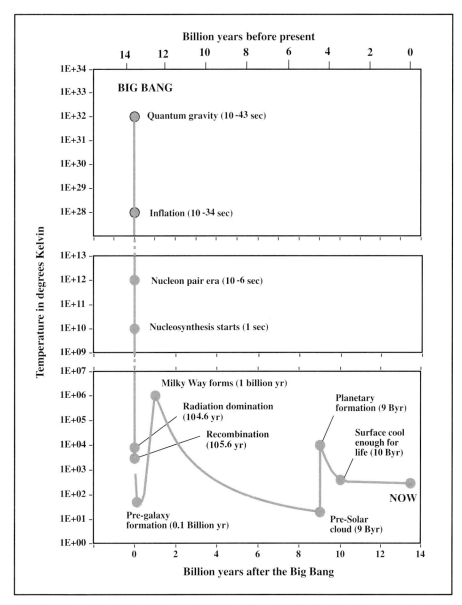

Figure 3.1 The thermal and climatic history of the Earth from the 'Big Bang' to the present day. Events in the aftermath of the 'Big Bang' (timings are shown after the 'Big Bang' and before present) are, in sequence: an era of quantum gravity, when normal ideas of space and time break down; the initiation of universe expansion; the mutual annihilation of protons and antiprotons, permitting the formation of nuclei of light elements; the end of the period when radiation is the dominant form of energy in the universe; the recombination of ionised protons and electrons to form atoms, permitting light to travel freely through the universe; the cooling of diffuse gases to a low temperature until galaxies begin to aggregate together under gravity, leading to heating in the cores of nucleating galaxies. The Sun and planets form after 11 billion years and subsequently cool in a way that on Earth, after 3.8 million years ago, permits life to develop with surface temperatures controlled within a narrow range by a natural thermostat. Until this time, the graph schematically shows the probable temperature history of planetary constituents. After this time, it shows the surface temperature. (Temperature notation: 1E+04=104=10,000; Degrees Kelvin = 273+degrees Celsius). It is suggested that intelligent life is the next likely step, but there is a great deal of contrary evidence!

this detritus around the star we call the Sun about 9 billion years ago, and the Earth and the other rocky planets around it began to form from the swirling dust of the nucleating solar system. Most of the atoms that make up this book formed in the intense heat and pressure deep within a star over 9 billion years ago.

The layered structure of the Earth that exists today is believed to have formed about 4.5 billion years ago when the Earth collided with a planetary object about the size of Mars. The energy of the impact created the Moon and melted the Earth, leading to segregation of a dense iron-rich core surrounded by siliceous mantle and an outer gaseous layer including water vapour, carbon dioxide and nitrogen. The water vapour condensed to form a primitive ocean, and Earth's gravity trapped the gases to form the thin and apparently fragile atmospheric veil that wreathed the Earth, and which dictated much of its subsequent evolution. The long history of a watery planet had begun.

3.2.2 Coupling between the surface and deep Earth

Heat generation within the Earth's core and mantle produces convection, in which hot material rises and, as it subsequently cools and becomes more dense, sinks again, though leaving some light materials on the surface to form embryo continents. The water on the surface of the planet has played a vital role in convection and the growth of continents. As water is carried down from the surface in the sinking arms of convection cells, it acts as anti-freeze in the mantle, producing water-rich magmas, which are light and fluid enough to rise under gravity, to crystallise as granites near the surface and progressively create continental plates with their typical granitic compositions. This water also weakens the rocks below and at the edge of plates, allowing them to slide easily past each other. Without it, plates would soon jam and plate tectonics would cease.

Water thus plays a vital role in facilitating plate tectonic processes that maintain the flow of deep re-crystallised rocks to the surface. These weather to form soil, and release fresh mineral nutrients to feed plant life and the food web which depends upon it. Without plate tectonics, surface nutrients would long ago have been exhausted, and the Earth's surface would have become barren, like that of Mars.

The first evidence of life on Earth dates from about 3.8 billion years ago, and the first bacteria, identical in form to modern bacteria, from about 3.5 billion years ago. These first organisms lived in the vicinity of hot springs, rich in the chemicals needed to create complex biological molecules and sources of the heat energy needed to drive chemical reactions. From this they may have evolved the capacity to use the Sun's energy for photosynthesis, which uses sunlight to create oxygen from carbon dioxide and water, and to build carbon-based skeletons. This would have permitted them to break free from volcanic zones, to colonise the rest of the Earth, and ultimately to create free oxygen in the atmosphere in increasing concentrations by about 2.1 billion years ago. As oxygen concentrations increased and spread into the upper atmosphere, sunlight led to dissociation of O_2 into oxygen atoms able to recombine to form an ozone (O_3) layer that absorbed much harmful solar radiation. The combination of an oxygenated atmosphere that permitted more complex organic structures to develop, and a protective ozone shield, were the conditions that permitted life to colonise the Earth and create the great biodiversity that has characterised it for the last 600 million years.

Whereas we previously supposed that the forces generated by the Earth's internal heat created most of the large-scale features of its surface, it has only recently been recognised that the surface Earth and the deep Earth are coupled, and that the penetration of surface water is able to stimulate upward movement of the fresh mineral materials that ultimately maintain life itself.

3.2.3 *The Earth's thermostat and the climate system*

One of the Earth's most remarkable attributes is the way in which it has maintained a relatively steady temperature since at least 3.8 billion years ago, between the freezing point and boiling point of water, even though the output from the Sun has increased through time (Figures 3.1 and 3.2). It is almost as if it had a thermostat. It does. It is the interaction between atmospheric gases (largely carbon dioxide), rock weathering and living organisms.

Short wave solar radiation is both absorbed by the Earth's surface and reflected from it back into space. However, when radiation is re-emitted from the Earth, it is re-emitted at longer wavelengths. This is absorbed by atmospheric gases, generating heat and warming the atmosphere. This is the so-called 'Greenhouse Effect'. If there were no atmospheric gases, there would be no such effect, the Earth would be about 30°C cooler, and we would not be here.

The vital gas is carbon dioxide. How is its concentration controlled so as to act as a thermostat? Volcanoes add carbon dioxide to the atmosphere, but the weathering of silicates and the growth of living organisms extract it from the atmosphere, the latter to build their skeletons. The balance between these processes plays a key role in determining the Earth's surface temperature. If Earth's temperature increases, the rate of silicate weathering increases, taking up atmospheric carbon dioxide and thus reducing the greenhouse effect and holding back temperature rise. The role of living organisms is more complex. A warming Earth will in general produce enhanced organic growth on the continents, which will absorb more atmospheric carbon dioxide, but the oceans are the dominant carbon dioxide sink, and their role, and the role of marine organisms in helping to control carbon dioxide concentrations is not yet entirely clear.

3.2.4 *The variability of climate*

Although the thermostatic mechanism ensures that the Earth's temperature remains within a band that is narrow by the standards of other planets in the solar system, it does not exert very strict control on climate. Figures 3.1-3.8 show how the Earth's climate appears to vary on all timescales. We can distinguish several frequencies of variation.

3.2.4.1 *Changes at tectonic frequencies*

Figure 3.2 shows that both 'ice ages'[1] and 'hot-houses' have occurred from time to time during Earth history. These probably reflect the varying efficiency of the Earth as a heat transmission engine. The Earth receives more solar heat than it re-emits in the equatorial region and emits more than it receives in the polar regions. The excess in the equatorial region is transported polewards by the oceans and the atmosphere to make up the polar deficit. If poleward heat transport is efficient, the equator-pole temperature gradient is small and the polar regions have a relatively high equilibrium temperature. If inefficient, the temperature gradient is high and the poles are relatively cold.

---

[1] An ice age is a period of time when a significant part of the Earth is covered by ice sheets. The Earth is therefore currently in an ice age.

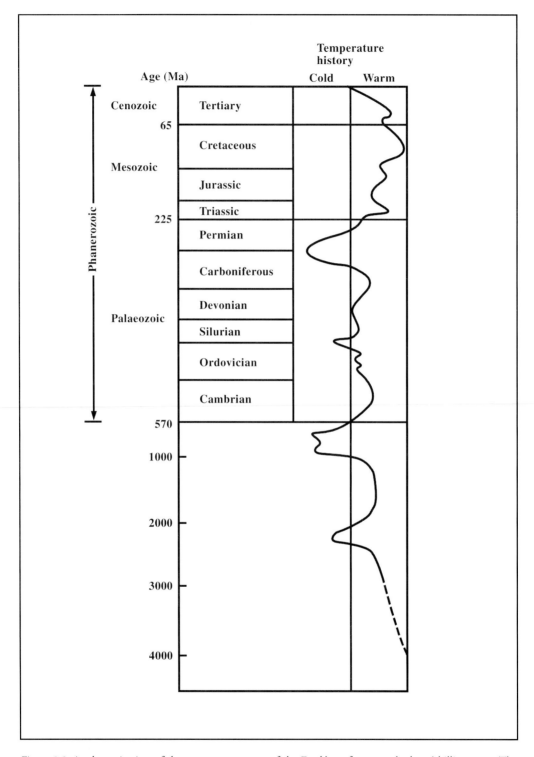

Figure 3.2 A schematic view of the mean temperature of the Earth's surface over the last 4 billion years. The range of variation in mean temperature over the last 3 billion years is unlikely to have exceeded 40°C, and is certainly less than 100°C.

From the early Tertiary, 50 million years ago, until the onset of the Quaternary ice age, about 2.5 million years ago (Figure 3.3), poleward temperature gradients have increased and the circum-polar regions have cooled. We believe that this reflects plate tectonic movements that have changed the geometry of the ocean basins in such a way as to create barriers to poleward flow of warm equatorial waters, thus producing a warmer tropical zone, colder circum-polar zones and growth of land ice in high latitudes (Barron, 1984). Plate tectonic movements have also led to strong uplift in Tibet, the alpine zones of Europe and the western American cordilleras during the last 10 million years. These uplifted zones have perturbed the atmospheric flow so as to generate large standing waves in their lee (Rosby waves), similar to those which occur in the lee of boulders in streams, that have the capacity to draw down polar air into middle latitudes (Ruddiman and Kutzbach, 1990). It seems that large-scale changes in Earth physiography driven by tectonic processes have changed the efficiency of heat distribution on the surface to produce major changes in global climate such as 'ice ages' and 'hot-houses'.

3.2.4.2 Changes at orbital frequencies

Tectonically driven climatic changes occur at frequencies of the order of millions and tens of millions of years. Evidence from cores from the deep ocean and ice sheets demonstrates the existence of powerful climatic changes at frequencies of tens to hundreds of thousands of years (Figure 3.4). It shows that during the last 750,000 years, there have been three dominant frequencies of change with cycle lengths of 100,000, 40,000 and 20,000 years. These cycles are of the same duration as cycles of variation in the intensity and geographic and seasonal distribution of radiation that the Earth receives from the Sun due to predictable changes in the geometry of the Earth's orbit around the Sun (so-called 'Milankovitch cycles'). We believe, therefore, that the frequencies apparent in the record shown in Figure 3.4 are determined by Earth orbital variations.

The 100,000-year cycles apparent in Figure 3.4 are the dominant climatic cycles of the Earth's current ice age. During its cold periods, so-called 'glacial periods', much of the northern continents (Eurasia, North America) are covered by great ice sheets similar to those of Antarctica and Greenland, wide zones beyond them suffer from permafrost, and ecological zones on the continents and in the oceans are displaced towards the equator compared with the present. The intervening warm periods, one of which we are now experiencing, are termed 'interglacials'. However, if we calculate the maximum changes in global mean temperature between glacial and interglacial periods due to orbital variations alone, it would be at most 0.5°C, whereas the geological record shows that the changes were in reality about 5°C. It is as if the Earth were a radio receiver and the Sun the transmitter. The receiver receives a signal from the transmitter with a certain frequency and reflects it in its output. However, there is also a volume knob, and something turns the volume knob so as to amplify the volume of the output signal so that it is about ten times greater than the input.

The probable cause of this amplification has become apparent in the last decade from borehole cores from the Antarctic and Greenland ice sheets (Figures 3.5 and 3.6). The centres of these ice sheets represent stratified accumulations of frozen atmospheric constituents providing a continuous record going back for 0.5 million years, with identifiable annual layers going back at least 30,000 years. Gas bubbles within the ice provide a reliable record

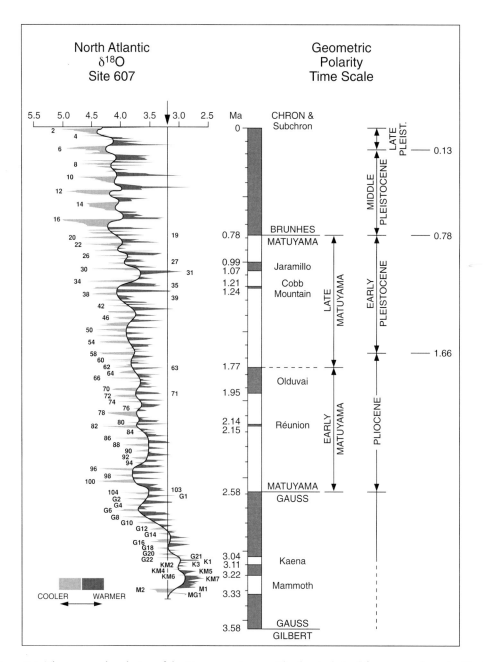

Figure 3.3 The onset and evolution of the Quaternary ice age. The data is derived from a core from the North Atlantic Ocean (data from Barendregt and Irving, 1998). The curve on the left shows the oxygen isotope composition of the shells of marine micro-organisms. On the right is shown the geomagnetic timescale in the core, which reflects reversals of the Earth's magnetic field. The strong cooling that led to the increase of large ice masses on the Earth's surface began about 3 million years ago. Subsequent average cooling reflects intensification of the cold periods. Hemi-cycles to the left show glacial periods, during which ice sheets grew on the mid-latitude continents of the northern hemisphere. Hemi-cycles to the right show interglacial periods similar to the present day. (Individual cycles are numbered as stratigraphic stages). Prior to 0.75 million years ago, complete glacial/interglacial cycles were about 40,000 years in duration; subsequently, they were about 100,000 years in duration. (Source: Barendregt and Irving, 1998).

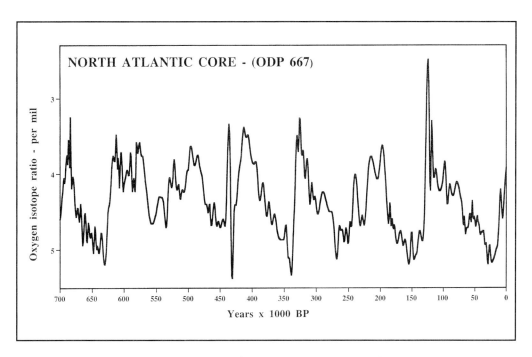

Figure 3.4 Data from a core from the North Atlantic Ocean showing details of change in the oxygen isotope composition of marine micro-organisms over the last 700,000 years. It reflects the temperature of the ocean surface. Low values (up) show warm conditions; high values, cold conditions. Interglacial periods were short (about 10,000 years); glacial periods were long (about 100,000 years).

of atmospheric gas composition from shortly after the ice accumulated on the surface, and the isotopic composition of the ice itself gives a reliable estimate of atmospheric temperature over the ice sheet centre at the time of precipitation[2]. Figure 3.5 shows the record of carbon dioxide and temperature from the Vostok ice core in Antarctica for the last 400,000 years. It shows that during warm periods similar to that which the Earth has experienced for the last 10,000 years, atmospheric carbon dioxide concentrations have been approximately constant at about 270-280 ppm, whilst during the coldest parts of glacial periods they were about 190-200 ppm.

The shifts between these two extremes reflect changes in global sources and sinks of carbon. Earth has two major natural stores which are able to release and absorb atmospheric carbon dioxide relatively rapidly, acting either as net sources or sinks: the oceans and the terrestrial biosphere. During periods of global cooling which have led to glaciation, upwelling of cold nutrient-rich water in the equatorial ocean increases planktonic productivity which draws down carbon dioxide from the atmosphere and reduces its concentration (Mix, 1989). During periods of global warming, this effect is reversed and the equatorial ocean becomes a carbon source, thus increasing atmospheric concentrations.

---

[2] It should be noted that the gas signal is not locked in until some time after formation of the ice containing it. As snow is buried and progressiveley compressed and metamorphosed into ice, gas-bearing pores are closed off and lose contact with the atmosphere. This may occur at depths of 10s or 100s of metres, equivalent to 10-100s of years after precipitation. The temperature signal is derived from oxygen isotope determinations on the ice. There is thus an appearance that carbon dioxide changes lag temperature.

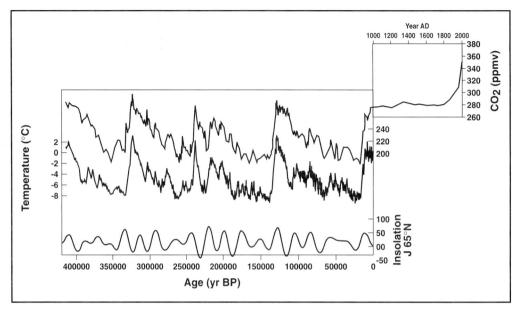

Figure 3.5 The climatic history of the last 0.5 million years preserved in an ice core from Vostok station in Antarctica (from Petit *et al.,* 1999). The lowest curve shows the intensity of June solar radiation at 65°N, the middle curve the variation in temperature, and the upper curve the variation in atmospheric carbon dioxide concentration. Radiation is probably the ultimate driver of change, though not in a simple linear fashion. Temperature and carbon dioxide concentration are very strongly correlated. Carbon dioxide concentrations are about 190 ppm during glacial periods and 270-280 ppm during interglacial periods. The inset at top right shows details of atmospheric carbon dioxide concentration during the last 1000 years, and the dramatic climb to a value of 350 ppm at 2000 AD because of burning of fossil fuel for energy after the onset of the industrial revolution.

It is suggested that the remarkable match between the palaeotemperature and palaeo-gas records reflects greenhouse gas amplification of the solar signal. If an increase in insolation increases Earth surface temperature, there is net exhalation of carbon dioxide from the oceans, atmospheric concentrations increase and further greenhouse warming occurs. This in turn increases carbon dioxide exhalation, and so on, in a positive feedback. The reverse process follows reductions in insolation.

3.2.4.3 *High frequency internal oscillations*
There is no strong evidence of any external process able to force climatic changes on timescales between those of Milankovitch changes and the annual cycle, and yet climate fluctuations do occur on such timescales. Figure 3.6 shows a detailed record of climate change from a core through the Greenland ice sheet during the last glacial cycle of about 120,000 years. During the glacial periods in particular, there are numerous strong climatic excursions that can build up very quickly, in a decade or so, and may last for a few hundred years. A number of processes have been invoked to explain these events:

- Mechanical instabilities may cause ice sheets to surge into the oceans, increasing sea levels, depressing ocean temperatures, changing ocean circulation, cooling the atmosphere, changing atmospheric circulation patterns and patterns of precipitation.

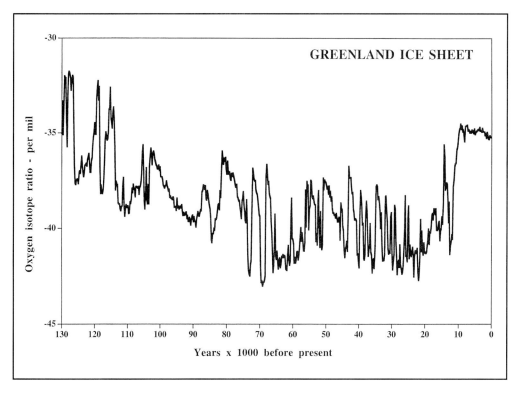

Figure 3.6 Details of the last glacial cycle as shown in the Greenland ice core record (from Dansgaard *et al.,* 1993). High values of oxygen isotope ratio (up) reflect warm conditions. There is a strong contrast between the last glacial period, when climate varied extremely rapidly, and the relatively stable conditions of the present interglacial, which has lasted about 10,000 years. The last interglacial (120,000 years ago) was significantly warmer than the present, and had a much more variable climate. This may be a warning about the potential for greater climatic instability in a warmer, greenhouse world.

- Meltwater from ice sheets produces a brackish water layer over the North Atlantic, stopping deep overturning of the ocean, preventing formation of deep waters and the penetration of warm equatorial waters into high latitudes and causing high-latitude cooling.
- A cool phase that produces large extensions of areas of sea ice or snow can so increase the reflectivity of the Earth's surface that any cooling is amplified, whilst storms, which are means of transporting atmospheric heat, tend to be steered away from such areas, producing yet further cooling. This phenomenon of 'persistence' can also intensify warming by the reverse processes.

A particularly interesting sub-Milankovitch phenomenon is seen in the Greenland ice core record (Figure 3.6) during the last interglacial about 120,000 years ago. It shows that the last interglacial was significantly warmer than the present, and although the present interglacial has only seen climate changes of small amplitude prior to the last century (Figure 3.7), the last interglacial showed variability of much greater amplitude. This may reflect greater storminess or other longer-term sub-Milankovitch changes in climate. Could it be a characteristic of warmer interglacials? And might it become characteristic of the modern Earth if global warming continues?

3.3 Humanity – a new geological agent

There is one last, novel process that has become fundamental to the operation of the Earth system during the last 200 years – the human race.

The traditional view implicitly assumed that there was a natural Earth, which behaved much as it always had, and there was human society, which simply lived in nature, used its resources, but did not otherwise affect it. We can now see that humanity has developed the same type of powerfully coupled relationship with the rest of the Earth system that I have described between the atmosphere, hydrosphere, the rest of the biosphere and the mineral Earth. The difference is that we have not sufficiently recognised human actions as powerful geological agents and have not yet tried to understand them in the way we do other parts of the Earth system. It is a major new challenge for the Earth sciences.

Although the magnitudes of human impacts are not sufficiently widely known, a few examples will suffice to demonstrate their significance:

- **In the lithosphere,** the average annual transport rate of rock and soil by man is now about 42 billion tons per year, equal to about half that transported by rivers, glaciers, oceans and wind together, and three times that created by mountain building (Hooke, 1994). The rate of loss of cultivatable soil by erosion is now greater than the rate of natural soil formation plus the amount brought into cultivation by forest clearance and land reclamation (Pimental, 1993) – we are stripping the Earth of its fertile topsoil.

- **In the hydrosphere**, we now consume about 18% of the total available freshwater runoff of the Earth, and redirect or appropriate 54% of it in one manner or another (Postel *et al.*, 1996).

- **In the atmosphere**, we have interfered fundamentally with the carbon cycle. We have taken carbon, in the form of petroleum, from deep within the Earth and burnt it a rate 1,000,000 times faster than would have happened naturally, with the consequence that the atmospheric carbon dioxide concentration has risen more precipitately and to a level that is greater than at any recent period of Earth history (Figure 3.5). Given the long residence time of carbon dioxide in the atmosphere (50-200 years), it is an effect that cannot quickly be reversed. We have thinned the protective ozone layer, and destroyed it over polar regions, through the use of CFCs. Even if the use of CFCs and their replacements were to cease immediately, their long residence times will ensure that the ozone layer will continue to thin for decades to come (Turco, 1997).

- **In the biosphere**, we have removed between 26% and 46% of global forests (Williams, 1994), vital scavengers of atmospheric carbon dioxide, by clearance for agriculture and more recently for logging. Biodiversity has decreased dramatically. The extinction rate of mammalian species in the twentieth century has been calculated as 40 times the 'natural' background rate, and 1000 times that rate for birds (Heywood and Watson, 1995; May *et al.*, 1995). We appear to be in the midst of a phase of mass extinction of a magnitude that has only happened five times before

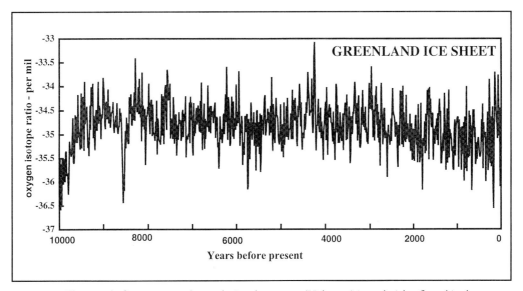

Figure 3.7 The record of temperature change during the present (Holocene) interglacial, reflected in the oxygen isotope record from the Greenland ice sheet (from Dansgaard *et al.*, 1993). It shows the end of the phase of strong warming at the end of the last glacial period, about 10,000 years ago. Although climate varies rapidly during the Holocene, the amplitude of change is small (see Figure 3.6). The core shows evidence of the 'Little Ice Age' during the 17th to 19th centuries and the subsequent warming at the end of the 19th and the beginning of the 20th century.

in Earth history (Manning, this volume). Its cause this time is quite different from before: the economic activity of a single species.

A further product of human activity has been to change the geochemistry not only of the Earth's atmosphere, but also of its land surface and its natural waters, by redistributing and concentrating natural chemical species and creating new ones. We urgently need to understand the impact on the environment of the disposal of waste from human activities. We dispose of our solid and liquid wastes in the shallow Earth without understanding adequately its properties or the processes of change within it. We probably understand the long-term, future impacts of deeply buried nuclear waste, with a toxic lifetime of tens of thousands of years, better than we do the potential impact in a 100 years or so of the landfill sites with which we now pepper the countryside around our cities or the pervasive pollution of ground and surface waters. They involve both natural and artificial solids, liquids, gases and chemical species that have never before been associated together in the history of the planet. Unlike natural materials, the history of whose associations on all timescales is reflected by the geological record, we have no empirical guide to the long-term behaviour of these new materials.

3.4 The challenge to the Earth sciences

Most sciences are valued in the long run for the material benefits and the insights they are perceived to bring to society. During the last 200 years, the value of Earth science has been perceived to be in the search for primary resources (metallic minerals, water, hydrocarbons). But the market for exploration for metallic minerals has now largely collapsed, water supply is now principally the province of engineers, and if progress is to be made towards the aspirations of the Kyoto summit for a carbon-neutral energy economy, the long-term future of hydrocarbon exploration and production is limited. Is the future for the Earth sciences similarly bleak? Not if we apply our understanding to the challenge of finding means of repairing past damaging human impacts on the planet, of mitigating future impacts and of finding strategies for sustainable use of the planet and its resources.

If we are to do this effectively, Earth scientists not only need to apply their understanding to new problems or old problems set in a new context, but also need to reconsider the way in which they conceive of the Earth system and to make the boundaries that they adopt for their individual disciplines more fuzzy and more interactive. Section 3.2 explains how the Earth can be understood as a complex system whose component parts interact on all timescales, and section 3.3 describes how human activity has become part of the system of the planet in such a way that it needs to be understood as one of the planet's fundamental components. Developing our understanding of the Earth in such terms has several important pre-requisites:

- **Cross disciplinary collaboration** is needed between geologists, geophysicists, biologists (Manning, this volume), cosmologists and, I shall argue, engineers, if we are to understand the Earth system better and apply that understanding effectively. But the role of humanity in the recent evolution of the Earth system also requires the involvement of those who study social, political and economic behaviour, which are ultimately key determinants of human impacts on the Earth.

- **Complexity, simulation and prediction.** Many of the great advances of science since the 17th century have been made as a consequence of experiments on phenomena that can be regarded as parts of simple closed systems in which relationships between cause and effect can be deduced to produce physical and chemical laws. These laws have then been made the basis of quantitative theories that are sufficiently robust to have predictive capability.

  Observational sciences such as traditional biology and geology have observed the patterns that are the outcome of complex interacting processes, and derived explanations for them. Darwin's theory of evolution and plate tectonic theory both belong to this category. They have poor predictive capability because of uncertainties about precise interactions between their components, the difficulty of gaining quantitative information on some system properties and the intractability of the complex computations required to simulate and predict their behaviour. However, new means of observation and measurement (section 3.2) permit us to monitor system interactions and measure system properties in ways not previously possible, and modern computers permit us to simulate the behaviour of complex systems.

  Is prediction possible? If we are able to test our understanding of the behaviour of a complex system by our capacity to simulate its past evolution known from geological information, then we have a basis for testing predictive capability. Arguably, the modern computer adds a third key tool, of simulation, to the scientist's classical toolkit of experiment and theory. It is a vital tool in understanding the Earth system.

- **Teaching and the curriculum.** The purpose of school education is not to produce specialists, but to give pupils an understanding of the environment in which they live, equip them with some of the basic conceptual tools which they will need to live in that environment and to provide them with the early stages of specialist knowledge that they may build on in subsequent employment or in further or higher education. The purpose of further and higher education is to develop deeper levels of understanding, which may be highly specialised or relatively broad. The end in both cases is to help individuals to be more effective citizens in a democratic society and to deploy high levels of skill in their employment. I would argue that a deeper understanding of the system of the planet on which they live should be a vital part of everyone's education, and that neither the school nor university curriculum currently do justice to that need.

The position of the discipline of geography is an interesting one. Whereas 'man-land' relationships seemed to be at the heart of much geography in the past, a gulf now seems to have developed between physical and human geography, such that it is difficult to see them as parts of an intellectually coherent single discipline, notwithstanding the value of its two parts. I suggest that the human role in the Earth system, and the consequential need for engagement between Earth science and sociology and economics, could provide an important agenda for modern geography.

3.5 Applying Earth science: the response to global change

The traditional applications of Earth science have been in the search for, and exploitation of, primary minerals and groundwater, understanding the processes that affect the Earth's surface and the hazards they pose, and as an aid to engineering construction. These will continue to be important, but the evidence of the past becomes increasingly important as we become aware of how quickly the Earth system can change, physically, chemically and biologically, and how much human society is intimately involved in these changes. This section addresses some of these key issues of global change.

3.5.1 Global change: applying the lessons of the past
3.5.1.1 The inevitability of change

The geological record gives a unique insight into the way in which global and local environments are continually changing in response to processes that operate on a wide range of frequencies. Any one period of net change in climate may be a consequence of several superimposed causes as is shown by the time spectrum of variation of climate in Figures 3.1 to 3.8. The present phase of global warming appears to be a consequence of changes that would have occurred without human intervention, upon which are superimposed human-driven changes. The inevitability of change is most vividly illustrated by the fact that for most Quaternary time, the last two million years of Earth history, Scotland has been almost unimaginably different from its present state. For 90% of that time it has been a land of tundra, glaciers and strong sedimentary and erosional activity. About every 100,000 years the environment has become, for a brief 10,000 years or so (Figures 3.4 and 3.5), one with a mild and relatively inactive landscape of temperate forest and grassland, similar to that of the present day, but without the artefacts of civilisation. The reality that immense environmental changes have accompanied the development of recognisably modern societies is brought home by the fact that Jericho was a thriving city, and its people were probably leading a normal, recognisable, urban existence, at a time when Fort William lay

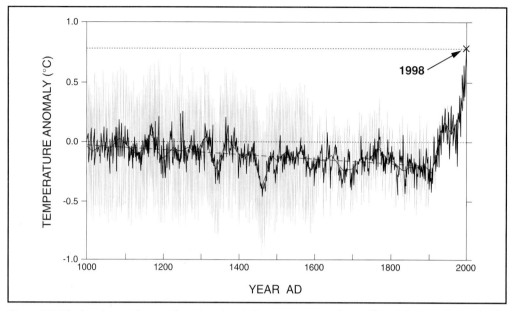

Figure 3.8 The last thousand years of northern hemisphere temperature change (from Mann *et al.*, 1999). The solid lines show the reconstructed temperature and the 40-year smoothed mean. The grey shading shows two standard error limits, and the dashed line the linear trends of mean temperature prior to 1900. It shows that although there have been regionally important events, such as the early mediaeval warm period and the 'Little Ice Age' in the North Atlantic sector, global mean temperatures have been very stable. However, the very strong warming during the 20th century seems anomalous. Is it connected to the unprecedented increase of atmospheric carbon dioxide during the last hundred years (see Figure 3.5)?

beneath a kilometre of ice and a glacier was invading what are now the northern suburbs of Glasgow. Even on the timescale of the last thousand years, Scotland has suffered significant local climatic adjustments to global change, leading to major changes in the regimes of rivers, in ecology and in agriculture.

Such a history illustrates several important principles:

- natural climate and environmental change can be very rapid, and can be extreme;
- great natural changes can occur in one geographical area that are not reflected in others;
- climatic and environmental changes take place on all timescales, and at any one time, processes of change which are occurring on several timescales may be superimposed; and
- complex networks of cause and effect characterise past climate change, and are also likely to characterise future change.

3.5.1.2 Forecasting the future?

The geological record demonstrates how Earth processes interact in complex ways to produce change and to vary the rate at which change occurs. To what extent are we able to evaluate potential future directions and rates of change? Although the development of a predictive science of the Earth able to forecast future trajectories in complex, natural, open systems is a daunting task, one powerful tool is already available. The geological record provides evidence about the ways in which Earth systems have evolved in the past, and can provide a guide to the way in which they might behave in future. Moreover, many systems that appear to be inherently complex show patterns of evolution that are so repetitive as to suggest that powerful self-organising processes are at work, which perennially steer the system along similar trajectories. For example, we know that complex series of processes are implicated in forcing and modulating the tempo and amplitude of climatic changes, but the consequent pattern can be relatively simple (e.g. Figure 3.5). Patterns of repetitive climatic change in the past, such as shown in Figures 3.4 and 3.5, can be statistically characterised and used for extrapolation into the future, as shown in Figure 3.9 (Dalgleish *et al.*, 2000). However, such forecasts of future change are based on statistical extrapolations of past climates from a time period when the human impact was small. If we introduce human impacts on the atmosphere into the system, for which we have no past precedent, simple extrapolation is no longer open to us, and it becomes necessary to develop global computer models that incorporate anthropogenic effects in their forecasts (Figure 3.10). The outcome suggests a dramatic impact over relatively short periods into the future, with a subsequent reversion to the 'natural trend'.

3.5.2 Global change – the anthropogenic component

Anthropogenic global change should not only be understood as change in climate caused by human impacts on the atmosphere, but also change in the operation of the Earth system by all the modes of human intervention summarised in section 3.3: in the hydrological cycle, in the fertility of soils, in pollution of surface and groundwaters, in the generation and disposal of geochemically complex wastes. However, the one that gives the greatest current cause for concern is the increase in atmospheric carbon dioxide produced as a waste gas from combustion; a change in atmospheric composition of a magnitude and speed that is unprecedented in the last 100 million years. From our understanding of the geological role of carbon dioxide, it would be surprising if such changes did not have major environmental and climatic impacts. Computer models designed to forecast the climatic consequences of increased atmospheric greenhouse gas concentrations have first been tested by their capacity to simulate known changes in the geological past, such as the 'icehouse' conditions of the last glacial period and the extreme 'greenhouse' conditions of the Cretaceous (Crowley, 1988).

Models in which the warming due to an anthropogenic enhanced greenhouse is computed without considering the carbon cycle have predicted (e.g. IPCC, 1996), under a business-as-usual emissions scenario, an atmospheric carbon dioxide concentration of about 700 ppm by 2100 (compared with about 280 ppm prior to the industrial revolution), producing a global temperature rise of up to 4.5°C. If the global carbon cycle is included in modelling (Meteorological Office, 2000), the land biosphere changes after 2050 from being a weak sink for carbon to a strong source, mainly due to loss of soil carbon as soils oxidise under warmer conditions. In this model, atmospheric carbon dioxide concentrations increase to about 1000 ppm by 2100, and global temperatures increase by up to 8°C[3]. High-resolution models suggest that because of the increased energy of atmospheric and oceanic circulation in the Atlantic sector, Scotland will become between 1.2 and 6°C

---

[3]   The variability of solar output has been shown to have a small, direct effect on climate (Tett *et al.*, 1999), although the direct effect may be amplified by the greenhouse effect. Some have claimed that it is the dominant control on the present phase of global warming.

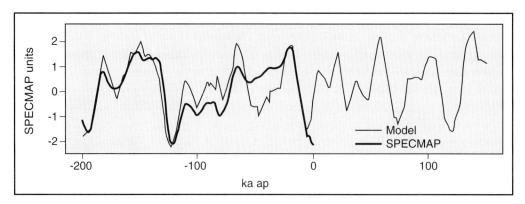

Figure 3.9 Statistical extrapolation from past to future. The heavy line shows the average oxygen isotope composition of bottom-living micro-organisms during the last 200,000 years taken from a large number of cores from the world's oceans. It is a proxy for global ice sheet volume. High values (up) reflect large ice sheet volumes. It is statistically matched by the thinner line, which also depends on solar radiation parameters, reflecting the ultimate driver for climate change. Using these parameters calculated for the future, the past record has been extrapolated for 150,000 years into the future. It suggests an imminent decline into glacial conditions. (Reprinted from *Quaternary Science Reviews*, 20, Dalgleish *et al.*, The ice age cycle and the deglaciations: an application of nonlinear regression modelling, 687-697, copyright 2000, with permission from Elsevier Science).

warmer during the next century, with more warming in winter than in summer months; that annual precipitation will increase by 5-20% (Kerr *et al.*, 1999), with the biggest increases in autumn and winter; that storminess and the frequency of extreme events will increase; and that sea levels will increase by 0.7 m. These are likely to favour enhanced growth rates of forest areas; increased frequency and severity of flooding along river valleys and in low-lying coastlands, together with major changes in river courses. In detail, the potential changes in ecology, water chemistry and biodiversity on land and in sea areas are much more difficult to assess. The complexity of the network of cause and effect are such that significant unanticipated consequences are likely. The present interglacial has, since the end of the last glacial period, 10,000 years ago, been remarkably stable climatically. Human society has adapted to this climatic stability. Unanticipated climatic surprises are likely therefore to be costly. Below are three examples of potential major surprises:

- The tempo of long-term climate change reflected in the geological record (e.g. Figure 3.5) suggests that without anthropogenic greenhouse warming, the Earth would be moving, possibly rapidly, towards the next glacial period (Figure 3.9). This was indeed the view until the early 1970s, before we became aware of a potential anthropogenic greenhouse warming. Whether the human influence will hold the natural tendency of climate at bay, or whether this will reassert itself is unknown (Figure 3.10). Indeed, if we have damaged our 'thermostat', we may be in unknown territory.
- The modern circulation of the North Atlantic is driven in part by the sinking, off Iceland, of saline sub-tropical water flowing north on the surface of the ocean which sinks as it cools and becomes denser. This circulation warms the fringing land areas, such as Scotland, whilst the zone of sinking is a major carbon sink where the global ocean 'inhales' atmospheric carbon dioxide. Twelve thousand years ago, a phase of

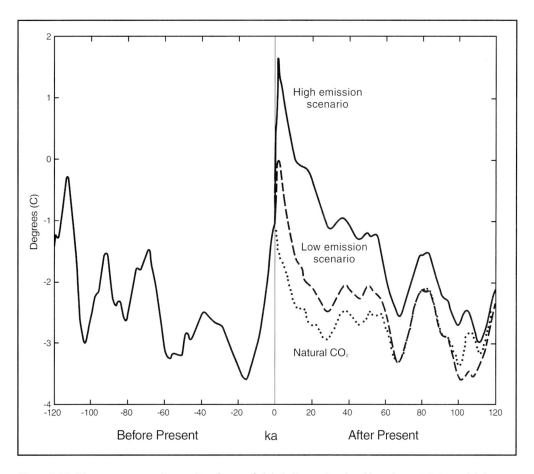

Figure 3.10 The recent past and immediate future of global climate simulated by a deterministic model that can include anthropogenic effects. A simulation of global temperature change during the last glacial cycle is shown to the left, which matches well with geological records of change (Figures 3.5 and 3.6). To the right it shows future forecasts. The dotted line shows a 'natural' forecast (without anthropogenic greenhouse gases). The other lines show forecasts based on different scenarios for atmospheric composition determined by anthropogenic greenhouse gas emissions. They forecast strong immediate warming and an extension of the length of the present interglacial. (Reproduced with permission from Burgess, 1998).

global warming enhanced the ingress to the North Atlantic of fresh water from melting ice sheets, thus suppressing the process of sinking of sub-tropical water, stopping the North Atlantic circulation, driving the climate temporarily back to a glacial state and having a major impact on atmospheric chemistry. Under conditions of enhanced global warming, sub-tropical waters may not cool sufficiently in the sub-polar North Atlantic to cause them to sink, a process that would be aided by increased run-off from the continents. This could suppress the North Atlantic circulation, with severe effects on the atmosphere and climates of flanking continents.

- The last interglacial, which occurred between 120,000 and 130,000 years ago, was significantly warmer than the present. The Greenland ice core record (Figure 3.6) shows this, but it also shows that the last interglacial had much greater climatic variability than the present interglacial has hitherto shown. It is possible, therefore, that increased global warming may drive the Earth into a climatic mode similar to that of the last interglacial, with much greater medium-term climatic instability, possibly driven by processes such as those described in the previous paragraph.

3.5.3 Coping with global change

Global climatic and environmental change, whether 'natural' or anthropogenic in origin, can have significant impacts on the mode of life of a human species that has become highly adapted to specific environmental niches. This is particularly true when our use of nature's resources (e.g. water supply, soil fertility) is so close to their current yield capacity. Our response to such changes in the context of the search for sustainability involves monitoring change, understanding the complex, interactive Earth system, reducing the anthropogenic forcing of change and anticipating and mitigating the consequences of change. Not only do substantial resources need to be expended by bodies such as Research Councils in improving our understanding of basic Earth processes, but Government and Scottish Executive Departments need to fund projects directed towards establishing mitigation options in specific areas of high risk, rather than the generic scoping studies that have been undertaken hitherto.

3.5.3.1 Energy – moving away from a carbon-based economy

The mode of energy generation is now regarded as a vital determinant of the anthropogenic impact on climate. The use of carbon-based fuels to produce cheap and readily useable energy has been the basis upon which much modern prosperity has been built. But there are now strong arguments for breaking this dependence because of evidence that the consequential increase of atmospheric carbon dioxide concentration will have major environmental effects with severe consequences for many human populations

Even if the international community is able to agree that there should be a decisive move away from a carbon-based economy, such a move will not be easily achieved and in a single step. It has already begun in the shift in energy generation from coal and petrol to gas in the UK and elsewhere, which has reduced the carbon intensiveness of economies. But the next step is not clear. Nuclear power generation is carbon free but creates wastes with long-lived toxicity, and is the subject of much public suspicion. Renewable energy from wind, from biomass burning, solar cells, photosynthesis and from hydro-electric schemes is also carbon free, but unlike petroleum and nuclear energy, these sources are land intensive, and as prospect turns to reality are meeting, or are likely to meet, increasing public opposition. There is therefore a question mark over the rate at which they can be developed to replace carbon-intensive energy generation. Wave energy is technically realisable, but its intermittency makes it unlikely to be a major, base-load contributor to the National Grid. There are possibilities for new technologies based on hydrogen or nuclear fusion, but their possibility and practicability are unproven.

Another pathway is through capture of flue gases prior to emission and their sequestration in underground formations in depleted oil or gas fields, or injection into the deep ocean. The former has been demonstrated to be technically feasible, and it could provide a valuable interim method of reducing emissions to the atmosphere during a period of adjustment to a less carbon intensive economy. It seems unlikely, given the current rate of global destruction of forest areas, and the uncertainties surrounding the carbon balances of forest areas during a period of global warming, that tree planting could be a reliable mechanism for reducing concentrations of atmospheric carbon dioxide.

If there is to be international agreement to restrain atmospheric carbon dioxide concentrations below 'business as usual' levels, the shift to a sustainable, renewable energy economy is likely to involve a basket of transitional measures involving sequestration, more intensive use of gas and possibly nuclear energy. Geologists and geophysicists have an important role to play in all these areas: in evaluating and determining the safety of underground strata as potential sites for carbon dioxide sequestration; in the exploration for new gas rather than petroleum fields; and in the demonstration that long-lived, toxic nuclear waste can be safely disposed of deep underground.

3.5.3.2 *Waste-understanding and mitigating the consequences of change*
The growth of population and increased material wealth of society during the last 150 years have dramatically increased the generation of wastes. We have as yet a limited understanding of the consequences of the potential geochemical impact in a hundred years or so of the growth of landfill sites around our cities. There is urgent need for Earth scientists to work on such problems. They pose a particular challenge to the development of a predictive Earth science.

An extreme problem of waste disposal is that of disposing safely of nuclear waste, some of which has a toxic lifetime in excess of 10,000-100,000 years. The problem is acute in Scotland, where 50% of the electricity supply is generated by nuclear power stations, all of which are due to be de-commissioned between 2010 and 2020. If we could be sure of being able to replace this capacity, and some of the capacity of carbon-based generation stations in order to meet more stringent emissions targets, by non-carbon based sources, then the problem of safely disposing of waste could be approached in a very measured fashion. If it proves necessary and acceptable to create new nuclear capacity as an interim measure in adjusting to emissions targets, then on the principle that new stations should not be created until a waste disposal strategy has been agreed (Royal Commission on Environmental Pollution, 1998), the latter would become a very high priority.

Although surface storage of nuclear waste is probably the best option in the short- to medium-term (say 50 years), deep sub-surface burial is currently the only rational long-term strategy. The challenge to Earth scientists is not only to find locations where leakage of radionuclide migration from a repository to the surface is unlikely to occur during the toxic lifetime of the waste, but one where the long-term risk can be evaluated. This will involve using geological evidence of past rates of fluid migration in the Earth as a guide to future rates of migration, an approach that has been termed 'palaeohydrogeology' (Boulton *et al.*, 2000). It is important to recognise, however, as in other matters of public concern, that scientific understanding of relevant processes, of uncertainty and of risk must be clearly expressed in the public domain, and that the policy decisions are not simply matters for science, but for society and its institutions.

3.5.3.3 *Hydrology: mitigating and adapting*
The hydrological system in Scotland has changed dramatically in the recent past. As little as 15,000 years BP (radiocarbon years before present), runoff from the land consisted of water melting from beneath the ice sheet that covered the land, channelled into powerful

subglacial streams that ultimately gave rise to the eskers on which some of Scotland's best golf courses are built. Between 12,500 and 10,000 years BP, the newly deglaciated land was sparsely vegetated and relatively unstable, so that rainfall ran off rapidly into flood-prone and unstable, sediment-laden, braided river systems. The invasion of early woodlands, tree birch by 10,000 years BP and Scots Pine by 8,300 BP, intercepted, reduced and slowed down runoff, permitting the river systems to adopt more stable courses, a trend enhanced in the lowlands by the spread of more varied mixed-oak forests after about 7000 BP. After about 6,000 BP, climate in Scotland became significantly wetter and after 4000 BP human forest clearance began to make major inroads into the forests. Taken together, these changes are likely to have produced faster runoff and more flood-prone rivers, although the evidence of actual river regimes from this period is slender. Deforestation reached its maximum by the 18th and 19th centuries; as little as 4% of the country being under woodland by AD 1750 (Edwards and Smout, 2000). This process, which mimicked the barer landscape of newly deglaciated Scotland, coupled with the climatic deterioration of the so-called 'Little Ice Age', generated increased flood frequencies and may have been the cause of the greater instability and tendency to river braiding in the 18th and 19th centuries (Macklin and Lewin, 1993). As a consequence, there was widespread engineering of lowland river courses in an attempt to control both flooding and course instability.

The increased precipitation and storminess, together with rising sea level, that we expect from continuing global warming are likely to create greater frequencies of flooding and greater river instability. In planning to mitigate potential changes and adapting land use to them, it is important to couple the study of geological evidence of past changes in river regime in relation to climate and land use with studies of modern hydraulic process. It is important to understand the thresholds for change in a river and catchment system and forecast the magnitude and frequency of flooding (Werritty and Ferguson, 1980). It should become an important part of land use planning in Scotland.

3.5.3.4 *Biodiversity and landscape ecology – understanding and managing change*
The ecology of the landscape and the diversity of life that it supports are at least as complex in their operation as the climate system. The mosaic of plant and animal life changes both as a consequence of external forcing by climate (or human activity) and the internal dynamics of the system that cause it to change without apparent external forcing because of interactions between biological, physical and geochemical processes. As in the case of climate, it is not easy to predict how the system will respond to external forcing, nor how spontaneous changes may arise merely as a consequence of its internal dynamics. It has sometimes been observed that nature reserves that had a particular character when first established appear to 'deteriorate' with time. This may reflect 'external' forcing by climate or human agency, or may be a consequence of unforced internal dynamic changes in the ecological mosaic.

Developing a deep understanding of these processes is particularly important during a period of potentially rapid climate change, both because plants may act as global carbon sinks or carbon sources (the recent upward revision of global warming estimates (Meteorological Office, 2000) is largely driven by the predicted dieback of the Amazonian forest due to drying out of soils), and because of the need for effective countryside management. In relation to the latter, the geological record of floral and environmental change contained in lake sediments, buried peat and peat bogs in Scotland offers an opportunity to understand how the floral mosaic and its associated biogeochemical environment has changed in the past both in response to climatic forcing and because of internal dynamics. It permits us to identify repetitive patterns through time that indicate chains of association, which should be explored in anticipating the consequences of future climate change. For example, during the present, Holocene interglacial, there is evidence of time periods during which climate is believed to have become more humid, and which may therefore be a helpful template in forecasting possible consequences of increased humidity induced by an enhanced greenhouse effect. There is evidence from Fife that increasing humidity during the earlier part of the present interglacial produced a strong response in the floral mosaic (Edwards and Whittington, 1997) associated with the extension of hazel and then alder (Figure 3.11). The capacity of sediment cores from inland lochs to yield rich evidence of floral change in space and time through much of the present interglacial has recently been demonstrated from the Oban area by Macklin *et al.* (2000). This is an area that is expected to receive a considerable increase in annual rainfall as global warming proceeds. Evaluations of future ecological responses could be greatly improved by detailed palaeoecological studies of this type. But analyses should also seek to assess associated patterns of change in hydro-geochemistry, in soil micro-organisms and in the hydrology and biology of rivers and lakes. They provide a route to better understanding of the chains of association underlying environmental response to climate change.

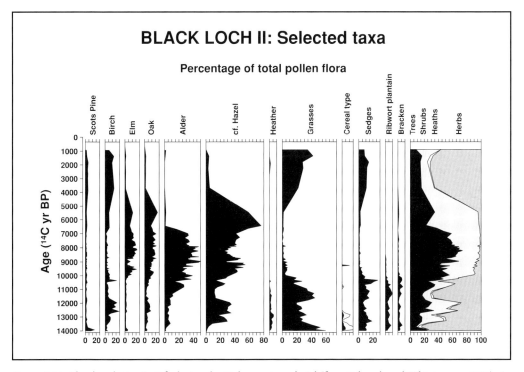

Figure 3.11 Floral evolution in Fife during the Holocene interglacial (from Edwards and Whittington, 1997). At the end of the last glacial period, between 13,000 and 9,000 radiocarbon years ago, open tundra and grassland were progressively replaced by forest; firstly birch, then pine, elm and oak. Hazel, then alder, reflected the onset of wetter conditions. Human impacts are seen by 4-5,000 years ago in forest clearance. They were the first steps in the creation of the human-engineered modern landscape, as tree-less as the later part of the glacial period, but warmer.

3.5.3.5 *Engineering <u>into</u> the environment: an imperative*

Engineering structures and interventions, be they buildings, bridges, roads, dams, agro-engineering enterprises of field drainage, blocks of forestry plantation, fertiliser campaigns or irrigation, have tended to be created within a narrow environmental perspective. A project has been assumed to be environmentally well conceived provided that it is safely constructed and that its immediate and short-term environmental consequences are not perceived to be severe. However, unintended and unexpectedly severe consequences are not uncommon. Many major dam constructions, such as those on the Volga, the Nile, the Colorado, the Indus, the Gambia River and many others have, notwithstanding the short-term economic gains they have brought, had major unintended consequences: salinisation; destruction of soils, vegetation and farmland; desertification; destruction of fisheries; coastal erosion; and acidification. They were the consequence of planning for a single purpose, such as electrification, irrigation or flood control without asking the larger environmental question: "how will the local Earth system behave when this dam is part of it?" Whether we are engineering a dam or a marine wind farm, we are engineering *into* the environment, and we should seek to understand what the consequences will be. We need a predictive environmental engineering, which in reality merges with the predictive Earth science that I argued for in section 3.4. It should be part of a holistic approach to Earth system science and engineering.

3.6 Science and society

The Earth system has been discussed above largely in terms of the need to understand it better. However, when the question is asked, "how should society use that understanding?", the issue is no longer one for scientists alone, but for society as a whole. It has become increasingly important to respect this distinction as scientific innovation has become increasingly rapidly translated into efficient and invasive technologies that not only place the natural system of the Earth under siege by changing the interconnected planetary ecosystem but also exert a powerful and pervasive influence on the lives of individuals and society.

Uncertainties in the minds of both scientists and governments about the role of scientists and science have led to a confused public view of their role. They are variously regarded as benign agents of public good, malign agents of suspicious corporate or government dealings or quixotic advocates of caution in human dealings with nature. Scientists have both claimed to make dispassionate and objective judgements and yet been passionate advocates of particular public policies, whilst purporting to speak with the authority of science and playing down uncertainty. Governments, particularly when faced with science-driven issues where there are uncertainties about risk of harm, have claimed that their policies will be determined by strictly scientific judgements, rather than accepting that it is Government's role, as guardians of the public good, to make judgements about cost, benefit and risk.

Scientists often lament the clamour and confusion that surrounds many science-driven issues of public concern as a reflection of lack of public understanding of science. We should rather welcome it. It is a recognition that science matters, and a reflection that science is now firmly embedded in the public domain. Scientists must realise that they cannot dictate the terms of the debate, but must find clear and distinctive ways of contributing to it. We must not make the fatal error of assuming that if only the public understood more science, they would agree with us. It is we who need to understand the public more and to base our public interventions on that understanding. We need to promote scientific understanding and understanding of science (the distinction is important) as integral parts of public and popular culture, not as mandarin activities. We need to draw clear distinctions between the roles of the scientist as advocate or as a disinterested source of scientific assessment and the role of scientific knowledge in the process of policy formation.

It is important to recognise that public concern about science-driven issues is greatest where scientific uncertainty is perceived to be large, and often reflected in strong disagreements amongst scientists, where the balance of benefit to the public is uncertain, as in a move away from a carbon-based economy, or where there is a perception of unquantifiable risk, as in the case of nuclear waste disposal. Scientists need to take great care in presenting their case publicly to ensure that: it is as clear as possible; any uncertainty is clearly expressed; risk is expressed in a comprehensible way that respects public perceptions; and that they do not stray over the line that separates a scientific judgement from a value judgement. (The definition of a Site of Special Scientific Interest, for example, is not a scientific judgement, but a societal judgement about the value of science set against the value of the site for other purposes). In contexts such as this, it is important that scientists collaborate with social scientists and economists in understanding the political, social, ethical and economic context of the debate.

Failure to respect these principles, governmental secrecy and conventional patterns of official reassurance have led to an erosion of public trust and confidence in existing processes and institutions. This has stalled the capacity of governments to make policy decisions in many science-driven fields, and made it difficult to break the impasse between extreme views about the consequences of any novel technology, process or environmental intervention. On the one hand, an extreme view of the precautionary principle[4] holds that uncertainty should lead to its abandonment; and on the other, that unintended consequences can always be subsequently engineered to remove or mitigate harm.

In this setting, it is doubtful that existing institutions are adequate to the task of resolving conflict in many areas where there is scientific uncertainty, disagreement about costs and benefits and differences in public values. There are new, deliberative approaches that need to be further developed (such as the 1994 Biotechnology and Biological Sciences Research Council Consensus Conference on plant biotechnology) that permit public values to be articulated in the context of scientific knowledge and analysis of costs and benefits. In Scotland, a new Parliament has created a unique, and probably short-lived, opportunity to forge institutions capable of tackling these new challenges. It should be grasped.

Although it is not possible to remove conflict from decision making, the present system conflates issues of national policy, science, technology and local land use. Over an issue such as the future of energy generation, for example, the absence of a national strategy makes it extremely difficult for bodies such as the Scottish Environment Protection Agency, Scottish Natural Heritage, local planning authorities and the Enterprise Network to discharge their responsibilities in a mutually coherent fashion. The development of a national strategy, informed by rigorous science and compatible with public values and interests, is a necessary pre-requisite for optimal decisions about specific proposals.

---

[4] The precautionary principle originated in Germany in the 1970s as the *Vorsorgeprinzip*. It required a balance to be found between economic effort and maintenance and improvement of environmental quality. " It is not so much a practical guide to decision making as a moral injunction not to ignore possible environmental impacts which cannot be proven" (Royal Commission on Environmental Pollution, 1998).

3.7 Humanity and nature

There has long been a dichotomy, both in philosophy and popular perception, between 'nature', which we presume not to include us, and humanity and its artefacts, which are 'unnatural'. There is now such overwhelming evidence that humanity is today a powerful geological agent, and as much a part of the system of the Earth as its glaciers and its flora, that we should discard the distinction between the 'natural' and 'human'. We should accept that we have been, though we little recognised it, engineering the planet. We cannot avoid continuing to do so. We cannot, by choice, retire from nature and become just another species. Our best hope is to adapt our behaviour so that it becomes 'sustainable', both at a local level, in Scotland, and globally, and in some balance with the rest of the biosphere. Inevitably it is humanity that will decide that balance. It implies that we must continue to engineer. We may not yet be good at it, and we will make mistakes, but we must try to learn. Earth and life scientists and engineers need rigorously to understand some of the complex processes of environmental evolution and their coupling to human activity and to develop predictive theories. These are exacting challenges and deserve the attentions of the best Earth scientists. A future exists for the Earth sciences in a rapidly changing setting in which science is much more in the public eye and subject to much more scrutiny than hitherto. It might be said to be arrogant, to 'interfere in the works of nature', but if we are to be realistic, humanity has done it in the past and will continue to do it in the future. It is far better that it is done consciously, with knowledge and understanding, rather than continuing to blunder on.

References

Baender, P. (ed.) 1973. *The Works of Mark Twain. What is Man? And Other Philosophical Writings.* University of California Press, Berkeley.

Barendregt, R.W. and Irving, E. 1998. Changes in the extent of North American ice sheets during the late Cenozoic. *Canadian Journal of Earth Sciences*, **35**, 504-509.

Barron, E.J. 1984. Climatic implications of the variable obliquity explanation of Cretaceous-Paleogene high-latitude floras. *Geology*, **12**, 595-598.

Boulton, G.S., Casanove, J., Kervevan, C., Delisle, G., Kosters, E., Schelkes, K., Thiery, D. and Vidstrand, P. 2000. Palaeohydrogeology and the impact of climatic change on deep groundwater systems. *In* Davies, C. (ed.) *Euradwaste 1999. Radioactive Waste Management Strategies and Issues.* European Commission EUR 19143, 497-504.

Broecker, W.S. 1985. *Building a Habitable Planet.* Lamont-Doherty Geological Observatory of Columbia University, Eldigio Press, New York.

Brown, G.C., Hawkesworth, C.J. and Wilson, R.C.L. (eds) 1992. *Understanding the Earth. A New Synthesis.* Cambridge University Press, Cambridge.

Burgess, P. 1998. Future climatic and cryospheric change on millenial timescales: an assessment using two-dimensional climate modelling studies. Unpublished PhD thesis, University of East Anglia.

Crowley, T.J. 1988 Paleoclimate modelling. *In* Schlesinger, M.E. (ed.) *Physically-based Modelling and Simulation of Climate and Climatic Change.* Kluwer, Amsterdam, 883-949.

Dalgleish, A.N., Boulton, G.S. and Renshaw, E. 2000. The ice age cycle and the deglaciations: an application of nonlinear regression modelling. *Quaternary Science Reviews*, **19**, 687-697.

Dansgaard, W., Johnsen, S.J., Clausen, H.B., Dahl-Jensen, D., Gundestrup, N.S., Hammer, C.U., Hvidberg, C.S., Steffensen, J.P., Sveinbjornsdottir, A.E., Jouzel, J. and Bond, G. 1993 Evidence for general instability of past climate from a 250-kyr ice-core record. *Nature*, **364**, 218-220.

Edwards, K.J. and Smout, T.C. 2000. *In* Holmes, G. and Crofts, R. (eds) *Scotland's Environment: the Future.* Tuckwell Press in association with the Royal Society of Edinburgh and Scottish Natural Heritage, East Linton.

Edwards, K.J. and Whittington, G. 1997. Vegetation change. *In* Edwards, K.J. and Ralston, I.B.M. (eds) *Scotland: Environment and Archaeology, 8000BC-AD1000.* Wiley, Chichester, 63-82.

Heywood, V.H. and Watson, R.T. (eds) 1995. *Global Biodiversity Assessment.* Cambridge University Press, Cambridge.

Hooke, R.L. 1994. On the efficacy of humans as geomorphic agents. *Geological Society of America, GSA Today,* **4**, 217-25.

Hutton, J. 1788. Theory of the Earth; or an investigation of the laws observable in the composition, dissolution, and restoration of the land upon the globe. *Transactions of the Royal Society of Edinburgh,* **1, ii,** 209-304.

IPCC 1996. *The Science of Climate Change 1995. Summary for Policymakers.* Cambridge University Press, Cambridge.

Kerr, A., Shackley, S., Milne, R. and Allen, S. 1999. *Climate Change: Scottish Implications Scoping Study.* Scottish Executive Central Research Unit, Edinburgh.

Lamb, S. and Sington, D. 1998. *Earth Story. The Shaping of Our World.* BBC Books, London.

Macklin, M.G. and Lewin, J. 1993. Holocene alluviation in Britain. *In* Douglas, I. and Hagedorn, J. (eds) *Geomorphology and Geocology. Fluvial Geomorphology. Zeitschrift für Geomorphologie,* Supplement Band, **88**, 109-122.

Macklin, M.G., Bonsall, C., Davies, F.M. and Robinson, M.R. 2000. Human-environment interactions during the Holocene: new data and interpretations from the Oban area, Argyll, Scotland. *The Holocene*, **10**, 109-121.

Mann, M.E., Bradley, R.S. and Hughes, M.K. 1999. Northern hemisphere temperatures during the past millenium: inferences, uncertainties, and limitations. *Geophysical Research Letters*, **26**, 759-762.

May, R.M., Lawton, J.H. and Stork, N. 1995. Assessing extinction rates. *In* Lawton, J.H and May, R.M. (eds) *Extinction Rates.* Oxford University Press, Oxford.

Meteorological Office 2000. *Climate Change: An Update of Recent Research form the Hadley Centre.* Meteorological Office, Bracknell.

Mix, A.C. 1989. Influence of productivity variations on long-term atmospheric CO_2. *Nature*, **337**, 541-544.

Petit, J.R., Jouzel, J., Raynaud, D., Barkov, N.I., Barnola, J.M., Basile, I., Bender, M., Chapellaz, J., Davis, M., Delaygue, G., Delmotte, M., Kotlyakov, V.M., Legrang, M., Lipenkov, V.Y., Lorius, C., Pepin, L., Ritz, C., Saltzman, E. and Steinhard, M. 1999. Climate and atmospheric history of the past 420,000 years from the Vostok ice core, Antartica. *Nature*, **399**, 429-436.

Pimentel, D. (ed.) 1993. *World Soil Erosion and Conservation.* Cambridge University Press, Cambridge.

Postel, S. 1996. Forging a sustainable water strategy. *In* Brown, L.R. *et al., State of the World 1996. A Worldwatch Institute Report on Progress Towards a Sustainable Society.* W.W. Norton & Co, New York and London.

Royal Commission on Environmental Pollution 1998. *Setting Environmental Standards.* 21st Reprint. HMSO, London.

Ruddiman, W.F. and Kutzbach, J.E. 1990. Late Cenozoic plateau uplift and climate change. *Transactions of the Royal Society of Edinburgh: Earth Sciences*, **81**, 301-314.

Tett, S.F.B., Stott, P.A., Allen, M.R., Ingram, W.J. and Mitchell, J.F.B. 1999. Causes of twentieth-century temperature change near the Earth's surface. *Nature*, **399**, 569-572.

Turco, R.P. 1997. *Earth under Siege: from Air Pollution to Global Change.* Oxford University Press, Oxford.

Werritty, A. and Ferguson, R.I. 1980. Pattern changes in a Scottish braided river over 1, 30 and 200 years. *In* Cullingford, R.A., Davidson, D.A. and Lewin, J. (eds) *Timescales in Geomorphology*. Wiley, Chichester, 53-68.

Williams, M. 1994. Forests and tree cover. *In* Meyer, W.B. and Turner, B.L. (eds) *Changes in Land Use and Land Cover: a Global Perspective*. Cambridge University Press, Cambridge 97-124.

PART TWO

EARTH SCIENCE AND THE NATURAL HERITAGE: FOUNDATION AND INTERACTIONS

Earth Science and the Natural Heritage: Foundation and Interactions

Geology and geomorphology provide the foundations of the landscapes and scenery of Scotland. In combination with the oceanic climate, they also exert a powerful influence on habitats and biodiversity through their interactions with soils, hydrology and topography. This is particularly apparent in coastal, freshwater and upland environments where there is a dynamic interaction between geomorphological processes and the natural heritage. The first chapter in this part describes the geodiversity of Scotland and its significance in landscape and Earth heritage terms. Against this background, the subsequent four chapters examine key interactions and case studies in these dynamic environments, including the effects of human activities.

Scotland is renowned for the diversity of its geology. Under the influence of global tectonics, Scotland has been at a 'crossroads' in geology for millions of years and has consequently experienced a wide range of geological environments. In turn, this is reflected in the diversity of the physical landscapes and landforms and in the presence of many classic geological localities. Trewin (Chapter 4) outlines the geological framework of Scotland and the significance of this inheritance. He describes how the characteristics of major landscape areas reflect the underlying geology.

Trewin notes the significant contribution that Scottish geologists and geological localities have made to the modern development of the subject, beginning with the seminal work of James Hutton. Many of these localities are now classic sites of international importance, an accolade which carries a wider Earth heritage responsibility that reaches beyond Scotland. This responsibilty requires that these sites remain available for scientific research and interpretation. Trewin emphasises the valuable tourist attraction and interpretation functions which many of these sites have, as well as the importance of greater site usage as part of raising public awareness, a theme which is developed in Part 4. He also alludes to the threats to the interest at some of these key sites, an issue which is explored further in Part 3.

Hansom and Angus (Chapter 5) address the links between coastal processes, human activities and the natural heritage in one of Scotland's most distinctive and internationally important coastal environments – the machair of the Western Isles. The issues involved reflect many of the wider concerns of coastal managers in Scotland. The machair lands demonstrate, perhaps more than anywhere, the symbiosis between physical processes, natural heritage and traditional land use. Maintenance of these interrelationships is fundamental to the future sustainable management of the machair.

Machair began to form in the mid-Holocene when large amounts of sand were moved onshore on to beaches and blown inland as sand dunes. In turn, the latter were eroded and the sand blown further inland to form the machair. Subsequent reduction in sediment supply led to a natural cycle of erosion and recycling of the dune and machair sands, which continues to maintain the machair today. However, this cycle is now being perturbed by enhanced wave erosion of the coastal edge, driven by a combination of increased storminess and rising sea level. Dune systems have been removed or overtopped, allowing erosion of the machair edge and flooding of the lower-lying machair. Hansom and Angus question whether the loss of machair is currently outstripping machair accretion under present conditions of restricted supply. This leads on to discussion of complex management issues. Localised coast protection would simply transfer the problem to adjacent stretches of coastline; more extensive protection would be prohibitively expensive. The dynamic nature of the machair is also underlined, in that coast protection would reduce the sand supply inland that feeds and maintains the machair. However, the agricultural system, on which so much of the natural heritage interest depends, may be made unworkable by overtopping and breaching of the dune corridor. In turn, this could lead to deteriorating landscape quality, with consequent impact on the tourist economy of the islands.

This case study emphasises that in dynamic coastal environments, issues cannot be addressed in isolation. As Hansom and Angus explain, the issues require careful integration of understanding of coastal processes and sediment budgets, as well as the socio-economic elements of land management. In immediate practical terms, the answer may be to do nothing and to let the natural processes run their course. However, the level of risk that such an approach entails is uncertain, because the sediment budget dynamics are unresolved. Given the significance of the natural heritage interests and the socio-economic and cultural value of the machair, this uncertainty deserves to be addressed.

Physical processes also underpin the biodiversity and ecological quality of dynamic freshwater systems. Soulsby and Boon (Chapter 6) emphasise that understanding spatial and temporal scales is crucial for sustainable management of the resource. In the spatial organisation of catchments, factors such as discharge regime, sediment characteristics and channel gradient combine to create complex 'patch' dynamics at almost any spatial scale, both along the length of a river and laterally within the river corridor. Temporally, the long-term evolution of present-day rivers reflects both the glacial inheritance and postglacial readjustments. Additionally, human interference has changed sediment inputs and altered hydrological regimes through, for example, forest clearance.

The geomorphological underpinning is also important in the management of freshwater systems. However, as noted by Soulsby and Boon, the management timeframe is usually based on human experience and not on the longer-term geomorphological perspective. They show how an understanding of geomorphological sensitivity provides a more secure basis for management. This may involve identification of boundary conditions and thresholds where management intervention may trigger instability. Instability in itself is part of the natural order and can be of value in maintaining biodiversity. Such natural instability, however, is usually unacceptable to river managers. It often results in *ad hoc* bank protection measures that are unsuccessful or transfer problems elsewhere, with consequent ecological and geomorphological damage. Soulsby and Boon illustrate many of these geo-ecological relationships and management issues in a case study of the Atlantic salmon.

The varied character of Scotland's montane landscapes reflects their geological history and the effects of glacial and postglacial processes, the oceanic climate and its effects on habitats, and episodic geomorphological processes associated with extreme weather phenomena. A range of human activities has also impacted to varying degrees over the last 5000 years, both on habitat condition and geomorphological processes such as soil erosion and podzolisation. The two chapters by Thompson *et al.* (Chapter 7) and Haynes *et al.* (Chapter 8) emphasise the dependencies between regolith, soils, geomorphological processes and vegetation. Thompson *et al.* argue the need to understand these dependencies as well as the interactions with human activities. This would allow conservation managers to be informed of the likely consequences of different natural and anthropogenic changes, and hence better able to assess the effectiveness of any management measures. The impacts of different pressures are related to the sensitivity of montane landscapes. In a case study of the Cairngorms, Haynes *et al.* show how the geomorphological sensitivity of different parts of the landscape may be used as a filter to identify the most vulnerable locations. This is developed further by Thompson *et al.* in a sensitivity matrix of the main topographical features and their principal vegetation types in relation to pressures arising from extreme weather events, grazing, burning, pollution trampling and built developments.

Both Thompson *et al.* and Haynes *et al.* stress the importance of palaeoenvironmental records in providing a longer-term perspective on geo-ecological processes, their natural range of variability and responses to perturbations over centennial and millennial timescales. Climate variability during the Holocene was greater than previously recognised, and there was a complex spatial and temporal interplay with human activities in driving landscape change. Change is a fundamental part of montane landscapes, and regardless of any management they will continue to evolve both gradually and episodically. However, there are now additional stresses from atmospheric pollution and local pressures, with the risk that human activity may be moving process systems closer to geomorphological and ecological thresholds than in the past. Unfortunately, as Thompson *et al.* point out, we still lack answers to some fundamental questions about montane geo-ecological systems in order to address the conservation and management implications.

The chapters in Part 2 highlight not only the links between geological and landscape diversity, but also emphasise the fundamental interplay between physical and biological factors, as well as the legacy of human intervention, in our most dynamic environments. This leads on to issues of sustainable management which are examined in Part 3.

4 SCOTLAND'S FOUNDATIONS: OUR GEOLOGICAL INHERITANCE

Nigel H. Trewin

Summary

1.   Scotland's geological inheritance is both historical and physical. The great variety of rocks and geological structure attracted the attention of the great pioneers of geological thought in the late 18th and 19th centuries. The stimuli were economic (coal and minerals), scientific curiosity and sometimes religious. From Hutton's time to the present, Scotland has contributed significantly to geological research, and boasts many sites of great historical importance to the geological sciences.

2.   The distinct geographical regions of Scotland such as the Southern Uplands, Midland Valley, N.W. Highlands and the Hebrides all have characteristic topographies reflecting the physical and chemical attributes of the underlying solid geology, and the resistance of the rocks to the forces of erosion. Major structural features such as the Great Glen and Highland Boundary faults are picked out by erosion and produce features which dramatically influence the landscape. On land, the evidence of ancient mountain chains, ocean closure, rifting and ocean creation is preserved. In offshore areas, Mesozoic and younger rocks fill sedimentary basins, the margins of which effectively control the coastline of Scotland.

3.   The physical and chemical attributes of the rocks and their reaction to weathering exert strong control on vegetation and hence on fauna, both on land and in freshwater. Thus the geology of Scotland underpins all other aspects of the natural environment.

4.   At the outcrop scale, Scotland is rich in localities where rocks, minerals or fossils are of international scientific importance. The management of such sites, both for research and public education, is essential. The geological wealth of Scotland is of world significance, and deserves to be displayed and interpreted for a wide audience. It is a major challenge to promote Scotland's geological inheritance for both education and sustainable conservation.

4.1   Introduction

Britain can be regarded as having more geological diversity than any other comparable area on Earth. This diversity stimulated geological studies and made Britain the cradle of geological knowledge. The Industrial Revolution, based on coal and ironstone, provided an economic stimulus for geological study as the subsurface was mined to greater depths. A general thirst for knowledge in the late 18th and 19th centuries was stimulated by collectors, by theological debate concerning the age of the Earth, and by biblical accounts of the creation and Noah's flood.

Scotland contains an extensive historical geological inheritance which has been fundamental in fashioning the landscape of northern Britain. Scotland has been at a crossroads in geology for millennia and bears the scars of mountain building, ocean closures, rifting and volcanic activity. Representative rocks of all geological periods are present, deposited in conditions ranging from deep ocean to shallow seas, and from tropical swamps to hot deserts and inland lakes. As the plates that make the Earth's crust have been driven over the surface of the globe, Scotland has ranged geographically from the equatorial belt to cool temperate regions.

The timespan covered by the rocks of Scotland covers nearly 3 billion years. This ranges from the Quaternary glaciations which shaped much of our landscape in the last 2 million years, back to the ancient Lewisian gneiss, parts of which were metamorphosed deep within the Earth's crust nearly 3 billion years ago (see the geological time scale (Figure 4.1) for further information on geological dates and events).

The geological inheritance of Scotland can be divided into three topics:

1. The Historical Inheritance. The important part played by pioneering geologists studying in Scotland during the 18th and 19th centuries has resulted in many sites which are of great historical significance for the development of geological science.
2. The Landscape Inheritance. The variety of rock types present in Scotland, and their broad division into geographical regions of distinct topography allows us to examine the relationships between the geology and the landscape and its fauna and flora. Comparison of the geological map (Plate 4) with a satellite image of Scotland (Plate 5) clearly shows the relationship. Thus our mountains, hills, valleys and coastline are closely controlled by the rocks and their resistance to erosion by the agencies of ice, water and wind.
3. The Classic Localities. Scotland abounds in geological localities, both large and small, which are of international scientific importance. The value may be in the broad structure seen in a cliff or quarry, or the presence of important rock types, fossils or minerals.

4.2 Historical inheritance

The most influential work for the subsequent development of Scottish geology was undoubtedly James Hutton's *Theory of the Earth*, published in 1788. Hutton believed in the uniformitarian principal of geological processes, and, unlike the Wernerians, the intrusive nature of granite and other igneous rocks. Hence the localities utilised by Hutton to demonstrate his views have enormous importance in the history of geology. 'Hutton's Unconformities' at Siccar Point, in Berwickshire, and the Cock of Arran, and intrusive phenomena in Glen Tilt and on Salisbury Crags in Edinburgh (Plates 1 and 2), lie at the roots of Scottish geology. Following Hutton, a succession of renowned geologists advanced knowledge of geology. The first account of Scottish geology, Boué's (1820) *Essai geologiqué sur l'Ecosse*, contains the earliest published geological map of the country. Others concentrated on regions, and MacCulloch's (1819) *Description of the Western Islands of Scotland* contains some wonderful geological maps and detailed observations, particularly on the intrusive Tertiary sills in the Jurassic of Trotternish on Skye.

Eras	Geological Period	Ages	Events mentioned in text
	Pleistocene	2	Glaciations of Scotland.
Tertiary	Pliocene	4	
	Miocene	24	Post-rift fill of the North Sea Basin.
	Oligocene	34	
	Eocene	55	
	Palaeocene	65	Volcanic centres and lavas of the Inner Hebrides and Arran. Atlantic Ocean opening.
Mesozoic	Cretaceous	142	Rifting in the North Sea and other offshore basins. Margins of some basins control present Scottish coastline e.g. Moray Firth.
	Jurassic	206	
	Triassic	248	Desert conditions - Red Sandstones of Mauchline and Elgin.
Palaeozoic	Permian	290	Coal swamps, deltas, shelf seas and volcanoes in the Midland Valley.
	Carboniferous	354	
	Devonian	417	The Old Red Sandstone, rivers and lakes, volcanoes from S. Scotland to Shetland.
			Caledonian mountain uplift and granite intrusion. Closure of Iapetus Ocean
	Silurian	443	Deep marine greywackes and shales, S. Uplands.
	Ordovician	495	Shelf limestones and quartzites, N.W. Highlands.
	Cambrian	545	
Proterozoic	(Pre-Cambrian)	1000	Torridonian Sandstone, N.W. Highlands.
		1400	
		2500	Metamorphic and intrusive episodes recorded in Lewisian Gneiss.
Archean		2900	

Figure 4.1 Geological timescale, with a selection of important events in the geological history of Scotland.

The structure of the North-West Highlands was a hotly contested issue, with Roderick Impey Murchison and James Nicol the main protagonists. Nicol's view eventually won the day (see Oldroyd, 1990). Nicol published a guide to Scottish geology in 1844, and Hugh Miller produced his classic work, *The Old Red Sandstone* in 1841. This brought the fossil fish of the Scottish Devonian to the attention of the world (Plate 7). Charles Lapworth (1879) introduced the Ordovician System, and through his work at Dob's Linn, near Moffat, demonstrated that graptolites could be used for stratigraphic zonation. This advance enabled him to unravel some of the complexities of structure in the Southern Uplands. The relation between geology and scenery in Scotland was elegantly demonstrated by Archibald Geikie in *The Scenery of Scotland*, first published in 1865. His examples, presented as engravings, are now published as colour photographs, but their relevance is undiminished.

Many famous geological names from the 20th century could be added to those mentioned above. Techniques, such as geophysics, isotopic analysis and offshore drilling, have allowed new or revised interpretations. Before offshore oil exploration began using sea-borne geophysics, few would have guessed that an enormous sediment-filled, oil-rich Mesozoic rift lay between the ancient metamorphic rocks of Scotland and Norway. We can only speculate about the geological revelations that future techniques might produce.

4.3 Landscape inheritance

It is not possible here to cover the full range of geologically controlled landscapes found in Scotland. The following broad generalisations are illustrated by a few of the more spectacular examples. The regions of Scotland (Figure 4.2) apparent on the geological map can be summarised as follows:

- the Southern Uplands;
- the Midland Valley;
- the Highlands south of the Great Glen Fault;
- the Northern Highlands;
- Caithness and Orkney - the Orcadian area;
- the Hebridean area; and
- the Offshore Basins.

There is a great variety within some of these regions, and the boundaries can be gradational. For example, the Mesozoic rocks of the Moray Firth Basin have narrow onshore outcrops, and the Hebridean area includes dissected Tertiary volcanoes and landscapes of ancient Lewisian gneiss. The Shetland Islands combine characteristics of the metamorphic rocks of the Northern Highlands and Old Red Sandstone of the Orcadian area, but in their northern isolation have a unique character. More information can be found in Craig (1991), and a useful and well illustrated account in plain language is given by McKirdy and Crofts (1999).

The Southern Uplands are dominated by greywacke sandstones and slates of Ordovician to Silurian age, deposited in deep marine environments and deformed during the closure of the Iapetus Ocean in the late Silurian. The old 'suture' probably passes under the Solway area. The topography of the area is one of rounded hills sculpted by glaciation, and the general uniformity of the rocks is reflected in the topography.

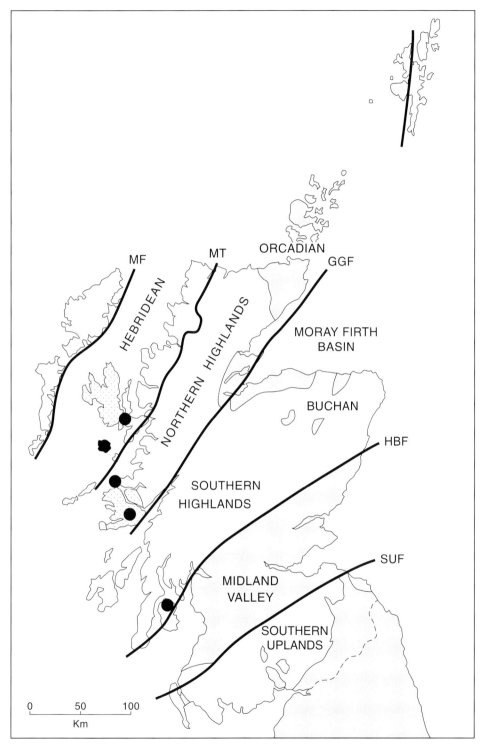

Figure 4.2   Distinctive geological regions and features of Scotland. SUF: Southern Uplands Fault.   HBF: Highland Boundary Fault.   GGF: Great Glen Fault.   MT: Moine Thrust.   MF: Minch Fault.   Shaded areas are dominated by Upper Palaeozoic sedimentary rocks. Tertiary volcanic centres are represented by spots and lavas by stipple.

The Midland Valley, bounded by major faults, is dominated by Carboniferous and Devonian sedimentary rocks and volcanics, with numerous intrusions in the form of sills and volcanic necks. The igneous rocks tend to have been the most resistant to erosion: Old Red Sandstone (Devonian) lavas shape the Sidlaws and Ochils, and volcanic necks - the eroded feeders of volcanoes - give rise to Arthur's Seat and the hills of East and West Lomond. Scarps are formed where the resistant dolerite of the Midland Valley sill caps hills. The lower land is generally underlain by the less resistant shales and sandstones of the Carboniferous and Devonian.

To the north of the Highland Boundary Fault, resistant metamorphic rocks and granite intrusions underlie the high ground of the Southern Highlands. Here, erosion has picked out the weaker rocks and the shattered rock of fault zones, to leave the resistant granites and quartzites which tend to form the higher mountains. Traced east to Buchan, the mountains die away. This can partly be ascribed to pre-Devonian erosion and the probability that a cover of Devonian existed over the eastern Grampian area, outliers of which still exist at Rhynie and Tomintoul. In Buchan, where effects of glacial erosion were minimal, deep weathering profiles remain from tropical conditions in Tertiary times. Furthermore, the high plateaux (e.g. Cairngorms) of the Highlands are probably remnants of uplifted and tilted erosion surfaces of Tertiary age (Hall, 1991), but could conceivably represent uplifted marine planation surfaces from the late Cretaceous. Hence the landscape includes inherited features from prior to the Pleistocene glaciations. Devonian uplift of the metamorphic basement was greater to the south west. Volcanoes punched through the metamorphic rocks, and their lava flows are preserved in Glen Coe and the Lorne Plateau.

The Great Glen Fault is a complex structure with a long history of activity, and erosion has picked out the shattered fault rock to give a spectacular linear glaciated valley with deep ice-gouged basins such as Loch Ness. This fault, and the Highland Boundary Fault are clearly visible on satellite images of Scotland (Plate 5).

In the Northern Highlands it is again the granites and metamorphic rocks which form the rugged topography, so clearly modified by glaciation. Here, too, the high plateaux represent old uplifted planation surfaces. These surfaces have been uplifted along the western margin and slope toward the North Sea. In Tertiary times, a drainage system carried debris from volcanoes in the Hebridean area to the North Sea basin.

A different topography of flat moorland and rolling hills takes over in Caithness and Orkney which are underlain by the flagstones of the Old Red Sandstone. These rocks were deposited in a large lake basin (Lake Orcadie) in the Middle Devonian. The rocks are generally flat lying and the cliffs provide numerous flat ledges for nesting seabirds as at Duncansby Head. The narrow geos (inlets) in the cliffs are generally eroded along faults and shatter belts, and the sea stacks became isolated from the main cliff by the sea eroding the weakest joints. The spectacular sandstone cliffs of Hoy and Dunnet Head are made of Upper Old Red Sandstone which gives rise to ground clearly identified on the satellite image (Plate 5) as a distinct shade representing similar vegetation and land use.

The Northern Highlands are bounded to the west by one of the most spectacular and historically important regions in British geology - the Moine Thrust Zone. The line of the Moine Thrust can be taken to divide our Northern Highland area from the Hebridean region. The metamorphic rocks of the Moine were uplifted and thrust westward over the Lewisian, Torridonian and Cambro-Ordovician rocks of the north-west in the Caledonian

Orogeny, and it was this thrust relationship that was first recognised by James Nicol. The Moine Thrust Zone extends from Eribol in the north to the Sleat of Skye in the south, and the complexities of the fault zone have been studied in great detail, particularly in the Assynt area. The succession to the west of the thrust zone is beautifully displayed in the mountains of the north-west. The ancient metamorphic rocks of the Lewisian gneiss (1800 - 2900 Ma) are eroded to a distinctive hummocky terrain, best seen in the Outer Hebrides. On the mainland and the islands of the Inner Hebrides, the Torridonian sandstone (about 1,000 Ma) rests unconformably on the Lewisian gneiss, and the Cambro-Ordovician (450 - 550 Ma) succession of quartzites and the Durness limestone in turn rest unconformably on Torridonian, or directly on the Lewisian. In places, the ancient pre-Torridonian erosion surface of the gneiss has been exhumed by removal of the Torridonian. These great unconformities are displayed in the mountain of Suilven, for example.

Within this area, there is a well marked contrast between vegetation on limestones and on the gneiss and Torridonian sandstones, and is due to the different chemistries and drainage characteristics of the rocks. This is a prime area where the geology can be mapped on the basis of the natural vegetation.

Whilst the scenery of the Assynt area so beautifully reflects the geology of the foreland of the Caledonian mountain chain, two other major rock groups are present in the Hebridean area. Mesozoic rocks, predominantly Jurassic, are exposed mainly on Skye, and form part of the fill of sedimentary basins underlying The Minch and the Sea of the Hebrides. They are included in this discussion as onshore fragments of basins which are dominantly offshore in nature. The main Jurassic outcrops of Skye are only preserved by protection under thick lavas of Tertiary age. These lavas were erupted from the 'Tertiary Volcanic Centres' which make up the 'Tertiary Volcanic Province'. Thus in Mull, Ardnamurchan, Rum, Skye, and further south on Arran, we see the eroded remnants of the roots of great volcanic centres active about 55 million years ago (Plate 3).

The arcuate concentric intrusions making up the centres weather to display the volcanic roots, and swarms of dykes radiate from them. The topography of Skye typifies the erosion patterns of the igneous rocks. The individual lava flows making up the pile of lavas that covers most of Skye north of the Cuillin consist of a hard resistant centre and softer top and base. When weathered, a stepped or 'trap' topography is produced, the flat tops of McLeod's Tables near Dunvegan being a prime example. The main igneous centre on Skye has two contrasting rock types as its main constituents. The jagged forms of the Black Cuillin are made of gabbro, cut by many dykes which erode as gullies. In contrast, the Red Hills are made of pale granite, are generally devoid of dykes, and weather to rounded forms. At the height of volcanic activity, volcanic debris was transported east to the North Sea, implying a watershed to the west of Skye in the early Tertiary.

The final division is the Offshore Basins, with little to see except water, but it must be appreciated that much of the coastline of Scotland is controlled by the presence of offshore Mesozoic to Tertiary basins, which contain the oil wealth of Scotland.

The most obvious examples of coastlines controlled by basins are the Moray Firth and the Minches. In the Moray Firth a fringe of Jurassic sediments is preserved on the north-west side of the Firth in the Brora-Helmsdale area adjacent to the Helmsdale Fault, and patches also exist in the Elgin area to the south. Underlying the Firth are Mesozoic sequences which exceed 2 km in thickness over much of the area. The basins in the

Hebrides area are also fault controlled, with a major fault at the western margin of the basin adjacent to the outer Hebrides. The vertical displacement across on this fault is possibly as much as 4 km in places. Apart from these clear examples of coastlines controlled by sedimentary basins, it must be remembered that at present, the North Sea is underlain by a subsiding basin which has over 300 m of Pleistocene to recent deposits in its centre, and up to 3 km of Tertiary muds and sands. To the west of Shetland and the Hebrides, other basins along the continental margin await further exploration.

This brief survey of geology and topography in Scotland masks the detail to be found in many areas. Geology can be related to topography, soils, flora and fauna at scales ranging from tens of kilometres to metres, and requires consideration in any assessment of the natural environment. Furthermore, many large scale features of our landscape are inherited from Tertiary and earlier times, and have been modified by the Pleistocene glaciations to give the composite landscapes preserved today.

4.4 Classic geological localities

Apart from the historical and regional aspects of the geological inheritance, Scotland has many localities of international importance which we have a duty to utilise in an educational and scientifically sustainable manner. Historically famous sites such as Hutton's unconformities at Cock of Arran and Siccar Point need only be conserved for access and explanation. The section of the Moine Thrust at Knockan Crag in the Northern Highlands provides a valuable focus for geological interest in the wider area, with a variety of geological phenomena displayed in an area of outstanding beauty (Plate 6). A visitor centre and geological trails demonstrate the essentially field-based nature of geology. The viewpoint of 'Kilt Rock' in Skye is a popular tourist stop for a view, but this experience is now enhanced by a geological explanation of the 'tartan' effect of vertical columnar jointing in a dolerite sill combined with horizontal bedding in the contrasting Jurassic sandstones.

More difficult situations arise with localities that are attractive to collectors of rocks, minerals or fossils. Some control is necessary, such as Scottish Natural Heritage exercises at Achanarras Quarry in Caithness - an internationally famous fossil fish site (Trewin, 1993). Responsible collecting has its benefits: two animals new to science, a fish and an arthropod, have recently been found at Achanarras. The negative attitude of closing such a site to collecting results in degradation by vegetation overgrowth, or tipping and filling of an 'abandoned' site. Old quarries are important sites, and their filling, or natural degradation is detrimental to geological interest. We could enhance the educational value of many more of our important sites by creating interpretive displays and linking these into geo-tour itineraries. By establishing site usage and public interest, it is easier to monitor activity and resist the landfillers!

Arguably our most significant fossil site of international importance is at Rhynie, a green field with no natural exposure of the famous Rhynie chert and its silicified early Devonian land plants and arthropods (Trewin, 1994). Here, research is expensive and involves deep drilling, coring and excavating holes to bedrock with a mechanical digger. In this and other cases, continued research is essential not only to determine the existing value of the site, but to enhance both scientific value and public interest. This is particularly true of localities that have not been studied or even excavated since the 19th century.

Scotland has many significant geological localities that require further investigation to realise the potential of this part of our natural heritage.

4.5 Conclusion

Scotland is rich in geological features relating to the history of geological science. This diversity provides a superb illustration of geological control on landscape, and consequently on soils and vegetation. Geological localities of world class provide the opportunity to create a countrywide network of geological educational sites. We have made a start, but a lot remains to be done in presenting Scotland's geological inheritance to her own people and to the world.

References

Boué, A. 1820. *Essai géologique sur l'Ecosse.* Paris.

Craig, G.Y. (ed.) 1991. *Geology of Scotland* (3rd edn). The Geological Society, London.

Geikie, A. 1865. *The Scenery of Scotland.* Macmillan, London.

Hall, A.M. 1991. Pre-Quaternary landscape evolution in the Scottish Highlands. *Transactions of the Royal Society of Edinburgh: Earth Sciences,* **82**, 1-26.

Hutton, J. 1788. Theory of the Earth. *Transactions of the Royal Society of Edinburgh,* **1**, 209-304.

Lapworth, C. 1879. On the tripartite classification of the Lower Palaeozoic rocks. *Geological Magazine,* **16**, 1-15.

MacCulloch, J. 1819. *A Description of the Western Islands of Scotland including the Isle of Man.* Constable, London.

McKirdy, A. and Crofts, R. 1999. *Scotland. The Creation of its Natural Landscape. A Landscape Fashioned by Geology.* Scottish Natural Heritage, Perth.

Miller, H. 1841. *The Old Red Sandstone.* Constable, Edinburgh.

Nicol, J. 1844. *Guide to the Geology of Scotland.* Oliver and Boyd, Edinburgh.

Oldroyd, D.R. 1990. *The Highland Controversy.* University of Chicago Press, Chicago.

Trewin, N.H. 1993. The Old Red Sandstone of Caithness. *In* Trewin, N.H. and Hurst, A. (eds) *Excursion Guide to the Geology of east Sutherland and Caithness.* Scottish Academic Press, Edinburgh, 123-156.

Trewin, N.H. 1994. Depositional environment and preservation of biota in the Lower Devonian hot-springs of Rhynie, Aberdeenshire, Scotland. *Transactions of the Royal Society of Edinburgh: Earth Sciences,* **84**, 433-442.

5 TIR A' MHACHAIR (LAND OF THE MACHAIR): SEDIMENT SUPPLY AND CLIMATE CHANGE SCENARIOS FOR THE FUTURE OF THE OUTER HEBRIDES MACHAIR

James D. Hansom and Stewart Angus

Summary

1. Machair is a distinct and unique environment found only in the western seaboard of Scotland and Northern Ireland. This paper discusses the distribution, evolution and present habitat of the Scottish machair, together with an assessment of its present and future status.

2. The initiation of machair surfaces began in the mid-Holocene when beach sand was blown landwards in quantity to produce large dune systems which themselves were then subject to deflation. Since then, a declining supply of sand has resulted in the recycling of dune sands into beaches, via beach erosion, and the ongoing deflation of older dune surfaces down to the water table or underlying gravels.

3. With increasing sea levels and storminess, many machairs are vulnerable to rapid change as a result of erosion and over-topping of the machair or dune edge, coupled with a landwards gradient and poor drainage conditions. This, together with the human response to such change, may impact negatively on the biodiversity and sustainability of many machair habitats that are already altering as a result of changes in traditional agrricultural practices.

5.1 Introduction

In common with many coasts around the world, the coastline of Scotland is characterised by a spectrum of environments ranging from open rocky shores to enclosed muddy estuaries, each displaying both direct and indirect links between structure, process and the habitats that these substrates support. Of these coastal environments, machair has a very limited world distribution and is restricted to Northwestern Ireland and Western and Northern Scotland on the extreme western fringes of Europe. Machair is a distinctive and unique coastal environment that encapsulates the symbiosis and interconnection between Earth science and the natural heritage. In addition, because of its strong links to human land use, images of the machair environment also capture something of the cultural essence of the western seaboard of the Scottish coast (Plate 15). However, as a result of ongoing natural processes, and the likely human reaction to coastal erosion associated with these processes, the machair environment may be under threat. This paper discusses the distribution, evolution, and present habitat of the Scottish machair, together with an assessment of its present and future status.

5.2 The machair system

Ritchie (1976) defined machair (*sensu stricto*) solely in terms of the machair plain and mainly characterised by:

- a base of blown sand with a high percentage of shell-derived sediment;
- lime-rich soils of pH greater than 7.0;
- a low-angled and almost level sand plain at a mature stage of geomorphological evolution;
- herb-rich grassland vegetation with a low frequency of sand-binding grasses;
- detectable current or historic biotic interference resulting from grazing, cultivation and fertilisation, trampling and, sometimes, artificial drainage; and
- a moist, cool, oceanic climate.

However, in a wider geomorphological and conservation context, the related habitats and transitions adjacent to the machair plain are considered to be integral parts of 'machair systems'. In this context, machair can be described as a gently sloping coastal dune-plain formed mainly by wind-blown, calcareous shell-sand, incorporating a mosaic of dunes to the seaboard and a species-rich grassland plain (managed by low-intensity traditional agriculture), wetland, loch and blackland (a mixture of sand and peat) to the landward (Angus, 1994, 2000).

There is also a strong correlation between the distribution of machair and the use of the Gaelic language in Ireland and, with the exception of Orkney and Shetland, in Scotland. Approximately 13,300 ha or about 64% of the global machair resource of 20,800 ha is found in western Scotland, with the remaining 7500 ha occurring in Northwestern Ireland (Angus, 2001) (Figure 5.1). However, all of the machair lands have similarities in their land use histories as well as language, and so it is likely that the present distribution and nature of machair systems owes as much to cultural factors as it does to the more usual biotic and abiotic influences.

Most machair systems are composed predominantly of shell sand derived from offshore, but the actual percentage of carbonate and non-carbonate sediment can be highly variable. For example, the carbonate content of machair sands in Tiree in the Inner Hebrides reaches 95%. In the Outer Hebrides, it reaches 83% in Hushinish, but can be as low as 1% in Grimsay (Mather and Ritchie, 1977). The sediment composition of machair systems should mainly reflect the composition and availability of the sediment sources. Since streams traversing machair on the western seaboard are rare and generally sediment-poor, Mather and Ritchie (1977) consider that they are not a major supplier of new sediment to machair systems and mainly serve to recycle limited amounts of sand from the dunes through which they flow (Figure 5.2). Although some mineral sand arrived at the coast from terrestrial sources in the early Holocene (Gilbertson *et al.*, 1999), the generally accepted principal source of mineral and carbonate sands supplied to Scottish beaches, and thence blown on to the machair, is from the nearshore and offshore during the middle and late Holocene (Hansom, 1988, 1999; Gilbertson *et al.*, 1999). Though it has been

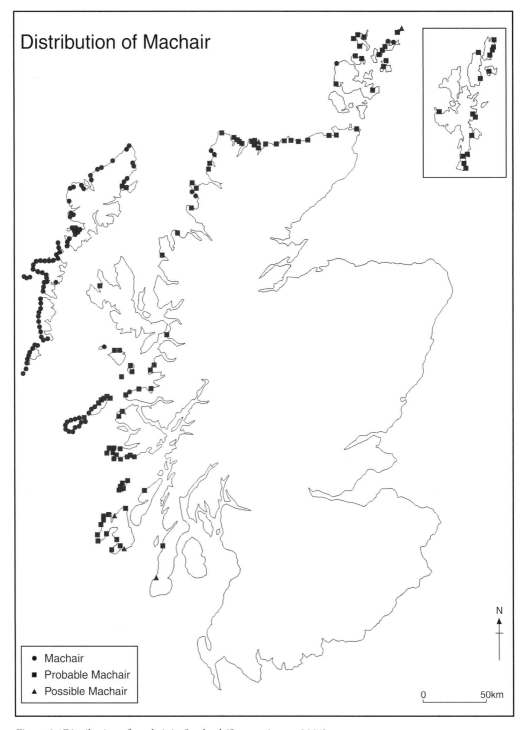

Figure 5.1 Distribution of machair in Scotland (Source: Angus, 2001).

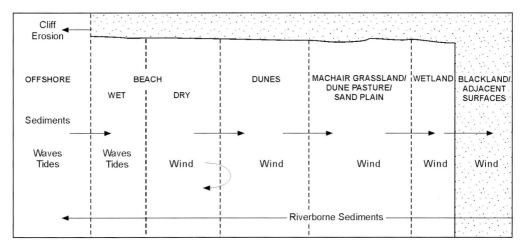

Figure 5.2 Sand transfer system from beach to machair. (Source: adapted from Mather and Ritchie, 1977).

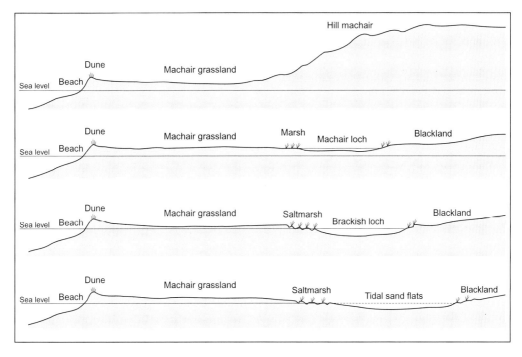

Figure 5.3 Changes in machair habitat with decreasing altitude inland. The two lower profiles assume a saline incursion. (Source: Angus, 2000).

suggested that the sand supply is still augmented by new shell material (Mate, 1991), the scale of such a contribution is unknown (Ritchie and Whittington, 1994). The availability of upper beach sand in a vigorous aeolian environment (the western and northern seaboard experiences the strongest winds in the British Isles, with hourly mean wind speeds of 4 ms[-1] exceeded for 75% of the time (Caton, 1976)) has resulted in extensive dune development and the migration of large amounts of blown sand on to adjacent land surfaces.

The dune cordon and machair grassland may be backed by a variety of habitats, depending on topography and altitude above sea level. These mainly reflect the deposition of aeolian sand on to machair surfaces and either the resultant impounding of fresh water in the form of machair marsh and lochs, or the varying inundation of low-lying land by tidal salt water (Figure 5.3). Both situations are usually flanked by wetland and backed on the landward side by blackland or moorland beyond (Ritchie, 1976; Angus, 1994).

5.3 Machair development

Whilst the present machair system is highly dynamic, both genesis and present status are rooted in its developmental history. Although peculiar to the western seaboard, the machair system is in essence a particular type of dune and sand plain complex produced from the normal cycle of deposition and erosion of sand dunes. However, it is important to note that Hebridean machair is at a very late stage in the dune system development sequence and is now eroding and recycling due to sediment deficiency. The generic dune development sequence is summarised by Pethick (1984) and Hansom (1988), but in essence depends on a surplus of upper beach sand being blown landward to be trapped at the strandline by specialist pioneer species such as sea rocket (*Cakile maritima*), common in the Western Isles. The presence of such plants enhances sand deposition and allows the developing embryo dune to develop in pace with vegetation growth. Once this dune grows in height, it is known as a fore-dune or mobile dune, and other specialist sand-trapping species, such as marram grass (*Ammophila arenaria*), allow it to expand rapidly, coalesce with adjacent dunes and form a continuous dune ridge semi-fixed by vegetation. As this dune ridge ages and grows, it becomes increasingly fixed by vegetation, although it continues to receive decreasing amounts of sand from seaward because of interception by the next generation of dunes forming above the strandline. However, it is also subject to loss of sand to landward, resulting from wind deflation of breaks in the vegetational cover. Such deflation results in the development of blow-outs, the end member of which is a sand plain produced from the deflation of the oldest dunes. In many machair systems, deflation continues to a low level, often coincident with the water table or basement of gravel or till (Ritchie, 1972, 1979). The resultant machair surface is often characterised by steep, eroded, shore-parallel inner escarpments located within low-lying and landwards-dipping deflation surfaces. In the more complex systems, higher dune surfaces may lie both to seaward and landward.

It is important to recognise that the above sequence is essentially depositional in its early phases and based on a positive sediment economy on the beaches that feed the dunes. As long as continuity of accretion is maintained, new dunes develop in front of older ones, producing in time a series of ridges, the oldest of which becomes starved of sand and subject to blow-out, deflation and machair plain development. This model attributes the development of the machair plain to a constant interplay of sands 'exhumed' from the oldest dunes, together with sand recycled from its own deflation. As a result, machair development is controlled by its position as the end member of an initially accreting system. However, in most machair systems, embryo and mobile dunes are now rare, and where they do occur, they occupy a restricted area, with strandline, embryo and mobile dunes 'telescoped' into each other. In most places, Hebridean machair is now characterised by wave-induced frontal erosion either of the mature dunes if these remain or, if they do not remain, of the machair plain itself, so that the 'successional' model is truncated.

5.4 Evolution of the machair system

The conditions that favoured a positive sand economy were widespread on the Scottish coast when the previously rapidly rising Holocene sea level began to slow between about 8,000 and 6,500 radiocarbon years BP. Waves were then able to accomplish substantial nearshore modification and bring some gravels, followed by large amounts of sand, from the nearshore shelf on to beaches (Carter, 1994). The sands were then blown into sand dunes (Figure 5.4a). However, the finite nature of this sediment supply led to a progressive reduction in sediment availability and a switch from surplus prior to 6,500 radiocarbon years BP, to deficit sometime after 6,500 radiocarbon years BP (Carter, 1988, 1994; Hansom, 1999). This widespread switch in sediment economy from surplus to deficit ultimately led to the replacement of the accreting system responsible for beach, dune and machair development by an erosional system (Figure 5.4b). Such a degradational cycle might be felt first in those areas subject to high energy wave conditions and exacerbated by isostatic submergence, conditions that are met on the north and north-western seaboards of Scotland (Hansom, 2001). The Western Atlantic coast of the UK is subject to wave heights that are significantly higher than in other parts of the UK coast (Lee and Ramster, 1981). In addition, increases in storminess over the last 30 years have resulted in a 2.5-7.0 mm per year increment in significant wave height in the North Atlantic (Gunther *et al.*, 1998). The

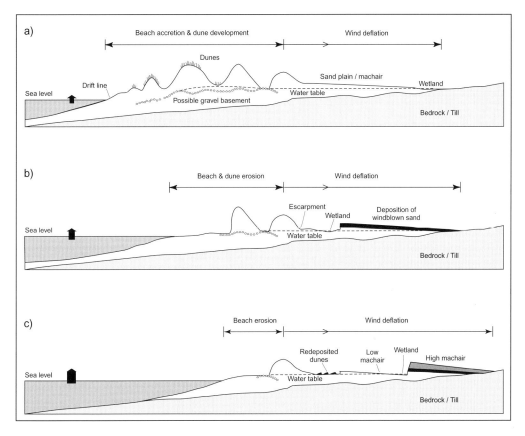

Figure 5.4 The Holocene development of machair from approximately 8.5k radiocarbon years BP to present. See text for explanation.

current ongoing sea-level rise in the Outer Hebrides is 1-2 mm per year (Pethick, 1999; Dawson *et al.*, 2000), and so erosion resulting from increases in sea level is probably masked by erosion resulting from increases in storminess. The net result of a combination of long-term sediment deficiency, increases in storminess and isostatic submergence in the Outer Hebrides is that erosion of the dune cordon in machair areas is now well advanced, and in places the machair plain itself is now eroding. For the last *c.* 6,500 radiocarbon years, the operation of a negative sediment economy has resulted in the progressive erosion and recycling of dune and machair plain sands (Figure 5.4c).

Support for the above geomorphological evidence of an initial surplus followed by declining sand supply comes from dating the sand layers in association with archaeological sites located originally within accreting dunes and now found on eroding coasts. Optically stimulated luminescence (OSL) dating of aeolian sands by Gilbertson *et al.* (1999) indicates that the carbonate sand of the Benbecula and North Uist machairs began to arrive from offshore about 8,700 years BP and in Barra about 6,800 years BP. At Northton in South Harris, the onset of sand deposition which buried Neolithic remains occurred from 4,500 radiocarbon years BP (Ritchie, 1979). Other archaeological sites in machair, such as Bornish, Baleshare and Paible in the Uists and Traigh Varlish in Vatersay, were established on aeolian sand dunes and subsequently abandoned due to wind-blow and instability (Ritchie, 1979; Gilbertson *et al.*, 1996). The discovery of exhumed archaeological sites within dunes is largely due to frontal erosion, although multiple cycles of erosion, deposition and deflation are concealed within this general erosional trend. However, in spite of the above, dating of the initiation of dune and machair formation in the Outer Hebrides remains problematic. Ritchie and Whittington (1994) report intertidal peats overlain by aeolian sands that date from 7,800 radiocarbon years BP at Cladach Mór in North Uist and from 7,700 radiocarbon years BP at the Landing Jetty in Pabbay. Yet other sites on these islands, for example at Quinish in Pabbay dating from 4,300 radiocarbon years BP and at Borve in Benbecula dating from 5,600 radiocarbon years BP, suggest that the arrival of aeolian sand and the initiation of machair development in the Hebrides were non-synchronous (Ritchie and Whittington, 1994). However, in the low and undulating coastal landscape of the Western and Northern Isles, rock basins close to sea level are likely to be affected by rising sea levels at different times and so the influences of local bathymetry and site factors represent important site-specific controls on the date of machair initiation.

Once established, the development of the machair plain is essentially erosion-driven, with new surfaces produced as old ones are consumed. However, there can be marked seasonal differences. For example, where deflation has exposed the water table, winter flooding may result in sand blowing on to wet surfaces and this results in a depositional flat surface rather than an erosional one. Archaeological studies provide evidence of fertile and stabilised sand surfaces around 2,000 radiocarbon years BP (Ritchie, 1966a, 1966b). Several sites ascribed to the Iron Age and later are located on the low flat surfaces of machair that have been produced following deflation of earlier machair surfaces (Ritchie, 1979). Gilbertson *et al.* (1996) document layers of thick organic palaeosols within the dunes and machair dating from Bronze Age to Mediaeval, together with periods of instability (particularly between the 9th and 13th centuries AD), as indicated from Viking settlements now buried below aeolian sand deposits (MacLaren, 1974). Historical evidence extends the above pattern of phased instability and stability of the machair into modern times. During the 16th century, machair surfaces were stable with well-established agriculture, but the 17th century brought widespread sand-blow on much of the Scottish coast and burial of machair surfaces and buildings in the Outer Hebrides (Ritchie, 1967, 1979; Lamb, 1991; Angus, 1997). Although probably more stable than it has been in the past, Hebridean machair is still actively forming and the present machair *surface* has probably formed over the same timescale as it has in the past, that is over periods of less than 100 years (Gilbertson *et al.*, 1999). Nevertheless, the present machair system as a whole represents the latest manifestation of a continuum of essentially similar processes operating since at least the middle Holocene.

5.5 Machair associations

The machair habitat and its structure closely reflect depositional history, the present level of aeolian activity and past and present land-use patterns. The vegetation now present on machair is a function of the interdependence of sand mobility and calcareous content, level of water table, and land management. Most machairs exhibit a landward gradient as follows (Mather and Ritchie, 1977):

- calcareous (shell) content rises from beach to dune crest then declines gradually landwards;
- sand mobility declines landwards;
- level of water table rises inland, often reaching the surface at a terrestrial transition and marked by a range of marshes or lochs (Figure 5.3); water levels also fluctuate seasonally, and the drainage pattern is much affected by artificial channels established in the 18th century;
- pH declines landwards;
- organic content rises landwards;
- recreation on beach and dunes, grazing on dune and near-dune machair, arable on far-dune landward end of machair grassland, and settlement on blackland.

5.5.1 Beach and strandline

Many beaches forming part of machair systems have strandlines accumulating large amounts of wave-torn marine algae, usually 'tangle' (*Laminaria hyperborea*) over winter, which is gathered and spread on the machair arable land as an organic fertiliser and sand-binding agent. Often there is more seaweed than can be removed, and the spring strandlines are generally rich in algal material which becomes buried by blowing sand. This material provides a breeding ground for invertebrates and a growing medium for vegetation, the winter and spring strandlines being marked by the linear growth of plants in characteristic strandline associations, notably *Cakile maritima-Honckenya peploides* (SD2) and occasionally *Tripleurospermum maritimum-Galium aparine* (SD3) in the National Vegetation Classification (NVC). Dargie (1998) has identified a third new strandline type, *Potentilla anserina* (SDx), found mainly on the Inner Hebrides machair strands.

5.5.2 Embryo dune and mobile dune

Where strandline, embryo and mobile dunes occur, they merge into each other over extremely short distances. Embryo dunes occur only when sand is locally available and so have a restricted distribution in the machair areas where they are characterised by *Elytrigia juncea* (SD4). Mobile dunes are also restricted and are almost all of the *Ammophila arenaria* type (SD6). In comparison to England and Wales, Dargie (2000) considers the small proportion of mobile dune within Scottish dune systems to be related to cool moist conditions which encourage fixation by rapid establishment of mosses and herbs. On machair, sand deficits, together with the extreme exposure of machair beaches, will also serve to restrict mobile dune extent.

5.5.3 Semi-fixed dune and fixed dune

The commonest type of semi-fixed dune in the machair areas is not described in the NVC, and has been named the *Ammophila arenaria - Festuca rubra* semi-fixed dune, provisional new *Galium verum* sub-community (SD7x), although in depressions close to the dune edge there is a variant rich in *Heracleum sphondylium*, believed to rely on nutrients from blown fragments of seaweed (Dargie, 1998). The dominant vegetation on calcareous machair fixed dunes is *Festuca rubra-Galium verum* (SD8), found mainly as the *Ranunculus acris-Bellis perennis* sub-community (SD8d) of dry machair and the *Prunella vulgaris* sub-community (SD8e) of wet machair (Dargie, 1988).

5.5.4 Wet areas

The machair usually becomes increasingly wetter inland, reflecting the landward slope of the machair surface towards the water table, and the associated transitions add considerably to the habitat diversity and conservation attributes of the machair system. The damp machair sub-community (SD8e) indicates areas which often flood in winter. Where conditions permit, low-lying areas may form mosaics including the vegetation of slacks (SD17), mires (M), or saltmarsh (SM), with sandflats in the lower intertidal areas (Figure 5.3).

5.5.5 Cultivation and grazing

The inland sectors of the dry machair and the seaward sectors of the wet machair are cultivated, in the Uists, using a traditional rotation that involves two or more years fallow following cropping. In some crofting townships, livestock are moved to hill ground for the duration of the growing season, coincidentally allowing them to pick up the trace elements that are absent from machair. The traditional cattle-based land management, of which the growing of winter fodder is such an integral part, is an important contributory element to maintenance of high biodiversity. Where cattle have been replaced by sheep, for example since the 1960s in Lewis and Harris, the biodiversity of the machair lands affected has suffered and its conservation value diminished (Angus, 2001). A lack of herbicides, combined with the patchwork of crops and different stages of fallow, also provides a highly varied habitat for invertebrates and breeding birds, including an assemblage of waders that breed in internationally important numbers (Figure 5.5), together with species now lost from most agricultural land elsewhere in UK, such as corncrake and corn bunting. There is an intensity of integration between human activity and the natural heritage in machair management which is now rare in the UK, and this positive interaction is not only pivotal to the international value of the habitat but is critical to its future. Maintenance of this interrelationship is the crux of any sustainable management strategy.

An additional grazing pressure on almost all the machair islands comes from rabbits, that were introduced in the Outer Hebrides in the late 18th century and are now widespread. Their grazing may lead to problems on machair areas already heavily grazed by livestock, while burrowing and, to a lesser extent, scraping, may initiate erosion by exposing sub-surface sand to wind blow (Angus and Elliott, 1992). Grazing and burrowing by rabbits may also lead to significant changes in vegetation (Dargie, 2000).

5.5.6 Transitions

The sequence of vegetation from beach to inland habitats is determined by a sequence of water table, organic content, pH and $CaCO_3$, but this sequence is now zonal rather than seral. The distributions of breeding birds reflect these changes, and together the transitions consititute a very important aspect of the habitat (Figure 5.5).

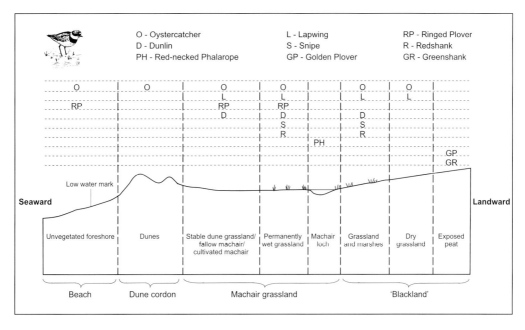

Figure 5.5 The intricate association of bird species with machair habitat from beach to blackland. (Source: modified from Fuller, 1982).

5.6 Erosional status of machair

At present, aeolian erosion of machair is probably not a major problem and there is extensive evidence to suggest that machair surfaces are now more stable than they have been historically (Angus and Elliott, 1992). In any case, because machair development relies upon exhumed and recycled sands from older dunes or machair, ongoing aeolian activity is essential to the future health of the system. However, frontal edge erosion of the mature dunes by waves presents more serious implications for machair. Such erosion is now widespread in machair areas and, in some cases, substantial dune cordons have been removed, allowing waves to impinge on the low edge of the machair plain itself, as at

Baleshare, North Uist, or to expose the gravel ridges that underlie some machairs, as at Stoneybridge, South Uist. Although wave activity will release more sand volume to the beach, this occurs via the loss of either dune or machair surfaces. Where the machair system is underlain by older beach gravels (see Figure 5.4), erosion results in exposure of these gravels on the upper beach and this also restricts beach and dune sand exchange. In general, the machair sand economy has been negative for a substantial period of time and the bulk of the available evidence relates to ongoing sediment redistribution and loss of machair edges (HR Wallingford, 2000). Whilst there is also evidence of sediment recycling inland, bay-infilling as a result of alongshore movement of sediment, and the contribution of an unknown amount of shell sand from the Hebridean shelf (Mate, 1991), it seems unlikely that machair losses are currently balanced by machair gains. An important research priority is to establish the validity of this assertion, but at present it appears more likely that the present area of machair is not sustainable within the current restricted sediment supply condition. In this respect, erosion and over-topping of the dune ridge and flooding of adjacent low-lying machair, as has occurred at Vallay Strand and Stoneybridge, can be interpreted in the medium-term as part of such a sediment redistribution process. However, as a result of the landward slope of the machair surface, over-topping could lead to either direct flooding of agricultural land downslope, or indirect flooding as a result of disruption of the network of ditches that drain such areas. With the removal of the remnants of the dune cordon in the future as a result of ongoing increases in wave height and sea level, many more such locations may become vulnerable to over-topping.

In situations where erosion or flooding is seen as a problem, protection of the eroding section of coast appears an understandable response particularly where valuable assets are threatened, such as has occurred at at Balivanich, Benbecula, in North Uist at Baleshare, in Harris at Northton and as has been proposed at Liniclate in Benbecula (Plate 16). However, it has been shown elsewhere that protection of short sections of eroding coastline leads, more often than not, to local beach lowering and an acceleration of adjacent erosion rates (Carter, 1988; Bird, 1996). Since such *ad hoc* responses are likely ultimately to fail, erosion of machair lands presents a dilemma. Failure to protect the eroding beach results in ongoing loss of machair edge and possible flooding but allows continuation of the sand supply to feed machair surfaces. Protection of the eroding beach not only accelerates losses of adjacent unprotected machair but arrests the sand supply to the protected machair.

Though over-topping and breaching of the dune cordon may recreate habitat and redistribute sand inland (possibly on to croft land), in all likelihood the agricultural regime may be so disrupted by water impoundment from blocked drainage networks that the present traditional system on which so much of the conservation value of machair depends may be abandoned due to operational or motivational difficulties. As a result of such *agricultural* disruption, the extraordinarily high biodiversity of the present-day machair is unlikely to be fully recreated elsewhere. The creation of new machair surfaces or wetlands elsewhere is unlikely to compensate for the loss of the biodiversity now provided by traditional cattle-based land management. The realisation that machair may be threatened by sand deficits, relative sea-level rise and flooding, complicated by the land management changes that these might force, represents a thorny problem for managers of the resource, be they crofters, conservation bodies or other agencies.

5.7 Machair conservation: a way forward?

Machair is regarded as a habitat of European importance, and 50% of Scottish machair has been proposed for designation as either Special Protection Area (SPA) or Special Area of Conservation (SAC) through the EC Directives on Birds and Habitats, respectively, with many systems qualifying for both. In Scotland, 80% of machair systems are protected as Sites of Special Scientific Interest (SSSI) by UK legislation.

Current opinion is that the Habitats Directive does not require member states to prevent natural change, yet of the coastal habitats in Scotland, machair (together with saltmarshes (Hansom *et al.*, this volume)) are perhaps the most at risk from future climate changes that involve a combination of flooding and sediment redistribution, possibly on a large scale. Opinions vary on the scale of projected sea-level rise and storminess (Dawson *et al.*, 2000), although if such changes result in increased machair erosion, there will be a temptation to protect. Although widespread protection from wave erosion is not a realistic option, there are means of addressing the worst consequences of flooding, by identifying the most vulnerable areas to allow regeneration of sand dunes and adjustment of drainage patterns (Angus, 2000). However, the threat is not only to dunes, habitats and wildlife, or to the socio-economic fabric of machair townships, but also to the infrastructure of these communities located on the economic periphery of the UK where alternatives to traditional agriculture are limited. Tourism is one such alternative and now contributes 14% of the gross domestic product of the Western Isles (Western Isles Tourist Board, 2000). However, because machair constitutes a significant part of the tourist attraction of the islands, any deterioration in the quality of the habitat would have negative effects on tourism and its infrastructure.

Conservation policies are required which acknowledge the wider sediment-machair system and fully embrace the socio-economic and cultural dimension of machair. Where people and their livelihoods are at the heart of such an integrated system, there is a duty of care when planning any actions that affect any part of the system. Machair is a rare global resource and its conservation quality is highest where traditional crofting is most active. Yet the agriculture, economy and culture which are so inextricably linked to this habitat may be under as much threat as the habitat itself. To be truly effective and to 'plan for real', the people of the machair townships need to be fully engaged in decision-making in the spirit of Agenda 21. This will provide a considerable challenge to crofters, conservation bodies and other agencies involved with machair over the next few decades.

Acknowledgements

The authors gratefully acknowledge the incisive but constructive comments of Professor Bill Ritchie and Dr. John Gordon on an earlier draft of the paper.

References

Angus, S. 1994. The conservation importance of the machair systems of the Scottish islands, with particular reference to the Outer Hebrides. *In* Usher, M.B. and Baxter, J. (eds) *The Islands of Scotland: a Living Marine Heritage.* The Stationery Office, London, 95-120.

Angus, S. 1997. *The Outer Hebrides: the Shaping of the Islands.* White Horse Press, Harris and Cambridge.

Angus, S. 2000. *The Outer Hebrides: Moor and Machair.* White Horse Press, Harris and Cambridge.

Angus, S. 2001. The conservation of machair in Scotland: working with people. *In* Houston, J.A., Edmondson,

S.E. and Rooney, P.J. (eds) *Coastal Dune Management: Shared Experience of European Conservation Practice.* Liverpool University Press, Liverpool, 177-191.

Angus, S. and Elliott, M.M. 1992. Problems of erosion in Scottish machair with particular reference to the Outer Hebrides. *In* Carter, R.W.G., Curtis, T.G.F. and Sheehy-Skeffington, M.J. (eds) *Coastal Dunes: Geomorphology, Ecology and Management for Conservation.* A.A. Balkema, Rotterdam, 93-112.

Bird, E.C.F. 1996. *Beach Management.* John Wiley & Sons, Chichester.

Caton, P.G. 1976. Maps of mean hourly wind speed over the UK 1965-73. *Climatological Memorandum,* No. 79. Meteorological Office, Bracknell.

Carter, R.W.G. 1988. *Coastal Environments.* Academic Press, London.

Carter, R.W.G. 1994. How the British coast works: inherited and acquired controls. *In* Stevens, C., Gordon, J.E., Green, C.P. and Macklin, M.G. (eds) *Conserving Our Landscape: Evolving Landforms and Ice-age Heritage.* Proceedings of the Conference on Conserving Our Landscape: Evolving Landforms and Ice-Age Heritage, Crewe 1992. Peterborough, 63-68.

Dargie, T.C.D. 1998. Sand dune vegetation survey of Scotland: Western Isles. *Scottish Natural Heritage Research, Survey and Monitoring Report,* No. 96.

Dargie, T.C.D. 2000. Sand dune vegetation survey of Scotland: national report. *Scottish Natural Heritage Commissioned Report,* No. F97AA401.

Dawson, A.G., Smith, D.E. and Dawson, S. 2000. Potential impacts of climate change on sea levels around Scotland. *Scottish Natural Heritage Research, Survey and Monitoring Report,* No.178.

Fuller, R.J. 1982. *Bird Habitats in Britain.* Poyser, Calton.

Gilbertson, D.D., Grattan, J. and Schwenninger, J.-L. 1996. A stratigraphic survey of the Holocene coastal dune and machair sequences. *In* Gilbertson, D., Kent, M. and Grattan, J. (eds) *The Outer Hebrides: the Last 14,000 years.* Sheffield University Press, Sheffield, 72-101.

Gilbertson, D.D., Schwenninger, J.-L., Kemp, R.A. and Rhodes, E.J. 1999. Sand-drift and soil formation along an exposed North Atlantic coastline: 14,000 years of diverse geomorphological climatic and human impacts. *Journal of Archaeological Science,* **26,** 439-469.

Gunther, H., Rosenthal, W., Stawarz, M., Carretero, J.C., Gomez, M., Lozano, I., Serrano, O. and Reistad, M. 1988. The wave climate of the northeast Atlantic over the period 1955-1994: the WASA wave forecast. *The Global Atmospheric and Ocean System,* **6,** 121-163.

Hansom, J.D. 1988. *Coasts.* Cambridge University Press, Cambridge.

Hansom, J.D. 1999. The coastal geomorphology of Scotland: understanding sediment budgets for effective coastal management. *In* Baxter, J.M., Duncan, K., Atkins, S.M. and Lees, G. (eds) *Scotland's Living Coastline.* The Stationery Office, London, 34-44.

Hansom, J.D. 2001. Coastal sensitivity to environmental change: a view from the beach. *Catena,* **42,** 291-305.

HR Wallingford 2000. Coastal cells in Scotland; Cells 8 & 9 - The Western Isles, *Scottish Natural Heritage Research, Survey and Monitoring Report,* No. 150.

Lamb, H.H. 1991. *Historic storms of the North Sea, British Isles and Northwest Europe.* Cambridge University Press, Cambridge.

Lee, A.J. and Ramster, J.W. 1981. *Atlas of the Seas around the British Isles.* Ministry of Agriculture, Fisheries and Food, Lowestoft.

MacLaren, A. 1974. A norse house on Drimore machair, South Uist. *Glasgow Archaeological Journal,* **3,** 9-18

Mate, I.D. 1991. The theoretical development of machair in the Hebrides. *Scottish Geographical Magazine,* **108,** 35-38.

Mather, A.S. and Ritchie, W. 1977. *The Beaches of the Highlands and Islands of Scotland.* Countryside Commission for Scotland, Battleby.

Pethick, J.S. 1984. *An Introduction to Coastal Geomorphology.* Edward Arnold, London.

Pethick, J.S. 1999. Future sea-level changes in Scotland: options for coastal management. *In* Baxter, J.M., Duncan, K., Atkins, S.M. and Lees, G. (eds) *Scotland's Living Coastline.* The Stationery Office, London, 45-62.

Ritchie, W. 1966a. The physiography of the machair of South Uist. Unpublished PhD thesis, University of Glasgow.

Ritchie, W. 1966b. The post-glacial rise in sea level and coastal changes in the Uists. *Transactions of the Institute of British Geographers*, **39**,79-86.

Ritchie, W. 1967. The machair of South Uist. *Scottish Geographical Magazine*, **83**,161-173.

Ritchie, W. 1972. The evolution of coastal sand dunes. *Scottish Geographical Magazine*, **88**, 19-35.

Ritchie, W. 1976. The meaning and definition of machair. *Transactions of the Botanical Society of Edinburgh*, **42**, 431-440.

Ritchie, W. 1979. Machair development and chronology in the Uists and adjacent islands. *Proceedings of the Royal Society of Edinburgh*, **77B**, 107-122.

Ritchie, W. and Whittington, G. 1994. Non-synchronous aeolian sand movements in the Uists: the evidence of the intertidal organic and sand deposits at Cladach Mór, North Uist. *Scottish Geographical Magazine*, **110**, 40-46.

Western Isles Tourist Board 2000. *Tourism in the Western Isles: Strategic Plan 2000-2004.* Western Isles Tourist Board, Stornoway.

6 FRESHWATER ENVIRONMENTS: AN EARTH SCIENCE PERSPECTIVE ON THE NATURAL HERITAGE OF SCOTLAND'S RIVERS

Chris Soulsby and Philip J. Boon

Summary

1. River systems in Scotland have developed in the post-glacial in response to changes in controlling variables such as climate and catchment land use.

2. This development has been paralleled by the evolution of ecological communities which are well adapted to the natural hydrological and geomorphological regimes. In many cases these communities have high levels of biodiversity and, in the case of salmon fisheries, important economic value.

3. Scottish river systems are often highly dynamic, reflecting high and variable levels of runoff, coarse sediment loads and steep channel gradients.

4. The processes of erosion and deposition which characterise such dynamism can cause river management problems which can affect various interest groups.

5. In a response to such problems, schemes to 'manage' river systems through engineering approaches are commonly attempted for a variety of purposes. Often these schemes are based on a poor understanding of the temporal scales that fluvial processes operate over and the spatial linkages within catchment systems. Consequently, such schemes are in many cases unsustainable.

6. The European Commission Water Framework Directive will dictate that integrated catchment management will become increasingly important in the coming decades. It is argued that an Earth science perspective will provide an important feature of this move towards a more sustainable approach in the management of river catchments.

6.1 Introduction

An Earth science perspective of Scotland's fresh waters suggests that their maintenance can only be understood in terms of their evolution in space and time. Spatially, freshwater environments, which include rivers, lochs and various types of wetlands, are inextricably linked to their surrounding catchment areas (Werritty *et al.*, 1994; Gilvear *et al.*, in press). Temporally, such environments are inherently dynamic, and fluvial landforms evolve and change over geological timescales (McEwen, 1997). Such insights help the understanding of those physical interactions that underpin the biodiversity and ecological quality of freshwater ecosystems (McEwen *et al.*, 1997). Moreover, the importance of processes operating over extensive spatial and temporal scales needs to be recognised if the management of such systems is to be truly sustainable (Rosgen, 1996).

This chapter focuses on Scotland's rivers, the most dynamic type of freshwater environment and one of the most valuable components of the nation's natural heritage

(Werritty and McEwen, 1997). Whilst biological conservation has steadily developed in Britain over the past 50 years, geomorphological aspects have taken rather longer to be brought within the nature conservation framework. With the publication of the Geological Conservation Review, fluvial geomorphological features and processes are now recognised as a priority for conservation, both in their own right and due to their dynamic role in forming aquatic habitats (Werritty and McEwen, 1997). Partly as a consequence of this dynamism, rivers also constitute environments where many management issues arise which are often difficult to resolve (Hey, 2000; Leys, this volume). An Earth science view of the ways that rivers function demonstrates that river processes are a fundamental part of landscape evolution at all spatial and temporal scales (Leopold, 1994). For example, the evacuation of water and sediments from terrestrial environments contributes to denudation of catchments and to the global sedimentary cycles which ultimately create new sedimentary rocks (Schumm, 1977). Similarly, the flux of dissolved materials carried during these hydrological and geomorphological transfers is an integral part of biogeochemical cycles at both the catchment and global scale (Schlesinger, 1997). Moreover, biological evolution has been intimately tied to this dynamic physical template, and it is increasingly recognised that the combined insights from both the Earth and life sciences are required in an interdisciplinary paradigm of Earth systems science (Skinner *et al.,* 1999).

This close relationship between dynamic geological and ecological processes helps explain the high levels of biodiversity associated with freshwater environments which, although covering less than 1% of the Earth's surface, are thought to hold 12% of the world's species (Allan, 1995). Consequently, human intervention in river systems has potentially profound implications for many aspects of the natural heritage and it is essential that river management is grounded within an Earth science context. This chapter explores some of the links between river ecology and geomorphology in Scotland. The information is necessarily selective and the reader is referred to other sources for a more detailed examination of fluvial geomorphology in general (Richards, 1982; Petts and Calow, 1996; Thorne *et al.,* 1997; Knighton, 1998) or for Scotland in particular (Werritty *et al.,* 1994; McEwen, 1997; Werritty and McEwen, 1997).

6.2 Spatial interlinkages

6.2.1 The catchment system

For Earth scientists operating in the disciplines of hydrology and geomorphology, the catchment forms the fundamental functional unit of the landscape where processes and landforms can be examined within a topographically defined area. A classical view of catchment systems, articulated by Schumm (1977), recognises a tripartite classification (Figure 6.1). The steeper upland headwaters act as the hydrological and sedimentary 'source' areas which drive catchment functioning. The delivery of the water and sediments from these source areas enters a second 'transfer' zone where gradients and energy levels fall and depositional processes operate alongside those promoting erosion. The 'depositional' zone is characterised by low energy levels, limited erosion, and landforms dominated by deposition. Moving downstream in such an idealised catchment, channel characteristics (such as width and depth), flows, and temperatures all change with distance as gradients tend to fall, and concomitant changes in hydraulic conditions (such as velocity and turbulence) also occur.

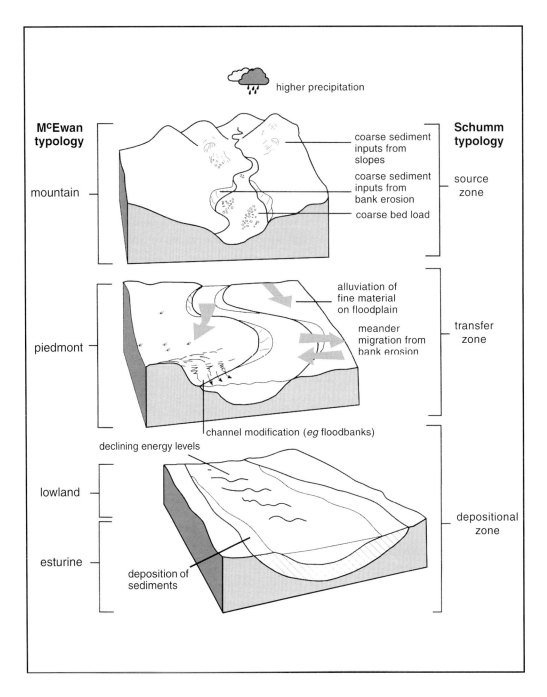

Figure 6.1 Schumm's 3-fold zonation of catchment systems (adapted from RPSB, NRA and RSNC, 1994).

Referring specifically to Scotland's rivers, McEwen (1997) similarly identified mountain and piedmont zones, which equate to Schumm's 'source' and 'transfer' zones, and differentiated 'lowland' and 'estuarine' environments within the 'depositional' zone (Table 6.1). Within each zone, McEwen identified a typology of channel types which may be found in contrasting geographical settings. Such generalised conceptual models are inevitably over-simplified, and hydrologists and geomorphologists are increasingly stressing the often dominant influence of local geographical conditions on river behaviour (cf. Newson *et al.*, 1997). These models, however, provide a powerful educational tool emphasising the spatial continuity in the flow of energy and matter in hydrological and geomorphological systems. They also demonstrate the links between changes in hydraulics or sedimentary characteristics and the habitat conditions that have been exploited by different aquatic organisms (Statzner and Higler, 1986). Moreover, they help find common ground for interdisciplinary collaboration with life scientists who, in recent years, have developed integrated models such as the river continuum concept (Vannote *et al.*, 1980; Cowx and Welcomme, 1998).

6.2.2 Nested hierarchies of habitats within catchments

If such views of river catchments provide a useful perspective on the overall spatial organisation of freshwater habitats, then at levels of increasing resolution, interlinked hierarchies of habitat conditions can be identified (Figure 6.2). These provide increasing levels of detail at which the geomorphological functioning of catchment systems can be understood and the interrelationships with aquatic ecosystems can be examined. For example, the range of channel patterns observed within an individual catchment vary in relation to factors such as discharge regime, sediment characteristics and channel gradient (Figure 6.3). These in turn create a range of different reach types within a catchment (see Table 6.1), each displaying contrasting habitat characteristics. Thus at the reach scale, different geomorphological features, such as pools, riffles and glides, may produce marked changes in hydraulic and sedimentary environments in close juxtaposition (Figure 6.2), which create contrasting habitat 'patches' utilised by different organisms (Gibbins *et al.*, 2000). However, even within the bounds of an individual habitat feature, hydraulic and sedimentary conditions can be highly variable, thus creating complex 'patch' dynamics at almost any spatial scale (Allan *et al.*, 1997).

It is important to recognise that such habitat hierarchies operate both longitudinally (from catchment source areas to depositional zones), and laterally as the river interacts with the surrounding valley slopes or 'river corridor' (Cowx and Welcomme, 1998). Moreover, it is increasingly recognised that surface waters form a continuum with groundwater discharging into the riparian zone at the base of a stream channel (Brunke and Gonser, 1997). These linkages in running-water ecosystems led Ward (1989) to describe rivers as 'four-dimensional', having longitudinal, lateral, vertical and temporal components. Indeed, it is only comparatively recently that the importance of ecotones such as the hyporheic zone has been fully recognised (Stanford and Ward, 1988; Soulsby *et al.*, in press). This continuum between groundwater and surface water in river corridors underlines the integrity of catchment systems and the need for a holistic perspective that recognises such linkages (Boon, 1992; Soulsby *et al.*, 1998).

Table 6.1 Types of river channel in Scotland (after McEwen, 1997).

Zone	Channel type	Channel characteristics	Geomorphological context	Activity
Mountain	Bedrock reach	Steep, narrow transportation zone with high rates of sediment throughput	Meltwater gorge	Very stable
	Mountain torrent	Steep channel, turbulent flows, coarse bedload.	Upland channel entrenched in glacio-genic or fluvioglacial sediment, partial bedrock control in upper reaches	Episodic activity; binary systems with high thresholds for sediment entrainment
	Alluvial basin	Gradual decrease in gradient and sediment size, usually with confinement above local base level	Glacially eroded valley with infill sediment	Varies downstream with different thresholds for entrainment and channel change
	Fluvio-lacustrine delta	Delta, with sediment fining downstream	Former ribbon lake.	Episodic switching of channel
Piedmont	Wandering gravel bed river	Low sinuosity, coarse grained; medium slopes; bedload active, incohesive banks	Local partial confinement by fluvioglacial terraces	Active; floods important as geomorphic agents; mobility depends on number of times per year that the bed becomes mobile
	Fluvio-lacustrine	Fine grained delta often with spits and strathlochans	Former ribbon lake	Alignment relatively stable; deposition of sediment builds up deltas, lochs act as major regulators of flow and sediment traps
Lowland	Meandering	Typically sand bedded rather than gravel bedded.	Restricted to coastal fringe	Highly stable
	Active meandering	Sand bedded, lack of confinement	Lack of confinement; reworked sediment from upstream sources	Active migration
	Bedrock controlled	Slot gorge	Meltwater gorge	Highly stable
Estuarine	Straight wide channel	Sand bedded, tidal limit reached	Links fluvial and coastal systems	Stable alignment with bars shifting

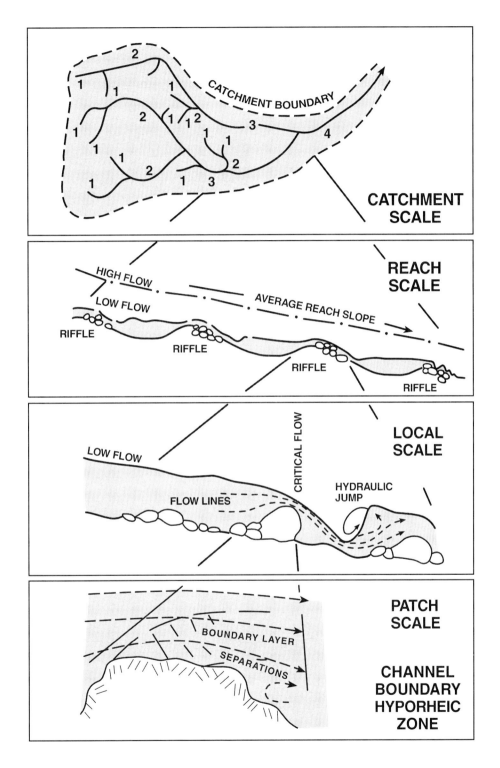

Figure 6.2 Nesting of habitats in catchments adapted from different spatial scales (adapted from Newbury and Gaboury, 1994).

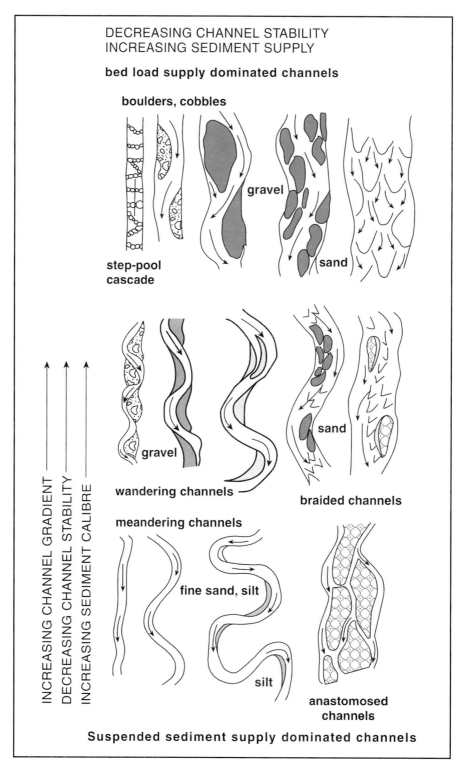

Figure 6.3 Channel types in relation to prevailing discharge and sedimentary regimes (adapted from Church, 1996; after Mollard, 1973 and Schumm, 1985).

6.3 Temporal context

6.3.1 Long-term evolution of freshwater environments

The long timescales over which organisms evolve is matched by the timescales over which geological and geomorphological change occurs. Werritty *et al.* (1994) showed how Scotland's contemporary river systems are evolutionary drainage networks whose spatial arrangements and controlling variables are changing over long (*c.* >1000 yr) timescales. Most obviously, today's river systems reflect the influence of the last glacial period and subsequent post-glacial adjustment (McEwen, 1997). However, these are just the latest developments in a long series of glacial and interglacial periods that have established the characteristics of drainage networks.

Over intermediate timescales (*c.* >100 yr), human influences on river channels become apparent. For example, widespread land-use change in the Scottish Highlands will have affected changes in the hydrological and sedimentary regimes that govern contemporary river systems (Acreman, 1985; McEwen, 1989). Often the response of rivers to such changes in boundary conditions occurs over timescales of decades or centuries (Hey, 2000). Thus, for example, the reduction in woody debris inputs into Scotland's rivers, resulting from reduced forest cover in the last several hundred years, will have led to major changes in their geomorphological functioning and habitat availability (Gurnell and Petts, 2000).

6.3.2 Short-term dynamics in river systems

The experiential observation of river systems by environmental managers and the general public does not generally incorporate such long-term perspectives. Rather, society experiences the fleeting dynamism associated with extreme events such as floods, where river channel forms and habitat conditions may change dramatically during the course of an individual flood event (Acreman, 1983). These events may exert a significant impact on river biota through the direct impact of increased flows as well as the re-structuring of channel form. In February 1998, a flood with a 100 year return period was recorded on the River Kerry, a medium-sized upland river in North-West Scotland. This river supports one of the largest populations of freshwater pearl mussels in the world (0.6-1.2 million) (Plate 18) and as a result has been proposed as a Special Area of Conservation (SAC) under the EC Habitats Directive. The flood, which in places caused large-scale movements of bed material, had a significant impact on the freshwater pearl mussel population, killing an estimated 50,000 individuals (Hastie *et al.*, 2001).

Although, from an Earth science perspective such short-term changes (*c.* <10 yr) following individual events usually have an infinitesimally small impact on catchment evolution, they can be cumulatively significant over geological time. Moreover, one flood may effect more change than is observed during an entire human lifespan (Acreman, 1991), and climatic variation can dictate that periods of marked geomorphological activity are interspersed by relatively inactive periods. For example, Werritty and Ferguson (1980) observed a 136% increase in the width of part of the River Feshie (northern Scotland) (Plate 11) between 1977 and 1981, when rates of bank retreat were as high as 10 m yr^{-1}. These rates of change were found to be much greater than those occurring over the preceding two centuries as identified from historical maps. Consequently, the frame of reference which provides a basis for managing rivers is usually related to timescales of human experience and is not rooted in an Earth science perspective.

6.4 Contemporary processes in Scottish rivers

6.4.1 Process context

The characteristics of river environments in any particular catchment can be understood in terms of interactive boundary conditions (Figure 6.4). At the large scale, the geology and climate of a catchment will strongly influence its topography, soils and land use, which will in turn also influence the prevailing hydrological and sedimentary regimes. These influences, when combined with the more localised effects of the channel gradient, and the composition and the nature of bed and bank material, produce an interacting set of controls on channel characteristics. Identification of such controls, along with quantitative assessment of channel dimensions, can help identify the channel characteristics which are usually in quasi-equilibrium with the prevailing conditions (Figure 6.3). Accordingly, the apparent stability of many riverine landscapes and the habitat patches that they sustain are underpinned by a quasi-equilibrium in both process and form. Table 6.2 summarises the main types of equilibrium observed in river systems. Often relatively long periods characterised by 'robust' or quasi-equilibrium conditions are separated by relatively short periods of 'sensitive' behaviour when a limiting threshold of a regulating boundary condition has been exceeded (e.g. during or after an extreme flood event). Assessment of channel characteristics and controlling boundary conditions can help identify when the channel is not in equilibrium and is undergoing adjustment in response - for example, to modified hydrological regimes or land-use change, or to direct channel intervention in river engineering schemes (Sear *et al.,* 2000).

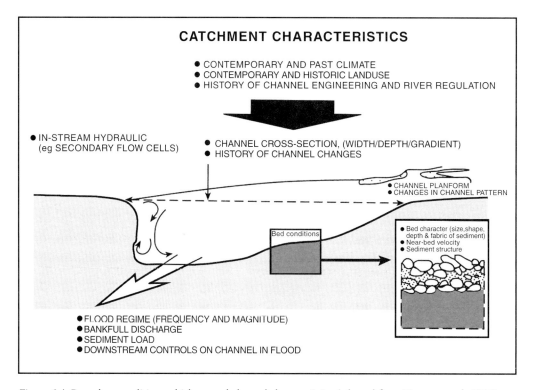

Figure 6.4 Boundary conditions which control channel characteristics (adapted from Newson *et al.,* 1997).

Table 6.2 Types of equilibrium in river systems (after Richards, 1982).

Equilibrium Type	Characteristics	Stability
Steady state equilibrium	Activity of channel maintains 'average' condition with limited fluctuation due to negative feedback controls.	Relatively stable channel exhibiting robust behaviour.
Dynamic equilibrium	Channel activity fluctuates around 'average' condition over short timescales but is trending towards different conditions in the longer term (e.g. land-use change, climate change, etc.).	Stable and robust but gradually changing.
Dynamic metastable equilibrium	Channel activity fluctuates around average conditions which are trending in the longer term. However, threshold effects can bring about marked 'step-like' changes in channel activity. This may relate to extreme flood events or channel intervention.	Generally stable, with gradual change, but sensitive to marked increases in activity.

6.4.2 Sensitivity and stability

Such conceptual and quantitative understanding of river behaviour can provide a sound basis for channel management. Identification of influential boundary conditions can help identify the differential sensitivity and subsequent stability of rivers to various types of management intervention. It can also help identify thresholds, in particular controlling variables which, once passed, may instigate channel instability. Sensitive rivers, including many gravel-bed rivers characteristic of Scotland, are usually in an almost continuous adjustment to changing controls which may operate over longer timescales (such as climate change), and to shorter, more dynamic events (such as floods or channel engineering). Thus, rates of erosion and deposition can be rapid and a channel unstable if such changes cross controlling thresholds.

The contribution of channel instability to maintaining biological diversity in dynamic rivers is well illustrated by a study of the River Feshie (Gilvear *et al.*, 2000). This river, which has an alluvial fan at its confluence with the River Spey, is considered to be one of the best examples of a near-natural, active, gravel-bed river in the UK (Plate 11). The fan and the nearby islands in the Spey contain some of the few remnants of Scotland's floodplain forest, and the whole area (protected as a Site of Special Scientific Interest) comprises a rare mosaic of woodland, grassland and unvegetated or partly vegetated gravel bars. Gilvear *et al.* (2000) showed that the diversity of vegetation is maintained by an intermediate level of disturbance. Artificially constraining the mobility of the channel within the alluvial fan (or conversely, increasing mobility excessively) will lead to a reduction in diversity and hence in the nature conservation interest for which the site was designated. A similar intermediate disturbance hypothesis has been suggested as being important in maintaining the diversity of macroinvertebrate communities in streams in the western Cairngorms, where floods, acid episodes and temperature extremes were identified as causing a turnover of species over short timescales (<3 months), but maintained robust, resistant communities over periods of a few years (Gibbins *et al.*, in press).

6.4.3 Intervention in river channel management

Such instability may, of course, be undesirable to river managers who often take short-term and localised action to prevent channel change (McEwen *et al.*, 1997; Leys, this volume), particularly if it involves loss of land or degraded fishing conditions (Cowx and Welcomme, 1998). Thus, revetments, flood embankments and various other management tools are often used to try to control river channel behaviour (Hey, 2000). Given, the spatial inter-linkages in fluvial systems and the long timescales over which they respond to changed boundary conditions, such management is often extremely crude and in many cases merely transfers a problem elsewhere. For example, an attempt at preventing erosion at one location, if undertaken in a piecemeal manner, often results in shifting the problem downstream, where a further piecemeal approach may be adopted to its management (Newson *et al.*, 1997; Sear *et al.*, 2000). As a consequence, it is not uncommon to see rivers in Scotland degraded by well-meaning but crude and unsuccessful channel management approaches which are, at best, unsustainable, and at worst extremely damaging to ecological quality (Northern Ecological Services, 1998).

6.5 Case study of the linkages between geomorphology and ecology: Atlantic salmon habitat in Scottish rivers

6.5.1 The salmon life cycle

The Atlantic salmon (*Salmo salar*) is a keystone species in many Scottish rivers; moreover, its presence has been exploited, initially as a food source, but more recently for game angling (Youngson and Hay, 1996). The different stages in the life cycle of the salmon have evolved to exploit many of the diverse and dynamic habitat conditions found in Scottish rivers. Spawning, for example, is often preferentially located in the transition between the end of pools and runs and the upper part of a riffle in headwater streams. In such areas, the accelerating flows and accumulation of appropriate sediments of gravel-cobble size allows female fish to excavate redds within quasi-stable bed sediments (Moir *et al.*, 1998). This provides a high probability that eggs will remain in a stable area where there is a continuous flow of clean, well-oxygenated water between spawning in the autumn and the hatching of eggs and emergence of alevins in the following spring (Soulsby *et al.*, in press; Malcolm *et al.*, in press).

After emergence, juvenile salmon are small and relatively weak and thus avoid exposure to high water velocities and turbulent conditions. Consequently they tend to occupy protected areas close to the stream bed or in the relatively still waters at the edge of river channels (Mills, 1991). Subsequently, with further growth the fish generally move downstream and occupy riffle habitats where invertebrate food sources are abundant and tend to be delivered in areas of hydraulic convergence. Complex social arrangements appear to develop which are driven by density-dependent competition in fish populations but also influenced by hydrological influences on food availability (Gilvear *et al.*, in press).

After 2-3 years in their natal streams, juvenile salmon undergo smoltification and leave for the main period of growth in the Atlantic Ocean. Usually after 2-3 years, fish return to their natal river system to spawn, though this may occur after only 1 year, or more exceptionally 4 years. If possible, the fish will usually return to the tributary where they spent the juvenile phase of their life cycle. However, spring salmon will enter the river system perhaps as much as 10 months before spawning. The upstream journey usually occurs in a relatively brief series of movements triggered by hydrological events. These are interspersed by long periods of inactivity where adult fish rest in deeper pools with good cover from predators and where lower water velocities minimise energy expenditure and cool conditions prevail (Webb and Hawkins, 1989). Eventually, close to spawning, the fish will approach their spawning tributaries and enter them during hydrological events when deeper water conditions allow access and provide cover from predators (Webb *et al.*, in press). Usually, post-spawning adult fish (kelts) die once the basis for a viable progeny has been established.

Interdisciplinary studies in the Girnock Burn, a 12 km long stream draining some 30 km^2 of the Dee catchment in Aberdeenshire, have provided insights into the dynamic relationships between habitat of Atlantic salmon and the geomorphological and hydrological characteristics of the catchment (Figure 6.5). At the broad scale, catchment geology and geomorphology exert a strong influence on the distribution of spawning sites. The upper stream, >6 km upstream of the fish traps at the catchment outfall (Figure 6.5), is underlain by granite and characterised by steeper glacial meltwater channels grading into an outwash plain created by meltwater from receding ice emanating from the Lochnagar massif to the south (Figure 6.5). In the middle reaches where metamorphic rocks predominate, a lower gradient associated with an alluvial basin behind some morainic deposits (approximately 4 km upstream of the fish traps) has created riffle areas and suitable spawning habitat (Figure 6.6). In these areas, there is a preponderance of spawning-calibre sediment, and hydraulic conditions (velocities and depths) that the fish use for spawning (Table 6.3). Consequently, detailed observations have shown that spawning tends to be concentrated in these areas, though suitable habitat is exploited throughout the catchment (Webb *et al.*, in press). In the lower reaches of the river (<3 km from the fish traps), gradients increase where glacial deposits have been cut through as the river reaches its base level at the confluence with the River Dee. In this sector, spawning habitat is sparse, though the steeper, riffle conditions create good juvenile habitat which is used by salmon at different life stages.

Although the spatial distribution of potential spawning habitat is largely fixed by the availability of spawning-calibre sediment, the ability of fish to utilise this habitat is a dynamic characteristic based on prevailing hydrological conditions during the spawning period (Moir *et al.*, 1998). Figure 6.7 shows that the flow duration curve during the spawning period exhibits higher flows than average. Thus, fish often spawn following small or moderate spate events where increased depths and water velocities increase access and availability of spawning habitat. Higher up the catchment, greater flows are required for spawning suitability owing to channel geometry and gradient (Webb *et al.*, in press). Although spawning habitat is more marginal in these upper reaches (Figure 6.7), often relating to individual patches of gravel, its importance to the ecological functioning of the stream is considerable. This is because juvenile fish tend to move downstream from

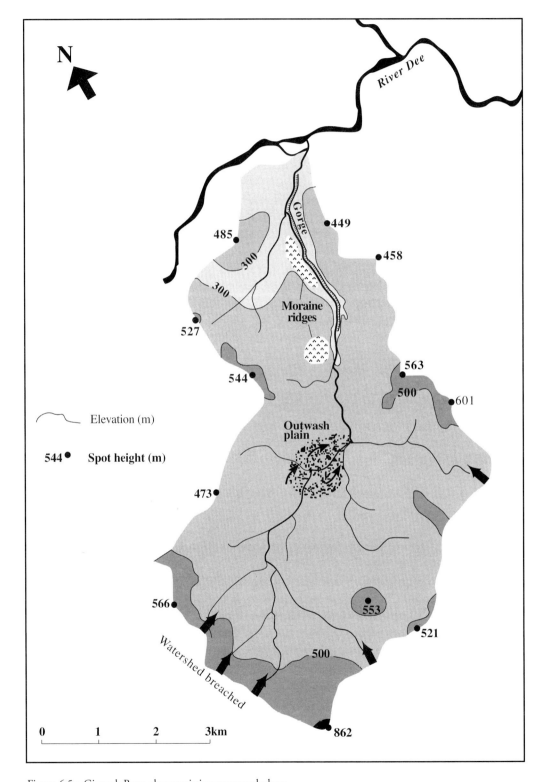

Figure 6.5a Girnock Burn characteristics: geomorphology.

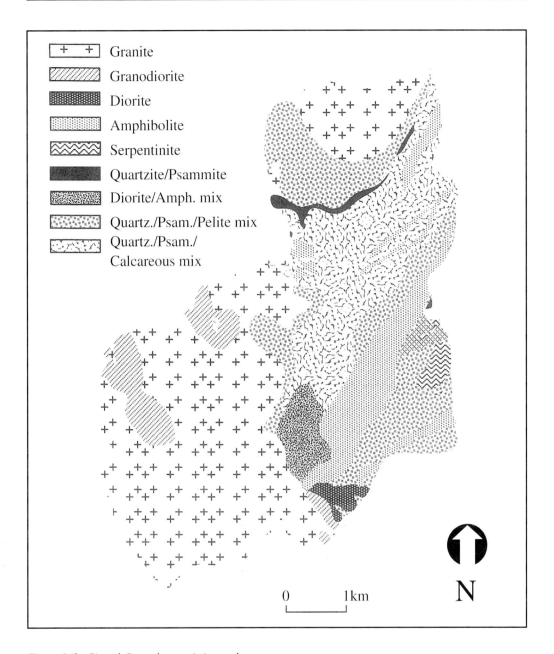

Figure 6.5b Girnock Burn characteristics: geology.

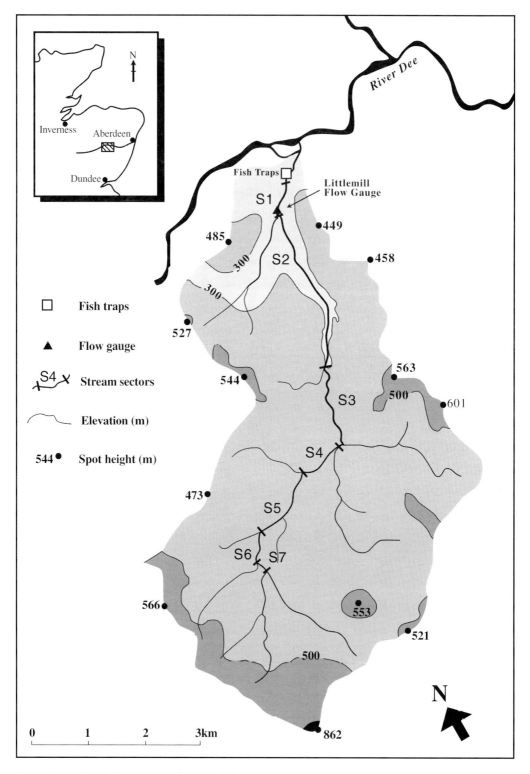

Figure 6.5c Girnock Burn characteristics: main habitat units.

Table 6.3 Sedimentary (n=12) and hydraulic characteristics (n=93) of spawning habitats in the Girnock Burn (from Moir *et al.*,1998).

Sediment size	Mean D_{50} (mm)	Range D_{50} (mm)	%<2mm	Sorting
	30.08	24.05-34.06	12.34	Moderate
Velocity	Mean utilised $(m\ s^1)$	Range utilised $(m\ s^1)$	Mean available $(m\ s^1)$	Range available $(m\ s^1)$
	0.536	0.2-0.95	0.546	0.01-1.25
Depth	Mean utilised (m)	Range utilised (m)	Mean available (m)	Range available (m)
	0.245	0.1-0.45	0.295	0.01-0.7

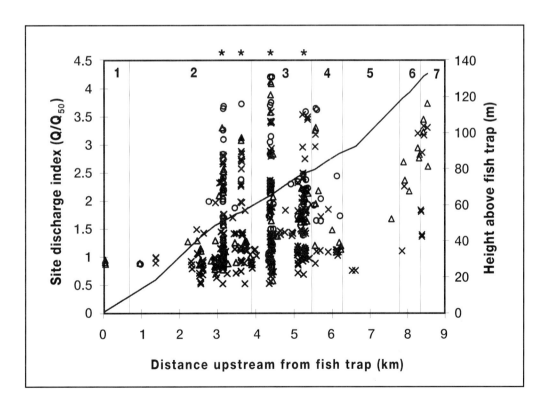

Figure 6.6 Distribution of spawning in relation to channel gradient and an index of stream flows. Points showing spawning locations upstream relative to the fish traps in three different years. The solid line shows the long profile of the channel relative to elevation above the fish traps on the secondary y-axis.

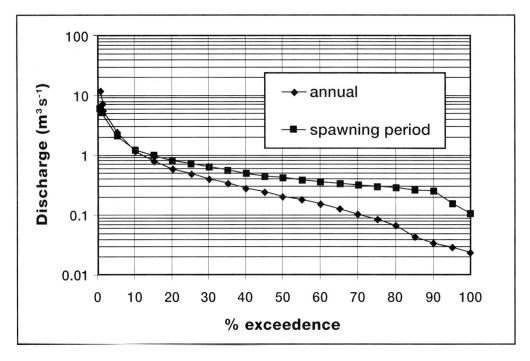

Figure 6.7 Flow duration curves for annual conditions and the spawning period.

spawning areas and exploit available habitat. Consequently, the further upstream spawning occurs, the greater the potential carrying capacity for salmon and for salmon productivity. Thus, the fish are adapted to spawning preferentially in the most suitable areas, yet opportunistically exploiting other habitat areas to maximise the chances of maintaining viable populations in a dynamic physical environment. This is not surprising given the likely colonisation of Scottish rivers in the post-glacial period and the establishment of populations over the same long timescales in which geomorphological processes operate. Such links reflect the longevity of evolutionary forces which irreversibly integrate biota with their abiotic environment.

6.5.2 Management of rivers for salmonids

At a general level the linkages between utilisation and habitat conditions are well known both to fisheries managers and to anglers (Mills, 1991). The decline of Atlantic salmon in Scottish rivers during the last few decades has been a matter of extreme concern, especially where game fishing is important to the local economy (Youngson, 1995). Although the source of the decline is widely believed to be related to the marine phase of the salmon's life cycle, many fisheries managers are understandably keen to maximise smolt production to try to arrest the decline in returning adult numbers (Youngson and Hay, 1996). Consequently, there is at present much interest in habitat 'improvement' schemes or rehabilitation of rivers for fish (Cowx and Welcomme, 1998). Such schemes often include many proposals that are eminently sensible, such as fencing to encourage tree growth and to prevent access by cattle to river banks and thus reduce erosion (Plates 25 and 26). However, in other instances, channel engineering works may be proposed - for example, to create or 'improve' spawning habitat or juvenile habitat. Moreover, as salmon become increasingly scarce and the prospects of successful angling are reduced, many 'improvement' schemes focus on improving fishing conditions rather than fish habitat. Consequently the use of croys, or direct excavation to create pools for adult fish during resting phases of the upstream migration, are becoming increasingly common (Plate 27).

The design of such habitat or fishing improvement schemes is usually the work of a consulting engineer or fisheries managers with relatively little Earth science training. Thus, engineers tend to be concerned with highly localised design criteria which fail to recognise the broader consequences upstream or downstream (Newson *et al.*, 1997). Fisheries managers usually take an instinctive approach based on their perceived understanding of river channel functioning which can often be erroneous. Such inappropriate intervention can, in extreme cases, destabilise sensitive channels (Maizels, 1985). Almost invariably such attempts at management create unnatural features which in less extreme cases reduce the amenity value of rivers, but more commonly can disturb the habitat of other freshwater species. There are few data to show that such habitat 'improvement' schemes have their desired effect of increased smolt production, and rarely are the broader environmental impacts ever assessed, either before or after such schemes. Consequently, even well-intentioned projects can inadvertently have an adverse affect on the very processes that maintain salmonid habitats.

6.6 Future management of rivers in Scotland

To secure the sustainable management of Scotland's rivers in the future, Earth scientists need to be more effective in communicating their perspectives at a range of different levels (Ziman, 2000). Professionally, it is only in the last decade or two that Earth scientists concerned with freshwater environments have been engaged in an active dialogue with life scientists with similar interests (RSPB, NRA and RSNC, 1994). The differences in approach, conceptualisation and language often frustrate such collaboration, but real progress is now being made in moving towards a functional understanding of freshwater ecosystems (Naiman *et al.*, 1995). However, further research efforts are required and these need to 'filter down' to influence the education and training of future environmental professionals (National Research Council, 1996). Specialist texts that seek to bridge disciplines such as hydrology and ecology (e.g. Gordon *et al.*, 1992) are also needed. However, an active outreach programme is essential to provide river managers, often with highly sectoral interests, with a sound conceptual understanding of river channel characteristics and controls on channel behaviour (River Restoration Centre, 1998).

The development of a range of river evaluation methods has helped in this regard. Tools such as River Habitat Survey (RHS) and the System for Evaluating Rivers for Conservation (SERCON) provide assessments of river channels designed to communicate their natural heritage value to planners and decision-makers, and indicate the ways in which they have been affected by management practices (Raven *et al.*, 1997, 1998; Boon, 1994; Boon *et al.*, 1997). Based on extensive surveys of channel characteristics, these schemes have often demonstrated marked degradation of the physical habitat of rivers (Northern Ecological Services, 1998).

The rehabilitation or restoration of degraded habitats is now receiving growing attention world-wide. Even where the motive for restoration schemes is specifically ecological, there is ample evidence that they are unlikely to succeed unless they are designed with an understanding of geomorphological *processes*, rather than merely attempting to mimic a particular channel *form* (Kondolf, 1998). Restoration planning must be sufficiently broad spatially to encompass catchment-level influences, and temporally to address long-term studies of channel history (Kondolf and Larson, 1995).

However, truly holistic, environmentally-sensitive river management and rehabilitation requires an even wider inter-disciplinary partnership that is not yet well developed in Scotland. A good example of the success of this approach is the Long Term Resource Monitoring Program of the upper Mississippi, where a variety of different agencies collaborate to assess trends in plant and animal populations, sediment and water quality, and in river morphology, before determining the causes of the trends and making recommendations for improved management (Petts *et. al.*, 2000)

Geomorphological classification of river channels may aid river habitat restoration in setting restoration priorities, defining targets for restoration, and for indicating the types of measures that might be successful (Kondolf, 1995). Classifications are nonetheless arbitrary divisions of continua and cannot be expected to provide a complete understanding of river functioning. In the UK, a recent attempt at classifying river 'types' based on their physical features was rejected in favour of a modelling technique in which the presence of habitat features at a site level (500 m) can be predicted from a set of environmental variables (Jeffers, 1998). This approach has considerable potential for reconstructing rivers according to the characteristics that they might be expected to contain in the absence of degradation.

The science and application of fluvial geomorphology is certain to play a crucial role in improving the way that rivers are managed. A particularly exciting recent development has been the evolution of specific geomorphological survey techniques that allow a geomorphological perspective to be presented in a highly visual but quantitative manner to help both channel assessment and design for management schemes (Rosgen, 1996; Newson *et al.*, 1997; River Restoration Centre, 1998). Such tools will lead to a better understanding of how fluvial systems function, so that sensitive river engineering techniques can deliver a more sustainable approach to river channel management.

6.7 Conclusions

Despite the greater autonomy that has come with devolved government in Scotland, environmental management decisions have to be made within a far wider context. European Commission Directives, in particular, are now shaping UK government policy on the environment, with the conservation and management of rivers very much part of the agenda. The Habitats Directive, for example, requires that Member States designate Special Areas of Conservation (SACs) for a range of listed habitats and species. Thus, in Scotland, there will be SACs to protect rivers with important populations of Atlantic salmon, otter, lamprey and freshwater pearl mussel.

The success of the conservation designation relies very much on finding the best solutions for river management. This is likely to be a challenging task, not only to harmonise the needs of protected species with the aspirations of people, but to seek management solutions that meet the varied ecological requirements of different species within the same river system. For example, salmon fishing rivers where both lamprey and salmon are present will need management practices that will maintain clean spawning gravels for salmon as well as silty regions for the development of lamprey larvae. An EC

LIFE-funded project on river SACs has recently begun in the UK, and it is hoped that catchment management strategies for each river will help to resolve problems such as this.

The EC Water Framework Directive (WFD) is likely to have far-reaching consequences for the management of all surface waters in Scotland. Indeed, the importance of maintaining and enhancing the ecological quality of rivers will become as important in the future as maintaining and enhancing chemical water quality has been in the past. The Directive intends that such policy changes will be underpinned by Integrated Catchment Management which, if it is to be sustainable, will require understanding of the spatial integrity of catchments and the temporal context of their evolution. The WFD will require Member States to aim to achieve 'good status' for their surface waters within a prescribed timescale, and defines 'status' not only chemically but also ecologically in terms of aquatic plants, invertebrates and fish. In addition, so-called 'hydromorphological' features must also be assessed because they are considered to support the biological elements. For running waters these features include 'hydrological regime' (quantity and dynamics of flow), 'river continuity', and 'morphological conditions' (river depth and width variations, structure and substrate of the bed, structure of the riparian zone), emphasising that disciplines such as ecology, hydrology, and geomorphology will each be needed to help implement the Directive.

Further to this research challenge, Earth scientists need to be engaged in effective communication with managers, scientists, and others and provide an Earth science perspective in education at all levels. The task of understanding and sustainably managing freshwater environments in Scotland will continue to provide considerable challenges and opportunities for Earth scientists in the foreseeable future.

Acknowledgements

The authors greatly appreciate the encouragement of John Gordon to complete this contribution and the cartographic skills of Alison Sandison and Jenny Johnson.

References

Acreman, M.C. 1983. The significance of the flood of September 1981 on the Ardessie Burn, Wester Ross. *Scottish Geographical Magazine,* **100**, 37-49.

Acreman, M.C. 1985. The effects of afforestation on the flood hydrology of the upper Ettrick valley. *Scottish Forestry,* **39**, 89-99.

Acreman, M.C. 1991. The flood of July 25th 1983 on the Hermitage Water, Roxburghshire. *Scottish Geographical Magazine,* **107**, 170-178.

Allan, J.A. 1995. *Stream Ecology.* Chapman & Hall, London.

Allan, J.A., Erickson, D.L., and Fay, J. 1997. The influence of catchment landuse on stream integrity across multiple spatial scales. *Freshwater Biology,* **37**, 149-161.

Boon, P.J. 1992. Essential elements in the case for river conservation. *In* Boon, P.J., Calow, P. and Petts, G.E. (eds) *River Conservation and Management.* John Wiley, Chichester, 11-33.

Boon, P.J. 1994. Nature conservation. *In* Maitland, P.S., Boon, P.J. and McLusky, D.S. (eds) *The Fresh Waters of Scotland: a National Resource of International Significance.* John Wiley, Chichester, 555-576.

Boon, P. J., Holmes, N.T.H., Maitland, P.S., Rowell T.A. and Davies, J. 1997. A system for evaluating rivers for conservation (SERCON): development, structure and function. *In* Boon, P.J. and Howell, D.L. (eds) *Freshwater Quality: Defining the Indefinable?* The Stationery Office, Edinburgh, 299-326.

Brunke, M. and Gonser, T. 1997. The ecological significance of exchange processes between rivers and groundwater. *Freshwater Biology*, **37**, 1-33.

Church, M. 1996. Channel morphology and typology. *In* Petts, G.E. and Calow, P. (eds) *River Flows and Channel Forms*. Blackwell Science, Oxford, 185-202.

Cowx, I.G. and Welcomme, R.L. 1998. *Rehabilitation of Rivers for Fish*. Blackwell Science, Oxford.

Gibbins, C., Jeffries, M.J. and Soulsby, C. 2000. Impacts of an inter-basin water transfer: distribution and abundance of *Micronecta poweri* in the River Wear, N.E. England. *Aquatic Conservation: Marine and Freshwater Ecosystems*, **10**, 103-115.

Gibbins, C., Dilks, C., Malcolm, R. and Soulsby, C. in press. Factors controlling long-term patterns in invertebrate community structure in four streams in the Cairngorm Mountains, Scotland. *Freshwater Biology*.

Gilvear, D.J., Cecil, J. and Parsons, H. 2000. Channel change and vegetation diversity on a low-angle alluvial fan, River Feshie, Scotland. *Aquatic Conservation: Marine and Freshwater Ecosystems*, **10**, 53-71.

Gilvear, D.J., Heal, K. and Stephen, A. in press. Hydrology and the ecological quality of Scottish river ecosystems. *Hydrology and Earth Systems Science*.

Gordon, N.D., McMahon, T.A. and Finlayson, B. L. 1992. *Stream Hydrology: an Introduction for Ecologists*. John Wiley, Chichester.

Gurnell, A. and Petts, G.E. 2000. Causes of catchment scale hydrological changes. *In* Acreman, M. (ed.) *The Hydrology of the UK: a Study of Change*. Routledge, London, 82-98.

Hastie, L.C., Boon, P.J., Young, M.R. and Way, S. 2001. The effects of a major flood on an endangered freshwater mussel population. *Biological Conservation, **98**, 107-115.

Hey, R. 2000. River processes and management. *In* O'Riordan, T. (ed.) *Environmental Science for Environmental Management*. Prentice-Hall, Harlow, 323-348.

Jeffers, J.N.R. 1998. Characterization of river habitats and prediction of habitat features using ordination techniques. *Aquatic Conservation: Marine and Freshwater Ecosystems*, **8**, 529-540.

Knighton, A.D. 1998. *Fluvial Form and Process*. Arnold, London.

Kondolf, G.M. 1995. Geomorphological stream channel classification in aquatic habitat restoration: uses and limitations. *Aquatic Conservation: Marine and Freshwater Ecosystems*, **5**, 127-141.

Kondolf, G.M. 1998. Lessons learned from river restoration projects in California. *Aquatic Conservation: Marine and Freshwater Ecosystems*, **8**, 39-52.

Kondolf, G.M. and Larson, M. 1995. Historical channel analysis and its application to riparian and aquatic habitat restoration. *Aquatic Conservation: Marine and Freshwater Ecosystems*, **5**, 109-126.

Leopold, L.A. 1994. *A View of the River*. Harvard University Press, Cambridge.

Maizels, J.K. 1985. The physical background of the river Dee. *In* Jenkins, D. (ed.) *The Biology and Management of the River Dee*. Institute of Terrestrial Ecology, Monks Wood, 7-22.

Malcolm, I.A., Soulsby, C. and Youngson, A.F. in press. Hyporheic zone temperatures in two salmon spawning streams; hydrological and ecological implications. *Fisheries Management and Ecology*.

McEwen, L.J. 1989. River channel changes in response to flooding in the upper Dee catchment, Aberdeenshire, over the last 200 years. *In* Carling, P. and Bevan, K. (eds) *Floods: Hydrological, Sedimentological and Geomorphological Significance*. John Wiley, Chichester, 219-238.

McEwen, L.J. 1997. Geomorphological change and fluvial landscape evolution in Scotland during the Holocene. *In* Gordon, J.E. (ed.) *Reflections on the Ice Age in Scotland*. Scottish Association of Geography Teachers and Scottish Natural Heritage, Glasgow, 116-129.

McEwen, L.J., Brazier, V. and Gordon, J.E. 1997. Evaluating the geomorphology of fresh waters: an assessment of approaches. *In* Boon, P.J. and Howell, D.L. (eds) *Freshwater Quality: Defining the Indefinable?* The Stationery Office, Edinburgh, 258-281.

Mills, D. 1991. *Ecology and Management of Atlantic Salmon.* Chapman and Hall, London.

Moir, H.J., Soulsby, C. and Youngson, A.F. 1998. Hydraulic and sedimentary characteristics of habitat utilised by Atlantic salmon for spawning in the Girnock Burn, Scotland. *Fisheries Management and Ecology,* **5**, 241-254.

Mollard J.D. 1973. Air photo interpretation of flurial features. *Proceedings of the 7th Canadian Hydrology Symposium*, 341-80.

Naiman, R.J., Magnuson, J.J., McKnight, D.M. and Stanford, J.A. 1995. *The Freshwater Imperative.* Island Press, New York.

National Research Council 1996. *Freshwater Ecosystems.* National Academy Press, Washington DC.

Newbury, R.W. and Gaboury, M.N. 1994. *Stream Analysis and Fish Habitat Design – a Field Manual.* Newbury Hydraulics Ltd, Manitoba.

Newson, M.D., Hey, R.D., Bathurst, J.C., Brookes, A., Carling, P.A., Petts, G.E. and Sear, D.A. 1997. Case studies in the application of geomorphology to river management. *In* Thorne, C.R., Hey, R.D. and Newson, M.D. (eds) *Applied Fluvial Geomorphology for River Engineering and Management.* John Wiley, Chichester, 311-363.

Northern Ecological Services 1998. *Restoration Opportunities in Degraded River Corridors.* Report to Scottish Natural Heritage (2 Volumes). Scottish Natural Heritage, Edinburgh.

Petts, G.E. and Calow, P. 1996. *River Flows and Channel Forms.* Blackwell Scientific Publications, Oxford.

Petts, G.E., Sparks, R. and Campbell, I. 2000. River restoration in developed economies. *In* Boon, P. J., Davies, B.R. and Petts, G.E. (eds) *Global Perspectives on River Conservation: Science, Policy and Practice.* John Wiley, Chichester, 493-508.

Raven, P.J., Fox, P., Everard, M., Holmes, N.T.H. and Dawson, F.H. 1997. River Habitat Survey: a new system for classifying rivers according to their habitat quality. *In* Boon, P. J. and Howell D. L. (eds) *Freshwater Quality: Defining the Indefinable?* The Stationery Office, Edinburgh, 215-234.

Raven, P.J., Holmes, N.T.H., Dawson, F.H., Fox, P.J.A., Everard, M., Fozzard, I.R. and Rouen, K.J. 1998. *River Habitat Quality: the Physical Character of Rivers and Streams in the UK and the Isle of Man.* Environment Agency, Bristol.

Richards, K.S. 1982. *Rivers: Form and Process in Alluvial Channels.* Arnold, London.

River Restoration Centre 1998. *Manual of Techniques for River Restoration.* River Restoration Centre, Silsoe.

Rosgen, D. 1996. *Applied River Morphology.* Wildland Hydrology, Colorado.

RSPB, NRA and RSNC 1994. *The New Rivers and Wildlife Handbook.* Royal Society for the Protection of Birds, Sandy.

Schlesinger, W.H. 1997. *Biogeochemistry – Analysis of Global Change.* Academic Press, London.

Schumm, S.A. 1977. *The Fluvial System.* John Wiley, New York.

Schumm, S.A. 1985. Patterns of alluvial rivers. *Annual Reviews of Earth and Planetary Science*, **13**, 5-27.

Sear, D., Wilcock, D., Robinson, M. and Fisher, K. 2000. River channel modification in the UK. *In* Acreman, M. (ed.) *The Hydrology of the UK: a Study of Change.* Routledge, London, 51-81.

Skinner, B.J., Porter, S.C. and Botkin, D.B. 1999. *The Blue Planet: an Introduction to Earth Systems Science.* (2nd edn). John Wiley, New York.

Soulsby, C., Chen, M., Helliwell, R.C., Ferrier, R.C. and Jenkins, A. 1998. Hydrogeochemistry of groundwater in an upland Scottish catchment. *Hydrological Processes*, **12**, 1111-1118.

Soulsby, C., Malcolm, I. and Youngson, A.F. in press. Hydrochemistry of the hyporheic zone in salmon spawning gravels: a preliminary assessment in a degraded agricultural stream. *Regulated Rivers: Research and Management.*

Stanford, J.A. and Ward, J.V. 1988. The hyporheic habitat of river ecosystems. *Nature*, **335**, 64-66.

Statzner, B. and Higler, B. 1986. Stream hydraulics as a major determinant of benthic invertebrate zonation patterns. *Freshwater Biology*, **16**, 127-139.

Thorne, C.R., Hey, R.D. and Newson, M.D. 1997. *Applied Fluvial Geomorphology for River Engineering and Management*. John Wiley, Chichester.

Vannote, R.L., Minshall, G.W., Cummins, K.W., Sedell, J.R. and Cushing, C.E. 1980. The river continuum concept. *Canadian Journal of Fisheries and Aquatic Sciences,* **37**, 130-137.

Ward, J.V. 1989. The four-dimensional nature of lotic ecosystems. *Journal of the North American Benthological Society,* **8**, 2-8.

Webb, J. and Hawkins, A.D. 1989. The movements and spawning behaviour of adult salmon in the Girnock Burn, a tributary of the Aberdeenshire Dee. *Scottish Fisheries Research Report,* No. 40. Department of Agriculture and Fisheries for Scotland, Pitlochry.

Webb, J., Gibbins, C., Moir, H. and Soulsby, C. in press. Spatial patterns of discharge utilisation by spawning female Atlantic salmon: implications for flow allocation. *The Journal of the Chartered Institute of Water and Environmental Management.*

Werritty, A. and Ferguson, R. 1980. Pattern changes in a Scottish braided river over 1, 30 and 200 years. *In* Cullingford, R.A., Davidson, R.A. and Lewin, J. (eds) *Timescales in Geomorphology*. John Wiley, Chichester, 247-259.

Werritty, A. and McEwen, L.J. 1997. Fluvial landforms and processes in Scotland. *In* Gregory, K.J. (ed.) *Fluvial Geomorphology of Great Britain*. Geological Conservation Review Series, No. 13. Chapman & Hall, London, 21-32.

Werritty, A., Brazier, V., Gordon, J.E. and McManus, J. 1994. Geomorphology. *In* Maitland, P.S., Boon, P.J., and McLusky, D.S. (eds). *The Fresh Waters of Scotland: a National Resource of International Significance.* John Wiley, Chichester, 65-88.

Youngson, A.F. 1995. *Salmon in the Dee Catchment: a Scientific Basis for Management*. Atlantic Salmon Trust, Pitlochry.

Youngson, A.F. and Hay, D. 1996. *The Lives of Salmon*. Swan-Hill, Shrewsbury.

Ziman, J. 2000. *Real Science*. Cambridge University Press, Cambridge.

7 MONTANE LANDSCAPES IN SCOTLAND: ARE THESE NATURAL, ARTEFACTS OR COMPLEX RELICS?

Des B. A. Thompson, John E. Gordon and David Horsfield

Summary

1. One of the most difficult questions facing Earth scientists and biologists working in mountain areas is: to what extent have natural and human-related pressures worked together or separately to shape the landscape?

2. This question is important because it addresses the underlying fundamental nature of landscape evolution and change, and because we need to understand interactions between the various pressures in order to address conservation and management issues.

3. Examples of sensitivities to natural and human-related pressures in Scotland's mountains are given.

4. The need for experiments and more detailed work on mountain landscape sensitivity is highlighted.

5. We raise some fundamental questions regarding the nature of landscape change and, in particular, the extent to which some mountain landscapes in Scotland are natural.

7.1 Introduction

"The cycle of change in all the communities is divisible into two parts, an upgrade and the downgrade. The upgrade series is essentially a process or set of processes resulting in a building up of plant material and of habitat potential and the downgrade a dispersion of these mainly by fungi, bacteria, insects, etc., but also by inorganic agents. At each stage, of course, there is both a building up and a breaking down, but in the upgrade series the balance is positive, in the downgrade negative."

(Alex. S. Watt, Presidential Address to the British Ecological Society on 11 January 1947).

In his brilliant presidential address to the British Ecological Society, given over 50 years ago, Alex. S. Watt (1947) laid down a major foundation block for our understanding of the functional ecology of plant communities. He drew evidence from seven plant communities to establish a framework for understanding patterns and processes underlying the plant community. Much of his paper was devoted to upland ecosystems and, in particular, work he and colleagues had done in the Cairngorms (see also Watt and Jones, 1948). This work had a radical impact on our understanding of interactions between soils, climate and vegetation change, and it is appropriate to dwell on this when considering the nature and sensitivity of mountain landscapes.

We now know considerably more about the soils, geomorphological processes and vegetation of mountains. Yet still there are a substantial number of unanswered questions, notably regarding the origins of different habitats, whether or not some of these cycle through time, and the extent to which natural and human-related pressures influence the soil-landform-vegetation mosaics we see today.

In this paper we address three issues. First, we consider the sensitivity of mountain landscapes to change, with a particular focus on high mountain areas in Scotland. Here, we have to reflect the dearth of detailed studies to date. Second, we classify natural versus human-related impacts in terms of scale and impact upon the landscape. Third, we point to the need for further research, and suggest that high mountain and blanket bog/wet heath habitats are particularly important candidates.

Our over-arching aim is to seek improvements in the level of information we have in order to advise on the conservation and management of mountain areas. Central to this is the need for clarity on the extent to which mountain landscapes are naturally or otherwise determined.

7.2 Scotland's mountain landscapes

In Britain, the uplands embrace all land lying above the upper limits of enclosed farmland, including the hills, moors and mountains. The natural altitudinal zonation in vegetation is largely absent today. In the middle Holocene, there would have been an upward sequence of forest, sub-alpine woods, scrub and medium shrubs, low-alpine dwarf shrubs, middle-alpine grasslands, moss and lichen heaths and communities associated with snow lie (Ratcliffe, 1977, 1981; Ratcliffe and Thompson, 1988; Thompson and Horsfield, 1990). The British upland landscape is largely a product of human influence and natural processes. Ratcliffe (1977) and Ratcliffe and Thompson (1988) use the term 'montane' to describe vegetation lying above the potential, former tree-line, and 'sub-montane' for habitats below this within the uplands, and including all vegetation derived from woodland (see Horsfield and Thompson, 1996).

7.2.1 Variability and complexity of the landscape

Scotland's mountain landscapes are a quintessential part of what makes Scotland so special. They are varied in character and setting, with each region having a distinctive appearance, beauty and setting (e.g. Scottish Natural Heritage, in press). A closer look reveals a much more complex picture, however, and several factors are particularly important in influencing the appearance of the mountain landscape today.

First, the character of the mountain landscape is the outcome of over three billion years of environmental change involving geological, climatic and, much more recently, human-related forces. Most of the underlying rocks are ancient, in global terms, with the oldest in the north and west. Each of the major rock types has a complex history, and in many parts of upland Scotland there is a mixture of older metamorphic and sedimentary rocks (gneisses, schists and sandstones) and relatively younger volcanic and intrusive rocks (lavas and granites) (see Craig, 1991). Such variations in geology, combined with the landform inheritance of the Quaternary glaciations and postglacial geomorphological processes, have endowed the uplands of Scotland with a remarkable geodiversity. This is apparent both at a regional scale (e.g. in terms of the contrasts between the North-West Highlands and the

Cairngorms) and at a local scale (e.g. in the detail of topography associated with the glacial deposits of the Highland glens or the variation of micro-relief across an assemblage of solifluction lobes). Such variations are frequently reflected closely in soils, hydrology, macro- and micro-climate and snow-lie patterns and consequently in plant communities and habitats (e.g. Haynes *et al.*, 1998).

Second, the global position of Scotland, at a high latitude within a particularly oceanic climate zone, results in cool, wet and windy conditions in the mountains (Ratcliffe and Thompson, 1988; Ballantyne and Harris, 1994). This has favoured the widespread development of podzolic soils which are inherently infertile, a wide range of soil erosion features, and open, exposed rocky landscapes (especially in the western Highlands). Extreme weather phenomena associated with periodic intense or prolonged rainfall, rapid snowmelts and high wind speeds play a significant part in initiating geomorphological changes, such as slope failures (Brazier and Ballantyne, 1989; Hinchliffe 1999; Curry, 2000a, 2000b) and floods (McEwen and Werritty, 1988). On the many exposed mountain summits, spurs and cols, the geomorphological effects of wind are particularly evident, in the form of deflation surfaces, spectacular wind-terraces, deposits of wind-blown sand and mobile vegetation patterns (e.g. Ball and Goodier, 1974; Goodier and Ball, 1975; Ballantyne and Whittington, 1987; Ballantyne and Harris, 1994; Ballantyne, 1998).

The flora is limited (in comparison with the European continental mainland), though local variation in vegetation diversity is marked, not least where flushing produces local nutrient enhancement effects, and where there is base-richness derived from calcareous parent materials (Ratcliffe, 1977; Thompson and Brown, 1992). Across the British Isles, there is a downward compression of life zones towards the north and west. Altitudinal boundaries between plant communities are several hundred metres lower in the North-West Highlands compared with eastern Scotland and northern England, and the altitudinal breadth of each zone is narrow in the north-west. Yet across the mountain landscape we see links with arctic, temperate, oceanic and even Mediterranean elements in terms of plant species, plant-soil relations, and some of the geomorphological processes (e.g. Ratcliffe and Thompson, 1988; Gordon *et al.*, 1998).

The third important facet of the mountain landscape is the complexity and range of human-related pressures on the land. Much of Scotland's past woodland cover has been lost, with the earliest major periods of upland deforestation occurring from around 3,900 ^{14}C years BP in the North-West Highlands and eastern Skye, to as recently as 300 - 400 ^{14}C years BP in the Grampians and the Cairngorms (Birks, 1988). Many upland areas cleared of forest became dominated by dwarf-shrub heaths and patches of grassland, with large areas of heath then giving way to acidic grasslands under widespread grazing and/or burning (e.g. McVean and Ratcliffe, 1962; Stevenson and Thompson, 1993).

In parts, grazing and, in particular, burning have been considered to account for widespread gullying and sheet erosion of blanket bogs (e.g. Tallis, 1985, 1997; Lindsay, *et al.,* 1988) and more rapid podzolisation (e.g. Innes, 1983; Stevenson *et al.,* 1990). More recently, parts of Scotland's uplands were managed as grouse moors (from the 1840s onwards) and for more intensive agricultural uses (from around the 1820s onwards) to carry more sheep (*Ovis aries*) and red deer (*Cervus elaphus*) (Ratcliffe and Thompson, 1988). Industrial acidification appears to have had impacts in Scotland in the last 150 years (e.g. Battarbee *et al.*, 1985; Lee *et al.,* 1988; Jones *et al.,* 1993). Since the 1920s, many upland areas have been re-afforested, largely with exotic conifers, with impacts on podzolisation, and downstream effects on water sediment loading and acidity. Finally, over the past 50 years there has been a marked increase in the recreational use of the uplands, in the mountains resulting in the creation of five downhill skiing developments and the proliferation of footpaths and localised erosion.

7.2.2 Land uses above and below the former tree-line

We have a great diversity of mountain landscapes in Scotland which endure oceanic climatic conditions, are variable in vegetation, soils and geomorphological processes, and which have been subjected to many human-related pressures. One important factor, however, distinguishes the high mountain landscape from the others. Below the former tree-line, lying between 700 - 800 m above sea level (asl) in the Cairngorms and central Highlands (but as low as 350 m asl in north-west Sutherland, and 200 - 300 m asl in the Northern Isles), human-related pressures have consisted largely of deforestation in upland districts, followed by agricultural impacts - not least, grazing and burning. Above this, however, deforestation and burning pressures were largely absent, with grazing being the main, widespread manifestation of human pressure. The montane (or alpine) landscape is therefore one of our more natural areas. Other factors have had impacts of course, such as pollution and recreational use, and do not necessarily differ below and above the tree-line, though we know that the impacts of acidic deposition on upland vegetation increase markedly with altitude (e.g. Lee *et al.*, 1988; Baddeley *et al.*, 1994; Leith *et al.*, 1999).

7.3 Examples of sensitivities to change: the interplay between geomorphological and habitat processes

Clearly, there is an interaction between natural and human-related pressures on the present-day nature of the mountain landscape. Gordon *et al.* (1998, 2001) provide examples of some of the consequences of the principal human-related pressures on mountain geomorphological and habitat features.

7.3.1 Impacts of different pressures

Recently, we have developed work to describe the impacts of the different pressures on geomorphological and habitat features in mountains (e.g. Thompson and Brown, 1992; MacDonald *et al.*, 1998; Gordon *et al.*, 1998, 2001; Haynes *et al.*, 1998, this volume; Legg, 2000). In Figure 7.1 we have summarised the degree and scale of impacts caused by the different human-related pressures. Unfortunately, this work shows just how little we still understand about the nature of these impacts. In some cases, the interplay between the human-related and natural pressures determines the impact on the landscape (Plate 30). Erosion, for instance, may be initiated by trampling by livestock or people, yet prevailing weather conditions and soil properties will have a marked impact on its severity (Plate 28).

7.3.2 Interplay between geomorphological and vegetation processes

Central to our understanding of the impacts of the different pressures on the landscape is the interplay between the influences of geomorphological and vegetation processes. Particularly striking examples of this interplay are found in solifluction terraces and gelifluction lobes, where there is a contrasting development of snow-loving (chionophilous)

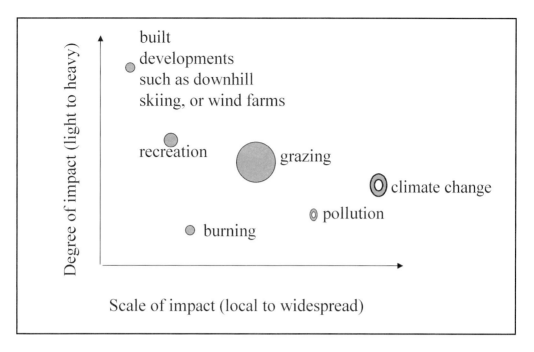

Figure 7.1. Schematic representation of the scale of impacts caused by different human-related pressures on mountain landscapes. The size of the symbol reflects the spatial scale of the impact; hollow symbols indicate uncertainty about impact (from Thompson and Brown, 1992; Gordon *et al.*, 1998, 2001).

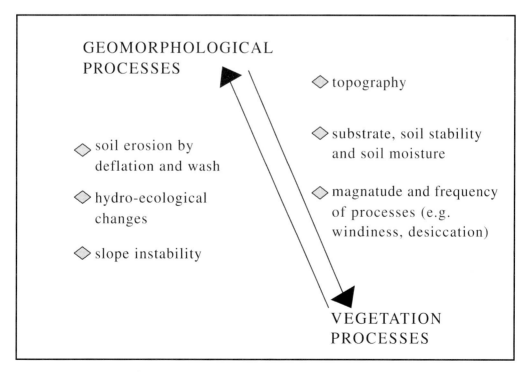

Figure 7.2. The interplay between geomorphological and vegetation processes in mountain ecosystems. The arrows indicate the influences of physical factors on the two sets of processes.

and snow-hating (chionophobous) vegetation occurring, respectively, in hollows and on exposed surfaces or riser edges. The interplay between the two sets of processes determines the physiognomy of the landscape. Figure 7.2 indicates at least six ways in which one set of processes influences the other. For instance, on exposed plateaux and ridges where snow is blown clear in winter, *Juncus trifidus* rush-heath (Ingram, 1958) and the wind-clipped dwarf-shrub heaths on the flat, open exposed areas are subject to wind-induced erosion as well as cryoturbation. In the more sheltered hollows, however, where snow tends to accumulate, snowbed vegetation is subject much less to geomorphological influences but more to the extremes of snow depth, absence of light, humidity and, during spring, the rate at which snow melts and ensuing flushing of minerals within the snow (e.g. Thompson and Brown, 1992; Woolgrove and Woodin, 1996). This interplay, in turn, has an important bearing on the impacts of human and non-human agents on the land and its vegetation. Hence, patches of lichen within exposed wind-clipped heaths on a mountain summit will be more prone to erosion under human trampling (or indeed local trampling by deer and sheep) than will vegetation within the snowbed, which is afforded more protection by the snow (Woolgrove and Woodin, 1996). But, after snowmelt, saturated soils and vegetation within and below the snowbed become highly susceptible to trampling until they dry out.

Gordon *et al.* (2001) have developed these arguments to suggest that the geomorphological sensitivity of different mountain landscape features will be determined by a particular trigger event, such as extreme weather, and that the actual response of the feature may be either robust or sensitive. The landscape may consist of some parts which, although dynamic, have retained relatively stable features in response to natural and human disturbances (e.g. distribution of gravel bars in a river bed), whereas at the other extreme, some parts may have changed fundamentally through the crossing of extrinsic thresholds (e.g. loss of soil cover following break-up of surface vegetation). The mountain landscape can be viewed in a similar way – some parts will be robust to change, whereas others are highly sensitive to even small perturbations.

7.4 Distinctions between natural and non-natural mountain landscapes

Several important studies in the uplands have made the distinction between natural and non-natural processes with regard to river channels. Werritty and Brazier (1994) and Brazier and Werritty (1994) have shown that river channels change in response to natural extreme events (which can occur locally, such as due to storm events throughout the post-glacial period) as well as to human intervention in the form of deforestation, and impacts of livestock in stimulating erosion on surrounding hill slopes. Higher up, on exposed mountain spurs and cols, weathering, periglacial processes, impacts of grazing, and trampling by livestock and humans vary with time, in space and in severity. Freeze-thaw effects (cryoturbation) can result in the churning up of the regolith and soil, which in turn can counteract the effects of leaching of nutrients, giving rise to a richer flora. A few nationally rare vascular plants such as *Artemisia norvegica* are favoured by such conditions. Some species favour disturbed sites, whether that disturbance is caused by freeze-thaw or by trampling.

On mountain slopes climate change, in the form of wetter conditions, may result in more frequent storms and the potential for erosion events. However, the moisture loading of the soil will influence its cohesion, and therefore susceptibility to erosion. Where there are discontinuities in soil structure, the local landform will be more susceptible to disturbance. For instance, grazing by sheep or deer will reduce the vegetation root hold and subsequently vegetation cover, which will then reduce the internal friction of the soil and, of course, may trigger an actual erosion event (e.g. Thompson *et al.*, 1987; Legg, 2000; Gordon *et al.*, 2001).

7.4.1 Classification of sensitivities to pressure

Building on the available, albeit limited, information on sensitivities to change of different mountain features, we have developed a classification of sensitivity to different pressures. Table 7.1 lists the main mountain topographic features, and gives their principal vegetation types. For each of these we have formed a judgement on the sensitivity to change in response to pressures ranging from extreme weather events to some of the more obvious physical manifestations of human influences such as grazing, burning and built developments. We have developed much of this analysis on the basis of work by colleagues and ourselves (cited in Table 7.1).

7.4.2 Topographical and habitat differences

Within the mountain ecosystem the different topographical features respond to environmental pressure in quite different ways. As Hobbs (1999) said of Australian ecosystems: "within a particular biophysical envelope, many different 'ecosystem states' may be possible, and the particular state in which we find the ecosystem may depend strongly on its response to past disturbance events and past management regimes". These sentiments certainly apply to mountains. Whilst parts of the summit plateaux (vegetated by moss heaths and blanket bogs) will be highly sensitive to extreme weather events, plateau valleys (with their medium-lie snow patches dominated by resistant graminoids) will be less sensitive. Grazing pressures also render the vegetation of parts of the summit plateaux, especially moss-dominated heaths, particularly sensitive. The corries are more varied in their sensitivity due to variations in slope, vegetation, soil, moisture levels and snow lie.

Building on knowledge of these sensitivities, we can form a view on the naturalness of some of the different parts of the mountain landscape. It is likely that snow-patch hollows are amongst the most natural features. These have experienced little disturbance from grazing and trampling. Yet the vegetation of the more exposed summit plateaux is probably less natural than some earlier studies have suggested (e.g. Thompson and Brown, 1992) because it is so sensitive to grazing and pollution. There is considerable grazing-induced variability in the floristics of these summit plateaux, and although there is little evidence of widespread modification through grazing in the Scottish Highlands, further south many of the stands have been much modified through grazing and possibly acidic deposition (e.g. Thompson and Brown, 1992; Baddeley *et al.*, 1994). Even in the Highlands, there is evidence locally that some mountain plateaux have been heavily modified by grazing pressure (e.g. parts of the Breadalbane Hills, Drumochter Hills and the Trotternish Ridge).

The natural tree-line with Scots pine (*Pinus sylvestris*) and birch (*Betula pubescens*) has all but disappeared from the mountains, surviving only in a few localities such as Creag Fhiaclach in the Cairngorms (Grace, 1997). Above the potential tree-line, montane scrub occurs as only fragmentary stands of the three principle communities in Scotland: alpine willow (*Salix* spp.) scrub; alpine juniper (*Juniperus communis*) scrub; and *Betula nana* scrub

Table 7.1. Sensitivity (low to high) to change from different pressures over the main topographical features, and their principal vegetation types, in montane areas. The grading from low to high is a judgement based on the severity and impact of the pressure (from Bayfield, 1979, 1980; Watson, 1985; Thompson *et al.*, 1987; Thompson and Brown, 1992; Gordon *et al.*, 1998, 2001; MacDonald *et al.*, 1998; Legg, 2000).

Topographic features	Principal vegetation types	Extreme weather (gales, rainstorms)	Global warming	Pollution	Built developments	Grazing	Burning	Trampling by people
High summit plateaux	Summit moss-heaths	high	high	high	high*	high	low*	high
Snow-patch hollows (long-lie)	Moss-dominated snow-beds	moderate	high	high	high*	moderate	low*	high
Low summit plateaux	Blanket bog	high	high	high	high	high	high	high
	Wet heath	moderate	moderate	moderate	moderate	moderate	moderate	moderate
Summit ridges, exposed spurs, cols and crests of corrie headwalls	Wind-clipped dwarf-shrub heaths	high	high	high	high*	moderate	high*	high
Corries	Flushed species-poor grassland	low	low	low	moderate*	low	low*	moderate
	Snow-bed dwarf-shrub heaths	low	moderate	moderate	moderate*	moderate	moderate	moderate
	Montane dwarf-herb communities and species-rich grasslands	low	moderate	moderate	moderate*	moderate	low	moderate
Plateau valleys and hollows (medium-lie snowpatches)	Snow-bed grasslands	low	moderate	low	low*	low	low*	low
	Springs and flushes	low	low	moderate	high*	moderate	low*	high

* denotes impact rarely or only very locally experienced in that part of the mountain

(Ratcliffe, 1981; Horsfield and Thompson, 1997). Alpine willow scrub is largely confined to ungrazed cliff ledges, steep rocky slopes, steep wet gravel and scree or rock outcrops. Alpine juniper scrub occurs very locally above the potential tree-line in the eastern Highlands (in the Cairngorms), mainly as *Juniperus communis-Oxalis acetosella* scrub; whereas *Calluna vulgaris-Juniperus communis* ssp. *nana* heath is confined to the North-West Highlands and Islands, where extensive stands occur in dry and wet heaths both below and above the former tree-line. Interestingly, the *Betula nana* scrub occurs very locally in blanket bogs and wet heaths in parts of the Scottish Highlands. Horsfield and Thompson (1997) made comparisons between montane scrub in Scotland with Norway to show the extent to which these scrub habitats in Scotland have been reduced in extent through human influence (see also MacKenzie, 2000).

The vegetation of the summit plateaux, consisting of summit moss-heaths, blanket bog and wet heath has one tendency in common - active erosion - though the extent to which natural and human pressures influences this is unclear. Current work by us and co-workers suggests that blanket bogs and wet heaths, in particular, may have been greatly reduced in extent. Stevenson *et al.* (1990) suggested that the 'Little Ice Age' may have stimulated major blanket bog erosion. More recently, Stevenson and Thompson (unpublished) have studied blanket bog hummocks and mounds in north-west Sutherland, and suggest that there may have been periods of mass peat erosion, leaving only remnants of peat bodies intact. There has even been the suggestion that vegetation crowns on large boulders, and other peat remnants, may be all that is left of once, much deeper peat deposits and indeed wet heath formations. Ongoing work indicates that prostrate juniper heaths (*Juniperus communis* ssp. *nana*) may be sparse and patchy over much of the North-West Highlands and Islands because they have been burnt out by fire, though it is also possible that the juniper has actually colonised exposed or eroded terrain.

7.4.3 Possibility of major responses in highly sensitive landscapes

At this stage we can do no more than point to anecdotal and very limited palaeoecological studies which suggest that some of the more open and extensive montane habitats may have endured more change than previously recognised. Whilst the mountain environment can indeed be viewed as episodically dynamic, varying in nature, rate and location of active landforming and vegetation processes (e.g. Gordon *et al.*, 2001), we still know little about trigger events or the effects of different natural and human-related pressures in forming the landscape we see today. As Hobbs (1999) stated: "An understanding of this historical component of ecosystems is thus essential, but is often incredibly difficult to develop."

Recent research points to the variability of climate change during the Holocene. Significant progress is being made in interpreting the climate record from montane bogs and lochs, including the recognition of cyclic patterns of climate change with series of 'wet shifts' over the last 5500 years (Chambers *et al.*, 1997; Anderson, 1998; Mauquoy and Barber, 1999; Barber *et al.*, 2000). Increased oceanicity resulting from climate change may present increased ecological stress (Crawford, 2000) as well as raise susceptibility to geomorphological change. It is also important to recognise that human interaction with the oceanic environment has also taken place over the timescale of such changes (e.g. Edwards and Whittington, 1997). This presents several difficulties in interpreting cause and effect in landscape sensitivity. With a few exceptions (Brazier *et al.*, 1988; Ballantyne and

Whittington, 1999), there is difficulty in disentangling human and natural effects (Ballantyne, 1991). There is difficulty also in relating geomorphic processes to such climate records, with growing evidence of the role of extreme events such as intense rainstorms (Hinchliffe, 1999; Ballantyne and Whittington, 1999; Curry, 2000a, 2000b). Also, different parts of the landscape may show different levels of geomorphological sensitivity and may respond in different ways to the same perturbations; for example Ballantyne and Whittington (1999) describe the contrasting behaviour of a river floodplain and a tributary alluvial fan in the central Grampian Highlands during the late Holocene, the former undergoing incision and the latter, episodic accumulation.

7.5 Implications for research, conservation and management
7.5.1 Range of research issues

Reflecting on the uncertainty regarding the 'natural' status of mountain landscapes, we feel that two types of research are needed. First, we need more work on the sensitivity of mountain landscapes. Palaeoenvironmental records may be particularly useful in this respect in providing a longer-term perspective on geo-ecological processes and addressing some of the problems identified in the previous section. Such records may allow contemporary ecological processes to be placed in their historical context (e.g. peat erosion in the uplands (Stevenson *et al.*, 1990) or the decline of heather moorland (Stevenson and Thompson, 1993)). They may also show how plant communities might respond to future environmental changes (Huntley, 1991). In particular, we need more detailed radiocarbon-dated records from different catchments to infer any associations between climate, erosion and vegetation changes. We do have a lot of such information for lowland/valley sites, but very little for high mountain peats.

Cyclicity in peat bogs and wet heaths remains a tantalising puzzle: to what extent is erosion in peat bogs at high altitude cyclical, variably fluctuating, or a 'one-off' event? On Skye there are areas of dissected blanket peat where the channels between the islands or tongues of deep peat appear to be actively healing up with near continuous vegetation cover and active peat formation in the hollows. This recovery process may have been triggered by reductions in stocking levels and cessation of burning 40-50 years ago. More investigations of palaeoenvironmental records of montane lochs would not only resolve climate records (e.g. Barber *et al.*, 1999), but also elucidate erosion events and patterns of landscape stability and instability.

We also need more dating of aeolian deposits which have accumulated in response to the stripping of plateaux vegetation and soils by deflation, notably on the Torridonian sandstone mountains of the North-West Highlands (Ballantyne and Whittington, 1987) (Plate 29), on Trotternish (Ballantyne, 1998), and in the Northern Isles (Ball and Goodier, 1974; Goodier and Ball, 1975). The presence of buried soils in these aeolian deposits suggests that the stripping has been episodic in the past. On many of these summits, the superficial deposits and the montane grasslands they support have been stripped down to a bare gravel lag, which suggests that a significant threshold may have been crossed, leading to irreversible loss. However, it is unclear to what extent the causes reflect natural processes, human activity or a combination of both. We also require further work on heavy grazing impacts on montane vegetation, along the lines advocated by Legg (2000).

The second area of research concerns experimental and restoration techniques. Here, we need experimental sites where we can mimic disturbance events and study subsequent geomorphological and vegetation processes. In particular, it would be valuable to study interactions between natural and human pressures. We also need to think more imaginatively about the geo-ecological 'restoration science'. To what extent do we understand the properties of resistance, degradation and erosion? Finally, here, can we develop means of restoring montane bogs and other sensitive features on the grand scale?

7.5.2 Thresholds of sensitivity and change: links to management

We have developed the theme that landforms, soils and vegetation are closely inter-related in the mountain landscape; changes in one element may trigger significant changes in the others. There appear to be uncertainties in knowledge about critical thresholds, timing and causes of threshold events, and here the distinction between robust and more gradual or sensitive responses to pressure is important. But to what extent can we really manage montane landscapes when so many questions appear to remain unanswered? Given the significance of the mountain natural heritage, we need to find ways of managing the pressures which have adverse impacts.

Any dynamic, changing environment presents a challenge for conservation management, but the mountains offer additional physical and indeed intellectual challenges. Until we address the scientific issues raised above, it is possible that some of the measures we take to reduce grazing pressures or more local human trampling impacts may be redundant (if the landform is already deteriorating to the extent that major reductions in human pressures are required). On the other hand, some landforms, notably the medium-lie snow-patch hollows and corries dominated by graminoids such as *Nardus stricta*, may be more ecologically resistant to pressure than previously recognised. The interaction between geographical position, climate change and grazing is particularly perplexing, for some of the changes in vegetation may actually raise the ecological carrying capacity of the land and its geomorphological stability. For example, the loss of bryophytes and lichen cover to graminoids may produce an inherently more stable complex – more robust to grazing and trampling and less liable to erode, but of lower nature conservation value. However, if there is more exposed regolith as a result of grazing impacts, then this could have a knock-on effect of greater erosion. There may thus be more erosion on the higher ground itself by wind and water if vegetation cover is temporarily reduced.

Related to this is the question of what sort of landscape we want. Erosion is a natural process which, through maintaining geomorphological diversity and heterogeneity, may be crucial in maintaining biodiversity (Gordon *et al.*, 2001). The 'ideal' landscape is perhaps one with minimal interference and modification that allows natural processes the scope to evolve. The lesson from the palaeoenvironmental record is that montane landscapes are dynamic, and regardless of management, will evolve both gradually and episodically. While palaeoenvironmental records may show the natural range of variability, and how different systems respond, there are now additional stresses from atmospheric pollution and intense local pressures from heavy grazing, human trampling and skiing.

There is also a risk that climate change may exceed past variability and that, cumulatively, human activity may be moving process systems closer to geomorphological and ecological thresholds. Conservation management can only respond to, and address, the local pressures, but these responses are currently constrained by a lack of answers to the sorts of questions raised above and a suitably informed geo-ecological management framework.

7.6 Conclusion

We feel that it is particularly important to recognise the sensitivity to change of the different components of the mountain landscape. If we carry out further, more detailed, palaeoecological and experimental work, we will be in a stronger position to manage these sensitive landscapes. Perhaps, after all, Alex Watt (1947) was providing us with an important hint when he closed his presidential address to the British Ecological Society with the following words: "What I want to say is what T.S. Elliot said of Shakespeare's work: we must know all of it in order to know any of it."

Acknowledgements

We thank Colin Ballantyne, John Birks, Tim Burt, Tony Stevenson, Angus MacDonald, Derek Ratcliffe, Ness Brazier, Rick Battarbee, Andrew Coupar, Iain Leith, John MacKay, Adam Watson and Aubrey Manning for discussions.

References

Anderson, D.E. 1998. A reconstruction of Holocene climatic changes from peat bogs in north-west Scotland. *Boreas*, **27**, 208-224.

Baddeley, J.A., Thompson, D.B.A. and Lee, J.A. 1994. Regional variation in the nitrogen content of *Racomitrium lanuginosum* in relation to atmospheric nitrogen deposition. *Environmental Pollution*, **84**, 189-196.

Ball, D.F. and Goodier, R. 1974. Ronas Hill, Shetland: a preliminary account of its ground pattern features resulting from the action of wind and frost. *In* Goodier R. (ed.) *The Natural Environment of Shetland*. Nature Conservancy Council, Edinburgh, 164-171.

Ballantyne, C.K. 1991. Late Holocene erosion in upland Britain: climatic deterioration or human influence? *The Holocene*, **1**, 81-85.

Ballantyne, C.K. 1998. Aeolian deposits on a Scottish mountain summit: characteristics, provenance, history and significance. *Earth Surface Processes and Landforms*, **23**, 625-641.

Ballantyne C.K. and Harris C. 1994. *The Periglaciation of Great Britain*. Cambridge University Press, Cambridge.

Ballantyne, C.K. and Whittington, G. 1987. Niveo-aeolian sand deposits on An Teallach, Wester Ross, Scotland. *Transactions of the Royal Society of Edinburgh: Earth Sciences*, **78**, 51-63.

Ballantyne, C.K. and Whittington, G. 1999. Late Holocene floodplain incision and alluvial fan formation in the central Grampian Highlands, Scotland: chronology, environment and implications. *Journal of Quaternary Science*, **14**, 651-671.

Barber, K.E., Battarbee, R.W., Brooks, S.J., Eglington, G., Haworth, E.Y., Oldfield, F., Stevenson, A.C., Thompson, R., Appleby, P.G., Austin, W.E.N., Cameron, N.G., Ficken, K.J., Golding, P., Harkness, D.D., Holmes, J.A., Hutchinson, R., Lishman, J.P., Maddy, D., Pinder, L.C.V., Rose, N.L. and Stoneman, R.E. 1999. Proxy records of climate change in the UK over the last two millennia: documented change and sedimentary records from lakes and bogs. *Journal of the Geological Society, London*, **156**, 369-380.

Barber, K.E., Maddy, D., Rose, N., Stevenson, A.C., Stoneman, R. and Thompson, R. 2000. Replicated proxy-climate signals over the last 2000 yr from two distant UK peat bogs: new evidence for regional palaeoclimate teleconnections. *Quaternary Science Reviews*, **19**, 481-487.

Battarbee, R.W., Flower, R.J., Stevenson, A.C. and Rippey, B. 1985. Lake acidification in Galloway: a palaeoecological test of competing hypotheses. *Nature*, **314**, 350-353.

Bayfield, N.G. 1979. Recovery of four montane heath communities on Cairngorm, Scotland, from disturbance by trampling. *Biological Conservation*, **15**, 165-179.

Bayfield, N.G. 1980. Replacement of vegetation in disturbed ground near ski-lifts in the Cairngorm mountains, Scotland. *Journal of Biogeography*, **7**, 249-260.

Birks, H.J.B. 1988. Long-term ecological change in the British uplands. *In* Usher, M. B. and Thompson, D. B. A. (eds) *Ecological Change in the Uplands*. Blackwell, Oxford, 37-56.

Brazier, V. and Ballantyne, C.K. 1989. Late Holocene debris cone evolution in Glen Feshie, western Cairngorm Mountains, Scotland. *Transactions of the Royal Society of Edinburgh: Earth Sciences*, **80**, 17-24.

Brazier, V. and Werritty, A. 1994. Conservation management of dynamic rivers: the case of the River Feshie. *In* O'Halloran, D., Green, C.P., Harley, M. and Knill, J. (eds) *Geological and Landscape Conservation*. The Geological Society, London, 147-152.

Brazier, V., Whittington, G. and Ballantyne, C.K. 1988. Holocene debris cone formation in Glen Etive, Western Grampian Highlands, Scotland. *Earth Surface Processes and Landforms*, **13**, 525-531.

Chambers, F.M., Barber, K.E., Maddy, D. and Brew, J. 1997. A 5500-year proxy-climate and vegetation record from blanket mire at Talla Moss, Borders, Scotland. *The Holocene*, **7**, 391-399.

Craig, G.Y. 1991 (ed.) *Geology of Scotland*. The Geological Society, London.

Crawford, R.M.M. 2000. Ecological hazards of oceanic environments. *New Phytologist*, **147**, 257-281.

Curry, A.M. 2000a. Holocene reworking of drift-mantled hillslopes in Glen Docherty, Northwest Highlands, Scotland. *The Holocene*, **10**, 509-518.

Curry, A.M. 2000b. Holocene reworking of drift-mantled hillslopes in the Scottish Highlands. *Journal of Quaternary Science*, **15**, 529-541.

Edwards, K.J. and Whittington, G. 1997. Vegetation change. *In* Edwards, K.J. and Ralston, I.B.M. (eds) *Scotland: Environment and Archaeology, 8000BC - AD1000*. John Wiley, Chichester, 63-82.

Goodier, R. and Ball, D.F. 1975. Ward Hill, Hoy, Orkney: patterned ground features and their origin. *In* Goodier, R. (ed.) *The Natural Environment of Orkney*. Nature Conservancy Council, Edinburgh, 47-56.

Gordon, J.E., Thompson, D.B.A., Haynes, V.M., MacDonald, R. and Brazier, V. 1998. Environmental sensitivity and conservation management in the Cairngorm Mountains, Scotland. *Ambio*, **27**, 335-344.

Gordon, J.E., Brazier, V., Thompson, D.B.A. and Horsfield, D. 2001. Geo-ecology and the conservation management of sensitive upland landscapes in Scotland. *Catena*, **42**, 323-332.

Grace, J. 1997. The oceanic tree-line and the limit for tree growth in Scotland. *Botanical Journal of Scotland*, **49**, 223-236.

Haynes, V.M., Grieve, I.C., Price-Thomas, P. and Salt, K. 1998. The geomorphological sensitivity of the Cairngorm high plateaux. *Scottish Natural Heritage Research, Survey and Monitoring Report*, No. 66.

Hinchliffe, S. 1999. Timing and significance of talus slope reworking, Trotternish, Skye, northwest Scotland. *The Holocene*, **9**, 483-494.

Hobbs, R. 1999. From our southern correspondent. *British Ecological Society Bulletin*, **30**, 20-22.

Horsfield, D. and Thompson, D.B.A. 1997. Ecology and conservation of montane scrub. *In* Gilbert, D., Horsfield, D. and Thompson, D.B.A. (eds) *The Ecology and Restoration of Montane and Sub-alpine Scrub Habitats in Scotland. Scottish Natural Heritage Review*, No. 83, 1-33.

Horsfield, D. and Thompson, D.B.A. 1996. The uplands: guidance on terminology regarding altitudinal zonation and related terms. *Information and Advisory Note*, No. 26. Scottish Natural Heritage, Battleby.

Huntley, B. 1991. Historical lessons for the future. *In* Spellerberg, I.F., Goldsmith, F.B. and Morris, M.G. (eds) *Scientific Management of Temperate Communities for Conservation.* Blackwell, Oxford, 473-503.

Ingram, M. 1958. The ecology of the Cairngorms. IV. The *Juncus trifidus* communities. *Journal of Ecology,* **46**, 707-737.

Innes, J.L. 1983. Lichenometric dating of debris-floor deposits in the Scottish Highlands. *Earth Surface Processes and Landforms,* **8**, 579-588.

Jones, V.J., Flower, R.J., Appleby, P.G., Natkanski, J., Richardson, N., Rippey, B., Stevenson, A.C. and Battarbee, R.W. 1993. Palaeolimnological evidence for the acidification and atmospheric contamination of lochs in the Cairngorm and Lochnagar areas of Scotland. *Journal of Ecology,* **81**, 3-24.

Lee, J.A., Tallis, J.H. and Woodin, S.J. 1988. Acidic deposition and British upland vegetation. *In* Usher M.B. and Thompson, D.B.A. (eds) *Ecological Change in the Uplands.* Blackwell, Oxford, 151-164.

Legg, C. 2000. Review of published work in relation to monitoring of trampling impacts and change in montane vegetation. *Scottish Natural Heritage Review,* No. 131.

Leith, I.D., Hicks, W.K., Fowler, D. and Woodin, S.J. 1999. Differential responses of UK upland plants to nitrogen deposition. *New Phytologist,* **141**, 277-289.

Lindsay, R.A., Charman, D.T., Everingham, F., O'Reilly, R.M., Palmer, M.A., Rowell, T.A. and Stroud, D.A. 1988. *The Flow Country: the Peatlands of Caithness and Sutherland.* Nature Conservancy Council, Peterborough.

MacDonald, A., Stevens, P., Armstrong, H., Immirzi, P. and Reynolds, P. 1998. *A Guide to Upland Habitats. Surveying Land Management Impacts.* Vol. 1. *Background Information and Guidance for Surveyors,* Vol 2. *The Field Guide.* Scottish Natural Heritage, Battleby.

MacKenzie, N.A. 2000. *Low Alpine, Subalpine and Coastal Scrub Communities in Scotland.* Highland Birchwoods, Munlochy.

Mauquoy, D. and Barber, K. 1999. A replicated 3000 yr proxy-climate record from Coom Rigg Moss and Felecia Moss, the Border Mires, northern England. *Journal of Quaternary Science,* **14**, 263-275.

McEwen, L.J. and Werritty, A. 1988. The hydrology and long-term significance of a flash flood in the Cairngorm Mountains, Scotland. *Catena,* **15**, 361-377.

McVean, D.N. and Ratcliffe, D.A. 1962. *Plant Communities of the Scottish Highlands.* HMSO, London.

Ratcliffe, D.A. (ed.) 1977. *A Nature Conservation Review.* Vol. 1. Cambridge University Press, Cambridge.

Ratcliffe, D.A. 1981. The vegetation. *In* Nethersole-Thompson, D. and Watson, A. (eds) *The Cairngorms.* Melven Press, Perth, 47-76.

Ratcliffe, D.A. and Thompson, D.B.A. 1988. The British uplands: their ecological character and international significance. *In* Usher M.B. and Thompson, D.B.A. (eds) *Ecological Change in the Uplands.* Blackwell, Oxford, 9-36.

Scottish Natural Heritage (in press). *A Vision for the Natural Heritage of Mountains and Moorland.* National Prospectus No. 1. Natural Heritage Zones Programme. Scottish Natural Heritage, Battleby.

Stevenson, A.C. and Thompson, D.B.A. 1993. Long-term changes in the extent of heather moorland in upland Britain and Ireland: palaeoecological evidence for the importance of grazing. *The Holocene,* **3**, 70-76.

Stevenson, A.C., Jones, V.J. and Battarbee, R.W. 1990. The cause of peat erosion: a palaeolimnological approach. *New Phytologist,* **114**, 727-735.

Tallis, J.H. 1964. Studies on Southern Pennine peats. III. The behaviour of S*phagnum. Journal of Ecology,* **52**, 345-353.

Tallis, J.H. 1985. Mass movement and erosion of a southern Pennine blanket peat. *Journal of Ecology,* **73**, 283-315.

Tallis, J.H. 1997. The southern Pennine experience: an overview of blanket mire degradation. *In* Tallis, J.H., Meade, R. and Hulme, P.D. (eds) *Blanket Mire Degradation. Causes, Consequences and Challenges.* Macaulay Land Use Research Institute on behalf of the Mires Research Group, Aberdeen, 7-15.

Thompson, D.B.A. and Brown, A. 1992. Biodiversity in montane Britain: habitat variation, vegetation diversity and some objectives for conservation. *Biodiversity and Conservation*, **1**, 179-208.

Thompson, D.B.A., Galbraith, H. and Horsfield, D. 1987. Ecology and resources of Britain's mountain plateaux: land use conflicts and impacts. *In* Bell, M. and Bunce, R.G.H. (eds) *Agriculture and Conservation in the Hills and Uplands*. Institute of Terrestrial Ecology, Grange-over-Sands, 22-31.

Thompson, D.B.A. and Horsfield, D. 1990. Towards a measurement of nature conservation interest in the British uplands. *In* Thompson, D.B.A. and Kirby, K. (eds) *Grazing Research and Nature Conservation in the British Uplands. Research and Survey Series*, No. 27. Nature Conservancy Council, Peterborough, 9-18.

Watson, A. 1985. Soil erosion and vegetation damage near ski lifts at Cairn Gorm, Scotland. *Biological Conservation*, **33**, 363-381.

Watt, A.S. 1947. Pattern and process in the plant community. *Journal of Ecology*, **35**, 1-22.

Watt, A.S. and Jones, E.W. 1948. The ecology of the Cairngorms. I. The environment and the altitudinal zonation of the vegetation. *Journal of Ecology*, **36**, 283-304.

Woolgrove, C.E. and Woodin, S.J. 1996. Effects of pollutants in snowmelt on *Kiaeria starkei*, a characteristic species of late snowbed bryophyte dominated vegetation. *New Phytologist*, **133**, 519-529.

Werritty, A. and Brazier, V. 1994. Geomorphic sensitivity and the conservation of fluvial geomorphology SSSIs. *In* Stevens, C., Gordon, J.E., Green, C.P. and Macklin, M. (eds) *Conserving our Landscape*. Proceedings of the Conference, Conserving Our Landscape: Evolving Landforms and Ice-Age Heritage, Crewe, 1992. Peterborough, 100-109.

8 Assessing Geomorphological Sensitivity of the Cairngorm High Plateaux for Conservation Purposes

Valerie M. Haynes, Ian C. Grieve, John E. Gordon, Peter Price-Thomas and Keith Salt

Summary

1.   In a dynamic landscape such as the high plateaux of the Cairngorms, the distribution of stable and unstable ground surfaces is closely linked with the physical properties of the regolith, geomorphological processes and vegetation communities.

2.   Conservation managers need to understand the likely consequences of different natural and anthropogenic changes, and to assess the effectiveness of any management measures. Assessment of the geomorphological sensitivity of process and form to the main types of changes envisaged allows the most vulnerable locations to be identified.

3.   Conservation management and protection of biodiversity in the area requires an integrated approach to the understanding of geomorphological, pedological and ecological processes and their sensitivities to change.

8.1 Introduction

The Cairngorm Mountains are located on the maritime fringe of Europe, an area that is potentially highly sensitive in terms of geomorphological and ecological responses to environmental change and human activities, such as grazing, trampling and pollution (Gordon *et al.*, 1998). The high conservation value of the Cairngorms for geomorphology stems from the diverse assemblage of landforms (Brazier *et al.* 1996; Gordon *et al.* 1998). Protection of this diversity is an important management aim. The principal landforms on the high plateau surfaces are relict and present-day periglacial forms, the development of which is strongly linked to exposure, snow-cover and vegetation communities. Conservation managers need to understand the likely consequences of different natural and anthropogenic changes, and to assess the effectiveness of any management measures. Thus, there is a need to assess the sensitivity of process and form to the main types of changes envisaged, and to identify the most vulnerable locations.

8.2 Geomorphological sensitivity and its assessment

The sensitivity of landscapes is defined by their resistance to change. *Sensitive* landscape systems readily cross extrinsic geomorphological thresholds into new process regimes

(Schumm, 1979). *Stable* landscape systems operate far from such thresholds, and weathering often dominates over erosion so that there is a vegetation and soil cover. *Robust* systems are subject to constant change within intrinsic thresholds, yet retain similar forms and processes as they maintain a dynamic equilibrium, with features moving across the landscape or reforming after disturbance (Werritty and Brazier, 1994).

A three-pronged approach to the assessment of landscape sensitivity has been adopted:

- analysis of present-day forces and resistances allows identification of critical geomorphological thresholds, which enables assessment of the potential effects of climate change;
- change within critical parts of the system is to be monitored over annual or decadal timescales in order to identify sites which are in dynamic equilibrium or subject to change;
- identification of changes which have occurred over centennial and millennial timescales allows present-day developments to be put into context and helps to disentangle the reasons why extrinsic thresholds are crossed.

8.3 The present-day geomorphological system

The main forces within the natural environment of the high plateaux are provided by climate and slope angle. The area experiences a maritime periglacial climate, with strong winds, frequent yet shallow frosts, very variable snow-cover and thaws, and periodic intense rainstorms. The regolith, derived from coarse-grained granite, is deficient in the most erodible grain-sizes. Surface horizons have become particularly depleted in fines by a combination of wind deflation, wash and frost processes. Lag gravels are dominated by 2-4 mm grains (Haynes *et al.*, 1998).

Many processes are effectively episodic (Table 8.1), as high magnitude events are combined with processes which have reduced the sensitivity of the surface layers. Wind action provides a good example. It is capable of disrupting previously intact vegetation and transporting sand and gravel (Plate 30). Depletion of fines and the development of deflation surfaces and wind-patterned ground can readily be understood by examining prevailing wind-speeds. Data from the automatic weather station on Cairn Gorm summit (Herriot Watt University, 1999) show that during the last decade, thresholds for movement of the lag gravels by creep (Chepil, 1945; Bagnold, 1954; Selby *et al.*, 1974) were crossed on *c.* 29 - 47% of each year, and for saltation of medium sands, 78-89% of each year. Actual transport may occur less often than this in mixed grain sizes, however, as finer grains are protected by coarser ones, and some of the high winds occur when the ground is frozen or protected by snow.

Table 8.2 shows a sensitivity matrix for the geomorphological environments of the high plateaux. Marked transects are being used to monitor a variety of critical sites, involving bare ground/vegetation boundaries and the wastage of regolith matrix from around boulders. This part of the study is ongoing.

Table 8.1 Processes and changes in the environment.

Process	Activity	Effects	Sensitive to	Direction of change
Weathering	continuous	regolith and soil development	temperature +/- soil moisture +/- soil pH +/-	+/- +/- +/-
Needle ice	seasonal, mainly on bare ground	disrupts seedlings; contributes to creep, wind action and sorting	temperature +/- (well within its climatic boundaries) snow cover +/- vegetation change +/-	+/- -/+ -/+
Frost heave and solifluction	seasonal, on frost-susceptible regolith; around snowpatches	terracettes and ploughing boulders	temperature +/- quantity of snow melt +/-	-/+ +/-
Debris flow	episodic, only on steepest slopes	debris flows/cones	intense rainstorms +/- trampling +/-	+/- +/-
Runoff processes (snowmelt is main source)	seasonal and episodic; only on bare ground	rills under snow patches and on paths; gravel transport	snow patch size +/- bare area +/- trampling compaction +/-	+/- +/- +/-
Wind action	episodic	can break vegetation mat; deflation of bare ground, deposition in vegetation and snow	magnitude and frequency of winds +/- vegetation cover +/-	+/- -/+

Table 8.2 Sensitivity matrix for different geomorphological contexts on the Cairngorm high plateaux.

Location	Sensitive to	Influencing characteristics	Overall sensitivity
Plateau surfaces (blockfields, deflation surfaces)	climate change (wind, snow-cover); vegetation change; trampling	summits experience more concentrated trampling	fairly robust, though thresholds crossed during Holocene
Crests of corrie headwalls	ditto	routeways, concentrated trampling; steep edge - regolith wastage and wind acceleration	more sensitive than plateau surfaces
Exposed spurs	ditto	routeways; steep slopes - regolith wastage and wind acceleration	sensitive
Cols	ditto	routeways; steep flanks; pockets of deep regolith; wind funnelling	sensitive; include transitions between process regimes
Plateau valleys and hollows (medium-lie snow patches)	climate change (snow-cover, rainfall intensity); trampling (especially when wet); grazing	turfy vegetation; more organic soils; deep regolith	fairly robust, though some sensitive sites (combinations of slopes; deep regolith; copious moisture; paths)
Long-lie snow patches	climate change (spring weather and snow duration); trampling (during thaws)	may be 'honeypot' locations	sensitive

8.4 Landscape development over centennial timescales

Currently there are three main process regimes on the plateau (Plate 30): stable vegetated areas, underlain by alpine podzols; areas with a mosaic of bare and wind-patterned ground, underlain by truncated podzols; and areas predominantly bare of vegetation, with little sign of any soil podzolisation. The truncated podzols are widespread. Vegetation loss and soil truncation represent the crossing of a geomorphological and ecological threshold in the past, resulting in a change in process regime. Profile characteristics suggest soil development over at least millennial timescales and a former, more complete vegetation cover. The loss of surface horizons, together with losses of soil carbon, from such sites suggests several centuries of disturbance (Haynes *et al.*, 1998). In many cols there is a distinct boundary between discontinuous and continuous vegetation, representing the transition between process regimes. Since these boundaries have shifted in the past, they are potentially sensitive locations at present, and may be subject to shifts in either direction.

8.5 Conclusion

The small-scale landforms and currently active geomorphological processes of the Cairngorm high plateaux are largely contained within the regolith, which leads to close links between landforms, soils, hydrology and ecology. The micro-relief created by these landforms is associated with a rich mosaic of plant and animal habitats, and the interplay of physical and biological processes controls the distribution of stable and unstable surfaces and the degree to which dynamic equilibrium is maintained. Conservation management and protection of biodiversity in the area requires an integrated approach to the understanding of geomorphological, pedological and ecological processes and their sensitivities to change.

References

Bagnold, R.A. 1954. *The Physics of Blown Sand and Desert Dunes.* Chapman & Hall, London.

Brazier, V., Gordon, J.E., Hubbard, A. and Sugden, D.F. 1996. The geomorphological evolution of a dynamic landscape: the Cairngorm Mountains, Scotland. *Botanical Journal of Scotland,* **48**, 13-30.

Chepil, W.S. 1945. The dynamics of wind erosion. *Soil Science,* **60**, 305-20, 397-411.

Gordon, J.E., Thompson, D.B.A., Haynes, V.M., Brazier, V. and MacDonald, R. 1998. Environmental sensitivity and conservation management in the Cairngorm Mountains, Scotland. *Ambio,* **27**, 335-344.

Haynes, V.M., Grieve, I.C., Price-Thomas, P. and Salt, K. 1998. The geomorphological sensitivity of the Cairngorm high plateaux. *Scottish Natural Heritage Research, Survey and Monitoring Report,* No. 66.

Herriot Watt University 1999. Cairn Gorm AWS database 1991-1999. Herriot Watt University Physics Department. www.phy.hw.ac.uk/resrev/aws/weather.htm

Schumm, S.A.1979. Geomorphic thresholds: the concept and its applications. *Transactions of the Institute of British Geographers,* NS**4***,* 485-515.

Selby, M.J., Rains, R.B. and Palmer, R.W.P. 1974. Eolian deposits of the ice-free Victoria Valley, Southern Victoria Land, Antarctica. *New Zealand Journal of Geology and Geophysics,* **17**, 543-562.

Werrity, A. and Brazier, V. 1994. Geomorphic sensitivity and the conservation of fluvial geomorphology SSSIs. In: Stevens, C., Gordon, J.E., Green, C.P. and Macklin, M. (eds) *Conserving our Landscape.* Proceedings of the Conference, Conserving Our Landscape: Evolving Landforms and Ice-Age Heritage, Crewe, 1992. Peterborough, 100-109.

PART THREE

Earth Science and the Natural Heritage: Pressures and Sustainable Management

Earth Science and the Natural Heritage: Pressures and Sustainable Management

The chapters in Part 3 examine pressures on the natural heritage from an Earth science perspective. They address pressures directly on the Earth heritage itself and those where effects on geology or geomorphological processes impact on the wider natural heritage in dynamic environments such as rivers and the coast. Several of the chapters also examine sustainable use of natural resources. Together, they demonstrate the potential value and applications of Earth science in integrated management.

Gordon and MacFadyen (chapter 9) and Goodenough *et al.* (chapter 10) focus on the site-based approach to Earth heritage conservation. They highlight the scientific importance and wider values of Scotland's Earth heritage and how the most important sites are being protected and documented, following the Geological Conservation Review. Threats are many and varied, but improved awareness and greater involvement are vital, in addition to statutory protection, in the conservation of Scotland's Earth heritage.

In more dynamic environments, an understanding of physical processes and the links with habitats and species is a crucial part of sustainable management, for example through the maintenance of sediment cycling at the coast or natural flow regimes in rivers. Several chapters and case studies dealing with the coast and rivers emphasise the value of maintaining natural processes and how working with, rather than against, them is essential. Hansom *et al.* (Chapter 11) show how coastal management presents particular problems because of the dynamic nature of the environment, the concentration of development in the coastal zone and the range of natural heritage interests. They emphasise the importance of understanding the underlying geomorphological processes in a study of the possibilities for managed realignment of the coast in the Forth Estuary. Allowing formerly claimed mudflats and salt marsh to be reclaimed by the sea in certain areas would help to restore the natural characteristics of the estuary. This would have benefits for conservation, through recreating natural habitats, and for managing the coastal response to predicted sea-level rise. This type of approach is already undergoing trials in England and reflects a growing recognition of environmentally sensitive management, as well as a certain degree of realism that maintaining existing flood embankments in many areas is not viable as a long-term management option.

Cressey (chapter 12) deals with the particular problem of an eroding coast which is yielding exposures of significant geological and archaeological interest. The dilemma is that continuing erosion is needed to maintain the exposures, but this erosion is leading to the loss of the interest. Various engineering solutions were considered and rejected on environmental and cost grounds. Instead it is proposed to monitor the erosion and to make a permanent record of new exposures.

In the coastal environment, there is often a close overlap between geomorphological and biological interests, most evident in dune and saltmarsh habitats. Laidler (Chapter 13) highlights a less obvious example of isolation basins, many of which contain valuable records of relative sea-level change as well as important habitat and species interests. Such basins have provided high-resolution data, particularly in North-West Scotland where other evidence of relative sea-level changes is often lacking. It is crucial that the conservation and management of such sites recognises their multiple interests.

The importance of maintaining natural processes is equally a central pillar of sustainable river management. As discussed by Leys (Chapter 14), management objectives for geomorphological systems require the continued operation of the active processes which shape the landforms, not necessarily the preservation of individual, transient features such as gravel bars and pools. Similarly, maintenance of natural flow regimes and processes is a crucial part of the management requirements for habitats and species diversity. The natural geomorphological processes that benefit habitats, species and Earth heritage conservation also interact with other land and water uses and therefore require integrated management at both catchment and reach scales. As with the coast, there is an urgency for convergence in management approaches not only for natural heritage interests, but also with wider planning of land and water use and management of natural hazards such as flooding. This is well illustrated by Leys in a case study of the River Spey. This river has important natural heritage interests, including a number of species that are rare or endangered across Europe. There are pressures from hydro-power and from river management works to enhance the salmon fishery. Water quality is an important consideration, both for public consumption and the whisky and food processing industries. Some settlements and agricultural land are at risk from flooding. The proposed designation of the river as a Special Area for Conservation under the EC Habitats Directive has initiated a process of integrated catchment management, which offers the potential for new consensus-based management across a wide geographical area and founded on an understanding of the natural processes. Such catchment-scale management is also likely to be driven by the EC Water Framework Directive.

Similar themes are reiterated in two further case studies. The close links between geomorphology, hydrology and ecology require that effective river restoration and enhancement must work as far as possible with 'near-natural' river processes. McEwen and McGhee (Chapter 15) show how a geomorphological and hydrological study was used as part of the River Ettrick Habitat Restoration Project to inform management planning and monitoring, particularly in relation to priority targets for restoration and enhancement. On the River Endrick, sediment and water quality are crucial for supporting internationally important lamprey populations. McEwen and Lewis (Chapter 16) were able to assess lamprey habitat potential from the sediment characteristics and to identify sensitive and robust areas as a basis for conservation management and monitoring.

The links between physical and biological systems and the sustainable use of natural resources are particularly evident in the soil. The soil is a non-renewable resource that performs a variety of functions. These include support for ecosystems and their biodiversity, agricultural and forestry production, biogeochemical cycling and recycling of organic wastes. The diversity of uses and requirements means that, like coasts and rivers, soil management has been approached on a sectoral rather than an integrated basis. Puri *et al.* (Chapter 17) outline the many pressures on the resource from agriculture, forestry and pollution, but note that soil quality is difficult to define and measure. Soil is not currently protected as an environmental medium in the same way as air and water. There is no primary legislation that addresses the soil, although there are various indirect measures, particularly relating to pollution controls, as well as codes of best practice for agriculture and forestry. A range of different organisations has responsibility for applying and implementing these measures and guidelines. Following the report of the Royal Commission on Environmental Pollution in 1996 on *The Sustainable Use of Soil*, the UK Government recommended the preparation of a national policy for soil protection. This is being progressed through the preparation of soil strategies for England and Wales, and Puri *et al.* note that it would be timely to develop such a strategy for Scotland.

One of the issues that a soil strategy might address is soil erosion. This can have a significant impact on the natural heritage, both directly through loss of habitat and indirectly through downstream effects, for example on fish spawning grounds. Lilly *et al.* (Chapter 18) argue that a systematic national evaluation of erosion risk is a basic requirement for the development of integrated land management strategies. They use a rule-based model and GIS to determine the inherent geomorphological risk of soil erosion by overland flow in Scotland. The results provide an indicative picture of erosion risk, that with further refinement would allow vulnerable areas to be targeted for appropriate management.

Two papers address the sustainable use of minerals and energy resources from a geological perspective. Lindley *et al.* (Chapter 19) examine sustainability in the aggregate industry, which in the past has left a legacy of environmental impacts. On a positive note, they recognise the significant changes in practice that have taken place, linked to more comprehensive planning guidelines and legislation. The latter reflect changes in public opinion and attitudes to the environment. The development of more integrated planning has also been notable, facilitated by resource surveys and techniques such as GIS. Significantly, the industry is now working more with environmental bodies, particularly in relation to after-use and restoration through Local Biodiversity Action Plans. It is apparent that the vision and guidelines are in place for more sustainable use, as reflected in Government policy. However, more is still required to convert the intentions into action, particularly in relation to recycling and re-use of quarry waste.

Johnson *et al.* (Chapter 20) note the existence of considerable reserves of fossil fuels in the form of coal, oil, gas and other non-renewables. However, their use is linked with air pollution, carbon emissions and enhanced greenhouse warming and climate change. Nuclear power has its own problems. Sustainable use of current energy is therefore questionable. A more sustainable future requires a combination of more efficient use, more efficient energy conversion, application of new technologies for reducing carbon emissions and greater use of renewables. The latter, however, may still have environmental costs; for example, windfarms and hydro-power schemes may have adverse visual impacts on landscape character, depending on their locations, and tidal barrage schemes can impact significantly on estuarine habitats and species. It is crucial that such developments are sensitively located so as not to impact on the natural heritage and landscape quality for which Scotland is famous. The implementation of strategic and integrated approaches is thus vital. Johnson *et al.* conclude that future decisions will involve a complex set of considerations, including the availability of different resources, the state of technology and the assessment of socio-economic and environmental cost-benefits.

A clear message is that sustainable management and use of natural resources depends on the effective application of Earth science knowledge and skills as part of the development of more integrated approaches. In a case study from Norway, Erikstad and Stabbetorp (Chapter 21) emphasise the importance of the timing of Earth science inputs to the development process, before technical and economic conditions are fixed. In particular, they show the value of natural areas mapping at an early stage in road planning before alternative routes are identified. The use of GIS also assists the planning authorities to take an integrated view.

Davidson *et al.* (Chapter 22) illustrate how integrated management is proceeding in Ontario, Canada, where different approaches are being developed through the Land Use Strategy and Natural Stewardship Program to meet the requirements and management challenges of different parts of the province. Crucially, consultation, consensus building, stewardship and education underpin these approaches. In addition, the development of integrated management is also being considered for specific, physiographically defined landscapes, as in the integrated resource management and protection strategy completed for the Oak Ridges Moraine.

At a similar strategic level, Mitchell (Chapter 23) describes an approach to integrated management being developed in Scotland by Scottish Natural Heritage, based on the concept of Natural Heritage Zones. The Natural Heritage Zones Programme provides a vision, objectives and action programmes based on needs and opportunities in areas that share similar natural heritage characteristics. Key goals are linked to specific actions which seek to deliver the vision over a 25 year period. The programme attempts to bring together socio-economic interests with environmental stewardship. It is not a blueprint but provides a framework, founded in the natural heritage, in which sustainable development may be progressed with other bodies and partners.

In sum, the chapters in Part 3 make a compelling case for the Earth science perspective within an integrated approach to sustainable management and use of natural resources. They show how Earth science has a crucial role to play, not only in understanding natural systems and developing environmentally sensitive management, but also in contributing to strategic planning and vision for the landscape. The challenge remains, however, to demonstrate the values of this role effectively to policy makers, planners and land managers.

9 EARTH HERITAGE CONSERVATION IN SCOTLAND: STATE, PRESSURES AND ISSUES

John E. Gordon and Colin C.J. MacFadyen

Summary

1.   Scotland's Earth heritage is important for its scientific value for modern studies in geology and geomorphology and in the historical development of Earth science. The most important Earth science localities in Scotland have been identified for conservation as part of the Geological Conservation Review.

2.   The wider value of Scotland's Earth heritage is apparent in the manner in which the Earth heritage underpins the diversity of Scotland's natural landscapes and habitats; in the sensitivity of the present landscape both in terms of the current processes which shape the coasts, rivers and mountains, and in relation to past changes recorded in landform, sedimentary and palaeoenvironmental archives; and in the growing recognition of the Earth heritage as a resource for education and tourism.

3.   Pressures on the resource arise principally from planning developments and land use changes. These may damage key features, impair their visibility and accessibility or fragment the interest.

4.   There is a need for better application of existing knowledge to enable the development of more integrated strategies and policies for sustainable management, based on working with, rather than against, natural processes. Equally there is a need for raised awareness of the benefits of such approaches among key interest groups and their advisors. Better awareness is also crucial to the development of opportunities for environmental education and tourism based on the links between Earth heritage, landscape and industrial heritage. The formation of partnerships between different interest groups and sectors will be fundamental in addressing these issues.

9.1 Introduction

For a relatively small area, Scotland has a tremendous diversity of rocks, fossils, landforms and soils. This reflects a rich and varied geological history of some 3 billion years and spans much of the geological record (Craig, 1991; Mitchell, 1997; Trewin, this volume). At different times, Scotland occupied positions on continental margins at the edges the Earth's plates where magmatic activity, volcanism, large-scale crustal deformation and mountain building were concentrated. Erosion and sedimentation have shaped the surface of the landscape and produced a range of sedimentary rock formations under different environments, including tropical and desert conditions. These changes were accompanied by evolving life forms preserved in the fossil record over the last 800 million years.

During the last two million years, the Quaternary ice ages have left an extensive imprint on the character of the landscape (Gordon and Sutherland, 1993). Patterns of glacial erosion and deposition have determined the physical form of topography and the characteristics of soil parent materials; relative changes in the levels of the land and sea and variations in sediment supply have produced a great diversity of coastal landscapes; and climate change has been accompanied by major variations in the types and patterns of vegetation. More recent changes at the coastline, in river channel positions and in slope mass movements reflect the continuing geomorphological evolution of the landscape today.

This geological diversity is of great scientific value in the study of modern Earth science. It also has a profound influence upon Scotland's natural heritage and is the foundation for many aspects of its landscapes, soils, habitats, species, land use and recreation. This chapter reviews the conservation value of Scotland's Earth heritage. It examines the impacts of human activities, with a focus on positive approaches to resolving problems. Some key issues for the future are also identified.

9.2 Scotland's Earth heritage

9.2.1 Scientific value

The science of geology was born in Scotland 200 years ago when James Hutton investigated the rocks around Edinburgh and further afield (McIntyre and McKirdy, 1997). His discoveries paved the way for the work of a long line of distinguished Scottish geologists, including John Playfair, Charles Lyell, Roderick Murchison, Hugh Miller, John Horne, Benjamin Peach, Archibald Geikie and James Geikie, who accomplished significant pioneering work in the science. Many of the fundamental principles of Earth science have been developed in Scotland and applied worldwide.

Today, Scotland's rocks and landforms constitute a key resource of national and international importance for studies in metamorphic, structural and volcanic processes, mountain building, plate movements and ice age processes (Table 9.1). Areas such as the North-West Highlands, Glen Coe, Rum and Arthur's Seat in Edinburgh have all provided crucial evidence for interpreting past geological processes of global significance. In the North-West Highlands and Western Isles, the work of Sutton and Watson (1951) on the

Table 9.1 Importance of the geology, geomorphology and soils of Scotland.

- geological diversity - reflecting length of the geological record, plate tectonics and palaeogeographies, palaeoenvironments and geological processes;

- Scotland's role in the history of geology;

- understanding past geological processes (volcanism, crustal deformation) and modern applications;

- records of palaeoenvironmental conditions, palaeogeography and structural evolution preserved in sedimentary rock formations covering the last billion years;

- rich and diverse fossil record that spans crucial moments in evolution;

- ice age environmental change and landscape modification;

- postglacial and contemporary geomorphological processes, including soil formation.

Lewisian Complex laid much of the groundwork for unravelling the geological history of poly-deformed gneissic terrains. Peach *et al.* (1907) first described the Moine Thrust (Plate 6), the most famous of the major Caledonian structures, and its significance for large-scale, higher level crustal deformation. Geological mapping of the Glen Coe area, early in the 20th century, revealed volcanic rocks of Devonian age attributable to cauldron subsidence, the first example of this type of volcanicity to be identified and described in the geological record (Clough *et al.*, 1909). The Tertiary volcanic geology of Rum (Plate 3) has yielded much information on the processes taking place in the environment of the magma chamber, with the development of theories relating to the origin of layering in igneous rocks (e.g. Wager and Brown, 1968). The Arthur's Seat volcanic complex (Plate 2) provided key evidence supporting the theories of James Hutton, which laid the foundations for the development of modern geology. Arthur's Seat is still regarded as perhaps the best example on Earth of a dissected ancient volcanic cone.

Scotland's rocks also provide outstanding records of palaeoenvironmental conditions, palaeogeography and structural evolution preserved in sedimentary rock formations covering the last billion years. For example, at Cailleach Head in Sutherland, a section through the youngest sediments of the Torridonian sandstone represents the best example of cyclothemic sedimentation in Britain (Craig, 1991). These 800 million year old sediments comprise around 20 sedimentary units of lake-bed shales and silts, interspersed with alluvial fan deposits.

Equally, Scotland's fossil heritage (Plates 7 and 8) has had a crucial role in studies of the evolution of the plant and animal kingdoms. Although more than half of Scotland's area is underlain by igneous and metamorphic rocks, the remaining sedimentary rocks, especially the Palaeozoic and Jurassic sequences, contain rich fossil assemblages of immense diversity, some of which are unique. These have yielded the world's oldest known vertebrate (Dineley and Metcalf, 1999), a rich diversity of early amphibian remains (Milner and Sequeria, 1993), the oldest known example of an *in situ* fossilised terrestrial ecosystem, in the form of the Rhynie Chert (Cleal and Thomas, 1995), and some of the earliest mammal remains (Waldman and Savage, 1972). The variety and richness of the fossil heritage reflects the many biofacies and types of preservation that have arisen during the country's long and varied geological history. The ecology, environmental controls and tectonic settings of fossil biotas are receiving increasing attention (Clarkson, 1985). Not only is this work fundamental in dating rock sequences and correlation with rock sequences world-wide, it allows the development of palaeogeographic, palaeoenvironmental and palaeoecological models stretching back more than 600 million years. Scotland is also of great importance in the history and development of palaeontology through the work and publications, for example, of Louis Agassiz and Hugh Miller on the fossil fishes of the Old Red Sandstone (Agassiz, 1835; Miller, 1840).

Evidence from Scotland is crucial for studies of the Quaternary ice ages. Scotland lies at the maritime fringe of NW Europe, in a region that is climatically sensitive due to its proximity to the atmospheric and marine polar fronts and the North Atlantic Drift. The diverse landform and depositional records of Scotland and the adjacent continental shelves are potentially of great value for understanding the coupling of the atmosphere, oceans, ice sheets and biosphere during periods of rapid climate change in this region (Gordon and Sutherland, 1993). In particular, there is the opportunity to link terrestrial and offshore evidence with the high resolution Greenland ice core and deep-sea records. The wealth of information relating to the period following the Last Glacial Maximum and the termination of the last glacial cycle, a time of remarkably rapid environmental change (Boulton, this volume), now provides unprecedented opportunities to reconstruct climate change and the sensitivity of geomorphological and biological systems, as reflected in glacier dynamics, sea-level fluctuations (Plate 10) and changes in terrestrial and marine biota (Walker and Lowe, 1997).

Palaeoenvironmental records preserved in loch and bog sediments are important in setting current environmental changes into a longer term context (e.g. Edwards and Whittington, 1997). From these records it is possible to understand how climate, physical processes and habitats have changed in the past and to provide baselines for predicted future changes. For example, such records should allow an assessment of the extent to which predicted changes arising from global warming are likely to lie within the range of natural changes that have occurred within the Holocene, or to what extent significant thresholds are likely to be crossed, which may have economic and social costs as well as environmental implications through increased frequency of storm events or flooding.

Many sites in Scotland are therefore of great importance to Earth science for their rocks, fossils and landforms, demonstrating important geological processes or events. This importance is reflected in the system of protected sites that has been established following the Geological Conservation Review (GCR), which identified the key sites for geology and geomorphology in Great Britain (Ellis *et al.*, 1996; Goodenough *et al.*, this volume). There are over 800 GCR site interests in Scotland (Table 9.2). Because of overlaps, these are encapsulated in some 500 SSSIs which are accorded statutory protection. Scientific results of the GCR are being published in a series of 42 volumes by the Joint Nature Conservation Committee (Ellis *et al.*, 1996). Although soils were not considered in the GCR, representative examples of most of the important soils types in Scotland occur in existing SSSIs (Gauld and Bell, 1997).

Table 9.2 Summary of GCR sites in Scotland.

Subject areas	*Sites*
Stratigraphy	135
Structural & Metamorphic	193
Igneous Petrology	162
Mineralogy	47
Palaeontology	84
Quaternary	136
Geomorphology	77
Total	834

9.2.2 Wider Values

There are many wider benefits beyond scientific research which follow from conserving our Earth heritage. The great variations in Scotland's rocks, landforms and soils have given rise to an equally varied biodiversity. At a broad scale, the distribution of uplands and lowlands, open coasts and estuaries, and rivers and lochs has contributed to the overall diversity of habitats. At a local level, soils reflect variations in rocks and glacial materials, as well as the slope and drainage of the landforms on which they occur. Internationally important habitats owe their origins and continued existence to physical processes; for example, wintering sites for geese on the saltmarshes and mudflats of the Solway estuary and the Montrose Basin; the unique machair habitats of the Western Isles; and the arctic-alpine vegetation of the Cairngorms.

Natural change is a feature of many of these habitats. At the coast, sediment circulation and patterns of wind and waves determine the changing locus of coastal erosion or the growth of sand dunes; for example, at Tentsmuir Point in Fife, the coastal edge has advanced seaward by up to 500 m since AD1812, providing valuable dune and links habitat (McManus and Wal, 1996). Habitat condition and stability can depend on maintaining geomorphological processes. Some landscapes are relatively stable and respond only to infrequent large events such as floods, whereas others respond more sensitively; for example in the uplands, wind and water erosion may reduce soil stability, leading to stripping of vegetation cover, loss of soil and changes in vegetation succession. Understanding the sensitivity of the landscape is vital to developing appropriate management strategies for the more dynamic habitats in the uplands, along rivers and at the coast.

Sites demonstrating key features of geology, geomorphology and soils are important not only for the training of professional scientists, but also have great potential for education at school level. The great diversity of Scotland's Earth heritage is reflected in the diversity of its landscapes and spectacular scenery. This geological legacy is evident at many levels; for example at a regional level in the contrast between the Precambrian landscapes of North-West Scotland and those of the Cairngorms, and at a local level within the Cairngorms in the landform and habitat variations from arctic plateau and corries to the complex pattern of glacial channels, deposits and kettle holes on the lower slopes. Such scenery also provides the basis for Scotland's tourist industry and for a range of recreation and leisure activities. There are many opportunities for developing Earth heritage interpretation and the links with cultural and industrial heritage (McKirdy *et al.*, this volume; McKeever and Gallagher, this volume). Even within Scotland's cities there are close links between urban landscapes and Earth heritage, for example in the volcanic features of Edinburgh (Plate 1) , the drumlin field in Glasgow and the use of local building stone.

Geology, geomorphology and soils are thus an integral part of the natural heritage. Not only is there a close link with landscape and scenery, there are also many dynamic links between physical processes and habitats. These links emphasise the need to consider the whole natural heritage in conservation management. Safeguarding the Earth heritage is one means to help maintain the diversity of habitats and the species they support. Equally, by understanding better the physical processes in the landscape, we will be better able to secure the sustainable management of these habitats.

9.3 State of the Earth heritage

9.3.1 State of the resource

The GCR process has involved assessment of the scientific interests of key sites and publication of descriptions of those interests. The more practical aspects of site documentation relating to management and monitoring have been undertaken separately as part of SNH's Earth Science Site Documentation Programme (Goodenough *et al.*, this volume). The results will allow SNH staff, landowners and others to develop a clearer understanding of each site and its conservation requirements. They also provide a baseline inventory for assessing changes in site condition. This will be done through a site condition monitoring programme for all SSSIs, which is currently being implemented.

Systematic coverage of site-related information is largely confined to GCR sites. With some exceptions (Table 9.3), there is little standard documentation of information or survey on the condition of other sites, areas which provide the context for the GCR site networks, or the wider landscape. At present, therefore, it is difficult to draw clear conclusions about trends in the state of the wider resource (e.g. in the extent of loss of glacial landforms through sand and gravel quarrying or the loss of palaeoenvironmental records through reclamation of lowland wetlands). Similarly, there is a lack of systematic long-term monitoring (e.g. at benchmark sites) of current changes and trends in dynamic systems such as beaches, river channels and slope mass movements.

Table 9.3. Summary of knowledge of the state of the resource.

Subject area	Knowledge	State and Quality
Geology and Palaeontology	• well covered by BGS (maps and memoirs) and in journal articles and theses	• systematic information on state and quality and any changes (e.g. degradation of exposures) is limited to GCR sites • site condition monitoring confined to SSSIs
Geomorphology	• no systematic national survey of geomorphology, comparable to geological and soils mapping; exceptions are beaches survey and (partial) landslides survey • systematic knowledge of process systems is patchy (e.g. sediment transport); coastal cells work provides useful starting point on the coast • knowledge of magnitude, rate and frequency of processes is limited to case studies	• systematic information on state and quality and any changes is limited to GCR sites • site condition monitoring confined to SSSIs
Soils	• physical aspects well covered at reconnaisance level (Soil Survey maps and memoirs; MLURI database), but updating required • poor knowledge of soil biology/biodiversity/biological functions	• information on acidification critical loads • no other systematic information on state and quality and any changes; very few monitoring studies undertaken, but no systematic framework for monitoring key indicators of quality or change

9.3.2 Pressures and impacts

The pressures and threats facing the Earth heritage are diverse but generated largely by development activities and land-use pressures (Table 9.4) at both site and wider landscape scales (Werritty and Brazier, 1991; Gordon and Campbell, 1992; Werritty *et al.*, 1994; Taylor, 1995; Lees *et al.*, 1998; McKirdy, in press). For example, these may arise through economic forces which determine the demand for minerals and changes in agri/forestry support measures which affect land use decisions. Other impacts may arise from the effects of global processes (e.g. climate change and sea-level rise) (e.g. Gordon *et al.*, 1998; Pethick, 1999). These can act directly through enhanced erosion of coastal or riverbank exposures, or indirectly through demands for coast protection or river management. The types of impact that can arise are physical damage, loss of visibility or access (Plate 12), fragmentation of the interest and loss of relationships between features, and interruption of natural processes. Wider off-site impacts on the natural heritage may also occur; for example, erosion downdrift of coastal defences (Lees *et al.*, 1998). The more dynamic elements of the landscape are also subject to natural perturbations of varying frequency and magnitude, which produce responses in the landforms and sediments (e.g. floods, landslides, soil erosion). It is generally not easy to decouple the effects of natural change and human impacts (Ballantyne, 1991).

In considering the state of the resource and its changes, it is important to distinguish between integrity and exposure sites (Ellis *et al.*, 1996). Integrity sites include finite or relict interests (e.g. fossil beds or glacial landforms) which, if damaged or destroyed, cannot be reinstated or recreated since the formative processes are no longer active. Exposure sites include rock units which are spatially extensive and for which a number of potentially representative sites exist or could be created by excavation. Geomorphological sensitivity is an important concept in evaluating the response of active systems to external disturbance (Werritty and Brazier, 1994; Werritty and Leys, 2001). Systems may be regarded as 'robust' where current processes are able to absorb the impact or self-repair in a relatively short time period through feedback mechanisms and continued operation of the processes (e.g. the re-formation of a gravel bar following a flood). In sensitive (or responsive) systems, a fundamental change in the nature and rate of the landforming processes occurs (e.g. deflation of soil cover following break up of surface vegetation).

9.3.2.1 Mineral extraction

Mineral extraction can have positive and negative impacts. On the positive side, many key sites are in former quarries where the geological interest would not otherwise have been exposed; for example at Boyne Limestone Quarry, near Banff, stripping of the overburden has revealed important sections in Quaternary deposits. The main negative impacts tend to be on integrity interests which cannot be replaced; for example the removal of an esker through sand and gravel quarrying. While there are benefits in terms of being able to examine the sedimentary architecture of the deposits, these are offset by the permanent loss of the landforms. A more systematic approach, involving inventories and conservation assessment of the value of different components of the Earth science resource at a regional scale, would allow the more important sites to be given appropriate recognition along with other conservation interests in strategic minerals planning. A start has been made by SNH in developing a GIS-based approach to evaluating the sensitivity of different components of

Table 9.4 Pressures on the Earth heritage.

Pressure	Examples of on-site impacts	Examples of off-site impacts
1. Mineral extraction (includes pits, quarries, dunes and beaches)	- destruction of landforms and sediment records - destruction of soils, soil structure and soil biota - may have positive benefits in creating new sedimentary sections - soil contamination - loss of soil structure during storage	- contamination of watercourses - changes in sediment supply to active process systems; extraction from rivers, leading to deposition or channel scour - disruption of drainage network (impacts on runoff) - dust (may affect soil pH)
2. Restoration of pits and quarries	- loss of exposures - loss of natural landform - habitat creation	
3. Landfill	- loss of sedimentary exposures - loss of natural landform; soil disturbance - detrimental effects of gases and other decomposition products on soils and soil biotas	- contamination of water courses - contamination of groundwater - redistribution of waste on beach/dune systems - leakage of contaminants to water courses or ground water
4. Reclamation of contaminated land	- improvement of soil quality	
5. Commercial and industrial developments	- large scale damage and disruption/loss of surface and sub-surface features, including landforms and soils - soil contamination - damage to soil structure - changes to soil water regime - loss of soil biota	- changes to geomorphological processes downstream, arising from channelisation or water abstraction - leakage of contaminants to water courses or groundwater
6. Coast protection	- loss of coastal exposures - destruction of active and relict landforms - disruption of natural processes	- changes to sediment circulation and processes downdrift
7. River management and engineering	- loss of exposures - destruction of active and relict landforms - disruption of natural processes	- changes to sediment movement and processes downstream - change in process regime
8. Afforestation	- loss of landform and outcrop visibility - physical damage to small scale landforms - stabilisation of dynamic landforms (e.g. sand dunes) - soil erosion - changes to soil chemistry and soil water regime - changes to soil biodiversity	- increase in sediment yield and speed of runoff from catchments during planting and harvesting - changes to ground water and surface water chemistry

Table 9.4 (*continued*)

Pressure	Examples of on-site impacts	Examples of off-site impacts
9. Agriculture	- landform damage through ploughing, ground levelling and drainage - soil compaction, loss of organic matter, reduction in biodiversity - effects of excess fertiliser applications on soil chemistry and biodiversity; changes to nutrient status - effects of pesticides on soil biodiversity - soil erosion	- changes in runoff response times arising from drainage - episodic soil erosion, leading to increased sedimentation and chemical contamination in lochs and river systems - pollution of groundwater
10. Other land management changes (e.g. drainage, dumping, construction of tracks)	- degradation of exposures and landforms - oxidation of soil organic material - changes to soil water regime - soil contamination	- changes in runoff and sediment supply - drying out of wetlands through local and distal drainage
11. Recreation (infrastructure, footpath development, use of all-terrain vehicles)	- physical damage to small-scale landforms and soils (compaction) - localised soil erosion - loss of soil organic matter	
12. Irresponsible fossil collecting	- loss of fossil record	
13. Soil pollution	- acidification of soils - accumulation of heavy metals - effects on soil biodiversity	- downstream impacts on watercourses - contamination of groundwater
14. Soil erosion	- deterioration of landforms - loss of organic matter	- enhanced sedimentation in streams and lochs - changes in water chemistry
15. Climate change	- changes in active system processes - changes in system state (reactivation or fossilisation)	- changes in flood frequency - changes in sensitivity of landforming environments (e.g. rivers, coasts), leading to changes in types and rates of geomorphological processes (e.g. erosion, flooding)
16. Sea-level rise	- changes in coastal exposures and landforms - enhanced flooding	- changes in wider patterns of erosion and deposition

the natural heritage to mineral extraction in the Midland Valley where development pressures are greatest (Scottish Natural Heritage, 2000).

9.3.2.2 Landfill and restoration of quarries

Quarries represent a significant geological resource. Planning conditions normally require restoration and landscaping, and frequently involve landfill. The economic value of landfill space frequently results in the loss of geological exposures. Much earlier dialogue between interested parties (e.g. quarry operators, local authorities, academics, and the conservation bodies) would help to ensure that, where practical, geological interests are incorporated into restoration schemes. This applies equally to sites of local importance, representing a resource for education and interpretation which could be developed through the Regionally Important Geological/Geomorphological Sites (RIGS) programme. Securing the geological interest in this way could form an integral part of a wider package of enhancement measures for restoration of mineral sites following the kind of guidance produced recently for England (English Nature *et al.*, 1999). Planning sustainable management of after-use through such partnerships can create opportunities for Earth heritage interpretation, habitat enhancement, contributions to Local Biodiversity Action Plans (LBAPs) and recreation.

9.3.2.3 River engineering

Dynamic river systems are a key part of the natural heritage both for the study of physical processes and for the habitats they provide (Soulsby and Boon, this volume; Leys, this volume). Traditional approaches to river management have often involved heavy engineering, usually leading to channelisation of the river through the use of rock armour or gabions. Such approaches not only constrain the natural dynamics of the river system, but can also damage river bank and in-channel species, as well as the habitats they support (Leys, this volume; Soulsby and Boon, this volume). From a conservation viewpoint, they should be restricted to protecting essential utilities, buildings and infrastructure. Elsewhere, alternative forms of river management are more appropriate. A range of methods has been identified for Scottish gravel-bed rivers and appropriate general guidance published (Hoey *et al.*, 1998). At a more strategic level, National Planning Policy Guideline (NPPG) 7 (The Scottish Office, 1995) provides national policy guidelines for mitigating the impact of floods through control of development on floodplains.

9.3.2.4 Coast protection

In the past, coast protection has typically involved a similar heavy engineering approach. This leads to well known effects, notably interruption of sediment supply and enhanced erosion downdrift, affecting both landform systems and habitats. In recent years, a fundamental shift in thinking in the UK, particularly in England, has led to solutions that are more in harmony with natural processes (e.g. Pethick and Burd, 1995; Hooke, 1998, 1999). Such approaches are now being considered and followed in Scotland. Several local authorities, including Fife, Angus and Aberdeen City Councils, have undertaken strategic studies that include assessment of environmental impacts and alternative solutions prior to embarking on coast protection. Crucially, such studies are undertaken at an appropriate scale that incorporates the natural dynamics of the whole coastal system or coastal cell concerned. Consequently, possible wider adverse effects can be predicted, areas of conflict identified and recommendations made on how more integrated management should be progressed. Such studies have been undertaken at Montrose Bay and Aberdeen Bay (Halcrow Crouch, 1998, 1999).

Serious consideration is also being given to alternative forms of coast defence, both on environmental and cost grounds. These include managed retreat (e.g. Hansom *et al.*, this volume) and beach recharge and dune re-profiling (HR Wallingford, 2000). For example, at Montrose, a policy of managed retreat between artificial rock headlands has already been adopted for the dunes fronting a golf course, where a shift in wind patterns has led to enhanced erosion (Plate 21). Installation of hard coast protection, which would have impacted significantly on dune systems downdrift if the sediment supply was reduced, was rejected on grounds of costs and environmental impacts. At Gairloch, a combination of sand fencing, dune reprofiling, dune grass planting and recycling of sand from the foreshore has successfully halted rapid erosion of the dune ridge behind the beach and has helped to maintain the natural landform and habitat, which would not have been the case had hard defences been employed (Lees *et al.*, 1998).

9.3.2.5 Fossil collecting

Irresponsible fossil collecting has been a problem at many palaeontological and stratigraphic sites. Mechanical excavators, explosives, crow bars and rock saws have all been used to excavate and remove fossil material, which has resulted in the destruction and loss of irreplaceable specimens and rock exposure (Plates 13 and 14). A major concern is a loop hole in the 1981 Wildlife and Countryside Act, which allows no control on third-party activity on protected sites.

MacFadyen (1999) outlined the current situation and future aspirations concerning conservation of the fossil heritage in Scotland. The consensus opinion is that responsible fossil collecting can promote the science of palaeontology and should be encouraged, with emphasis on the *Code of Good Practice*. The role of commercial collectors in conserving the fossil heritage is also recognised. Commercial collectors are encouraged to work with palaeontological specialists and museum curators so that every opportunity is taken to maximise the scientific gain from their collecting and to guarantee that material goes to a suitable repository. Although, the consensus view is that the total prohibition of collecting at any site is unjustified (Wimbledon, 1988), a set of measures is being developed in Scotland to regulate collecting at the small number of very vulnerable fossil sites where there is a limited resource of high scientific and heritage value (MacFadyen, 1999). Collaboration and partnerships involving academics, collectors, museums, landowners and others with a stake in conserving the fossil heritage will be important in implementing such measures.

9.4 Key issues

Site protection and management, although fundamental, are only one strand in Earth heritage conservation (Gordon and Leys, this volume). There is a need for much wider recognition of the inter-dependencies of habitats and species on geology, geomorphology and soils to enable the development of integrated strategies and policies for sustainable management at a zonal scale (Mitchell, this volume) and in National Parks, integrated catchment management and shoreline management planning. Equally, there is a requirement for the development of alternative, less interventionist approaches to the management of sensitive coasts, rivers, and upland areas, based on an understanding of physical processes. The type of approach being developed in relation to coastal management (e.g. application of coastal cells in preparation of shoreline management plans) provides an important pointer for the future. Proposals for a national soil protection strategy will provide a more integrated approach to safeguard the interests of semi-natural soils and the vast, but largely unknown, biodiversity which they host (Puri *et al.*, this volume). At a local level there are also new opportunities for Earth heritage to be given a much higher profile through the RIGS initiative and LBAPs (Leys, this volume).

Geology and geomorphology contribute significantly to the understanding of the modern landscape, not just its origins but also the manner in which it continues to change. This has important implications for planning and sustainable land management; for example in relation to land stability, coastal erosion, river flooding, soil erosion and management of valued habitats. Understanding the physical environment and the sensitivity of geomorphological processes is a key part of sustainable management of land and water resources. There is a need to adopt new approaches that are more sustainable and that work with natural processes rather than against them. For example, the disruption of sediment supply through inappropriately sited coastal defence works or river bank protection may convert a local erosion problem into a more widespread one along the coast or downriver.

Natural change is a feature of many habitats. For example, at the coast, sediment circulation patterns and patterns of wind and waves determine the changing locus of coastal erosion or the growth of sand dunes. Habitat condition and stability can thus depend on maintaining geomorphological processes. Some landscapes are relatively stable and respond only to infrequent large events such as floods; others respond more sensitively - for example in the uplands, wind and water erosion may reduce soil stability, leading to stripping of vegetation cover, loss of soil and changes in vegetation succession. Understanding the sensitivity of the landscape is thus vital in developing appropriate management strategies for more dynamic habitats in the uplands, along rivers and at the coast.

Crucially, there is a need to raise awareness of the benefits of working with natural systems among key interest groups and their advisors (Crofts, this volume). To some extent, this is already taking place place, for example through the Forth Estuary Forum and in the development of pilot Shoreline Management Plans in Fife and parts of the Moray Firth coast; the latter represent important strategy documents for the management of coastal erosion based on an understanding of the natural processes at work on these coastlines. In relation to rivers, partnership approaches are now in place that are working towards integrated catchment management for the Tweed and Spey (Leys, this volume). However, more remains to be done to promote and demonstrate the long-term benefits of such approaches .

Finally, there is still a need for greater public awareness and involvement. Although the academic sector is generally well informed about the value of Earth heritage conservation, wider public awareness and appreciation remain much lower. Scottish Geology Week, development of the Knockan Centre and various publications (McKirdy *et al.*, this volume) are good examples of what can be done to raise awareness. However, there are many more opportunities to promote education and tourism based on our Earth heritage and its links with landscapes, habitats and the industrial and built heritage, particularly at a local level and involving joint ventures between local authorities, tourist boards and RIGS Groups.

9.5 Conclusion

The scientific, cultural and landscape importance of Scotland's Earth heritage is firmly established. At one level, there is a responsibility to future generations to ensure that the best sites and features continue to be protected and monitored. However, Earth heritage conservation is not merely about site protection, but has much wider value and relevance. Geology, geomorphology and soils are an integral part of the natural heritage. Not only is there a close link with landscape and scenery, there are also many dynamic links between physical processes and habitats. These links emphasise the need to consider the whole natural heritage in conservation management. Safeguarding the Earth heritage is one means to help maintain the diversity of habitats and the species they support. Equally, by understanding better the physical processes in the landscape, we will be better able to secure the sustainable management of these habitats.

Better public understanding, awareness and involvement are crucial, particularly within a wider framework of integrated management. Emphasis on such management in river catchments, at the coast, in Natural Heritage Zones and in the proposed National Parks will promote sustainable management of the Earth heritage and demonstrate the value of applying existing knowledge about physical processes. The development of existing and new partnerships will be fundamental. There is particularly a need to encourage greater involvement at a local level through LBAPs and RIGS.

Acknowledgements

We thank Ed Mackey for comments on the text.

References

Agassiz, J.L.R. 1835. On the fossil fishes of Scotland. *Report of the British Association for the Advancement of Science*, No. 4, 646-649.

Ballantyne, C.K. 1991. Late Holocene erosion in upland Britain: climatic deterioration or human influence? *The Holocene*, **1**, 81-42.

Clarkson, E.N.K. 1985. A brief history of Scottish palaeontology. *Scottish Journal of Geology*, **21**, 389-406.

Cleal, C.J. and Thomas, B.A. 1995. *Palaeozoic Palaeobotany of Great Britain*. Geological Conservation Review Series, No. 9. Joint Nature Conservation Committee, Peterborough.

Clough, C.T., Maufe, H.B. and Bailey, E.B. 1909. The cauldron-subsidence of Glencoe and associated igneous phenomena. *Quarterly Journal of the Geological Society of London*, **65**, 611- 676.

Craig, G.Y. 1991. (ed.) *Geology of Scotland*. The Geological Society, London.

Dineley, D.L. and Metcalf, S.J. 1999. *Fossil Fishes of Great Britain*. Geological Conservation Review Series, No. 16. Joint Nature Conservation Committee, Peterborough.

Edwards, K.J. and Whittington, G. (1997) Vegetation change. *In* Edwards, K.J. and Ralston, I.B.M. (eds) *Scotland. Environment and Archaeology, 8000BC-AD1000*. Wiley, Chichester, 62-82.

Ellis, N.V., Bowen, D.Q., Campbell, S., Knill, J.L., McKirdy, A.P., Prosser, C.D., Vincent, M.A. and Wilson, R.C.L. 1996. *An Introduction to the Geological Conservation Review*. Joint Nature Conservation Committee, Peterborough.

English Nature, Quarry Products Association and Silica & Moulding Sands Association 1999. *Biodiversity and Minerals. Extracting the Benefits for Wildlife*. Entec UK Ltd.

Gauld, J.H. and Bell, J.S. 1997. Soils and nature conservation in Scotland. *Scottish Natural Heritage Review,* No. 62.

Gordon, J.E. (ed.) 1997. *Reflections on the Ice Age in Scotland: Recent Advances in Quaternary Studies.* Scottish Association of Geography Teachers and Scottish Natural Heritage, Glasgow.

Gordon, J.E. and Campbell, S. 1992. Conservation of glacial deposits in Great Britain: a framework for assessment and protection of Sites of Special Scientific Interest. *Geomorphology,* **6**, 89-97.

Gordon, J.E., and Sutherland, D.G. (eds) 1993: *Quatenary of Scotland.* Geological Conservation Review Series, No.6. Chapman and Hall, London.

Gordon, J.E., Thompson, D.B.A., Haynes, V.M., MacDonald, R. and Brazier V. 1998. Environmental sensitivity and conservation management in the Cairngorm Mountains, Scotland. *Ambio,* **27**, 335-344.

Hooke, J. (ed.) 1998. *Coastal Defence and Earth Science Conservation.* The Geological Society, London.

Hooke, J. 1999. Decades of change: contributions of geomorphology to fluvial and coastal engineering and management. *Geomorphology,* **31**, 373-389.

Halcrow Crouch 1998. Montrose Bay Shoreline Management Study. Unpublished report to Angus Council and Glaxo Wellcome (2 vols).

Halcrow Crouch 1999. Aberdeen Bay Coastal Protection Study. Final Report. Unpublished report to Aberdeen City Council, Scottish Natural Heritage and Grampian Enterprise.

Hoey, T.B., Smart, D.W.J., Pender, G. and Metcalfe, N. 1998. Engineering methods for Scottish gravel bed rivers. *Scottish Natural Heritage Research, Survey and Monitoring Report,* No. 47.

HR Wallingford 2000. *A Guide to Managing Coastal Erosion in Beach/Dune Systems.* Scottish Natural Heritage, Perth.

Lees, R.G., Gordon, J.E. and McKirdy, A.P. 1998. Coastal erosion, coastal defences and the Earth heritage in Scotland. *In* Hooke, J. (ed) *Coastal Defence and Earth Science Conservation.* The Geological Society, London, 133-150.

MacFadyen, C.C.J. 1999. Fossil collecting in Scotland. *SNH Information and Advisory Note,* No. 110. Scottish Natural Heritage, Battleby.

McIntyrc, D.B. and McKirdy, A.P. 1997. *James Hutton - The Founder of Modern Geology.* The Stationery Office, Edinburgh.

McKirdy, A.P. in press. Environmental geology. *In* Trewin, N.H. (ed.) *Geology of Scotland.* 4th edition.

McManus, J. and Wal, A. 1996. Sediment accumulation mechanisms on the Tentsmuir coast. *In* Whittington, G. (ed.) *Fragile Environments: the Use and Management of Tentsmuir National Nature Reserve, Fife.* Scottish Cultural Press, Edinburgh, 1-15.

Miller, H. 1840. The Old Red Sandstone. *The Witness,* series of seven articles on 9, 12 and 16 September, and 3, 10, 14 and 17 October, 1840.

Milner, A.R. and Sequeira, S.E.K. 1994. The temnospondyl amphibians from the Visean of East Kirkton, West Lothian, Scotland. *Transactions of the Royal Scociety of Edinburgh: Earth Sciences,* **84**, 331-361.

Mitchell, C. 1997. The geology of Scotland. *In* Gordon, J.E. (ed.) *Reflections on the Ice Age in Scotland. An Update on Quaternary Studies.* Scottish Association of Geography Teachers and Scottish Natural Heritage, Glasgow, 15-30.

Peach, B.N., Horne, J., Gunn, W., Clough, C.T., Hinxman, L.W. and Teall, J.J.H. 1907. *The Geological Structure of the North-West Highlands of Scotland.* Memoir of the Geological Survey of Great Britain. HMSO, Glasgow.

Pethick, J. 1999. Future sea-level changes in Scotland: options for coastal management. *In* Baxter, J.M., Duncan, K., Atkins, S.M. and Lees, R.G. (eds) *Scotland's Living Coastline.* The Stationery Office, London, 45-62.

Pethick, J. and Burd, F. 1995. *Coastal Defence and the Environment. A Guide to Good Practice.* Ministry of Agriculture Fisheries and Food, London.

Scottish Natural Heritage 2000. *Minerals and the Natural Heritage in Scotland's Midland Valley.* Scottish Natural Heritage, Perth.

Sutton, J. and Watson, J. 1951. The pre-Torridonian metamorphic history of the Loch Torridon and Scourie areas in the North-west Highlands and its bearing on the chronological classification of the Lewisian. *Quarterly Journal of the Geological Society of London,* **106**, 241-307.

Taylor, A. (ed.) 1995. Environmental problems associated with soil in Britain. *Scottish Natural Heritage Review,* No. 55.

The Scottish Office 1995. *Planning and Flooding. National Planning Policy Guideline NPPG 7.* The Scottish Office, Development Department, Edinburgh.

Wager, L.R. and Brown, G.M. 1968. *Layered Igneous Rocks.* Oliver and Boyd, Edinburgh.

Waldman, M. and Savage, R.J.G. 1972. The first Jurassic mammal from Scotland. *Journal of the Geological Society,* **128**, 119-125.

Walker, M.J.C. and Lowe, J.J. 1997. Vegetation and climate in Scotland, 13,000 to 7000 radiocarbon years ago. *In* Gordon, J.E. (ed.) *Reflections on the Ice Age in Scotland. An Update on Quaternary Studies.* Scottish Association of Geography Teachers and Scottish Natural Heritage, Glasgow, 105-115.

Werritty, A. and Brazier, V. 1994. Geomorphic sensitivity and the conservation of fluvial geomorphology SSSIs. *In* Stevens, C., Gordon, J.E., Green C.P. and Macklin, M. (eds) *Conserving our Landscape.* Proceedings of the Conference, Conserving Our Landscape: Evolving Landforms and Ice-Age Heritage, Crewe, 1992. Peterborough, 100-109.

Werritty A. and Leys, K.F. 2001. The sensitivity of Scottish rivers and upland valley floors to recent environmental change. *Catena,* **42**, 251-274.

Werritty, A., Brazier, V., Gordon, J.E. and McManus, J. 1994. The freshwater resources of Scotland: a geomorphological perspective. *In* Maitland, P.S., Boon, P.J. and McLusky, D.S. (eds) *The Freshwaters of Scotland: a National Resource of International Significance.* John Wiley, Chichester, 65-88.

Wimbledon, W.A. 1988. Palaeontological site conservation in Britain: facts, form, function and efficacy. *In* Crowther, P.R. and Wimbledon, W.A. (eds) *The Use and Conservation of Palaeontological Sites. Special Papers in Palaeontology,* No. 40, 40-54.

10 PROTECTING THE BEST: CONSERVING EARTH HERITAGE SITES IN SCOTLAND

Kathryn M. Goodenough, Colin C.J. MacFadyen and Fiona Mactaggart

Summary

1. The geological diversity of Scotland forms a crucial resource for Earth science education and research.
2. A network of sites was selected for the Geological Conservation Review to represent this diversity and provides the basis of statutory Earth science conservation in Scotland.
3. Improved awareness and education are crucial, in addition to statutory protection, in the conservation of Scotland's Earth heritage.

10.1 Scotland's Earth heritage

For a small country, Scotland contains an exceptionally rich variety of Earth heritage features. The geological record begins with the oldest rocks in Europe, over 3000 million years old, and includes evidence for the appearance and disappearance of ancient seas, deserts and mountain chains as Scotland moved across the Earth's surface. Relict geomorphological features record in detail the palaeoenvironments and palaeogeography of Scotland since the retreat of the last ice sheet began around 15,000 years ago, whilst dynamic systems such as rivers and coasts are still developing and changing at the present day. All these features are crucial for Earth science education and research. In addition, many Earth science localities in Scotland are also important for historical reasons - much of the present-day understanding of Earth science was first developed through geological study in Scotland. Clearly, conservation and management of all the aspects of Scotland's Earth heritage requires many differing approaches. This paper discusses one approach - the establishment of a network of key Earth science sites through the Geological Conservation Review.

10.2 The Geological Conservation Review

Between 1977 and 1990, a series of 834 localities in Scotland was identified in a systematic site selection process, the Geological Conservation Review (GCR), conducted across the whole of Great Britain (Ellis *et al.*, 1996). These localities, which are known as GCR sites, make up a network which represents all the key features of Scotland's Earth heritage. The GCR network now forms the basis of statutory Earth science conservation in Britain.

The GCR sites were selected according to firm criteria, with each site falling into at least one of three categories:

1. sites of international importance for research. These include global reference sites for boundaries or biozones, such as Dob's Linn; internationally significant type localities for particular rock types or mineral and fossil species, such as East Kirkton Quarry; and historically significant type localities where important Earth science processes or features were first described, such as Siccar Point and Glencoe.
2. sites containing exceptional features. Sites within this category, such as the Rhynie Chert and the Parallel Roads of Glen Roy (Plate 9), have features which are unique or rare within Britain. These sites form the highlights of Scotland's Earth heritage.
3. networks of sites which are representative of features, events and processes that are crucial to our understanding of the geological history of Britain. Examples include representative sites for Quaternary stratigraphy (Gordon and Sutherland, 1993) or Caledonian igneous rocks (Stephenson *et al.*, 1999).

All the GCR sites in Scotland fall into one of 28 GCR 'blocks', with titles such as *Mineralogy of Scotland, Jurassic-Cretaceous Reptilia, Quaternary of Scotland* and *Fluvial Geomorphology*. The results of the GCR are being published in a set of 42 technical volumes which describe all the GCR sites in some detail. These volumes are intended to provide a public record of the features and localities of importance. Although aimed at those with some prior knowledge of Earth science, such as the professional and academic communities, students, teachers and amateur geologists, they will also be of value to local authority planners.

10.3 Threats to the Earth heritage

Although the need to take active measures to conserve our Earth heritage may not be obvious to all, a wide variety of threats exists. It is often forgotten that much of Scotland's Earth heritage is utterly irreplaceable; once a rare mineral vein, fossil bed or glacial landform is destroyed, it is lost forever.

Many types of large-scale development can affect Earth heritage sites (Nature Conservancy Council, 1990): landfill can permanently obscure sites of geological interest in quarries, old mines and caves; casual tipping of waste can obscure exposures (Plate 12); coastal defences can change the processes operating along a coastline, so that natural coastal landforms are destroyed and rock exposures obscured; and extraction of sand and gravel can completely destroy relict landforms. Smaller scale, but equally damaging, threats include irresponsible collecting of rare fossil and mineral specimens (Plates 13 and 14). Even developments which appear more 'environmentally friendly', such as tree-planting or landscaping of quarry sites, can locally impede access and reduce the visibility of key Earth science features, thus reducing the resource available for study or interpretation. On the positive side, however, some engineering works can produce new Earth heritage sites; the GCR network in Scotland includes quarries, road cuttings and dam spillways, all of which have provided superb new exposures of rocks and sediments. Examples of these include road cuttings along the A9 and the Quoich dam spillway in Lochaber.

10.4 Protecting and managing the Earth heritage

Many of Scotland's GCR sites have now been notified as Sites of Special Scientific Interest (SSSIs) and are therefore safeguarded through statutory planning procedures and the Wildlife and Countryside Act 1981. This means that SNH has some measure of control over potentially damaging operations within the sites.

In 1991, SNH instituted a project to provide clear, comprehensive documentation for all Earth science SSSIs in Scotland. This project has produced some 640 Site Documentation Reports which describe the geological or geomorphological features of each site in clear, simple language. Each report also includes a dossier of photographs which provide the baseline for future monitoring of the condition of the site. Associated with each report is a Site Management Statement which gives a practical prescription for the management and conservation of the site. The full set of Site Documentation reports for all Earth science SSSIs will be completed by the end of March 2001. These reports have a dual function: they enable SNH Area Officers to develop a clearer understanding of the interest of Earth science sites, and of the possible threats; and they also help raise awareness of the Earth heritage among landowners and land managers. Improved awareness of the significance of the GCR sites should mean a decrease in unintentional damage.

10.5 Earth Heritage conservation in the future

It is clear that, as demands on land and resources continue to increase, Scotland's Earth heritage will be put under even greater pressure. A combination of statutory protection and increased awareness is crucial to ensure the continued protection of Scotland's GCR sites. The fundamental requirement, however, is improved awareness and education: the greater the public understanding of the significance and relevance of our Earth heritage, the greater the support will be to conserve it. Education and interpretation should therefore be at the forefront in 'protecting the best' and conserving Scotland's Earth heritage.

References

Ellis, N.V., Bowen, D.Q., Campbell, S., Knill, J.L., McKirdy, A.P., Prosser, C.D., Vincent, M.A. and Wilson, R.C.L. 1996. *An Introduction to the Geological Conservation Review.* Geological Conservation Review Series, No. 1. Joint Nature Conservation Committee, Peterborough.

Gordon, J.E. and Sutherland, D.G. 1993. *Quaternary of Scotland.* Geological Conservation Review Series, No. 6. Chapman & Hall, London.

Nature Conservancy Council 1990. *Earth Science Conservation in Great Britain - A Strategy* and *Appendices - A Handbook of Earth Science Conservation Techniques.* Nature Conservancy Council, Peterborough.

Stephenson, D., Bevins, R.E., Millward, D. Highton, A.J., Parsons, I., Stone, P. and Wadsworth, W.J. 1999. *Caledonian Igneous Rocks of Great Britain.* Geological Conservation Review Series, No. 17. Joint Nature Conservation Committee, Peterborough.

11 Coastal Dynamics and Sustainable Management: the Potential for Managed Realignment in the Forth Estuary

*James D. Hansom, R. George Lees, John Maslen,
Cathy Tilbrook and John McManus*

Summary

1. Effective and sustainable coastal management initiatives rely on a clear understanding of the dynamics of coastal processes. This is particularly well illustrated in the application of managed realignment of the coast.

2. Approximately 50% of the former intertidal area of the Forth Estuary has been claimed for agriculture and development over approximately the last 400 years. The potential advantages of restoring some of this area to its former intertidal condition are discussed. These include not only benefits for nature conservation and estuarine functioning, but also for the management of ongoing and future sea-level rise.

3. Though many claimed areas in the Forth are unsuitable for managed realignment on account of current land uses, some are potentially suitable in terms of their physical settings and processes. The methodology used to identify such areas is presented, together with an assessment of the relative merits of pursuing managed realignment at each.

11.1 Introduction

There are few environments in Scotland where the need for understanding of geomorphological processes is as pressing and central to effective management as in the case of the coastline. This is partly on account of the extreme dynamism of many coastal environments and their capacity for rapid change, but also because of the concentration of development and diversity of activities that exist along an essentially linear boundary zone between land and sea.

The links between physical process and human response are particularly obvious in the fields of coastal protection, where an understanding of sediment transport pathways is crucial in the planning of sustainable defences, and in sediment extraction, where an understanding of the coastal sediment economy is crucial in determining whether sediment removal is in any way sustainable.

An understanding of the dynamism of coastal processes is no less important in areas such as:

- development control - where identification of areas susceptible to coastal flooding or erosion is central to sustainable coastal development;

- nature conservation - where an understanding of the scales of natural change within coastal habitats is essential to the identification of non-natural and potentially damaging changes; and

- climate change - where an understanding of how coastlines have developed throughout the Holocene is vital if we are to predict how they might change in the future as a consequence of sea-level rise and possible increases in storminess (see Hansom and Angus, this volume).

Since the mid-1990s, voluntary partnerships have been established within most of Scotland's firths to improve the management of the complex range of interests and concerns which exist within these areas. Virtually all of these fora have identified, as a fundamental issue, the need to understand the coastal processes affecting the areas concerned (Solway Firth Partnership 1996; Cromarty Firth Liaison Group, 1998; Forth Estuary Forum, 1999; Moray Firth Partnership, 1999).

11.2 Land claim and managed realignment

The fundamental linkage between coastal processes and coastal management is clearly illustrated within firths and estuaries where large expanses of low-lying land co-exist, often uneasily, with large-scale human development. In such areas, any future rises in sea level may have a major impact on the way in which the coast is managed.

It has long been recognised that large proportions of former inter-tidal mudflat or saltmarsh in UK estuaries have been claimed from the sea through the construction of flood embankments (Burd, 1995). The Firth of Forth is no exception (Cadell, 1929a, 1929b; Gostelowe and Browne, 1986; McClusky, 1987). In the Forth (Figure 11.1), the land enclosed by these embankments over the last four centuries has been mainly under

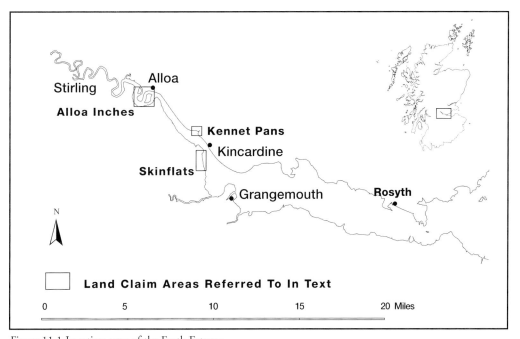

Figure 11.1 Location map of the Forth Estuary.

agricultural use but, in some locations, it has also been used for industry, housing and for industrial and domestic waste disposal.

Land claim such as this has many adverse consequences. Firstly, there is an initial loss of former intertidal mudflat and saltmarsh habitat, and the feeding resource which this provides for both birds and fish (McClusky, 1987). Secondly, land claim constrains the natural functioning of the estuary. It is now recognised that the intertidal mudflats and saltmarsh surfaces within estuaries perform a vital role in the attenuation of tidal energy (Knutson *et al.*, 1990). The tide is an exceptionally long-period wave similar to wind-waves, in that energy loss occurs as the wave shoals and traverses the intertidal slope, resulting in reductions in wave amplitude and, in consequence, maximum tidal level. Conversely, the removal of mudflat and saltmarsh from the intertidal profile by embankments results in the tidal amplitude being enhanced over its natural condition (Burd, 1995). Thirdly, land enclosed by embankments is no longer able to respond to enhanced tidal elevations and flooding by raising its surface level via the routine deposition of silt and mud. Embankments and defences prevent this, creating a progressively greater height difference between the landward surfaces, which lower as the sediment is subject to dewatering and compaction, and the seaward surfaces which continue to accrete. Finally, once embankments are constructed, there remains an on-going maintenance requirement, especially if the land enclosed has since been developed.

Sea-level rise compounds these concerns. In this region, sea levels are influenced by two components, global sea-level change and local effects resulting from isostatic readjustment of the crust following deglaciation.

There is widespread agreement that over recent centuries global sea levels have risen by 1-2 mm per year (Hansom, 1999; Pethick, 1999). Over the same time period, local isostatic readjustment of the crust in the Firth of Forth has, broadly speaking, elevated land levels at an approximately similar rate (Firth *et al.*, 1997). Since it appears almost certain that global sea-level rise will begin to accelerate over the next century on account of climate change (Hulme and Jenkins, 1998), this will result in rates of land uplift throughout the Firth of Forth being outpaced by sea-level rise (Pethick, 1999). In defended areas, several implications arise from this scenario. Further intertidal habitat loss will ensue as Low Water levels rise while High Water levels are constrained against embankments, leading to 'coastal squeeze'. In such circumstances, mid- to upper-saltmarsh, in particular, will be affected, often the most diverse and ecologically valuable components of that habitat. Because of the prevalence of defences, impacts on estuarine functioning will also be exacerbated as the estuary will be unable to migrate landward as a natural response to the rising sea levels (Figure 11.2) (Pethick, 1999). As a result, there will be increased pressure on existing defences and more extensive impacts on land areas should they breach.

One response to these pressures (Pethick and Burd, 1993; Burd, 1995), is to allow managed realignment of the coastline; i.e. to move back the existing flood defence in areas of claimed farmland to an appropriate position further inland, such as a natural rise in ground levels or closer to built development (Figure 11.3). This approach has been developed in North America in recent years and a few trial sites in England have been initiated, contributing to the UK Government's commitment under its Biodiversity Action Plan (Anon., 1994) to "undertake further research to assess the scope for habitat creation through managed retreat of the coast" (task 14).

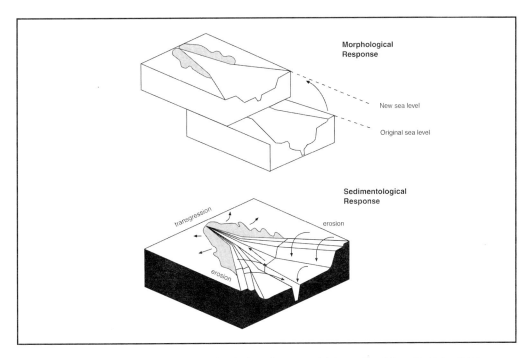

Figure 11.2 Estuarine response to rising sea level: the roll-over model (reproduced from Pethick, 1999).

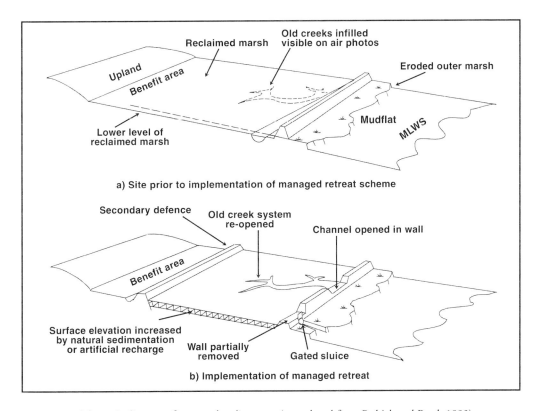

Figure 11.3 Schematic diagram of managed realignment (reproduced from Pethick and Burd, 1993).

The crux of this approach is that it attempts to restore as much of the intertidal area of the estuary to its former condition as possible. This has the advantage of recreating natural habitat and, crucially, restoring natural functioning to the estuary. The natural functioning is enhanced by increasing the area over which dissipation of tidal energy is possible, so reducing tidal amplitude. If this is possible, then not only is there a reduced need to maintain coastal defences to the heights required before realignment, but also future increases in sea level due to climate change may, at least in part, be counteracted. For example, the hypothetical restoration of the entire former intertidal area of the Humber is estimated to be capable of reducing high tide levels in the estuary by around 1m, or, counteracting 1m of future sea-level rise (J. Pethick, pers. comm.).

11.3 Assessment of potential for managed realignment in the Forth Estuary

11.3.1 Introduction
A legacy of extensive embankments and habitat loss, together with development pressure now and in the future, has been identified as placing increasing strains upon management within the Forth estuary (Forth Estuary Forum, 1998a, 1998b). Recognising the possible benefits of managed realignment within estuaries, a research project was therefore initiated through the Forum to assess the potential of this approach to the future management of the Forth Estuary. By mapping the extent of land claim and establishing the *physical* suitability of claimed areas to managed realignment, it was hoped to identify how the conservation interest of the estuary might be enhanced, whilst embarking on a possible route towards sustainable management of both flood risk and sea-level rise (GeoWise Ltd and Coastal Research Group, 1999). Consideration of the socio-economic, planning and legal issues that might arise from a managed realignment scheme was not addressed at this stage in the project design.

11.3.2 Physical background and conservation interest of the Forth Estuary
The estuary of the Firth of Forth is situated in south-east Scotland (Figure 11.1), stretching upstream of the Forth Bridges and Queensferry in the east to its head at Stirling, a distance of some 48 km (McClusky, 1987). The planform upstream of the Forth Bridges is essentially that of a classic trumpet-shaped estuary which progressively telescopes landwards. Tides in the Forth estuary are semi-diurnal and meso-tidal in range. Detailed tidal records have been kept for Rosyth since 1964 (Emery and Aubray, 1990) and show tidal range there to be 5 m at springs and 2.6 m at neaps (Wallis and Brockie, 1997). Water depths are generally shallow, with extensive areas of intertidal mudflats which dry to altitudes of about 1 m OD. However, deep channels exist where the flow is constrained. For example, in the vicinity of Kincardine Bridge depths of 9.28 m below OD are reached, and close to Alloa depths of 6.9 m below OD occur (Tay Estuary Research Centre, 1991). Elsewhere, the depths at MLWS lie about 2-3 m below OD.

The Forth is recognised as being one of the most outstanding estuaries in Britain for the diversity of its estuarine habitats and species (Forth Estuary Forum, 1998a), containing a number of international, national and local designations. In particular, the Forth Estuary has been identified as a potential SPA and Ramsar site due to its importance as an over-wintering area for many species of birds such as shelduck, redshank and knot. In addition, there are 5 SSSIs designated for their botanical and ornithological interest, covering 2455 ha of inter-tidal mudflats and sandflats, saltmarsh, reedbeds, brackish lagoons and coastal grassland (Forth Estuary Forum, 1998a).

11.3.3 Methodology

The most suitable areas for managed realignment in the Forth are areas of former saltmarsh which, over the last four centuries, have been enclosed for agricultural use by flood embankments and separated from the sea. Since land and sea levels in this area have risen at broadly similar rates over this period, former intertidal areas should, in the absence of embankments, have the capability to revert to modern intertidal habitat. In addition, it was anticipated that such areas should possess the most suitable soil structure for the recreation of saltmarsh habitat.

All known maps depicting the shoreline of the Forth Estuary were obtained, and those of sufficient accuracy transferred on to a GIS to allow the determination of shoreline changes over time. The earliest reliable survey of high and low water marks was obtained from an Admiralty Chart of the seabed surveyed in 1851 and published in 1860. Comparison with recent surveys provides an accurate record of change over the last 150 years. However, because considerable land claim had already been undertaken before 1851, shoreline positions were also noted from the maps of William Roy's Military Surveys which were prepared in the 1750s at a scale of 1:36,000. The Roy maps were not digitised, but aided delineation of certain claimed areas and 'fine-tuning' of shoreline locations plotted from other maps and data.

Historical accounts show that some land claim had been conducted prior to the 18th century (Cadell 1929a, 1929b) and these accounts were cross-referenced to the 1:25,000 drift geological map prepared by the British Geological Survey in the 1980s, which identifies areas of "reclaimed inter-tidal flats" based on a combination of field survey and analysis of sediment cores (Gostelowe and Browne, 1986). Overlay of current OS 1:10,000 digital data upon the spatially rectified images from the above sources allowed shoreline changes to be determined (Table 1).

Table 11.1 Summary of shoreline changes.

Estimated total intertidal area in 1600	56.12 km²
Estimated loss of intertidal area, 1600 - 1850	14.85 km² (26.4%)
Loss of intertidal area, 1850 - Present	13.75 km² (24.5%)
Estimated loss of intertidal area, 1600 - Present	28.6 km² (50.9%)

Potential sources of error in the above methods include, for example, unrecorded seaward shifts in the position of the low water mark (MLWS) since land claim commenced and unrecorded variations in the course of the main channel. Bearing these in mind, the best estimate of loss of intertidal area in the Forth Estuary over the last 400 years due to land claim is in the region of 51±5%.

Figure 11.4 shows all areas of land claim in the Forth Estuary. Clearly many of these have, since first claimed, been developed or built upon and so would be inappropriate for managed realignment. However, visual inspection of the maps and aerial photographs, bearing in mind contemporary land uses, suggested 18 possible sites where realignment might be feasible and these were then subjected to a more rigorous study and field assessment.

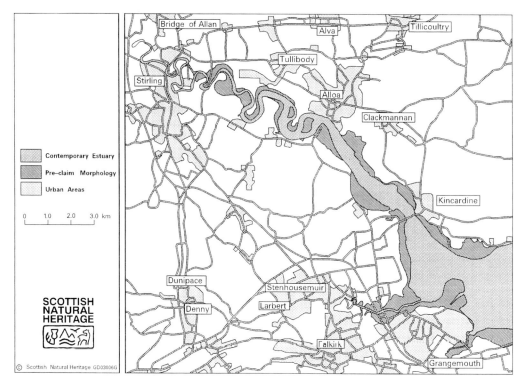

Figure 11.4 Overview of the Forth Estuary indicating all areas of land claim.

In order to make an objective assessment of site suitability, a system was devised which allocated points to each one based on its ability to meet certain essential or desirable criteria. The criteria were split into three categories related to:

- enhancement of estuarine functioning (primary attributes);
- susceptibility to adverse effects (secondary attributes); and
- disruption and cost (tertiary attributes).

The points were weighted towards the primary (i.e. functional) attributes and were awarded for each criterion met by the site concerned. These were then summed to provide a final figure. The scoring allocations are thus indicative only but allow for the *relative* suitability of all the sites in the Forth Estuary to be assessed. It is important to note that most of the attributes are used for indicative purposes only and these are not necessarily applicable to other estuaries in different physical settings; more detailed limits and thresholds are currently the focus of on-going research.

<u>Functional (primary) Attributes (2points)</u>
Related to restoration and enhancement of estuarine functioning
- **The site must be a former inter-tidal area, preferably of saltmarsh or mudflat.**
- **Once realigned, the site should form part of the present-day estuarine system.**

- **The site should have an upper or middle estuarine location for maximum dissipation of the tidal wave.** Since the amplitude of the tidal wave reduces up-estuary, then smaller areas may be required there, relative to lower estuarine locations, to affect amplitude significantly and thus influence estuarine functioning. However, the upper estuary is also characterised by narrow channel widths that are dominated by mainly fluvial processes and this reduces the relative importance of tidal processes. The seaward end of the estuary is subject to greater tidal amplitudes, and so wider intertidal areas may be required for realignment to affect estuarine processes in outer estuarine locations. Unfortunately, because the Forth narrows and becomes more rocky towards the Bridges, there is little scope there for realignment. In spite of the fact that the estuarine transgression model proposed by Pethick (1999) (Figure 11.2) indicates a need for managed realignment in both upper and middle estuarine locations, there is greater scope in the Forth for realignment in the middle estuary to affect the tidal wave, and so this location is preferred.
- **Once realigned, the free connection with the estuary should be of a shape which contributes to maximum energy dissipation of the tidal wave**. Although unproven, it seems likely that long, broad and shore-parallel surfaces are preferable for realignment, such shapes providing more resistance to tidal flow per unit increase of tidal prism than those which are narrow and shore-normal. If this assumption is valid, then this argument favours the removal of long lengths of embankment (bank realignment) rather than small breaches in embankments (breach realignment).
- **The altitude of the site should ensure regular inundation and preferably slope with a regular and low angle falling towards the estuary.** Surfaces which are too high will fail to be regularly inundated and so will contribute little to enhanced estuarine functioning, whereas sites that are too low will be inundated very frequently and may revert to mudflat rather than saltmarsh (Knutson *et al.*, 1990). Ideally, a range of heights will allow for a range of potential pioneer plants and thus habitats to be re-created, that range from high saltmarsh to mudflat (Zedler, 1984).

Secondary Attributes (1point)
Related to containment of possible adverse effects
- **The site should be backed by a rise in ground height, at least to the altitude of the present bank elevation, preferably by a natural slope.** This forms the new line of defence and is necessary to avoid possible flooding of assets or development inland. In the Forth this is most often the 4-5 m OD edge of the raised carse cliff formed earlier in the Holocene, depicted on the drift geology map (see Gostelowe and Browne, 1986).
- **The site should not be exposed to severe wave activity and should ideally be fronted by mudflat and saltmarsh to minimise wave erosion (and favour vegetation colonisation) of restored marsh.** However, since managed realignment aims to allow transgression of saltmarsh landwards under a rising sea level, then some erosion of the outer edge is acceptable as long as this is compensated by re-creation of saltmarsh either at the landward margin or in the upper estuary.
- **Realignment should entail only a minimal increase in the tidal prism of the estuary to mitigate any potential increases in erosion elsewhere.** Re-creation of

intertidal areas increases the total volume of water flooding in and out of the estuary on each tidal cycle (the tidal prism), and so the velocity of tidal currents downstream of the site may be increased. The effect may be offset by the enhanced attenuation of the tidal wave as it advances over the new intertidal surfaces of the realigned area.

<u>Tertiary Attributes (½ point)</u>
Related to site disruption and cost
- **Minimal need for engineering works.** Sites backed by natural rises in ground levels require minimal secondary defence. Other sites may require only short stretches of bank construction behind the realigned site.
- **Ideally the land should be in agricultural use.** Such areas are ideally suited to regeneration of habitat. Built sites would require rehabilitation prior to realignment.

Following this analysis and examination of the sites in the field, three sites achieved the maximum score of 14 points and so were considered *physically* well suited for realignment. Only these highest scoring sites are discussed below. A number of other sites achieved scores of 13 or 12 but, although physically well suited, these have greater practical problems for managed realignment.

11.3.4 Results
<u>The Forth Inches (Border of Middle and Upper Estuary) (45.3 ha)</u>
Tullibody Inch and Alloa Inch are islands within the estuary channel located either side of the meander loop at Longcarse, adjacent to Alloa (Plate 23), although the channel between Tullibody Inch and Longcarse is gradually becoming infilled through sedimentation. Though both islands are surrounded by flood embankments, these have been breached and have fallen into a state of disrepair. Both sites have probably been affected by subsidence from the Polmaise coal mine which underlies the estuary at this point.

The Inches are now regularly inundated by high tides and are naturally reverting to saltmarsh and reedbed habitats. On Alloa Inch, spring tides drown the land surface to a depth of 1 m. Much of this tidal water floods the island via a 30 m wide breach of the embankment on its northern flank, thought to have been formed in the early 1980s. Removal of further lengths of bank down to ambient ground level could allow enhanced tidal incursion and an important increase in the effect of the Inch on tidal friction and estuarine width. In many respects the enhancement of the tidal prism has already occurred via the breach but without the compensating effect of an enhancement of tidal width and attenuation. Removal of even small lengths of bank in a breach realignment would have the effect of reducing the velocities in the main breach in the north. The Inches are well located in the middle estuary and so would contribute positively to estuarine functioning. They have saltmarsh species growing on the site in conditions of moderate salinity.

Both Inches are designated within the Alloa Inches SSSI for their botanical and ornithological value. The SSSI extends along the estuary channel from South Alloa almost as far as the Devon confluence, including both islands together with brackish habitats fringing the channel. The islands are owned by the Scottish Wildlife Trust who manage them as a nature reserve.

Kennet Pans (Middle Estuary) (8.7 ha)

Kennet Pans is a small inlet, about 600 m long and 150 m wide, on the north bank of the estuary about 1.5 km upstream of the Kincardine Bridge. It is sited between two creeks, adjacent to an area of land claimed for the site of the Kincardine power station, and is backed by the edge of the carse cliff at approximately 5 m OD. The site undulates behind a low turf bank which has been undermined in places, giving rise to small seepage scars on the estuary side, the largest of which is a few metres across. The entire site is fronted by a saltmarsh which is accreting in the east and thus reaches its widest extent adjacent to the land-claim rip-rap wall of the power station.

To the west of the site lie the ruined masonry walls, wharves and warehouses of Kennet Pans, together with a large mining spoil heap at the rear of a 100 m stretch of gravel beach. The spoil heap is being undermined by waves and locally contributes coarse sediment to the beach. This erosion, together with the undermining of parts of the turf embankment, suggests that wave activity at high tide may give rise to restoration problems. However, such wave action may only be effective at the extreme west of the site, and the development of an active saltmarsh at the eastern end suggests that fairly rapid adjustment might be possible over much of any rehabilitated site. The degree of shelter provided by the hardened end of the power station rip-rap ensures that any frontal erosion of the saltmarsh edge will be limited to the north of the site.

Although a small site that would contribute in only a minor way to estuarine functioning, its middle estuary position and shape and the existence of healthy saltmarsh within a high salinity environment make it an ideal candidate for a small managed realignment project. The site also supports high bird numbers.

Skinflats (Middle Estuary) (71.4 ha)

Skinflats is an extensive area of high, mostly claimed saltmarsh which extends south-east of the Kincardine Bridge for almost 3 km along the southern bank of the estuary (Plate 24). Now arable farmland, the area originally formed the saltmarsh zone of a wide intertidal bay which extended between the 4-5 m OD carse cliff promontories at Higgins Neuk in the north and Kinneil in the south, bisected by the deltaic mouth of the River Carron.

Much of the area between the Carron mouth and Kincardine Bridge is now protected by embankments, but these are of varying heights and quality and on some stretches are entirely absent. The highest banks at 5 m OD occur between Orchardhead and Powfoulis, and present a rectangular promontory which juts into the bay. The lowest embankments are at Island Farm at 4 m OD, though an area of unbanked foreshore stretches over 500 m south from the Kincardine Bridge access road. At this site, saltmarsh extends from the outer mudflat in an unbroken sequence to the carse cliff.

The carse cliff in this area provides a complete secondary defence line at about 4 m OD at the rear of the site. A small number of properties, however, lie on land below 5 m OD, albeit above the carse cliff: the Powfoulis Hotel and its extensive walled gardens, Hardlands Farm and the now deserted Pocknave Farm. In addition to these, there is the SERC experimental drilling station on the claimed land north of Powfoulis Hotel, although this appears to be disused. Detailed levelling would therefore be required to establish the precise planform of any restored shoreline, particularly in the vicinity of these properties and in the valley of the Muirdyke Burn which runs inland between the Pocknave and Hardlands farms. Limited construction of secondary defences may be required to mitigate risk of flooding under a realignment scheme here.

Plans to extend deep coal mining from Longannet under the Forth into the Skinflats area have raised public concerns about possible subsidence effects. Any such impacts on the Skinflats area would have to be assessed carefully in advance of any potential managed realignment scheme in the area.

The site, as defined by the line of the carse cliff, appears well located in the middle estuary from a functional point of view, and the long and narrow shape would contribute to attenuation of the tidal wave. Salinity is high in this area and the adjacent unbroken saltmarsh sequence in the north shows the type of result that might be achieved where conditions are suitable for colonisation. The site is backed by the carse cliff, and the land is in agricultural use. The existence of embankments fitted with one-way clapped drains that divide the site into sections allows for a sequential restoration programme, if required.

Disadvantages of the site include the probable requirement for minor secondary defences, and the potential for mining subsidence to lower the altitudes and gradients.

The inter-tidal area of this whole stretch of coastline is situated within the much larger Skinflats SSSI, totalling 536 ha and notified for its botanical and ornithological value. The RSPB also lease 413 ha of the area and manage the site as an RSPB Reserve.

11.4 Conclusions

In summary, realignment of these three sites would be likely to result in the following:

- the re-creation of *c.* 125 ha of inter-tidal saltmarsh and mudflat habitat;
- enhanced attenuation of the tidal wave, as a result of the largely middle estuarine location of the sites (the Inches are on the border of the Upper Estuary), but only a small increase in tidal prism;
- reduction of tidal levels which would serve to reduce the impact of sea-level rise;
- minimal modification to existing embankments; and
- few secondary defences.

Though apparently well suited to realignment from a physical perspective, it is clear, indeed imperative, that a number of further studies, consultations and considerations are conducted before such an approach can be realised. These include discussions with landowners and local residents, detailed site evaluation, including topographic survey, engineering design and hydrodynamic studies, review of planning considerations and consents, environmental impact assessment and last, but not least, financial arrangements both for project implementation and compensation, as necessary.

Notwithstanding the requirement to carry out such studies, a full appreciation of whether or not this represents an effective and sustainable form of coastal management will only be gained when a demonstration project is initiated and the results assessed. There is a strong economic argument to act now to assess the suitability of such schemes, since delays may prove costly. Certainly, maintaining the *status quo* does not appear to be an option, as sea levels rise and the altitudinal disparity of land on either side of existing embankments continues to grow. Our options for mitigating the environmental and socio-economic impacts which future sea-level change will bring to UK estuaries are severely limited. If managed realignment schemes are not to be pursued, then the alternatives are by no means clear.

Acknowledgements

The authors gratefully acknowledge advice, assistance and data provided in the course of this study by many individuals and organisations and, specifically, Donald McClusky (Stirling University), Richard Leafe (English Nature), the Scottish Environment Protection Agency, the Royal Society for the Protection of Birds and the British Geological Survey.

References

Anon. 1994. *Biodiversity: The UK Action Plan.* HMSO, London.

Burd, F. 1995. *Managed Retreat: a Practical Guide.* English Nature, Peterborough.

Cadell, H.M. 1929a. Land reclamation in the Forth Valley. I. Reclamation prior to 1840. *Scottish Geographical Magazine,* **45,** 7-22.

Cadell, H.M. 1929b. Land reclamation in the Forth Valley. II. Later reclamation schemes and the work of the Forth Conservancy Board. *Scottish Geographical Magazine,* **45,** 81-100.

Cromarty Firth Liaison Group. 1998. *Cromarty Firth Management Strategy.* Cromarty Firth Liaison Group, c/o Cromarty Firth Port Authority, Port Office, Invergordon IV18 0HP.

Emery, K.O. and Aubray, D.G. 1990. *Sea Levels, Land Levels and Tide Gauges.* Springer-Verlag, New York.

Firth, C.R., Collins, P.E.F. and Smith, D.E. 1997. Coastal processes and management of Scottish estuaries. IV. The Firth of Forth. *Scottish Natural Heritage Review,* No. 87.

Forth Estuary Forum 1998a. *Nature Conservation Topic Paper.* The Forth Estuary Forum, Exmouth Building, Port of Rosyth, Rosyth, Fife KY11 2XP.

Forth Estuary Forum 1998b. *Coastal Defence Topic Paper.* The Forth Estuary Forum, Exmouth Building, Port of Rosyth, Rosyth, Fife KY11 2XP.

Forth Estuary Forum 1999. *The Forth. Integrated Management Strategy.* The Forth Estuary Forum, Exmouth Building, Port of Rosyth, Rosyth, Fife KY11 2XP.

GeoWise Ltd and Coastal Research Group 1999. *Use of GIS to Map Land Claim and Identify Potential Areas for Coastal Managed Realignment in the Forth Estuary.* Unpublished report to Scottish Natural Heritage and the Forth Estuary Forum. 3 volumes.

Gostelowe, T.P. and Browne, M.A.E. 1986. Engineering geology of the Upper Forth Estuary. *BGS Report,* No. 16.8. British Geological Survey, Edinburgh.

Hansom, J.D. 1999. The coastal geomorphology of Scotland: understanding sediment budgets for effective coastal management. *In* Baxter, J.M., Duncan, K., Atkins, S.M. and Lees, R.G. (eds) *Scotland's Living Coastline.* The Stationary Office, London, 34-44.

Hulme, M. and Jenkins, G.J. 1998. *Climate Change Scenarios for the UK. Scientific Report.* UK Climate Impacts Programme Technical Report, No 1. Climate Research Unit, Norwich.

Knutson, P.L., Allen, H.H. and Webb, J.W. 1990. *Guidelines for Vegetative Erosion Control on Wave-Impacted Coastal Dredged Material Sites.* US Army Corps of Engineers, Department of the Army, Washington DC.

McLusky, D.S. 1987. Inter-tidal habitats and benthic macrofauna of the Forth Estuary, Scotland. *Proceedings of the Royal Society of Edinburgh,* **93B,** 389-399.

Moray Firth Partnership 1999. *The Moray Firth: Management Guidelines and Action Programme.* Moray Firth Partnership, c/o Scottish Natural Heritage, 27 Ardconnel Terrace, Inverness, IV2 3AE.

Pethick, J. 1999. Future sea-level changes in Scotland: options for coastal management. *In* Baxter, J.M., Duncan, K., Atkins, S.M. and Lees, R.G. (eds) *Scotland's Living Coastline.* The Stationary Office, London, 45-62.

Pethick, J. and Burd, F. 1993. *Coastal Defence and the Environment. A Guide to Good Practice.* MAFF Publications PB 1191. Ministry of Agriculture, Fisheries and Food, London.

Solway Firth Partnership 1996. *Solway Firth Review.* Solway Firth Partnership, c/o Scottish Natural Heritage, Carmont House, The Crichton, Bankend Road, Dumfries, DG1 4ZF.

Tay Estuary Research Centre 1991. *Chart of the Upper Forth: Alloa to Kincardine Bridge.* Tay Estuary Research Centre, University of Dundee.

Wallis, S.G. and Brockie, N.W.J. 1997. Modelling the Forth Estuary with MIKE11. *In* McLusky, D.S. (ed.) *Coastal Zone Topics: Process, Ecology and Management. 3. The Estuaries of Central Scotland.* Joint Nature Conservation Committee (JNCC), Peterborough, 1-10.

Webb, A.J. and Metcalfe, A.P. 1987. Physical aspects, water movements and modelling studies of the Forth Estuary, Scotland. *Proceedings of the Royal Society of Edinburgh,* **93B**, 259-272.

Zedler, J.B. 1984. *Saltmarsh Restoration: a Guidebook for Southern California.* California Sea Grant College, University of Southern California, Los Angeles.

12 Management Options for the Newbie Cottages and Broom Knowes Shoreline, Inner Solway Firth, South-West Scotland

Michael Cressey

Summary

1. Palaeoenvironmental research at sections in an eroding cliffline in Quaternary sediments in SW Scotland has provided a detailed record of Holocene sea-level change.

2. The cliffs contain bog-oaks, and sub-fossil stumps have been radiocarbon dated to the Mesolithic and Neolithic periods. The site has produced the second earliest dendrochronological timber in Scotland.

3. This paper evaluates possible options for future conservation management of the Earth science interest: whilst rapid coastal erosion is maintaining the sections, it is also leading to progressive loss of scientific interest.

4. Several management options were considered to mitigate the erosion. These included bio-engineering, rock armouring/hard sea defence measures, and allowing the cliff to recede ('monitor and re-survey'). Each option is discussed.

12.1 Introduction

The study area comprises a stretch of coastline, about 800m in length, cut into Quaternary deposits on the northern shore of the inner Solway Firth between the village of Powfoot and the mouth of the River Annan, SW Scotland (Figure 12.1). It is characterised by some of the fastest rates of coastal erosion in the Solway estuary, locally up to 1 m per annum (Cressey and Toolis, 1997; Cressey et al., 1998). Sections exposed in the retreating cliffs have been the focus of very detailed palaeoenvironmental research, resulting in the construction of detailed records of Holocene sea-level change (Jardine 1975, 1980; Dawson et al., 1999). The cliffs also contain large bog-oaks which have been exposed recently at the high water mark at the base of the cliffs. The sub-fossil stumps have been radiocarbon dated to the Mesolithic and Neolithic periods, and the site has also produced the second earliest dendrochronological timber in Scotland (Crone, 1998). The scientific importance of the area is recognised in its inclusion in the Geological Conservation Review (GCR) (Gordon and Sutherland, 1993). The GCR site is also part of a larger Site of Special Scientific Interest (SSSI), notified for its estuarine tidal flat and saltmarsh environments.

The aims of the present study were to document new exposures, undertake palaeoenvironmental investigations and to evaluate possible options for future conservation management of the special interest (Cressey et al., 2001). The last of these is described here.

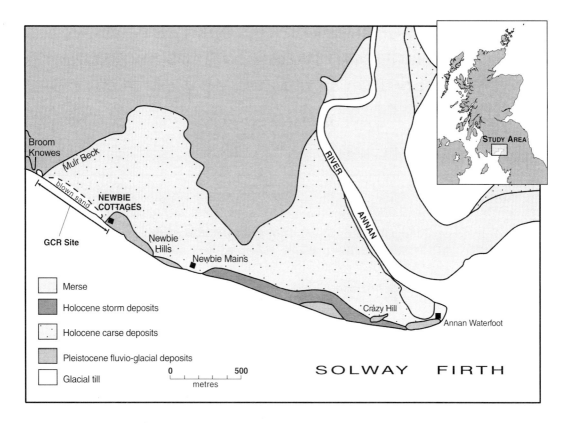

Figure 12.1 Quaternary geomorphology of the Annan Area, inner Solway Firth (after Jardine, 1980).

12.2 Management options

The principal management issue at the site is the rate of coastal erosion. Although this erosion is maintaining the sections, it is also leading to progressive loss of scientific interest. The difficulty is to achieve an appropriate balance. A secondary management issue is the use of inappropriate coastal defence measures in the past, particularly the tipping of rubble at the coastal edge. This rubble is now being dispersed by longshore drift. Several management options to address the issue of erosion were considered.

12.2.1 Bioengineering

Bio-engineering combines mechanical, biological and ecological principles to construct protective systems to prevent slope failure and erosion. This option was rejected principally on the grounds that the area is affected by high wave-energy.

12.2.2 Rock armouring/hard sea defence measures

These could involve some form of groyne or boulder dump defensive works. Given the length of coastline involved, the cost of such works would be considerable. Other factors such as the potential impact on the SSSI were also taken into account. This option was also rejected.

12.2.3 Allow the cliff to recede ('monitor and re-survey')
This might include the following elements:

1. Allow the cliff to recede and monitor the recession until such a time as an appropriate threshold is exceeded, say after 3 m, at which point a programme of section logging could be implemented to provide a permanent record of the new exposures.
2. Undertake a survey to establish the landward extent of the key deposits. This would allow acceptable limits of coastal erosion to be set for the protection of the scientific interest.
3. If, at some stage in the future, coast protection is deemed necessary on planning grounds or to maintain the scientific interest, then alternative methods to rock armouring should be considered. These might include foreshore revetments or establishing artifical headlands (e.g. HR Wallingford, 2000).

Option 3 was recommended on grounds of cost, maintaining access to the scientific interest and potential impacts on the wider SSSI of the use of 'hard' coast protection methods.

12.3 Conclusion

Establishing and implementing appropriate conservation and erosion mitigation measures on coastal sites which are continually under threat from erosion is both costly and time-consuming. A balance has to be struck between allowing some erosion to maintain open sections, loss of some of the interest through erosion and implementation of adequate recording of palaeoenvironmental and archaeological information in the changing sections. For the site at Newbie, it was recommended that erosion be monitored on an annual basis over the next five years to provide an early warning of new exposures and to trigger the formal recording of newly exposed palaeoenvironmental information, such as intertidal peat or sub-fossil wood stumps, after a fixed amount of cliff retreat.

Acknowledgements

The present study was funded by Historic Scotland, Scottish Natural Heritage and the Society of Antiquaries of Scotland.

References

Cressey, M. and Toolis R. 1997. Solway Coastal Assessment. *CFA Report*, No. 312. Centre for Field Archaeology, Edinburgh.

Cressey, M., Dawson, A., Dawson., S., Milburn, P., Long, D. and Bunting, M. J. 1998. Solway Firth Coastal Assessment Survey, Phase 2 1997. *CFA Report*, No. 384. Centre for Field Archaeology, Edinburgh.

Cressey, M., Milburn, P. and Crone, A. 2001. Solway Firth Environmental Assessment and Coastal Management Survey (Newbie Cottages to Broom Knowes, near Powfoot). *Scottish Natural Heritage Research, Survey and Monitoring Report*, No. 172.

Crone, B.A. 1998. Dendrochronology of four timbers from the Solway Firth. Unpublished report for the Centre for Field Archaeology, Edinburgh.

Dawson, S., Dawson, A., Cressey, M., Bunting, J., Long, D. and Milburn, P. 1999. Newbie Cottages, inner Solway Firth: Holocene relative sea level changes. *In* Tipping, R.M. (ed.) *The Quaternary of Dumfries and Galloway. Field Guide.* Quaternary Research Association, London, 98-104.

Gordon, J.E. and Sutherland, D.G. (eds) 1993. *Quaternary of Scotland*. Geological Conservation Review Series, No. 6. Chapman & Hall, London.

HR Wallingford 2000. *A Guide to Managing Coastal Erosion in Beach/Dune Systems*. Scottish Natural Heritage, Perth.

Jardine, W.G. 1975. Chronology of Holocene marine transgression and regression in south-western Scotland. *Boreas*, **4**, 173-196.

Jardine, W.G. 1980. Holocene raised coastal sediments and former shorelines of Dumfriesshire and eastern Galloway. *Transactions of the Dumfriesshire and Galloway Natural History and Antiquarian Society*, **55**, 1-59.

13 HYDROLOGY, PALAEOHYDROLOGY AND CONSERVATION OF ISOLATION BASINS IN NORTH-WEST SCOTLAND

P. Damien Laidler

Summary

1.   Isolation basins (saline lagoons) are significant for both their geomorphological and microfossil interests. Understanding the links among environmental conditions and microfaunal and microfloral communities is crucial in interpreting palaeoenvironmental records and changes in relative sea level.

2.   The use of isolation basins in sea-level research has allowed the collection of high-resolution data in areas seemingly lacking in evidence of relative sea-level change, such as North-West Scotland, where great precision is required given the relatively small vertical changes in sea level during the Holocene, and the resultant prolonged isolation process.

3.   Saline lagoons are important for nature conservation and are the only priority marine habitat in the EC Habitats Directive. Some of the issues involved in conservation of these important natural heritage features are highlighted, using Loch Maddy as a case study.

13.1 Introduction

Isolation basins (including some types of saline lagoon) are natural coastal rock depressions which may, at various times in their history, be isolated from or connected to the sea by changes in relative sea level or, more recently, by anthropogenic activity. They may be classified as silled, isolated or sluiced types (Joint Nature Conservation Committee, 1996), depending upon the nature of the material separating the lagoon from the sea, and the degree of water exchange within the basin.

From an Earth science perspective, isolation basins are significant for both their geomorphological and microfossil interests. Understanding the links in modern basins between environmental conditions and microfaunal and microfloral communities is crucial in interpreting palaeoenvironmental records and changes in relative sea level.

13.2 Geomorphological significance of isolation basins

Rebound of the Earth's surface following deglaciation has led to some basins rising out of the level of tidal influence and, in the process, moving through a succession from saline to brackish to freshwater environments. Changes in relative sea level, and often climate, are recorded in the substrate and/or in the microfossil assemblages of fossil isolation basins. The study of these basins has emphasised their importance as depositories providing a detailed chronology of local relative sea-level changes (e.g. Shennan *et al.*, 2000). The use of isolation basins in sea-level research has allowed the collection of high-resolution data in areas seemingly lacking in evidence of relative sea-level change, such as North-West Scotland, where great precision is required given the relatively small vertical changes in sea level during the Holocene, and the resultant prolonged isolation process (e.g. Shennan *et al.*, 2000).

The aim of work in progress by the author is to clarify some, as yet, poorly constrained sea-level records, through the use of modern analogue saline lagoons (i.e. those still within the range of tidal inundation). It seeks to identify the precise reference tide level (e.g. MHWNT, MHWST, HAT) at which isolation of any given basin would have taken place, and to increase the knowledge of relationships between environmental conditions (water chemistry, and particle size and organic content of the substrate) and associated assemblages of foraminifera (uni-cellular marine organisms, with the test (shell) composed of secreted minerals or agglutinated particles). This approach will allow development of a more precise understanding of the mechanisms of the isolation process and of the association between relative sea-level change and concomitant transformations in the microfossil communities.

Some initial results from the Outer Hebrides, although not yet subject to statistical analysis, appear to show that the presence or absence of foraminifera in particular samples is, to a large extent, controlled by the dominant particle size in the substrate. However, samples have a low species diversity relative to fossil sites, and many of the species that are present would traditionally be classified as brackish or estuarine types. One would not, therefore, expect a large variation in species between samples within a given basin. The area behind the rock sill or sluice often shows the greatest species diversity (though not necessarily the highest actual number of foraminifera present), primarily owing to the allotrophic nature of the foraminifera assemblage (dead foraminifera washed into the basin by the sea).

13.3 Biological significance and conservation of saline lagoons

The importance of saline lagoons in the natural heritage of Scotland is reflected in the fact that they are the only priority marine habitat in the 1992 EC Habitats Directive. Scotland has the largest amount of this habitat type in the UK, with the majority of lagoons to be found in the Western Isles. The Habitats Directive set out approaches for planning the conservation of the terrestrial and marine environment, and included a new set of international site designations for nature conservation, Special Areas of Conservation (SACs). These have a marine environment variant (Scottish Natural Heritage, 1996).

A survey of saline lagoons throughout the UK, undertaken as part of the Marine Nature Conservation Review (MNCR) (Hiscock and Connor, 1996), has provided information in support of the implementation of the Habitats Directive. The survey produced descriptions of 41 different biotopes present within Scottish lagoons, ranging from soft muds with *Ruppia* spp., to the less common rocky entrances, often with tidal rapids at certain stages of the tide, which have become habitats for communities including sponges and sea squirts (Covey, 1999).

Under the terms of the Biodiversity Framework, a costed Habitat Action Plan was formulated for saline lagoons in the UK. This involved an examination of the current status of, and factors affecting, this unique environment (greatly assisted by information collected during the MNCR survey of saline lagoons), and of the action being taken to protect lagoons. It concluded with the development of an action plan (involving liaison with a number of agencies) and proposed targets for the future management and safeguarding of areas of saline lagoon habitat, all with estimated resource costs to the public sector up to the year 2010.

13.4 Case study from North Uist, Western Isles

Loch Maddy, a large shallow inlet and bay including saline lagoons, reefs and intertidal sandflats and mudflats, is an example of a large marine candidate Special Area of Conservation (marine cSAC) which includes some isolation basins. Part of the area is also a biological SSSI, qualifying on the grounds of its size, species diversity, the level of naturalness of the lagoons, the rarity of the habitat and its potential fragility (Joint Nature Conservation Committee, 1996).

Many smaller lagoons on North Uist are also of potential scientific value. As would be expected, none has heavy direct pressures arising from human activity, and some may have been enhanced, to a degree, by the addition or increase in size of sluices. Lagoons modified in such a way may lose some of their 'natural' state, but they should achieve an equilibrium state quite rapidly.

Most existing pressures appear to be of a physical nature, including the cutting of peat (for fuel), the grazing of sheep, the use of all-terrain vehicles around some of the sites, and the discarding of refuse around the immediate catchment of some sites, the disturbance of flora and fauna by fish farms, and road construction (involving the introduction or enlargement of culverts, and the possible removal of the natural rock sill controlling the marine input). The possible effects of these pressures on isolation basins include changes in the input of freshwater from surface run-off, changes in the level of marine input, and the washing in of sediments from the surrounding land, which may also lead to possible chemical changes. With the insecurity currently surrounding livestock farming, some farmers are considering a move to commercial afforestation (A. Rodger, *pers. comm.*), which would have a much greater (and variable) effect on drainage and sediment inputs, depending upon the stage of plantation rotation.

Potential impacts of a chemical nature on isolation basins include changes in pH and drainage of freshwater into individual basins (affecting salinity), which may result from peat-cutting, fish farms, septic tank discharge, sheep droppings and the use of sheep-dips, which are likely to be washed in from any surrounding saltmarsh areas when inundated by high tides. The effects of acid deposition are also reported to have become increasingly noticeable in many lochs throughout Scotland. This can lead to major changes in, or damage to, the flora and fauna (Howells, 1990). From a brief comparison of earlier published articles with MNCR reports (e.g. Thorpe *et al.*, 1998), no particular evidence of such change appears to have been found in lagoons in the Uists, although their catchments do not have significant relief.

13.5 Conclusion

Although inlets, such as the main component lochs of the Loch Maddy marine cSAC, are relatively stable environments with built-in inertia from their large water mass, the isolated, silled, and sluiced types of lagoon tend to be of smaller dimensions and their habitats are, therefore, more vulnerable to impacts from human activity and climate change.

The larger basins are often protected through European and UK site designations because of the high level of species diversity within complex lagoon systems. Many smaller basins, however, also merit consideration for conservation on the strength of their value as palaeoenvironmental archives for research and education on changes in relative sea level and climate.

Acknowledgements

This research is being undertaken through a NERC studentship (GT/04/98/66/MS) in a CASE partnership with Scottish Natural Heritage, and is supervised by Drs Antony Long, Jerry Lloyd (University of Durham) and John Gordon (SNH).

References

Covey, R. 1999. The saline lagoon survey of Scotland. *In* Baxter, J.M., Duncan, K., Atkins, S.M. and Lees, R.G. (eds) *Scotland's Living Coastline*. The Stationery Office, London, 150-165.

Hiscock, K. and Connor, D. 1996. Scope and structure of the Marine Nature Conservation Review. *In* Hiscock, K. (ed.) *Marine Nature Conservation Review: Rationale and Methods*. Joint Nature Conservation Committee, Peterborough, 45-50.

Howells, G. 1990. *Acid Rain and Acid Waters*. Ellis Horwood, New York.

Joint Nature Conservation Committee 1996. *Guidelines for the Selection of Biological SSSIs: Intertidal Marine Habitats and Saline Lagoons*. Joint Nature Conservation Committee, Peterborough.

Scottish Natural Heritage 1996. *Natura 2000: a Guide to the 1992 EC Habitats Directive in Scotland's Marine Environment*. Scottish Natural Heritage, Perth.

Shennan, I., Lambeck, K., Horton, B., Innes, J., Lloyd, J., Mcarthur, J., Purcell, T. and Rutherford, M. 2000. Late Devensian and Holocene records of relative sea-level changes in northwest Scotland and their implications for glacio-hydro-isostatic modelling. *Quaternary Science Reviews*, **19**, 1103-1135.

Thorpe, K., Dalkin, M.J., Fortune, F. and Nichols, D.M. 1998. *Marine Nature Conservation Review Sector 14. Lagoons in the Outer Hebrides: Area Summaries*. Joint Nature Conservation Committee, Peterborough.

14 THE SUSTAINABLE USE OF FRESHWATER RESOURCES: A CASE STUDY FROM THE RIVER SPEY

Katherine F. Leys

Summary

1.   The conservation of dynamic river systems is important for holistic (process, habitat and species) conservation management.
2.   Scotland's dynamic river systems are subject to a range of human pressures, such as pollution and engineering works, which can cause a decline in their ecological status.
3.   The Spey is a high quality river with important populations of Atlantic salmon, sea lamprey, otter and freshwater pearl mussel. These species are the reason for its designation as a Site of Special Scientific Interest (SSSI) and its proposal as a European Special Area of Conservation.
4.   The Spey is not immune to those development pressures seen elsewhere in Scotland, although currently the pressures here are less acute.
5.   The European designation has initiated a process of integrated catchment management. This process, and the eventual catchment management plan, will provide an opportunity to reduce conflict between different interests and lead to agreed management approaches.
6.   Integrated catchment management also has the capacity to generate environmental improvements for the whole catchment, and in particular, to protect and enhance the river and its species.

14.1 Introduction

The conservation of dynamic river systems is important for scientific reasons and for their value in land and water management. Such systems aid our understanding of past, current and future hydrological and geomorphological processes. This understanding helps us find effective ways of managing our environment (Hooke, 1994). In Earth heritage conservation, management objectives are achieved by maintaining the active geomorphic processes which shape the landforms, not by preserving the form of individual pools, riffles and bars (Gregory, 1997). Maintenance of active processes is best achieved by minimising both direct human intervention in the river system and indirect impacts from land management changes in the catchment.

The management of dynamic river systems for habitat and species conservation is a complex balancing act. The integrity and management of river ecosystems relies on a balance between all the main physical, chemical and biological parameters and the identification of links between them. Current hydro-ecological models suggest that the best in-channel regimes for river ecosystems are natural regimes which depend on the operation of natural processes (Richter *et al.*, 1996). Thus, natural geomorphic processes benefit habitats, species and Earth heritage conservation and, as the basis for river ecosystems, are important for biodiversity. Maintaining the operation of active processes, whilst balancing development pressures and landuse interests, requires an integrated approach to catchment management (Werritty, 1995). Hence, in Scotland we are now beginning to see a convergence in management approaches, not only for Earth heritage, habitats and species, but also for wider land management issues.

In this chapter, the factors which combine to create dynamic, natural river systems in Scotland, are briefly identified. The state of Scottish river systems, in relation to water quality, quantity and habitat, is briefly examined to identify the problems and issues relating to the use of freshwater resources. The importance of active river processes in creating and maintaining a suitable natural habitat in the River Spey is presented as a case study which highlights the need for integrated conservation management.

14.2 Geomorphic processes forming Scottish river systems

Scotland's freshwater resources include around 27,000 lochs larger than 0.0001 km^2, approximately 100,000 km of river length (when measured on a 1:50,000 scale map), and significant groundwater resources (SEPA, 1999). The abundance of freshwater resources is related to high annual precipitation. In the west, annual precipitation totals can be greater than 3000 mm, whilst the east is significantly drier with annual totals less than 700 mm. Also significant are the low evapo-transpiration rates, with runoff in Scotland generally being around 50-75% of precipitation (Ward, 1981). This east-west precipitation and run-off gradient combines with the asymmetric location of the main east-west watershed, which is relict from the Tertiary (Sissons, 1967), to create short, steep rivers flowing west from the divide in the Highlands, and river systems with large catchments such as the Spey and the Tay, which flow east. It is only in the Southern Uplands that the drainage divide between the Tweed and the Clyde is more centrally located (Werritty and McEwen, 1997).

Within this general pattern, there is significant local variation, which mirrors Scotland's geological and glacial diversity (Werritty *et al.*, 1994). Bedrock outcrops within the stream bed create stepped long profiles and wide shallow alluvial basins upstream, and the abundance of glacial and fluvio-glacial deposits on the floodplain maintains a high sediment input to the rivers and streams (Werritty and McEwen, 1997). The variety of fluvial forms and processes that are present in Scotland has created diverse riverine habitats.

14.3 The state of Scottish rivers

14.3.1 Water quality

Land and water resources in Scotland have to serve many purposes, including water supply, industry and agriculture. Landuse is intimately related to the nature of underlying rocks, soils and landforms, to human activities and to natural geomorphic processes such as erosion and deposition (Ellis *et al.*, 1996). Sustainable use of finite land and water resources depends on being able to find a balance between encouraging new development in the catchment, delivering affordable conservation and environmental improvements, and protecting existing resources (SEPA, 1999).

Water quality in Scotland's rivers is currently high overall, with 91% of sampled sites having 'excellent' or 'good' water quality in 1996 (SEPA, 1999). The remaining 4000 km of sampled rivers defined as being 'polluted' are variously located in Scotland's populated central lowlands, in urban, industrial and agricultural areas. The geographical distribution of water quality has been related to a range of factors, including the differing population density across Scotland, the distribution of agricultural land, the topography of the country and the industrial history of the catchment (SEPA, 1999). Many of those rivers which support important nature conservation, fishery and potable water resources, such as the River Spey, are found in relatively undisturbed natural catchments in the north of Scotland (SEPA, 1999).

The actions of the Scottish Environment Protection Agency (SEPA) and its predecessor bodies have led to an overall improvement in the water quality of Scotland's rivers, particularly in the period since 1975. This has largely been generated by improvements to point source discharges such as sewage or colliery waste outfalls. Improving the quality of the remaining 4000 km of polluted river will mainly involve the treatment of diffuse forms of pollution such as agricultural run-off (SEPA, 1999).

14.3.2 Habitat quality

Answering the question 'what constitutes good habitat?' is complex, and depends on the requirements of particular species (Maitland, 1997). Research on the interaction between river flow, water quality and ecological patterns (e.g. Petts and Maddock (1996), and Thoms and Swirepik (1998)), and hydro-ecological models (e.g. Richter *et al.*, 1996) generally confirms that the best in-channel regimes for river ecosystems are 'natural regimes', where the operation of natural geomorphic and hydrologic processes, and the presence of a naturally formed channel, are important. Two survey methodologies are commonly used in Scotland to assess the physical structure and naturalness of water courses: River Habitat Survey (RHS) (see Fozzard *et al.*, 1997) and System for Evaluating Rivers for Conservation (SERCON) (Boon *et al.*, 1997). The results of these surveys are used as a means to assess the overall quality of the aquatic environment.

The results from 779 RHS sites surveyed in Scotland between 1995 and 1997 showed that just under 50% of sites were classified as semi-natural (SEPA 1999). The geographical distribution of modified sites reflects the impacts of agriculture, industry, hydro-electricity schemes, fishery management and urban development. Whilst the majority of sampled sites on Scotland's rivers are semi-natural or predominantly unmodified, schemes which impact on only a small reach of the river can have significant and widespread consequences off-site (Hoey *et al.*, 1998). In addition, RHS does not consider explicitly the effects of development on the floodplain and riparian zone. Whilst National Planning and Policy Guideline 7 (The Scottish Office, 1995) advises against new developments on floodplains vulnerable to inundation, there remains a legacy of older developments vulnerable to flooding which require the construction of flood embankments to afford protection.

14.4 A case study of the River Spey

14.4.1 The River Spey SSSI

The main stem of the River Spey, a major river in northern Scotland, was designated as a Site of Special Scientific Interest (SSSI) in November 1998 for its important populations of freshwater pearl mussel, sea lamprey, otter and Atlantic salmon. These species are becoming increasingly rare in Europe and the River Spey SSSI is one of the largest riverine sites proposed in Scotland as a Special Area of Conservation (SAC) under the *Conservation (Natural Habitats, &c.) Regulations 1994*, commonly known as the 'EC Habitats Directive'. The European designation will require land and river management activities to be carefully scrutinised to ensure that activities likely to have a significant effect on the important species are prevented.

Although the SSSI designation was made on the basis of species interests, the River Spey has significant Earth heritage interests: the Lower River Spey SSSI is one of the most extensively braided river systems in the UK (Plate 22); one section of the River Feshie SSSI is a large, low-angle tributary fan at the confluence of the Feshie with the Spey, the upper part an extensive braided reach (Plate 11); Loch Insh is a large kettle hole; there are noted earth pillars near Fochabers; and the Spey itself is misfit within a larger valley relict from glacial times (Werritty and McEwen, 1997). A further Earth heritage interest, which is fundamental to habitats and species conservation, is the dynamic nature of the Spey along much of its length. Erosion, sediment transport and deposition are natural processes which provide the mechanism for moving water and sediment from the uplands to the sea. The continued operation of these processes, and the creation and reworking of the pools, riffles and bars they create, is fundamental to the maintenance of the species interests.

14.4.2 The state of the River Spey SSSI

The River Spey is one of Britain's cleanest big rivers (NERPB, 1995). High water quality within the catchment is important for many whisky distilleries and two major food processors located along the tributaries and main stem. Drinking water for public supply is abstracted from alluvial gravels at Fochabers, near the river mouth, and Loch Einich in the upper catchment. The River Spey also supports an important salmon fishery with an estimated value of around £10-15 million annually to the local economy.

However, the system is not entirely natural. The pressures for modification of natural channels seen elsewhere in Scotland are present. British Alcan operates a hydro-power scheme in the upper part of the main stem, with water from the Spey catchment being impounded at Spey Dam and transferred into Loch Laggan (part of a west draining hydro scheme) (Payne, 1988). Hydro-power schemes are also operated on the River Mashie, River Tromie and the River Truim, all upstream tributaries. Gilvear (2000) found evidence of bed aggradation downstream of Spey Dam, with the geomorphic and habitat changes being consistent with those identified by Gregory and Park (1974) in Somerset.

The salmon fishery has traditionally generated a programme of river works aimed at fishery enhancement. These works have usually been in the form of flow deflection structures (croys), or have involved the excavation of gravel to create or increase pools, and the placement of large boulders in the channel to create lies and areas of shelter. Bank repair work, usually undertaken to protect land from flooding or erosion, has also been undertaken. The recent and widespread decline in salmon numbers (SERAD, 2000), particularly the decline in the spring salmon stocks, has raised awareness of the need to take great care over any in-river engineering works.

The Spey catchment is largely rural in nature. Agriculture is a major landuse in Scotland which has been shown to place pressure both on water quality, through diffuse pollution, and on channel and bank integrity, as a result of animal trampling or rubbing and foraging of riparian vegetation. In the Spey, agriculture has little effect on water quality through nutrient inputs, but inputs from pesticides, including sheep dip, may be more significant. Trampling is localised in extent on the Spey, but can be significant in those areas where it occurs (Plates 25 and 26).

There are only around 23,000 permanent residents of the Spey catchment, but the Strathspey area around Grantown and Aviemore has a large number of holiday visitors in winter and summer. The settlement pattern is traditionally one of planned towns such as Kingussie, Fochabers, Kingston, Aberlour and Grantown, which are all set back from the river edge. Many of these small towns have retail and light industry. There are numerous small villages of less than 500 residents (e.g. Carrbridge, Craigellachie and Garmouth). Only Aviemore, in the height of the tourist season, has a population exceeding 3,000 inhabitants (Spey Catchment Steering Group, 2000). Flood events, particularly those in 1989, 1990, 1992 and 1993, showed that some settlements, such as Aviemore, are vulnerable to inundation during periods of high flow. Agricultural fields are also vulnerable to flooding, and in consequence, some are protected by flood embankments.

14.4.3 The role of active processes in creating and maintaining habitat

The provision of habitat for key species at all stages of their life cycle is fundamental for conservation management. This requires an understanding of the habitat requirements of individual species and the river processes that will create and maintain them.

There has been comparatively little research on freshwater pearl mussel ecology (see Hastie *et al.* (2000) for information on the Scottish population). Current research suggests that freshwater pearl mussels usually occur in the lee of boulders or towards the slower-flowing stream margins of fast-flowing rivers (Plate 18). Sufficient current is needed to transport organic food particles and maintain oxygen levels in the water during summer, whilst preventing excess sediment transport and deposition (especially in areas where juvenile mussels settle). Adult freshwater pearl mussels lie partly buried in coarse sand or fine gravel, and juveniles are rarely found in silty or muddy conditions.

Mussel rivers are typically poor in calcium, mildly acidic, low in nutrients and suspended solids, well-oxygenated, have low levels of conductivity, and have temperatures not exceeding 20°C (Young, 1991). The presence of young salmon and trout is essential to the pearl mussel because the larvae (glochidia) attach to fish gills in the summer and remain there until the following spring when they drop off and settle into the substrate.

Sea lamprey ammocoetes (young) are usually found in rivers with silty beds. The optimum bed sediment size for ammocoetes is thought to be 0.18 - 0.38 mm, including silt and sand fractions. The extent of channel shading and in-stream flow velocity are also important in determining habitat suitability. In Britain, most populations are found where the average stream gradients are 1.9 to 5.7 m/km, and lampreys are rarely found where gradients exceed 7.8 m/km (Maitland and Campbell, 1992).

Little is known about the freshwater habitats occupied by adult sea lampreys. Most adults found in freshwater are either migrating to spawn or dying after spawning. The ability of the lamprey to migrate to suitable spawning beds is important, and barriers to migration include high waterfalls, weirs, dams and pollution (Maitland and Campbell, 1992). Spawning nests are normally built in areas of flowing shallow water among sand and gravel of varying particle size. After hatching, larvae leave the nest and drift downstream, distributing themselves amongst suitable silt beds. Sea lampreys usually spawn in late May or early June, when the water temperature reaches at least 15°C (Maitland and Campbell, 1992).

The key habitat requirement for otters is to be in or near water. Otter populations in freshwater areas are also strongly related to the distribution of prey species. Kruuk *et al.* (1995) found that otter utilisation of foraging habitat is correlated with fish biomass, and that otter populations may be food-limited. Although all species of fish are taken by otters, they appear to have a preference for species with high lipid content, such as salmonids and eels. Otters use both narrow and wide rivers and so occupy tributaries and main stem rivers. Streams at higher altitudes are less important as they tend to be less productive of prey than lower altitude streams. Kruuk *et al.* (1995) also identified that otters living in freshwater areas in north east Scotland often use riverine islands and reed beds (where they are present) as rest sites.

Atlantic Salmon spawn in fresh water and require adequate spawning and nursery areas and holding pools for adults to provide sufficient recruitment of young fish to maintain the population. Most spawning takes place in the upper reaches and tributaries, but, in keeping with most other Scottish rivers, it also occurs in the main stem of the Spey. A 15-20 cm deep redd (nest) is hollowed out of the gravel or cobbles by the female's tail, the eggs are laid and simultaneously fertilised by the male, then the hollow is refilled with gravel. Most redds are found in swiftly flowing, usually shallow water (Maitland and Campbell, 1992). The tail end of pools, and other areas, are also utilised.

After hatching, the alevins remain in the redd for several weeks before emerging as fry. The strongest fry remain in the shallow flowing water around the redds, displacing the weaker ones to sites downstream in search of food and habitat. The food supply in a typical salmon spawning stream is limited, so there is a high mortality rate in the first few weeks of life. The growth in fresh water is slow from fry to parr (they are generally termed parr by the end of their first summer) and 2-3 years may pass before they make their way to the sea as smolts. During this time the parr become well dispersed throughout the river in search of food (mainly aquatic insect larvae and wind borne aerial and terrestrial insects), and they tend to favour the riffles and runs rather than the pools, although this varies with season. After 1-3 years at sea, salmon or grilse return to freshwater to spawn. They do not feed in freshwater at this time but often rest in deeper pools on their journey upstream (Maitland and Campbell, 1992).

14.4.4 *Pressures on the natural heritage resource*

The high water quality and important populations of the designated species indicate that anthropogenic pressures are less intense on the River Spey than in many other Scottish rivers. However, issues arising before, during and since SSSI designation show that the natural riverine processes of the Spey are potentially under pressure from bank protection works, flood alleviation measures, agriculture, forestry and, to a lesser extent in recent times, river engineering.

Erosion is a natural part of active river behaviour and is necessary for habitat, but it can be exacerbated by human activities adjacent to the river and elsewhere in the catchment, such as afforestation (Maitland *et al.*, 1990). A dynamic river is not always compatible with static land and river ownership, in situations where banks form boundaries for land ownership, or where the number and location of pools has an economic value. Erosion or deposition in these instances can have serious economic consequences, and the desire to prevent channel change can lead to the installation of hard engineering structures which also prevent the operation of natural processes.

Unlimited stock access to river banks limits tree growth, destroys bank vegetation, weakens bank structure and can accelerate bank erosion (Hoey *et al.*, 1998). Bank erosion is usually addressed subsequently by the installation of revetment. Whilst revetment to protect agricultural land is often relatively small scale, over time, the cumulative impact of stabilising parts of the bank can be significant. It can change the balance between sediment input to the system and the dissipation of energy downstream, which impacts on habitat creation and maintenance, and is thus detrimental to existing species. If bank erosion has been exacerbated by agricultural activity, afforestation or landuse change elsewhere, the use of revetment at an erosion site treats the symptoms rather than the cause, and as such will reduce the likely success of any engineering scheme.

Informal discussions with fishery proprietors have shown that they perceive the sediment load in the Spey system to be high, and that the volume of sediment in motion appears to have increased. They cite the infilling of named fishing pools, that have existed over time, as evidence for this. Although this has not been studied formally, many blame the increased sediment on landuse change and increased disturbance of the river bed through other engineering schemes upstream. Whilst accepting that current fishery and landuse management practices may be partly to blame, some feel that the resultant pool infilling and deposition is sufficiently negative for fishery management to require them to undertake their own engineering (which propagates the problem downstream).

River engineering for fishery management purposes typically involves the creation of flow deflection structures (croys), boulder emplacement and re-excavation of pools. Croys (Plate 27) act to create areas of deep water within the channel. If wrongly sited they can locally increase bank erosion, and they can accelerate the rate at which sediment is moved through the reach, which may exacerbate deposition downstream. The emplacement of boulders can involve the local disruption of the stable bed armour and the loosening of sediment. The excavation of pools can liberate fine sediment and cause a net loss of sediment to the overall system through gravel removal (Hoey *et al.*, 1998). Machinery in the channel can cause physical damage to habitats and species (particularly mussels) through compaction. These management techniques can change the operation of natural processes and so have the potential to alter the relationship between process, habitat and species.

Sediment transport is a natural process which occurs at high flows competent to transport bed material (Shields, 1936). In contrast, river bank and bed engineering is usually undertaken during low flow for safety reasons. Engineering works can cause the release of silts and gravels, which blanket the bed downstream. This silt blanket can persist until the next period of high flow (which, in summer, could be weeks away). The infilling of pore spaces between the gravels can be fatal to young salmon and is potentially damaging to freshwater pearl mussel.

The River Spey is being constrained in locations vulnerable to flooding by flood embankments and bank repair works, which have been built to protect agricultural land or floodplain developments. Whilst flood embankments are important for the protection of vulnerable land and property, they separate the channel from the floodplain. This can reduce access to suitable riparian and floodplain habitat for otters. Embankments can prevent the periodic wetting that many riparian habitats and species depend upon and reduce the input of nutrients and invertebrates from riparian vegetation. They can also isolate flows in the channel from floodplain storage, leading to increased flood peaks downstream and increased channel erosion (Hoey *et al.*, 1998).

Water quality within the River Spey is currently high, but a significant proportion of the catchment is under agricultural production, a landuse which SEPA cite as being a major factor in determining water quality in Scotland (SEPA, 1999). Diffuse pollution, in the form of run-off containing fertilisers, pesticides and other farm wastes, is obviously a potential concern, although the water quality of the Spey is currently high and agriculture does not appear to be having a significant effect at present. Preventing future pollution in the Spey is of social, economic and conservation importance, and the support and assistance of the agricultural sector will be vital in achieving it.

14.4.5 The benefits of integrated catchment management

The River Spey is currently a river of very high quality, supporting a number of species that are rare or endangered across Europe. However, section 14.4.4 demonstrates that the river is subject to many of the same pressures on water and habitat quality that are present elsewhere across Scotland. The majority of activities and developments undertaken in the Spey catchment are entirely lawful, but individual practices have the potential to impact on the river and riparian area locally and more widely, and can also impact on other people.

In the recent past, land and river managers on the Spey looked upstream to areas outwith their own land ownership for the cause of any changes in river behaviour. Being able to link cause and effect was not a significant management tool, because individual owners or interests were unable to exert any influence on the way others behaved, even if their legitimate interests were being impacted upon by the activities of others. Now, however, the proposed SAC designation has initiated a process of integrated catchment management (ICM) (Werritty, 1995) for the River Spey, which offers the potential for new consensus-based management across a wide geographical area.

ICM is a process which takes a holistic view of the catchment area and tries to balance the requirements of economic interests, environmental improvements, land ownership and interests such as recreation, access and tourism, in order to develop a management plan for the benefit of the catchment as a whole. A number of competent authorities (as defined by the Habitats Regulations) have formed 'The Spey Catchment Steering Group' to promote and develop a catchment management plan. Membership presently includes SEPA, SNH, The Highland Council, The Moray Council and The Spey Fishery Board, with input from the Scottish Executive. The Steering Group will work with land and river managers and local people to drive forward the process of developing a catchment management plan. A public consultation, launched in April 2000, seeks people's views on the key issues affecting the Spey and invites them to become involved in the process of developing a catchment management plan.

There are a number of examples of good landuse practice already happening in the Spey catchment. For example, the use of riparian buffer strips, as advocated in current agri-environment schemes, offers a mechanism whereby run-off from the wider catchment (which could be carrying chemicals) can be prevented from reaching the river. The increased bankside vegetation cover has a dual benefit as it increases bank stability and reduces erosion, whilst reducing nutrient input to the system. Riparian buffer strips also illustrate the complexity of landuse management. Buffer strips improve water quality, reduce erosion, increase invertebrate input to the river and create habitat. However, riparian fences and tree or shrub growth can be a hindrance to casting whilst angling, the buffer strips themselves involve the loss of prime agricultural land, and the creation of linear riparian strips can look artificial. Balancing these competing interests is an example of a situation where a balanced, agreed approach to land and river management (in a catchment management plan), would prove beneficial.

A further development which will affect the management of the Spey is the proposed EC Water Framework Directive. Negotiations on UK implementation of the Directive are ongoing and it is anticipated that this will include a statutory requirement for ICM through the creation of the River Basin Management Plan. River Basin Management Plans will probably be at the scale of SEPA regions. Sub-Basin Plans, which are likely to be at the scale of large individual catchments such as the Spey, will also be required for practical management. The work on the Spey, whilst in its infancy, provides an example of the principle in practice.

14.5 Conclusion

The River Spey has a number of sites with Earth heritage interest and is of conservation importance for otter, sea lamprey, Atlantic salmon and freshwater pearl mussel. The active processes that have created the geomorphological features are fundamental in creating and maintaining habitat for these and other species. The continued operation of geomorphic processes is a vital component of the natural heritage. Future sustainable management of the Spey will have to be linked to an understanding of these natural processes.

The Spey currently has high water quality and is relatively unmodified, but the system is not entirely natural. It is subject to the same sorts of development, landuse and river management pressures as other parts of Scotland, albeit on a reduced scale. The Spey's recent designation as a Site of Special Scientific Interest and its proposal as a European Special Area of Conservation have provided an opportunity and impetus for integrated catchment management. It is hoped that this process, whilst still in its infancy, will provide a mechanism for future sustainable use by balancing conservation with development, resource protection, and the delivery of affordable environmental improvements.

References

Boon, P.J., Holmes, N.T.H., Maitland, P.S., Rowell, T.A. and Davies, J. 1997. A system for Evaluating Rivers for Conservation (SERCON): Development, Structure and Function. *In* Boon, P.J. and Howell, D.L (eds) *Freshwater Quality: Defining the Indefinable.* The Stationery Office, Edinburgh, 299-326.

Ellis, N.V., Bowen, D.Q., Campbell, S., Knill, J.L., McKirdy, A.P., Prosser, C.D., Vincent, M.A. and Wilson, R.C.L. 1996. *An Introduction to the Geological Conservation Review.* Geological Conservation Review Series, No 1. Joint Nature Conservation Committee, Peterborough.

Fozzard, I.R., Davidson, M. and Moffett, G. 1997. River Habitat Survey in Scotland. *In* Boon, P.J. and Howell, D.L (eds) *Freshwater Quality: Defining the Indefinable.* The Stationery Office, Edinburgh, 235-240.

Gilvear, D.J. 2000. An assessment of reported aggradation within the upper River Spey SSSI. Unpublished report to Scottish Natural Heritage.

Gregory, K.J. 1997. An introduction to the fluvial geomorphology of Britain. *In* Gregory K.J. (ed.), *Fluvial Geomorphology of Great Britain.* Geological Conservation Review Series No. 13. Chapman and Hall, London, 3-18.

Gregory, K.J. and Park, C. 1974. Adjustment of river channel capacity downstream from a reservoir, *Earth Science Processes and Landforms,* **10**, 363 –374.

Hastie, L.C., Young, M.R., Boon, P.J., Cosgrove, P.J. and Henninger, B. 2000. Current density/size estimates and observed age structures of Scottish *Margaritifera margaritifera* (L.) populations. *Aquatic Conservation: Marine and Freshwater Ecosystems,* **10**, 229-248.

Hoey, T.B., Smart, D.W.J., Pender, G. and Metcalfe, N. 1998. Engineering methods for Scottish gravel-bed rivers (edited by K. Leys). *Scottish Natural Heritage Review,* No 47.

Hooke, J. M. 1994. Conservation: the nature and value of active river sites. *In* Stevens, C., Gordon, J.E., Green C.P. and Macklin, M. (eds) *Conserving our Landscape.* Proceedings of the Conference, Conserving Our Landscape: Evolving Landforms and Ice-Age Heritage, Crewe, 1992. Peterborough,110-116.

Kruuk, H., Conroy, J.W. and Carss, D.N. 1995. Identification of key habitat types essential to otter populations and an assessment of methodological techniques. Unpublished report to Scottish Natural Heritage.

Maitland, P.S. 1997. 'Freshwater Quality': the use of the term in Scientific literature. *In* Boon, P.J. and Howell, D.L (eds) *Freshwater Quality: Defining the Indefinable.* The Stationery Office, Edinburgh, 24-38.

Maitland, P.S., Newson, M.D. and Best, G.A. 1990. The impact of afforestation and forestry practice on freshwater habitats. *Focus on Conservation,* No. 23. Nature Conservancy Council, Peterborough.

Maitland, P.S. and Campbell, R.N. 1992. *Freshwater Fishes of the British Isles.* Harper Collins, London.

NERPB 1995. River Spey Catchment Review. North East River Purification Board, Aberdeen

Payne P.L. 1988. *The Hydro.* Aberdeen University Press, Aberdeen.

Petts, G.E. and Maddock, I. 1996. Flow allocation for instream needs. *In* Petts, G.E. and Calow, P. (eds) *River Restoration.* Blackwells, Oxford, 60-79.

Richter, B.D., Baumgartner, J.V., Powell, J. and Braun, D. P. 1996. A method for assessing hydrologic alteration within ecosystems, *Conservation Biology,* **10**, 1163-1174.

SERAD 2000. Protecting and Promoting Scotland's Freshwater Fish and Fisheries: a Review. Scottish Executive Rural Affairs Department, Edinburgh.

SEPA 1999. *Improving Scotland's Water Environment. State of the Environment Report.* Scottish Environment Protection Agency, Stirling.

Shields, A. 1936. Anwendung der Ähnlichkeitmechanik und der Turbulenzforschung auf die Geschiebewegung. *Mitteilung der preussichen Versuchsanstalt für Wasserbau und Schiffbau, Heft* **26**, Berlin.

Sissons, J.B. 1967. *The Evolution of Scotland's Scenery.* Oliver & Boyd, Edinburgh.

Spey Catchment Steering Group 2000. River Spey: towards a catchment management plan. Invitation to contribute, April 2000. Spey Catchment Steering Group, Inverness.

The Scottish Office 1995. Planning and Flooding. National Planning and Policy Guideline 7. The Scottish Office Development Department, Edinburgh.

Thoms, M. C. and Swirepik, J. 1998. Environmental flow management in New South Wales, Australia. *In* Wheater, H. and Kirby, C. (eds) *Hydrology in a Changing Environment.* Volume 1. John Wiley, Chichester, 281-287

Ward, R. C. 1981. River systems and river regimes. *In* Lewin, J. (ed.) *British Rivers.* George Allen and Unwin, London, 1-33.

Werritty, A 1995. Integrated catchment management: a review and evaluation. *Scottish Natural Heritage Review,* No. 58.

Werritty, A., Brazier, V., Gordon, J.E. and McManus, J. 1994. The freshwater resources of Scotland: a geomorphological perspective. *In* Maitland, P.J., Boon, P.J. and McLusky, D.S. (eds) *The Fresh Waters of Scotland: a National Resource of International Significance.* John Wiley, Chichester, 147-170.

Werritty, A. and McEwen, L.J. 1997. Fluvial landforms and processes in Scotland. *In* Gregory K.J. (ed) *Fluvial Geomorphology of Great Britain.* Geological Conservation Review Series, No. 13. Chapman & Hall, London, 21-32.

Young, M.R. 1991. Conserving the freshwater pearl mussel (*Margaritifera margaritifera* L.) in the British Isles and continental Europe. *Aquatic Conservation: Marine and Freshwater Ecosystems,* **1**, 73-77.

15 GEOMORPHOLOGICAL AND HYDROLOGICAL ASSESSMENT FOR THE RESTORATION OF FLOODPLAIN WOODLAND: THE ETTRICK WATER, SCOTTISH BORDERS

Lindsey J. McEwen and Willie McGhee

Summary

1.   As part of the Ettrick Habitat Restoration Project, a geomorphological and hydrological study was conducted to inform management planning and monitoring, particularly in relation to priority targets for restoration and enhancement.
2.   The close links between geomorphology, hydrology and ecology require that effective restoration and enhancement must work as far as possible with 'near-natural' river processes.

15.1 Introduction

Riparian woodland and floodplain forests are depleted but valuable ecological resources within the UK uplands (e.g. Petts, 1990). Integrated catchment management strategies need to address their requirements, particularly where there is good potential to restore or enhance semi-natural floodplain processes and the indigenous woodland resource.   Such a strategy has been developed for the upper Ettrick Water, a tributary of the River Tweed (Figure 15.1), which has undergone direct and indirect human alteration in the 18th - 20th centuries.   The Ettrick Habitat Restoration Project, co-ordinated by the Borders Forest Trust, aims to restore and enhance this woodland habitat to increase its conservation value. The project, which commenced in 1997, involves partners including Millennium Forest for Scotland, World Wildlife Fund (Scotland and UK), Forest Enterprise, Scottish Natural Heritage and the Tweed Foundation, and support from private landowners.

15.2 Environmental setting

The mainstream upper Ettrick is a typical, active, sinuous gravel-bed river in a low-angle, wide, upland alluvial basin, characteristic of the Scottish Borders (a reach of c. 3 km). Specific enhancements involve re-creation of 25 ha of native woodland, restoration of 30 ha of floodplain habitat (including scrub, fen, hay meadows and wetlands), management of 15 ha of willow scrub and conversion of 30 ha of conifer plantation to native broadleaves.

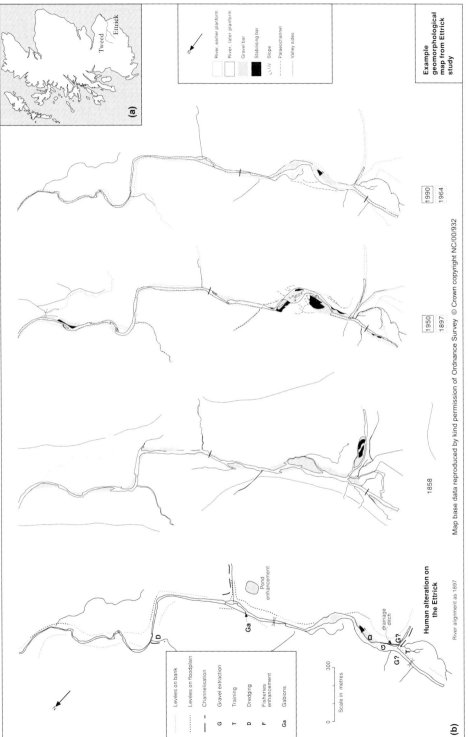

Figure 15.1 (a) General location; (b) example geomorphological map from the Ettrick study.

15.3 Project aims

As part of the Ettrick Habitat Restoration Project, a geomorphological and hydrological study was conducted to establish the links between habitats and natural processes (McEwen, 1998).

The aims of the study were to:

1. establish the scientific input to a baseline assessment of river, corridor and floodplain character, which will effectively inform management planning and monitoring. This includes evaluating the relationship between channel character/adjustment and habitat characteristics, establishing propensity for channel changes and the sensitivity to human intervention.
2. use the information from (1) to establish effective enhancement targets that will ensure sustainable management of the floodplain woodland resource.

15.4 Geomorphological assessment: methodology, criteria and outcomes

Geomorphological assessment was based on field, map and literature sources and is replicable as a baseline for a monitoring programme (Table 15.1). Landforms present were evaluated in terms of their diversity, degree of naturalness, representativeness/rarity and sensitivity to change across a range of flow conditions (see McEwen, 1997; McEwen, *et al.*, 1997). Summary outcomes are shown in Table 15.2.

Table 15.1. Material to be integrated in a geomorphological assessment.

Method	*Aim*
Detailed site description and morphological evaluation (proforma developed for SNH's SERCON project; McEwen, 1997)	to assess the relationship between river, corridor, floodplain and catchment.
Geomorphological mapping (1:10,000)	to describe the current nature and range of landforms evident within the channel, its margins, corridor and floodplain.
Photographic survey	to record key geomorphological and hydrological features of the study area.
Examination of archival sources (historical maps and estate plans)	to establish the geomorphological, sedimentological and ecological indicators of erosion, deposition and sediment transport rates.
Human impact map (1:10,000)	to identify the extent of past alterations that disrupt the connectivity of the river system.

Table 15.2 Criteria for geomorphological assessment.

Physical diversity	Significant spatial variations in channel pattern are evident, reflecting progressive downstream changes in channel controls. Key factors are discontinuities in slope and sediment availability associated with bedrock control and sediment inputs from tributaries. Floodplain units of different ages (representing diverse ecotones) are linked to progressive and episodic channel pattern adjustments.
Naturalness	Detailed investigation provides considerable evidence for piecemeal alterations, including levees, channel re-routing and sectioning. The history of alteration reflects national policies for river management (e.g. the merits of drainage against wetlands).
Representativeness and rarity	Landforms evident are typical of a partially-managed, alluvial basin in the Scottish borders. Characteristic downstream changes in channel character are evident - from steeper, stable coarse-grained channels through active, low sinuosity channels to lower gradient, more sinuous planforms. Features that are rarer (a sequence of meander cut-offs) enhance site value.
Sensitivity to change	Propensity for adjustment varies spatially with downstream changes in sediment character/availability and confinement, which determine local thresholds for change. They also control the timescale for any channel adjustment to reduced human intervention that aims to increase river/floodplain connectivity.

15.5 Links between geomorphology, hydrology and ecology

To carry out effective enhancement, the links between floodplain development and ecology need to be understood thoroughly. Different woodland resource patches identified along the Ettrick enhancement reach include disturbance patches (determined by rate of lateral channel erosion and deposition), meander palaeochannels, flood channel and local avulsions, areas of floodplain storage and seasonally flooded marshlands.

The floodplain is locally subject to regular seasonal inundation but to an extent reduced from the seasonally-flooded ecotones of the 17th century. The legacy of past levée systems (mainly late 19th century onwards) has significantly altered floodplain storage during more moderate floods. The history of channel migration explains the diversity of alluvial surfaces within the corridor, floodplain and valley floor - linked to repeated rejuvenation of successions associated with channel erosion and deposition. Ecological resource patches are delimited by the seasonal flood inundation but also by soil permeability (controlled by e.g. sediment size and depth). Both the seasonal inundation of the river corridor and the impact of extreme floods in sediment transfer are important in establishing a spatial and temporal variety of floodplain surfaces and associated habitats.

15.6 Restoration and enhancement – priority targets?

There is high potential for increasing the geomorphological and ecological value of the Ettrick floodplain through enhancement. Indicative management targets for restoration and enhancement on the Ettrick are to:

1. target channel segments that demonstrate past floodplain reworking for managed retreat (particularly those linked to tributary confluences);

2. increase the connectivity between different woodland resource patches, particularly those which have been artificially detached by human intervention; and

3. conserve palaeochannel features and maintain a natural flow regime that allows periodic inundation and sedimentation of these zones.

15.7 Conclusions

1. It is important to establish the discharge and sediment transfer relationships between the river, its corridor and floodplain, since these determine the potential ecological resource.

2. There is a need to determine the propensity for 'natural' change in channel and floodplain character. This involves assessing the geomorphological response and sensitivity of river landforms to flows of different magnitudes.

3. The past history of artificial intervention in river processes must be unravelled, along with the nature and rate of channel response, as essential background to enhancement.

4. Key woodland resource patches need to be identified, which have high potential value for enhancement due their process history.

5. It should be noted, however, that there are problems in establishing cause and effect, due to other climate and landuse changes over the same time-period, and that the baseline survey must be used to inform an effective monitoring programme.

6. Effective restoration and enhancement must work as far as possible *with* 'near-natural' river processes and be underpinned by a sound understanding of these processes. Good practice from the Ettrick project has significant potential to be extrapolated to upland environments elsewhere in the UK and so inform integrated river management. Here, geomorphological information has been used successfully to inform priority targets for restoration and enhancement.

Acknowledgement

The work reported here was commissioned by the Borders Forest Trust as part of its site management programme.

References

McEwen, L.J. 1997. SERCON module for geomorphological assessment: development of a field-based proforma. *Scottish Natural Heritage Research, Survey and Monitoring Report,* No. 90.

McEwen, L.J. 1998. Baseline hydrological and geomorphological survey for the upper River Ettrick enhancement reach. Unpublished report for Borders Forest Trust, Jedburgh.

McEwen, L.J., Brazier, V. and Gordon, J.E. 1997. Evaluating the geomorphology of freshwaters. *In* Boon, P.J. and Howell, D.L. (eds) *Freshwater Quality: Defining the Indefinable.* HMSO, Edinburgh, 258-281.

Petts, G.E. 1990. Forested river corridors: a lost resource. *In* Cosgrove, D. and Petts, G.E. (eds) *Water, Engineering and Landscape.* Belhaven Press, London, 12-34.

16 A Sediment Budget Approach to Inform Sustainable Habitat Management for Lampreys: the Endrick Water Catchment, Scotland

Lindsey J. McEwen and Simon G. Lewis

Summary

1.   This study demonstrates the value of a sediment budget approach as part of integrated conservation management at the catchment scale.

2.   The sediment budget approach allowed the identification of areas of potential habitat for lampreys and their likely sensitivity to disturbance such as gravel extraction. It can therefore provide a basis for conservation-sensitive management and monitoring.

16.1 Introduction

Integrated catchment planning is crucial to sustainable ecological management. As scientific underpinning, the latter requires evaluation of the linkages between hydrological, geomorphological and ecological resources at catchment level. Only then can the impacts of human and climate-induced changes on river discharge and sediment supply be determined. This study demonstrates a sediment budget approach to integrated resource evaluation, using as a case-study the Endrick Water (McEwen and Lewis, 1999). This catchment (271 km^2; Figure 16.1a/b), which drains into Loch Lomond, has exceptional conservation value. It is a Site of Special Scientific Interest (SSSI) and candidate Special Area of Conservation (cSAC), supporting strong populations of the internationally important river lamprey (*Lampetra fluviatilis*) and the brook lamprey (*Lampetra planeri*), which are listed in Annex II of the EC Habitats Directive. Quality sediment and water resources are required for healthy lamprey populations and so must be key elements in a catchment-level, conservation-sensitive management strategy.

16.2 The Endrick catchment – natural and human-induced controls

The Endrick is characterised by high geomorphological quality. The river changes in character from a steep, coarse-grained, relatively confined channel upstream of Low Bridge, through sinuous middle reaches (with a legacy of channel alteration linked to milling), to a relatively natural, small-scale, actively meandering channel in the lower reaches (Bluck, 1971; McEwen and Werritty, 1997). The catchment, however, has had a number of artificial alterations during recent and historical time, including channel changes associated with the milling industry and water abstraction linked to the Loch Carron reservoir. Localised, small-scale, private gravel extraction takes place at various locations along the Endrick.

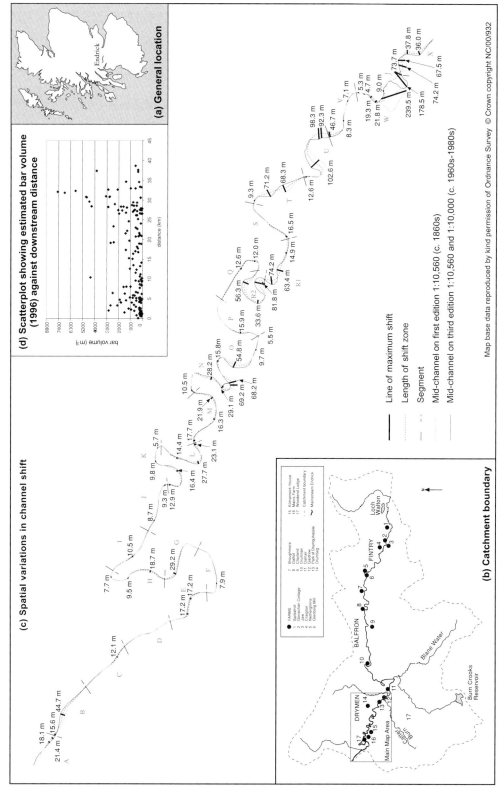

Figure 16.1 River Endrick. (a) General location; (b) catchment boundary; (c) location and scale of channel shift; (d) bar volume against downstream distance.

16.3 Project aims

The aims of the project were to:

1. provide a semi-quantitative analysis of the principal sediment sources, sinks and pathways within the Endrick catchment;
2. assess the impact of sediment removal from the channel and floodplain on the interest features of the SSSI and cSAC;
3. develop a conservation-sensitive management strategy for sediment input and extractions to the Endrick Water SSSI/cSAC, with reference to the requirements of lamprey habitats.

16.4 The approach

Geomorphological assessment (based on map, aerial photograph and field survey) was undertaken along 74 channel segments (each 500 m long) between Loup of Fintry and the efflux to Loch Lomond. Modified geomorphological proformas from the SNH SERCON project were used (McEwen, 1997). A Geographical Information System (Map Info - Version 5) was used to overlay historic channel planform and bar information (dated 1859/1860, 1896, 1969/1980 and 1996). Bar volumes and long-term rates of channel shift and sediment volumes input to the channel were estimated, ground-truthed and fed into a simple sediment budget model (with sediment inputs, storage and outputs; Figure 16.1c/d) using a Microsoft Excel spreadsheet. First order estimates of tributary inputs and the residence time of sediment within the channel and bars were obtained. Some elements could only be considered in qualitative terms, including the scale of colluvial or glacigenic inputs (Rose, 1981).

16.5 Results

Sediment balance data for each segment were plotted against downstream distance and the following observations noted.

1. *Dominant sediment sources vary downstream.* In the upper reaches, glacigenic and colluvial sources are reworked from tributary inputs and local incision of the mainstream Endrick. In the upper middle to lower reaches, sediment is mainly obtained from reworked floodplain sources and local tributary inputs.
2. *Major sediment stores are found at a number of locations downstream.* These include clusters of segments between Spittalhill to Netherglinns (upper to middle river) and below Dalnair to Drymen Bridge (lower river). The model indicates their relative size and gross composition.
3. *Areas of relative sediment depletion occur where there are low sediment inputs from tributaries and floodplain sources* (segments from below Broughmore to above Endrick Cottage Bridge).
4. *Bar sediment storage is important in terms of the overall sediment balance.* This is closely linked to volumes of sediment input from reworked floodplain sources, in the form of significant gradual and episodic injections of sediment. Annual sediment inputs from floodplain sources are much lower than the volume of sediment storage in bars.
5. *Annual sediment inputs from tributaries are a relatively small element in the sediment balance.* Inputs from the Blane Water, Altquhur Burn and Catter Burn (increasing

catchment area by 102.9 km²), however, cumulatively make a major contribution to the large sediment stores within bars downstream on the lower river.

16.6 Lamprey habitats

The geomorphological and sedimentological character of river channels required as river and brook lamprey habitats alters with the life cycle of the lamprey. For example, during spawning, adults require gravel/cobble stretches with unpolluted running water, riffles and immersed bar forms (for more detail see Maitland, *et al.*, 1994; Gardiner *et al.*, 1995). Using the sediment budget information, good lamprey habitat potential can be identified, based on known optimal sediment and slope characteristics. It is also possible to locate river sections that are both sensitive and more robust to artificial changes, such as gravel extraction.

16.7 Management strategy

The sediment budget model was used to assess the impact of sediment removal from the channel and floodplain on lamprey habitats, using baseline extraction data from riparian owners. Although individually the amounts extracted on the upper to middle river are generally low, cumulatively over space and time the quantities become more significant. The impacts will vary with spatial and temporal variations in natural sediment storage. Areas downstream of Netherglinns increase in vulnerability due to the decreasing amounts of gravel in the river.

A code of conduct is required for gravel extraction, that considers the relative sensitivity of different river/floodplain locations or limits the scale of the impact by various means. Conservation-sensitive management should, for example, require that a given depth of gravel is taken from the landward edge of the bar. This would allow the production of temporary backwaters, which can enhance the quality of the river environment for fish. Gravels could also be derived from those areas of the upper catchment with larger quantities of sediment available and where slopes exceed the normal limits for lamprey spawning habitats.

16.8 Way forward

A simple sediment budget approach can therefore be used to assess the scale and impact of gravel extraction on lamprey habitats and can form the basis for developing a sustainable, catchment-scale, conservation-sensitive management and monitoring strategy. The analysis generates further questions in fine-tuning the model that merit more detailed investigation. The approach can be usefully extrapolated to other small- to medium-sized catchments with geomorphological and ecological conservation value.

Acknowledgements

This work was commissioned by Scottish Natural Heritage as part of its commissioned research programme.

References

Bluck, B.J. 1971. Sedimentation in the meandering River Endrick. *Scottish Journal of Geology*, **7**, 93-138.

Gardiner, R., Taylor, R. and Armstrong, J. 1995. Habitat assessment and survey of lamprey populations occurring in areas of conservation interest. Unpublished report to Scottish Natural Heritage SNH/080/95AEB April, 1995.

McEwen, L.J. 1997.   SERCON module for geomorphological assessment: development of a field-based proforma. *Scottish Natural Heritage Research, Survey and Monitoring Report*, No. 90.

McEwen, L.J. and Lewis, S.G. 1999. Sediment budget of the Endrick Water catchment. Unpublished report for Scottish Natural Heritage.

McEwen, L.J. and Werritty, A. 1997. Endrick Water, Stirling. *In* Gregory, K.J. (ed.) *Fluvial Geomorphology of Great Britain.* Geological Conservation Review Series, No. 13.   Chapman & Hall, London, 48-51.

Maitland, P.S., Morris, K.H. and East, K. 1994. The ecology of lampreys (Petromyzonidae) in the Loch Lomond area. *Hydrobiologia,* **290**, 105-120.

Rose, J. 1981. Field guide to the Quaternary geology of the south-eastern part of the Loch Lomond basin. *Proceedings of the Geological Society of Glasgow,* **122/123**, 12-28.

17 THE SUSTAINABLE USE OF SOIL

Geeta Puri, Toby Willison and Paula Woolgar

Summary

1.   Soil is a key natural resource which performs many important functions both for society and the environment. However, it is a finite resource which needs to be used in a sustainable manner in order that it continues to provide these functions in the future.

2.   Scotland has a large and varied soils resource, including the majority of the UK terrestrial soil carbon reserves. In order to protect this resource effectively, an integrated approach to sustainable soil use is required in accordance with the conclusions of the 19th Report of the Royal Commission on Environmental Pollution in 1996. This stated that "soil, air and water are the three essentials for life on land but environmental policies have largely taken soil for granted".

17.1 Introduction

Soil is the unconsolidated surface of the Earth, formed from rock weathering and biological activity. One of its most important functions is as a medium for plant growth. Soil is usually considered in terms of its functions for the environment and society rather than its intrinsic properties. It fulfils a multitude of roles which include:

- the supply and store of nutrients for vascular plants;
- storage and filtration of surface and groundwater and removal of contaminants;
- gaseous exchange with the atmosphere, including CO_2 and NO_2 release and absorption;
- buffering the environment from contaminants by adsorbing or reacting with potentially toxic elements from diffuse and point sources;
- the source of raw materials for buildings and foundations;
- a store of biodiversity, being home to a varied, complex and relatively unknown population of microflora, microfauna and larger soil organisms.

How soil is perceived depends to a large extent on a specific function that is required of the resource, whereas in reality it is performing many of the above functions simultaneously. It is for this multitude of functions that soils are valued from different perspectives, such as the farmer, engineer, ecologist and regulators concerned with environmental pollution. Soil is not currently protected in the same manner as water or air, where specific targets are set for quality, and there is legislation to enforce sustainable use (Royal Commission on Environmental Pollution, 1996). This may be due to the fact that soils have so many functions or roles, and links to human health are more indirect than for other environmental media. Scotland has a diverse soils resource and a multitude of links with the natural heritage (Taylor *et al.*, 1996a). This paper reviews the various functions that this resource performs, the pressures on it and the management responses and requirements.

17.2 Soil and agriculture

From an agricultural perspective, soils are valued for their function in providing a medium for crop growth and how effectively they sustain crop production. A relatively small proportion (5.7% of the land surface) of Scottish soils is suited to intensive arable cultivation as determined by land capability criteria (Paterson, 1998), which consider soil properties, topography and climate in order to asses suitability for cultivation. This means that high-grade agricultural soils are a scarce resource in Scotland, and hence maintaining or sustaining their productivity and extent is important for Scottish agriculture. Cultivation entails manipulation of soils to provide favourable conditions for crop growth, which can sometimes have negative, long-term effects such as erosion of topsoils, compaction, nutrient enrichment and contamination from pesticides and fertilisers (SOAEFD, 1997). In Scotland, although intensively cultivated soils are a small component of the whole resource, intensive cultivation has impacts on the wider environment as well as on soils themselves. In localised areas, issues such as eutrophication of lochs and rivers (Wild, 1993) and wind and water erosion from arable land (Grieve *et al.*, 1994) are of concern for their effects on the wider environment.

Apart from site-specific case studies, there has been no systematic national evaluation of the impact of agriculture on the soils resource, such as erosion rates, soil structural effects, impacts on soil chemistry and biology and associated off-site impacts. A recent (1999) EU ban on dumping sewage sludge at sea will have a potential risk for agricultural soil quality as the pressure to dispose of more sewage sludge to land may lead to contamination by heavy metals and pathogens. Many Scottish soils are acidic, and excess sewage applications could have significant effects on soil condition. New methods of treating sludges and how and where they are applied to soils are being investigated by the Scottish Executive Rural Affairs Department (SERAD) funded research so that the risk to soil sustainability is reduced.

17.3 Soil and forestry

Forestry is a large and significant sector of the Scottish economy. However, commercial plantations can affect soil sustainability through erosion of soils during planting and felling operations and from roadways, acidification of soils, damage to soil structure and leaching of nutrients to watercourses. There has been no systematic evaluation of the effects of forestry on the Scottish soils resource, but guidelines have been produced to reduce adverse effects (The Forest Authority, 1998).

17.4 Soil as a terrestrial carbon reservoir

Scottish soils contain approximately 71% of the UK soil carbon reserve (Milne and Brown, 1997), stored as organic matter or peat. These soils are vulnerable to climate change and human activities which may accelerate the decomposition of soil organic matter, potentially releasing large quantities of terrestrial carbon dioxide to the atmosphere. Practices such as drainage of wetlands, afforestation and peat extraction can all affect the balance of carbon, as well as predicted changes to climate. Measures to protect peatlands and to restrict commercial afforestation and drainage are already in place to some extent. However, the land use sector is a large source of CO_2 in Scotland and has a high potential in the UK as source of greenhouse gases. Therefore, as part of the sustainable use of soils in Scotland, it is important to be able to evaluate and monitor the effects of activities such as agriculture and forestry in this area.

17.5 Soil and environmental pollution

Industrial processes and urban areas also affect soil sustainability, as soils can be polluted, contaminated, eroded, degraded, truncated and lose their ecosystem function as a result of urbanisation, mineral extraction and industrial development and processes (Puri and Gordon, 1998). Soils have been afforded some indirect protection through planning legislation and controls on waste disposal and industrial activity (Table 16.1).

Table 16.1. Indirect safeguards for soils.

Legislation	*Measures*
The Pollution Prevention and Control (Scotland) Regulations 2000	requires that permitted installations are restored to a satisfactory state on cessation of activity
The Sludge (Use in Agriculture) Regulations 1989	provides guidelines for levels of PTEs in sludge applied to land
Groundwater Regulations 1998	controls application of certain hazardous substances to land to protect groundwater
Waste Management Licensing Regulations 1994	controls the disposal of wastes to land
The Conservation (Natural Habitats) Regulations 1994	contains obligations to avoid pollution of habitats designated under EC Habitats Directive
Part IIA of the Environmental Protection Act 1990	includes requirement to inspect and identify contaminted land; provides a framework for identification and remediation of contaminated land
The Protection of Water against Agricultural Nitrate Pollution (Scotland) Regulations 1996	includes requirement to monitor and control nitrate input to surface and groundwaters from agricultural sources
The Control of Major Hazard Regulations 1999	places duties on operators of major hazard sites to minimise harm arising from accidental releases

Scotland's industrial activity over the past 200 years has left a legacy of some 14,000 ha of registered vacant and derelict land, most of which is concentrated in the central belt and some of which has damaged the most valuable agricultural soils. UK Government is encouraging the remediation and re-use of these brownfield sites and restricting the consumption of greenfield sites (Quality of Life Counts, 1999). There is no systematic, broad ranging evaluation of the loss of soils to development and/or contamination and these issues should form part of an overall strategy for sustainable soil use. Remediation, re-instatement and re-use of brownfield sites in a planned approach is an important aspect of sustainable soil use.

17.6 Soil and nature conservation

In addition to the agricultural and industrial functions that soils perform, they are important and integral parts of terrestrial habitats that sustain our semi-natural environments (Puri and Gordon, 1998; Bullock *et al.*, 1999). The majority of Scotland consists of upland environments which support a semi-natural or extensively managed agricultural system. Soils sustain the vegetation and water quality of these environments and are therefore fundamental to protecting the natural heritage.

Some soils also have value for their 'benchmark' status (Ball and Stevens, 1981); others are important from a historical and cultural viewpoint, such as *plaggen* soils (Simpson *et al.*, 1998). In Scotland, many upland areas contain a significant amount of terrestrial carbon either as peat or peaty soils, often associated with habitats of high natural heritage value. Nature conservation has traditionally focused on species without giving due regard to how ecosystems are maintained. However, it is becoming more widely recognised that soils play a significant role in supporting our valued habitats, and that in order to manage them, we need to understand better what the relationships are, and what soil properties or attributes are important for maintaining above-ground diversity. This applies particularly where land is reclaimed or being reinstated for nature conservation purposes.

The large biodiversity contained within our soils resource is also of significant nature conservation interest. Maintaining biodiversity in all spheres of our environment is considered to be important, and this includes soils which currently contain the largest unknown pool of biodiversity (Meyer, 1993).

17.7 Soil quality

In the preceding sections we have discussed the role and functions of soil in relation to land use and highlighted where sustainable soil use could be addressed. The quality of a soil is closely linked to its intended function and this is a central focus of soil protection and sustainable use since it is the function which dictates how we perceive its sustainable use. In reality soil performs a multitude of functions, but in terms of land use it is for a specific role or function that soil is valued. A farmer perceives soil quality from the perspective of those soil attributes which affect crop growth, such as pH, organic matter, texture and base cation status, and it is this perception of quality that we are most familiar with in relation to land capability for agriculture. We can identify acceptable pH values and textural properties of soil which suit particular crops and evaluate soil quality from a single perspective. For the ecologist, soil quality has a different meaning since quality relates to supporting ecosystems and biodiversity. In some cases, properties of the soil deemed to be important may even be extreme chemical or physical parameters which support unique habitats and soil biota, for example on the ultrabasic soils on Unst in Shetland and the bings of central Scotland. The engineer perceives soil quality in terms of the mechanical properties of soil such as shrinkage, swelling and shear strength. For waste disposal, soil properties considered desirable may be related to hydraulic conductivity and structure. It is clear that function dictates what is required from soils in terms of its perceived quality and this has traditionally translated into properties such as chemical and physical characteristics. Since soil information has historically been closely related to evaluating land for agriculture, many of the soil properties that are familiar and routinely measured by various surveys are those that relate to, and affect, crop yields. This is a valid perception of soil quality but we need to expand soil quality to include functions such as water storage, carrying capacity for contaminants, supporting habitats and providing a building resource, and for each of these functions we need to consider whether current land use is sustainable. The quality of water and air is well regulated and investigated, and it is a relatively straightforward exercise to set threshold values for human and environmental impacts. For soil we are not at the stage where we can provide indicators for soil quality or even clearly define what is meant by soil quality for certain functions (Paterson, 1998). This is the challenge for effective protection of soils and ensuring their sustainable use.

17.8 Indicators of soil quality

An indicator is a tool used to measure a feature or process, which in this case relates to the quality of soil for a specified function. Indicators are meant to have some of the following characteristics – be easy to measure and replicate, provide results that can be interpreted and translated, have defined limits of acceptability (thresholds), be relatively cheap, be representative of a number of properties and processes occurring, and have baseline information on natural temporal variation. For some functions, such as agriculture, the desirable qualities and hence indicators of soil quality are relatively well defined and documented for a large number of soils. Table 17.2 highlights some of the more generally accepted measures of soil quality which primarily relate to the agricultural function of soil, taken from Quality of Life Counts (1999), and those which could be applied to a wider number of functions (Paterson, 1998). For some of these measures we have broad threshold values, above or below which it is assumed that significant negative effects occur or that any recovery would be over the long term.

Table 17.2 Selection of soil indicators.

Soil Indicators selected for Quality of Life Counts (1999)

- Loss of soils to hard development
- Concentration of organic matter in agricultural topsoils

Soil Indicators proposed in Paterson (1998)

- Soil pH
- Organic carbon
- N, P, K status
- Soil strength

Soil resilience refers to how robust the soil is at recovering from a variety of stresses, such as contamination, compaction and loss of biodiversity. Soils are inherently very resilient and are capable of recovery from extreme events such as droughts and contamination. The great biodiversity in soils also suggests biological resilience, in that important biological functions are undertaken by a number of organisms, with a high degree of redundancy (Schimel, 1995). However, it is not clear how this resilience is expressed or what the thresholds are for a number of soil characteristics, such as organic matter content or contaminant loads, which may affect the resource over the long term or permanently. Issues such as permanent loss of the resource by erosion and development should be seen as unsustainable where loss exceeds soil development which is generally over hundreds, if not thousands of years. Indicators currently available are to some extent a historical reflection of soil survey work, but we need to identify and select those appropriate for a full range of soil functions, not only those for evaluating agricultural soil quality.

17.9 Soil protection

Both in the UK and Europe, soil protection is a topical issue. The European Soil Bureau aims to co-ordinate soil information and has set up a Soil Forum to address soil protection issues throughout EU member states. Some countries such as The Netherlands, Germany, France and Denmark have some form of strategy or policy which aims to protect soils. In the UK, the impetus has come from the 1996 report by the Royal Commission on Environmental Pollution on *The Sustainable Use of Soil* which recommended to Government that a policy for soil protection should be produced. Government accepted many of the findings of this report (Department of the Environment, 1997). Currently the Department of the Environment, Transport and the Regions and the Welsh Assembly are drafting soil strategies for England and Wales, respectively. The Scottish Executive has yet to draft a strategy, and both SEPA and SNH have recommended that it is timely and appropriate for this to be undertaken.

An appropriate focus for a strategy for Scotland would be the sustainable use and management of all soils in relation to their many different uses and functions. Such a strategy a would bring together a diverse set of existing guidelines, indirect legislation and codes of practice (Taylor *et al.*, 1996b) and would be of great value for the natural heritage, agriculture, forestry, the environment and society. Ideally it would:

- ensure adequate and explicit protection for soils from pollution from all sources;
- maintain the extent and diversity of the soils resource in Scotland, including agriculturally valuable soils and soils with high habitat and conservation value, as well as the significant peat and organic matter resource of Scottish soils;
- ensure that the use of soil is consistent with the aims of sustainable development and is based on a sound understanding of soil processes and the condition of the resource;
- ensure that soils are maintained and restored to their respective ecosystem functions;
- co-ordinate a national approach to monitoring the condition of the soils resource; and
- ensure that the importance of maintaining and improving soil quality is fully recognised by all interests.

An integral part of this process will be to define soil quality for a variety of purposes and to report on soil condition (Taylor *et al.*, 1996b). This will require to be supported by research at a UK level to evaluate soil quality for a wide range of functions and to identify threshold values or values of acceptable limits for soil indicators which can then be used to monitor the sustainable use of soils nationally.

17.10 Conclusion

Soils are a key natural resource and have many important values and uses. Over thousands of years, soils may be regarded as renewable resources, but over the timescale of human lifetimes, they are effectively non-renewable. Hence sustainable use is essential if soils are to continue to perform all their crucial functions effectively. However, soil receives only implicit protection through legislation designed to regulate water and air quality, urban development, waste disposal and contaminated land, and it is the only environmental medium not protected in its own right. It is therefore appropriate and timely that Scotland should begin to prepare an integrated strategy for soils which would emphasise sustainable use of the resource.

The views expressed in this chapter are those of the individual authors and do not necessarily represent those of their respective organisations.

References

Ball, D.F. and Stevens, P.A. 1981. The role of ancient woodland in conserving undisturbed soils in Britain. *Biological Conservation,* **19**, 163-176.

Bullock, P., Jones R.J.A. and Montanarella, L. 1999. *Soil Resources of Europe.* European Soil Bureau Report, No. 6. EUR 18991 EN. Office for Official Publications of the European Communities, Luxembourg.

Department of the Environment 1997. *Sustainable Use of Soil: Government Response to the 19th Report of the Royal Commission on Environmental Pollution.* Department of the Environment, London.

Grieve, I.C., Hipkin, J.A. and Davidson, D.A. 1994. Soil erosion sensitivity in upland Scotland. *Scottish Natural Heritage Research, Survey and Monitoring Report,* No. 24.

Meyer, O. 1993. Functional groups of microorganisms. *In* Schulze, E.D. and Mooney, H.A. (eds) *Biodiversity and Ecosystem Function.* Ecological Studies, 99. Springer, Berlin, 67-96.

Milne, R. and Brown, T.A. 1997. Carbon in the vegetation and soils of Great Britain. *Journal of Environmental Management,* **49**, 413-433.

Paterson, E. 1998. Development of a framework for soil monitoring for state of the natural heritage reporting. *Scottish Natural Heritage Commissioned Report* F98AC112B.

Puri, G. and Gordon J.E. 1998. Soils and sustainability - a natural heritage perspective. *In Contaminated Soil '98. Proceedings of the Sixth International FZK/TNO Conference on Contaminated Soil, 1/-21 May 1998. Edinburgh, UK.* Vol. 1. Thomas Telford, London, 1-5.

Quality of Life Counts 1999. *Indicators for a Strategy for Sustainable Development for the United Kingdom: a Baseline Assessment.* HMSO, Norwich.

Royal Commision on Environmental Pollution 1996. *Sustainable Use of Soil.* Royal Commision on Environmental Pollution, 19th Report. HMSO, London.

Schimel, J. 1995. Ecosystem consequences of microbial diversity and community structure. *In* Chapin, F.S. and Körner, C. (eds) *Arctic and Alpine Biodiversity.* Ecological Studies, 113. Springer, Berlin, 239-254.

Simpson, I.A., Dockrill, S.J., Bull, I.D. and Evershed, R.P. 1998. Early anthropogenic soil formation at Tofts Ness, Sanday, Orkney. *Journal of Archaeological Science,* **25**, 729-746.

SOAEFD 1997. *Prevention of Environmental Pollution from Agricultural Activity: a Code of Good Practice.* Scottish Office Agriculture, Environment and Fisheries Department, Edinburgh.

Taylor, A.G., Gordon, J.E. and Usher M.B. (eds) 1996a. *Soils, Sustainability and the Natural Heritage.* HMSO, Edinburgh.

Taylor, A.G., Usher, M.B., Gordon, J.E. and Gubbins, N. 1996b. Epilogue: the way forward – soil sustainability in Scotland. *In* Taylor, A.G., Gordon, J.E. and Usher M.B. (eds) *Soils, Sustainability and the Natural Heritage.* HMSO, Edinburgh, 295-305.

The Forest Authority 1998. *Forests and Soil Conservation.* The Forestry Commission, Edinburgh.

Wild, A. 1993. *Soils and the Environment: an Introduction.* Cambridge University Press, Cambridge.

18 INHERENT GEOMORPHOLOGICAL RISK OF SOIL EROSION BY OVERLAND FLOW IN SCOTLAND

Allan Lilly, Richard V. Birnie, Gordon Hudson, Paula L. Horne, John E. Gordon and Geeta Puri

Summary

1.   Soil erosion by overland flow is a naturally occurring process which has been recorded in many places around Scotland, although there has been no systematic national evaluation of erosion risk.

2.   Many factors affect soil erosion risk in Scotland other than overland flow induced by rainfall intensity. These factors vary both spatially and temporally.

3.   A rule-based model was developed to determine the inherent geomorphological risk of soil erosion by overland flow from a consideration of potential runoff over unvegetated soils. The model was applied, in GIS, to two existing national-scale soils and topographic datasets. This produced an estimate of the erosion risk throughout Scotland.

4.   From an estimated total land area of 77,000 km^2, over 40,000 km^2 (53.4%) of Scotland are classified as having a moderate inherent risk of erosion by overland flow, and a further 25,000 km^2 (32.1%) have a high risk.

18.1 Introduction

Soil erosion by overland flow is a naturally occurring process. Its rate, intensity and location can be altered by land management. Erosion can impact significantly on the natural heritage; for example, degradation of spawning grounds through streambed aggradation or increased turbidity, increased flood risk and eutrophication of rivers and lochs.

Although there have been recorded instances of severe erosion in Scotland (Hulme and Blyth, 1985; Spiers and Frost, 1985; Watson and Evans, 1991; Birnie, 1993; Kirkbride and Reeves, 1993; Davidson and Harrison, 1995; Wade and Kirkbride, 1998), there has been no systematic national evaluation of erosion risk. Only through assessing the underlying, inherent erosion risk and its spatial distribution can effective and targeted land management strategies be put in place to reduce the impact on the natural heritage.

18.2 Factors affecting soil erosion risk

Soil erosion by overland flow depends on the mechanical stability of the soil, the nature and extent of vegetation cover and the occurrence of triggering events such as rainfall and snowmelt. Soil erosion in Scotland is known to be triggered by events such as rapid snowmelt (Wade and Kirkbride, 1998), high intensity rainfall (Hulme and Blyth, 1985; Davidson and Harrison, 1995; Frost and Spiers, 1996) and prolonged low intensity rainfall

(Kirkbride and Reeves, 1993). This indicates that rainfall intensity is not a good indicator of the erosion risk in Scotland. Erosion by overland flow occurs when the soil's storage capacity is exceeded and runoff is initiated. As slopes increase, any potential runoff that is generated will have a greater ability to erode.

Soil particle detachability is the process by which soil aggregates disintegrate into their constituent parts that can then be transported. It is a complex attribute influenced by the amount and type of clay and by the amount of organic matter. In many soil erosion models (e.g. Wischmeier and Smith, 1978; Flanagan and Nearing, 1995; Morgan *et al.*, 1998), soil texture is used as a surrogate for this attribute or as a carrier of this information. As roots can have a binding action on the soil, soil particle detachability is generally determined on bare soil. Therefore, a rule-based model was developed to determine the inherent geomorphological risk of soil erosion by overland flow from a consideration of potential runoff over unvegetated soils.

18.3 Development of the rule-based model

A transparent, rule-based model was developed (Lilly *et al.*, 1999) which combined slope angle and percentage runoff (Table 18.1) to give a simple ranking of the erosive power of overland flow (ranked a-g). The erosive power was then combined with soil surface texture to produce a number of erodibility classes for both mineral soils (Table 18.2) and organic surface horizons (Table 18.3). These numbered erodibility classes (1-9 for mineral topsoils and I-VIII for organic topsoils) were subsequently grouped into six erosion risk classes (low, moderate and high for both mineral and organic topsoils).

Table 18.1 Slope versus runoff to derive erosive power of overland flow.

Percentage Runoff	Slope categories (degrees)					
	<2	2-4.9	5-9.9	10-17.9	18-30	>30
<20	a	b	c	d	d	slopes
20-40	b	c	d	e	f	unstable
>40	c	d	e	f	g	

Table 18.2 Erodibility classes for mineral soils.

Soil texture class	Erosive Power						
	a	b	c	d	e	f	g
Fine	1	2	3	4	5	6	7
Medium	2	Low	4	Moderate	6	High	8
Coarse	3	4	5	6	7	8	9

Table 18.3 Erodibility classes for soils with peaty or organic surface layers.

	Erosive Power						
	a	b	c	d	e	f	g
Peaty or	I	II	III	IV	V	VI	VII
humus topsoil		Low			Moderate		
Organic soils (Peats)				High	VIII		

18.4 Implementation of the rules within a GIS

The model was applied to two existing national scale soils and topographic datasets to produce an estimate of the erosion risk throughout Scotland. Each map unit depicted on the 1:250,000 scale national soil map of Scotland (MISR, 1991) was allocated to a topsoil texture class and to a runoff category. Runoff was predicted from the Hydrology of Soil Types classification (Boorman *et al.,* 1995). The slope coverage was derived from the 1:50,000 scale Ordnance Survey digital elevation model. These coverages were combined following the rules to produce a map of the soil erosion risk with a resolution of 50 m (Plate 31).

18.5 Results and conclusions

From an estimated total land area of 77,000 km^2, over 40,000 km^2 (53.4%) of Scotland are classified as having a moderate inherent risk of erosion by overland flow, and a further 25,000 km^2 (32.1%) have a high risk. The map depicts the dominant erosion class in each 50 m grid cell. As significant areas of Scotland have continuous and permanent vegetation cover, the *actual* area where erosion occurs will be less.

The classification gives a baseline estimate of the inherent geomorphological risk of soil erosion by overland flow in Scotland. Future work will aim to incorporate land use data into the rule-base, allowing the development of management plans to help minimise the instances of erosion in sensitive areas. As climate is not yet an integral component of the rule-base, future work will also aim to incorporate climate data such as rainfall seasonality, intensity and duration in relation to soil moisture content, plant growth and land use.

References

Birnie, R.V. 1993. Erosion rates on bare peat surfaces in Shetland. *Scottish Geographical Magazine,* **109**, 12-17.

Boorman, D.B., Hollis, J.M and Lilly, A. 1995. *Hydrology of soil types: a hydrologically-based classification of the soils of the United Kingdom.* Institute of Hydrology Report, No.126. Institute of Hydrology, Wallingford.

Davidson, D.A. and Harrison, D.J. 1995. The nature, causes and implications of water erosion on arable land. *Soil Use and Management,* **11**, 63-68.

Flanagan, D.C. and Nearing, M.A. 1995. USDA-Water Erosion Prediction Project: hillslope profile and watershed model documentation. *NSERL Report,* No. 10. USDA-ARS National Soil Erosion Research Laboratory, West Lafayette.

Frost, C.A. and Spiers, R.B. 1996. Soil erosion from a single rainstorm over an area in East Lothian. *Soil Use and Management,* **12**, 8-12.

Hulme P.D. and Blyth A.W. 1985. Observations on the erosion of blanket peat in Yell, Shetland. *Geografiska Annaler,* **67A**, 119-122.

Kirkbride, M.P. and Reeves, A.D. 1993. Soil erosion caused by low-intensity rainfall in Angus, Scotland. *Applied Geography,* **13**, 299-311.

Lilly, A., Hudson, G., Birnie, R.V. and Horne, P.L. 1999. *The inherent geomorphological risk of soil erosion by overland flow in Scotland.* Report prepared for Scottish Natural Heritage. Macaulay Land Use Research Institute, Aberdeen.

Morgan, C., Quinton, J.N., Smith, R.E., Govers, G., Poesen, J.W.A., Auerswald, K., Chisci, G., Torri, D., Styczen, M.E. and Folly, A.J.V. 1998. *The European Soil Erosion Model (EUROSEM): Documentation and User Guide.* Silsoe College, Cranfield University.

MISR 1981. Soil map of Scotland: scale 1:250 000. Macaulay Institute for Soil Research, Aberdeen.

Spiers, R.B and Frost, C.A. 1985. The increasing incidence of accelerated soil water erosion on arable land in the east of Scotland. *Research and Development in Agriculture*, **2**, 161-167.

Wade, R.J. and Kirkbride, M.P. 1998. Snowmelt-generated runoff and erosion in Fife, Scotland. *Earth Surface Processes and Landforms*, **23**, 123-132.

Watson, A. and Evans, R. 1991. A comparison of estimates of soil erosion made in the field and from photographs. *Soil and Tillage Research*, **19**, 17-27.

Wischmeier, W.H. and Smith, D.D. 1978. Predicting rainfall erosion losses. *USDA Agricultural Handbook*, No 537. United States Department of Agriculture, Washington D.C.

19 SUSTAINABILITY AND USE OF NON-ENERGY MINERAL RESOURCES

Ian Lindley, Alan P. McKirdy and Andrew A. McMillan

Summary

1. Sustainability and use of mineral resources is at first reading a conflict of terms. Drawing from the diverse backgrounds of the co-authors, this paper presents views on the definition of 'sustainable development' in relation to non-energy minerals, and considers the place of sustainable mineral working in current land use planning.

2. The minerals industry continues to extract large quantities of aggregates from Scotland each year. Although the principles of sustainability have been acknowledged by the industry, more could be done to convert policy into best practice. However, there are good examples of well-conceived site development plans in which restoration has resulted in enhanced physical and biological natural habitats, presenting new opportunities for education and recreation. Increased use of demolition and construction wastes will inevitably reduce the demand for primary aggregates, and the introduction of the Aggregate Levy will enhance that process.

3. These issues play a crucial part in the strategic planning process which seeks to balance the need for mineral production with a wide variety of competing uses for land. They are discussed with reference to current practice, guidance and legislation.

19.1 Introduction

This paper examines the extraction and use of non-energy minerals (especially construction minerals such as sand and gravel, crushed rock aggregate and building stone) in the United Kingdom and considers the criteria by which sustainable use of these materials can be assessed. The concept of sustainable development and the continued use of mineral resources may at first appear to be entirely incompatible. Past economic imperatives to build our economic infrastructure required that resources, non-renewable on a human timescale, such as sand and gravel, have been already consumed in considerable quantities. So is sustainable development achievable in reality, and if so, what changes in current practice are necessary to realise this goal?

Magnus Magnusson, past Chairman of Scottish Natural Heritage, in his address to the Natural Environment Research Council in November 1992 (Magnusson, 1993), argued that market forces will tend towards over-consumption, and the exploitation of the reserves that are cheap to work will be targeted with less consideration given to the impact on the environment. The demand for minerals is driven by the expectation of society. People expect good homes, an efficient transport infrastructure, modern learning establishments and hospitals. That same society also demands that the built historic and natural heritage enjoys protection. This is one of the many challenges that we face at the start of the third millennium, but it is surely not beyond us to make adequate provision for both.

19.2 Defining sustainable development

The World Commission on Environment and Development (1983) defined sustainable development as "development that meets the needs of the present without compromising the ability of future generations to meet their own needs. At a minimum, sustainable development must not endanger the natural systems that support life on Earth: the atmosphere, the waters, the soils and the living beings".

The UK Government response to the United Nations Conference on Environment and Development held in 1992 (the Rio Earth Summit) was comprehensively set out in the paper, *Sustainable Development - The UK Strategy* (Department of the Environment, 1994). The Strategy advocates waste minimisation, encourages recycling and endorses the effective protection of high quality landscapes and wildlife from development in all but exceptional circumstances. With reference to mineral resources, the Strategy recognises that mineral working can have a significant environmental impact and often takes place in areas of attractive countryside. The document also contains the indication that Government wished to see indigenous mineral resources developed within its broad objectives of promoting economic growth, assisting the creation and maintenance of employment and protecting the environment.

These broad themes were then taken forward by the Scottish Office, with the issue of sustainability, in the minerals context, placed firmly on the agenda in *National Planning Policy Guideline NPPG 4 - Land for Mineral Working* (The Scottish Office, 1994). NPPG 4 acknowledges the difficulty of assessing whether the exploration of a non-renewable resource constitutes a sustainable activity and also poses the key question - whether the asset created through the use of the minerals will be of greater value to society than the natural asset that is lost. NPPG 4 also reaffirms the framework for sustainable mineral development contained within *Sustainable Development - The UK Strategy*, the particular issues being:

- to conserve minerals as far as possible, while ensuring adequate supply to meet the needs of society;
- to minimise production of waste and to encourage efficient use of high quality materials and recycling of wastes;
- to encourage sensitive working practices during minerals extraction and to preserve the overall quality of the environment once extraction has ceased; and
- to protect designated areas of critical landscape or nature quality from development, other than in exceptional circumstances where it has been demonstrated that development is in the public interest.

More recently, Alan Meale MP (1999), outlining the UK Government's vision of sustainable development, highlighted four broad objectives:

- social progress, ensuring better health, good education and a reasonable standard of living for everyone;

- effective protection of the environment, ensuring that people's health does not suffer from poor air quality or other pollution, and protection of wildlife and the countryside;
- prudent use of natural resources, ensuring that we use resources efficiently and minimise waste; and
- maintenance of high and stable levels of economic growth and employment, so that everyone can share in high living standards and greater job opportunities, and to generate income and wealth needed to pay for essential infrastructure and future investments.

Each of these elements of the vision has potential consequences for the way in which minerals are developed and used. They also ensure that proper consideration is given to the changing demand for minerals, the potential for re-use of quarry wastes and that recycling of construction materials is encouraged.

19.3 Defining resources and reserves in Scotland

Mineral resources come in a variety of forms, from materials that can be worked and used directly (e.g. gravels and hard rock aggregate for construction and building) to those which require to be processed for industrial use (e.g. limestone and brickclay). With the exception of timber, virtually all materials used to construct the built environment (e.g. homes, schools and roads) originate in one form or another from the Earth's crust. Thus an 'inventory' of the geological deposits both on land and offshore is essential to determine the distribution of potentially useful minerals throughout the country.

The landscape of Scotland is determined by the distribution, structure and composition of the varied underlying geology formed over at least 3000 million years (Trewin, this volume). The opening and closing of oceans, intermittent volcanic activity, the incursion of shallow seas, the development of major river systems and extended episodes of glaciation can all be inferred from this record of the rocks. The glacial processes are responsible for some of the most recent modifications to the landscape and have left an extensive mantle of superficial deposits.

This geological legacy has provided indigenous resources ranging from metalliferous minerals, extensively exploited in previous centuries, to constructional and industrial minerals, including hard rock suitable for crushed aggregate and deposits of sand and gravel. Over the last five millennia, this rich and varied resource has been expoited for many end-uses, but primarily for the purposes of construction, in one form or another. Until the 1920s, much of the built heritage of Scotland was dependent upon the availability of good quality, indigenous stone, the local supplies of sandstone, flagstone, granite, slate and limestone (for lime mortar) once supplying the bulk of the nation's building requirements (McMillan, 1997). Quarrying of building stone resources may be regarded as a sustainable activity. The key to economic success of many pre-20th century quarries lay in the proximity to market of suitable, easily won resources. When compared with commonly used modern building materials, such as brick and concrete, the processing energy requirements (excluding transport) of stone production were, and still are, relatively low (Historic Scotland, 1997). Furthermore, maximum use was made of the total resource, so that the best material was cut for ashar (dimensioned stone) and poorer quality stone used as rubble for a variety of purposes including walling. Most of these materials were capable of recycling, for example granite and dolerite setts. The modern revival of the use and re-use of setts and flagstones for streetscapes constitutes a sustainable activity, provided that the design and technical specification of stone paving are well understood (McMillan, 2000).

The working of other mineral resources was less sustainable. These include the coal, oil-shale, ironstone, fireclay and limestone resources of the Midland Valley of Scotland, which fed the Industrial Revolution of the 19th century. Extensive mining and quarrying of these minerals left its legacy in the form of changed landscapes, groundwater pollution and subsidence problems, especially, but not exclusively, in the urban fringes of the major cities (Browne *et al.*, 1986).

19.4 Mineral extraction and the environment with reference to aggregates

The concept of sustainability is difficult to reconcile with the working of aggregates. It is self-evident that these resources are non-renewable on a human timescale and that particularly, in terms of sand and gravel, much of the easily exploitable reserve has already been removed in areas close to the primary markets. What remains is often situated in areas of highly valued countryside where the extraction process is considered to be a threat to the landscape or other environmental attributes.

With regard to crushed rock supplies within Scotland, demand continues to be met largely by local quarries serving predominantly local markets, with transport distances usually under 25 miles. However, the demand for materials of high quality and specification has led to the transport of these materials over greater distances. Indeed, the wider pattern of UK supply and demand is more complex. The major market of south-east England is naturally devoid of hard rock supplies and is thus a major importer from a wide geographical area. To meet the demands for crushed rock aggregate, one option considered in NPPG 4 (The Scottish Office, 1994) was the development of large coastal quarries (superquarries). It was argued that environmental disturbance associated with such quarries would be concentrated in clearly defined and often remote areas, high levels of production could be guaranteed over substantial periods of time and, in the case of coastal locations, bulk movement by ship to the heart of the market could significantly reduce the environmental impacts of transport. To date the sole UK example of such a development is at Glensanda on the Morvern peninsula, western Scotland.

19.5 Resources and land-use planning

In the broadest sense, a mineral resource includes materials that are potentially workable but not necessarily currently economically exploitable (McKelvey, 1972; Cook and Harris, 1998). This contrasts with reserves, which can be defined as that part of a resource that can be economically worked. One key aspect that may seem self-evident, but needs to be borne in mind, is that minerals can only be worked where they occur (Fish, 1972). Land-use planning must therefore be guided by a detailed knowledge of the distribution and character of the geological resource, so that informed decision-making is possible.

Since the Second World War, the rapid rise in demand for constructional minerals inevitably led to land-use conflicts. In the late 1960s the pressing need for aggregate resources in south-east England (Verney Advisory Committee on Aggregates, 1976) led to a programme (funded by the Department of the Environment) of systematic regional resource assessment to provide an objective background against which both local and national planning policy could be determined (Thurrell, 1981). Such surveys were undertaken by the Institute of Geological Sciences (now British Geological Survey) and extended across the UK. These surveys also provided a basis for understanding inter-regional and national patterns of supply and demand.

Following the completion of these resource surveys, and recognising the need to make informed land-use planning decisions, the Department of the Environment funded an environmental geology mapping programme (Monro and Hull, 1986). The key to this approach was the production of maps with information on different attributes of the mapped area, such as geology, former quarrying and mining activity and resources (Browne *et al.*, 1986; Monro and Hull, 1986). The thematic geological mapping approach became the recognised means of providing geological information for the formulation of Local Plans and Structure Plans (Brook and Marker, 1987) and land-use planning (Culshaw *et al.*, 1990; Smith and Ellison, 1999).

Advances in digital technology now enable analogue information to be readily translatable into Geographic Information Systems (GIS) for rapid retrieval of relevant datasets, so that GIS plays an increasingly important part in informing land-use planning decisions. An example of this approach is presented in the recently published guidance for minerals in the Midland Valley of Scotland (Scottish Natural Heritage, 2000). This document outlines the creation of sensitivity maps and strategic datasets that define the distribution of mineral resources based on British Geological Survey (BGS) data, Earth heritage and nature conservation sensitivity areas, landscape data and recreational and access data. GIS enables appropriate layers of information to be combined to inform input to Development Plans (Structure Plans, area-based Plans and Mineral Subject Local Plans).

19.6 The aggregate industry today

Demand for the UK's aggregate (crushed rock and sand and gravel) resources rose during the post-Second World War period, 1945-1970. Since 1965, production of these materials has since fluctuated between about 150 and 300 million tonnes and is currently (1998 statistics) about 220 million tonnes (Figure 19.1; British Geological Survey, 1999). Currently the UK minerals industry has an annual turnover of £3 billion, and 90% of its output is used by Britain's construction industry, which itself contributes about one-tenth of the country's Gross Domestic Product. Aggregate output in Scotland during the period 1980-1988 has grown, but in the 10 years from 1989-1998, output has been relatively stable at an average of approximately 33.5 million tonnes per annum (British Geological Survey, 1999). Quarrying occupies only 0.35%, in areal terms, of England and Wales and a lower proportion of land within Scotland.

19.6.1 Mineral planning permissions

There are many instances where opportunism to meet demand from the nearest available source took no account of environmental considerations. As an example, consider the public outcry that would result if it were proposed to open a quarry in Holyrood Park, Edinburgh. Yet, historically, quarries at and near Salisbury Crags provided sandstones for use in the construction of Holyrood Palace and whinstone (dolerite) for paving the streets of the city (McMillan *et al.*, 1999). It was only after 400 years of activity that mineral

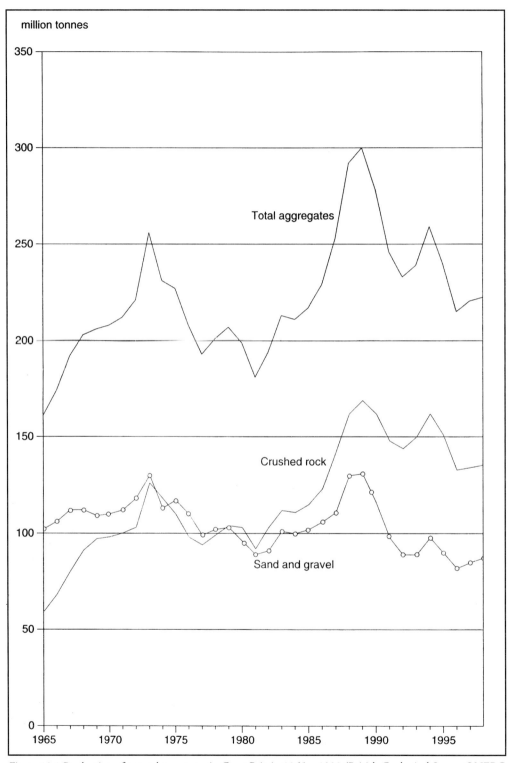

Figure 19.1 Production of natural aggregates in Great Britain 1965 – 1998 (British Geological Survey ©NERC 1999).

extraction in such a prominent location became unacceptable to society and the subject of legal action to terminate the practice.

The modern extractive industry is facing similar changes in public opinion in relation to the acceptability of some contemporary operations. The surrender of several extant planning permissions within the National Parks, for example at Furness Quarry in the Peak District, is indicative of the industry's response to this change in public mood.

The Review of Mineral Working procedures introduced by the Environment Act 1990 requires the regular review of mineral planning permissions and provides the opportunity to adopt modern planning conditions and schemes of working and to agree high quality restoration proposals. By working in close co-operation with the Mineral Planning Authority, this process will continue to bring significant improvements in standards of operation, with proper account being taken of environmental matters, particularly with respect to site restoration.

The surrender of working rights in sensitive areas and the comprehensive review and updating of older mineral planning permissions illustrates the commitment of the minerals industry to moving its existing business forward in a responsible and sustainable manner.

19.6.2 New approaches to minerals planning and recycling of wastes

Over many years, one of the difficulties in adopting sustainable minerals extraction policies has been the 'predict-and-provide' planning regime (Oliver, 2000). The identification of land for quarrying to meet forecasted demand for material has inevitably increased the pressure to work the minerals on allocated ground even when the forecast is inaccurate. In future, for site selection, it may become increasingly important to adopt the sequential approach of planning, monitoring and managing (PMM). This approach, set out in *Planning Policy Guidance Note, No. 3 – Housing* (Department of the Environment, Transport and the Regions, 2000; Oliver, 2000), enables policies to be devised to plan for the environment and social and economic objectives, to monitor progress by means of targets and to manage the policy by adjusting to changing circumstances. By this means it may be possible to avoid the most environmentally sensitive sites.

The use of quarry wastes is another area that could be improved to meet both profitability of quarrying operations and sustainability criteria (Harrison, 1999). Quarry wastes are thus reduced and use of the resource is optimised. During the early 1990s, in England and Wales some 10% of all bulk construction material was derived from the existing pool of secondary and recyclable wastes, whereas in Scotland only 2% of equivalent materials were used (Arup Economics and Planning, 1991). In 1998, Scottish local authorities reported that just over 5 million tonnes of construction and demolition waste were disposed to landfill (Scottish Environment Protection Agency, 1999). This was some 2 million tonnes less than arose in 1997 (a possible consequence of the impact of the Landfill Tax). However, "the strong dependence on landfill for waste management is not sustainable since it involves the depletion of both renewable and finite natural resources" (Scottish Environment Protection Agency, 1999).

19.6.3 Biodiversity, education and industry best practice

NPPG 4 (The Scottish Office, 1994) recognises the requirement to ensure continuity of supplies to meet the needs of society within a framework of sustainable mineral development. NPPG14 on *Natural Heritage* encourages the adoption of "policies which promote and afford protection to species and habitats identified as priorities in Local Biodiversity Action Plans" (The Scottish Office, 1999a). The industry also recognises that conserving the UK's biodiversity is an essential requirement for sustainable development. This 'unlikely' relationship between biodiversity and mineral extraction is described in a joint publication by English Nature, the Quarry Products Association and the Silica & Moulding Sands Association (English Nature *et al.*, 1999).

Because identified resources often potentially fall within environmentally sensitive areas or close to urban populations, there is an increasing need for integrated solutions to land-use planning. In Scotland, this is reflected in local authority Structure Plans and also in a limited number of the Local Biodiversity Action Plans. However, this situation is changing rapidly and, with the establishment of the Scottish Biodiversity Group (see The Scottish Office, 1999b, 2000 update), the links between geodiversity (the physical components of the natural heritage) and biodiversity (the biological processes) are now firmly recognised. The West Lothian Biodiversity Action Plan (West Lothian Council, 1998) is a good example where the influence of geology on the landscape and its ecology is given prominence. The Edinburgh Biodiversity Action Plan (Edinburgh Biodiversity Partnership, 2000) highlights how past quarrying activities have created new habitats and new opportunities for educational initiatives, for example through local geological societies and the Regionally Important Geological Sites (RIGS) Scheme (Royal Society for Nature Conservation, 1999) which offers non-statutory protection of sites.

There are many examples where restoration proposals have allowed research on key sites to continue. These include the Blakeney Esker, Norfolk, where the afteruse spinoff for education and tourism has also been recognised (Gray, 1992). The SSSI status of the Carstairs Kames, Lanarkshire, for long a major source of sand and gravel, clearly was a factor in preserving the integrity of the associated landforms (Jenkins, 1992). Nevertheless, the excavations have over the years offered much scope for research and it is clear that the scientific interest which these and similar deposits have generated has encouraged developers to argue the research benefits to be gained from exploitation of the resource. The balance between retaining prime examples of geomorphological features and opening new sections is an important consideration.

English Nature, the Silica & Moulding Sands Association and the Quarry Products Association have established a *Minerals and Nature Conservation Forum*; a Scottish version of this forum is currently under consideration. These organisations have also signed a joint Statement of Intent aimed at achieving environmentally sustainable management of mineral sites. Over 600 Sites of Special Scientific Interest (SSSIs) in England are former quarries, now managed to promote biodiversity. However, there is further scope to improve environmental management, and the recently published guide seeks to assist in this process (English Nature *et al.*, 1999). It identifies, within the context of the latest developments in biodiversity planning, good practice and new ideas to develop. Key points in this process are summarised in Table 19.1.

Table 19.1 Good practice in planning quarrying activities.

Quarrying activity	Actions
Planning and Site Selection	• work in partnership with statutory natural heritage bodies, the Wildlife Trusts, the RSPB and others • identify potential mineral sites that, through restoration, can contribute to biodiversity action plan targets without causing significant damage to existing biodiversity • make this potential contribution an important criterion in site selection • plan habitat creation based on the "habitat network" concept • treat environmental assessment as a process that parallels and links to scheme design
Operating Sites	• monitor sites to identify new species and habitats that appear during operation • wherever possible implement working practices to accommodate these species/habitats • implement working practices that reduce noise, dust and other impacts that can indirectly affect wildlife
Managing Restored Sites	• put in place management measures for restored sites that meet the long-term needs of biodiversity conservation • implement the management needed to conserve valuable habitats or to restore degraded areas on non-operational land
Other Activities	• consider preparing corporate statements of commitment to biodiversity and company biodiversity action plans • encourage staff to attend training courses geared to biodiversity and minerals • contribute to research on biodiversity • share experience in habitat creation, restoration and management • encourage educational and recreational use of restored and non-operational sites (where this does not cause damage) through, for example, the Regionally Important Geological Sites Scheme

Most of the points outlined in Table 19.1 are being actively incorporated into current industry business practice. For example:

- There is consultation with external organisations and wildlife groups during the site planning process.
- The preparation of restoration proposals for beneficial after-use is an important part of the overall design process.
- Environmental assessment issues are closely related to design.
- Species monitoring is routinely undertaken and there is a growing number of sites where specific works are undertaken to accommodate species.
- Minimisation of noise and dust is a major focus of attention and improvements continue to be made.
- Long-term management measures for restored sites are common, often involving wildlife groups and other organisations.
- Significant inroads are being made towards restoration of historic sites and improved environmental management of non-operational lands.

- Company environmental policy statements are now commonplace and detail the environmental parameters of operations over many areas and not solely biodiversity.
- Training courses covering all areas of environmental matters are regularly held to ensure the spread of knowledge and adoption of best practice.

Also, in its response to Government on a proposed aggregates tax, the Quarry Products Association, the trade association for the aggregates, asphalt, surfacing and ready mixed concrete industries whose members produce 90% of crushed rock and sand and gravel production in the United Kingdom, put forward in its 'New Deal Package' a proposal that a Sustainability Foundation should be established. This would have been funded by a 10p per tonne levy which would have produced some £20 million a year to fund initiatives which enhance sustainability. However, the Chancellor rejected the New Deal proposals and instead announced in the March 2000 Budget that an Aggregates Levy would be introduced in April 2002. The Aggregates Levy will apply to sand, gravel, crushed rocks and material dredged from the sea bed within UK territorial waters at a rate of £1.60 per tonne. It is being introduced with the clear intention of reducing demand for virgin aggregate and encouraging the use of recycled material.

19.7 Conclusions

The various initiatives outlined in this paper illustrate that the extractive industry has acknowledged the need for sustainable development and that greater emphasis is now given to environmental concerns generally. It is inevitably 'work in progress' and this momentum must be maintained to ensure that the central principles become enshrined in industry best practice. Efforts must also continue to reduce the demand for primary aggregates, and where the requirement for construction material remains, it should be met by increased use of recycled and secondary materials. Crucial to the success of these initiatives is an enhanced public awareness of the principles of sustainability and the practice of good environmental management, as the standards adopted by the minerals industry are demonstrably driven by changes in the public mood.

Acknowledgement

A.A. McMillan thanks Dr C.G. Smith (BGS, Edinburgh) for constructive criticism of this paper. Mr McMillan publishes with permission of the Director, British Geological Survey (NERC).

References

Arup Economics and Planning 1991. *Occurence and Utilisation of Mineral and Construction Wastes*. Department of the Environment Geological and Minerals Planning Research Programmes. HMSO, London.

British Geological Survey 1999. *United Kingdom Minerals Yearbook 1998: Statistical Data to 1997*. British Geological Survey, Keyworth, Nottingham.

Brooks, D. and Marker, B.R. 1987. Thematic geological mapping as an essential tool in land-use planning. *In* Culshaw, M.G., Bell, F.G., Cripps, J.C. and O'Hara, M. (eds) *Planning and Engineering Geology*. Geological Society Engineering Group Special Publication, No. 4, 211-214.

Browne, M.A.E., Forsyth, I.H. and McMillan, A.A. 1986. Glasgow, a case study in urban geology. *Journal of the Geological Society of London*, **143**, 509-520.

Cook, P.J. and Harris, P.M. 1998. Reserves, resources and the UK mining industry. *International Mining and Minerals*, May 1998, 120-133.

Culshaw M.G., Foster, A., Cripps, J.C. and Bell, F.G. 1990. Applied geological maps for land-use planning in Great Britain. *In* Price, D.G. (ed.) *Proceedings of the Sixth International Congress of the International Association of Engineering Geology, Amsterdam, August 1990.* Vol. 1. A.A. Balkema, Rotterdam, 85-93.

Department of the Environment 1994. *Sustainable Development - The UK Strategy.* HMSO, London.

Department of the Environment, Transport and the Regions 2000. *Housing. Planning Policy Guidance Note No. 3.* Department of the Environment, Transport and the Regions, London.

Edinburgh Biodiversity Partnership 2000. *The Edinburgh Biodiversity Action Plan.* City of Edinburgh Council, Edinburgh.

English Nature, Quarry Products Association and Silica & Moulding Sands Association 1999. *Biodiversity and Minerals. Extracting the Benefits for Wildlife.* Entec UK Ltd.

Fish, B.G. 1972. Road materials and quarrying. *Quarterly Journal of Engineering Geology*, **5**, 1995-2004.

Gray, J M. 1992. The Blakeney Esker, Norfolk: conservation and restoration. *In* Stevens, C., Gordon, J.E., Green, C.P. and Macklin, M. (eds) *Conserving our Landscape.* Proceedings of the Conference, Conserving Our Landscape: Evolving Landforms and Ice-Age Heritage, Crewe, 1992. Peterborough, 82-86.

Harrison, D. 1999. Re-use of quarry wastes: developing saleable by-products. *Earthwise*, **13**, January 1999, 32.

Historic Scotland 1997. *A Future for Stone in Scotland.* Historic Scotland Research Report prepared by Hutton and Rostron. Historic Scotland, Edinburgh.

Jenkins, K. 1992. Preservation versus investigation: earth scientists and conservation at the Carstairs Kames, Lanarkshire, Scotland. *In* Stevens, C., Gordon, J.E., Green, C.P. and Macklin, M. (eds) *Conserving our Landscape.* Proceedings of the Conference, Conserving Our Landscape: Evolving Landforms and Ice-Age Heritage, Crewe, 1992. Peterborough, 75-81.

McKelvey, V.E. 1972. Mineral resource estimates and public policy. *American Scientist*, **60**(1), 32-40 (reprinted in *US Geological Survey Professional Paper*, No. 820, 1973).

McMillan, A.A. 1997. Quarries of Scotland. *Historic Scotland Technical Advice Note,* No. 12. Historic Scotland, Edinburgh.

McMillan, A.A., Gillanders, R.J. and Fairhurst, J.A. 1999. *Building Stones of Edinburgh.* Edinburgh Geological Society, Edinburgh.

McMillan, P. 2000. Road surfacing: natural selection. *Surveyor*, 1 June 2000, 14-15.

Meale, A. 1999. Sustainable development. *Earthwise*, **13**, January 1999, 4-5.

Monro, S.K. and Hull, J.H., 1986. Environmental geology in Great Britain. *In* Bender, F. (ed) *Geo-Resources and Environment.* Proceedings of the Fourth International Symposium on Geo-Resources and Environment, Hannover, Federal Republic of Germany, 1985. E. Schweizerbart'sche Verlagsbuchhandlung (Nägele u. Obermiller), Stuttgart, 107-124.

Magnusson, M. 1993. Sense and sustainability: homage to Frank Fraser Darling. The 1992 NERC Annual Lecture by Magnus Magnusson. *NERC News*, January 1993.

Oliver, H. 2000. Sustainable minerals planning: the way ahead. *Mineral Planning*, **83**, June 2000, 3-5.

Royal Society for Nature Conservation 1999. RIGS Handbook. 1st edition. Royal Society for Nature Conservation, Newark.

Scottish Environment Protection Agency 1999. *National Waste Strategy: Scotland.* Scottish Environment Protection Agency, Stirling.

Scottish Natural Heritage 2000 *Minerals and the Natural Heritage in Scotland's Midland Valley.* Scottish Natural Heritage, Perth.

The Scottish Office 1994. *Land for Mineral Working. National Planning Policy Guideline NPPG 4.* The Scottish Office, Environment Department, Edinburgh.

The Scottish Office 1999a. *Natural Heritage. National Planning Policy Guideline NPPG 14.* The Scottish Office, Development Department, Edinburgh.

The Scottish Office 1999b. Scottish Biodiversity Group Local Biodiversity Action Plans in Scotland, Sector Guidance Note 1: Geodiversity (2000 update). *In: Local Biodiversity Action Plans: a Manual and Guidance Notes.* The Scottish Office, Edinburgh.

Smith, A. and Ellison, R.A. 1999. Applied geological maps for planning and development: a review of examples from England and Wales, 1983-96. *Quarterly Journal of Engineering Geology,* **32**, S1-44.

Thurrell, R.G. 1981. The identification of bulk mineral resources; the contribution of the Institute of Geological Sciences. *Quarry Management and Products,* **8**, 181-193.

Verney Advisory Committee on Aggregates 1976. *Aggregates: the Way Ahead.* HMSO, London.

West Lothian Council 1998. *Planning for Biodiversity Action in West Lothian.* Consultation Report of West Lothian Council, Linlithgow.

World Commission on Environment and Development 1983. *Our Common Future.* Oxford University Press, Oxford.

20 EARTH RESOURCES AND FUTURE ENERGY USE IN SCOTLAND

Howard Johnson, Dominic Counsell, Martyn F. Quinn, Susan J. Stoker, Joanne E. Cavill and David Long

Summary

1.   Currently, most of the energy consumed in Scotland comes from fossil and nuclear fuels. Considerable reserves of fossil fuels remain onshore and offshore Scotland, although the quantification of future resources is fraught with uncertainties. New ways of exploiting fossil fuels within the Midland Valley of Scotland may include the extraction of coalbed methane and coal gasification. Possible deposits of gas hydrates on the Atlantic Margin, and geothermal resources within the Midland Valley, may be exploitable in the longer term.

2.   Notwithstanding current estimates of resources, the burning of oil and coal is linked with air pollution and global climate change, and there are uncertainties over future use of nuclear power. These problems raise doubts about the sustainability of current energy usage.

3.   Steps to reduce the environmental problems of fossil fuel use include the underground sequestration of CO_2 and, potentially, the splitting of methane into clean hydrogen fuel and disposable CO_2. Research into safe underground storage for radioactive waste material aims to resolve environmental problems associated with nuclear power generation.

4.   Scotland has large resources of renewable sources of energy. Although their exploitation would avoid the environmental effects linked with fossil fuels, they can have significant impacts on landscapes, habitats and amenity. Development of renewable energy resources should not be permitted to compromise Scotland's natural heritage, which has considerable economic significance for tourism. A strategic approach to the future exploitation of renewable energy is required which takes account of natural heritage sensitivities.

5.   All energy usage affects the environment. The future energy mix in Scotland will be determined within the context of a complex range of economic, technological, political and environmental factors.

20.1 Introduction

Developed societies have a dependence upon high levels of energy use, but problems associated with sustainable development and the environment raise questions about the balance of costs and benefits resulting from the way energy needs are met. Currently, about 46% of the annual generated output of electricity in Scotland derives from fossil fuels, with

44% from nuclear, 9% from large-scale hydro and less than 1% from new renewable sources (Fellows and Snodin, 1999). There is effectively no contribution from oil for electricity generation, though current forms of transportation would be impossible without petroleum products.

This review concentrates on geoscience issues associated with Scotland's non-renewable energy resources, but recognises that these issues cannot be tackled in the absence of consideration of the natural environment. The potential contribution of renewable energy resources is outlined, along with the impacts these developments can have upon the natural heritage. Finally, selected solutions are outlined that could mitigate some of the environmental impacts associated with fossil fuel consumption and disposal of nuclear waste, and a way forward is suggested for a strategic approach to some aspects of planning for renewable energy.

20.2 Non-renewable energy resources

Significant amounts of oil, gas and coal are produced from onshore and offshore Scotland. A number of emerging fuels and technologies also offer other potential for energy supply.

20.2.1 Oil and gas

Much of the UK North Sea Basin lies offshore Scotland and contains over 100 producing oil and gas fields (Figure 20.1). The exploration and development of this petroleum province is now considered to be at a mature stage. In contrast, the extensive UK Atlantic Margin is a lightly explored frontier province, though the discovery and development of the major Foinaven and Schiehallion oilfields in the Faroe-Shetland Basin provides encouragement for the future.

One aspect of future decision-making regarding energy provision is estimation of our existing hydrocarbon resources, although it is important to recognise the uncertainties related to reserves estimation. On the UK Atlantic Margin, these uncertainties reflect the relative paucity of exploration information over much of the area, and difficulties in imaging effectively beneath a widespread and thick buried layer of lava and associated extensive sill complexes, which obscure the deep structure of the sedimentary basins. Past predictions for the UK have tended to underestimate the amounts of oil and gas expected to be produced (Figure 20.2). The indications are that considerable oil and gas reserves remain *in situ*. Current predictions suggest a future decline in UK oil and gas production from a peak at or near year 2000 (Figure 20.2).

The extent and rate of future exploration and development on the Atlantic Margin will reflect a number of influences, including the price of oil, the success ratio of wells, technological advances related to operating in a harsh environment, the fiscal regime and environmental protection issues. On the UK Atlantic Margin, the oil companies with licensed acreage are working together and with regulators and researchers to produce comprehensive regional environmental surveys, rather than adopting the piecemeal environmental approach originally used in the North Sea (Ferguson *et al.*, 1997).

20.2.2 Coal

Significant coal and lignite resources lie onshore and offshore Scotland (British Geological Survey, 1999). At April 1998, the total UK reserves of opencast coal, that have been proved

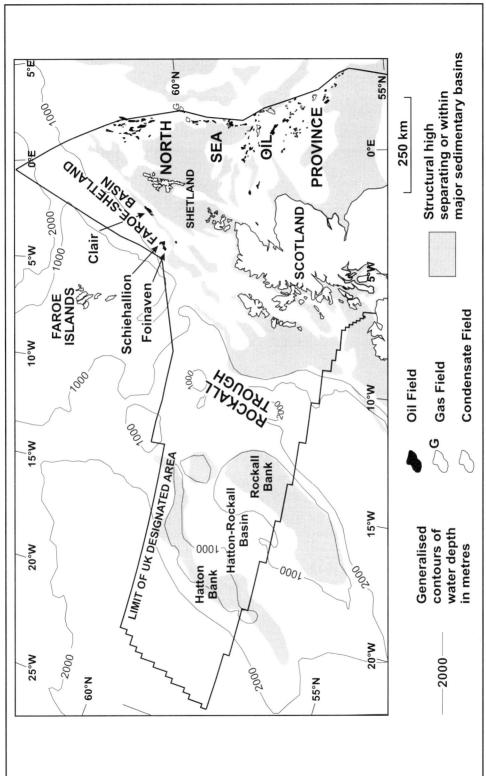

Figure 20.1 The distribution of oil, condensate and gas fields offshore Scotland.

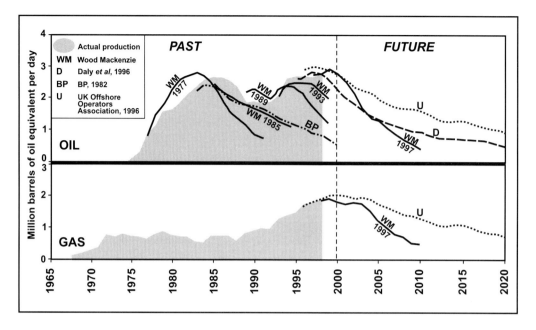

Figure 20.2 The amounts of oil and gas produced from the UK and its continental shelf compared with predicted amounts of production (modified after Daly *et al.*, 1996).

by drilling and for which planning permission for their extraction is in place, are estimated at approximately 89 Mt (International Mining Consultants Ltd, 1999); of this nearly 50% lies within Scotland.

Over the last few years there has been a marked decline in UK coal production, from over 90 Mt in 1990 to 44 Mt in 1998. Within Scotland, however, coal outputs have increased during this period, from 5.4 Mt to 8.2 Mt, with all of the increase coming from relatively low-cost opencast mining (Figure 20.3). Scotland has the capacity, and planning approval, to produce about 9.0 Mt per year for more than another 5 years.

However, opencast mining can affect sensitive landscapes, local amenity, and/or biodiversity. Scottish Natural Heritage (SNH) has considered a methodology for assessing the various natural heritage impacts which can derive from opencast developments within Scotland, and advocates a strategic approach to planning (Scottish Natural Heritage, 2000).

Longannet is the last major deep mine within Scotland (Figure 20.3), and supplied 1.8 Mt of coal to the electricity industry in 1997 (International Mining Consultants Ltd, 1999). While there are thought still to be major reserves under the Clackmannan and Fife coalfields, the future prospects for Longannet depend primarily upon planning considerations and technical issues related to the extraction of the coal.

20.2.3 Other non-renewable energy resources
Coalbed methane, coal gasification, gas hydrates and geothermal energy are all potential non-renewable energy sources that may be exploitable onshore and offshore Scotland in the

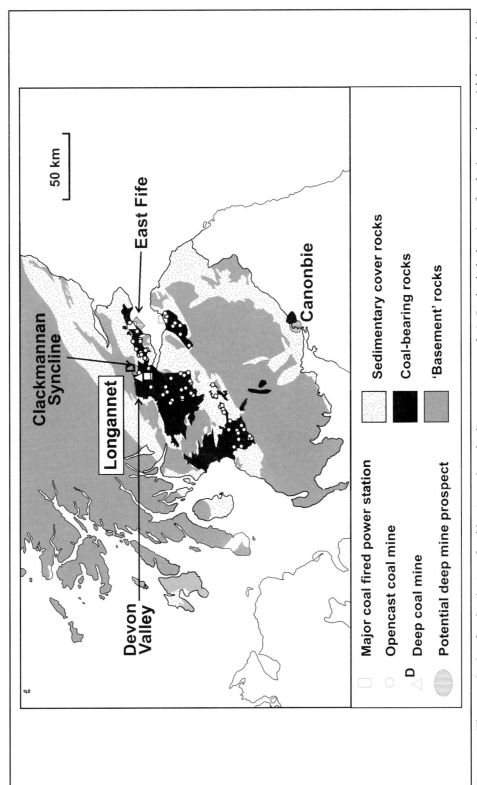

Figure 20.3 The generalised surface distribution of coal-bearing rocks and sedimentary cover rocks in Scotland; the locations of coal mines and potential deep coal mine prospects are indicated (modified after International Mining Consultants Limited, 1999; British Geological Survey, 1999; and Friends of the Earth Scotland, 1999).

future (Office of Science and Technology, 1998; Department of Trade and Industry, 1999a). Methane can be recovered from unworked coals, from working mines and from abandoned workings. The principal limitation on development at the moment is the generally low permeability of the UK coal seams, though techniques such as fracturing of the seams and horizontal drilling may improve efficiency. To put the size of the potential resource into perspective, unpublished information suggests that coalbed methane could account for about 1–2% of UK gas production by 2020. Initial testing of coalbed methane production is currently proceeding at Airth, near Stirling.

Underground coal gasification, though still in the development stage, may be of importance in the future. It involves very accurate directional drilling to the coal, which is then subject to a controlled burn that produces a usable gas combustion product.

Gas hydrates are ice-like crystalline accumulations that form under conditions of high pressure and low temperature and which can hold large quantities of methane (1 m^3 of methane hydrate contains up to 164 m^3 of methane at standard temperature and pressure). Despite major environmental and technological issues that need to be addressed, such large potential deposits of methane make gas hydrates attractive as a potential energy resource for the future and major research programmes have begun in many countries. However, the lack of suitable production technology implies that wide-scale exploitation, if proven to be feasible, is unlikely to take place for 20 years or so. Theoretically, gas hydrates could occur on the UK Atlantic Margin, though no evidence has yet been reported.

Within Scotland, there is some potential for the development of geothermal energy from low enthalpy hot groundwaters in Palaeozoic sedimentary basins and from radiothermic granites acting as Hot Dry Rock (HDR) reservoirs (British Geological Survey, 1988; Barker *et al.*, 2000). This resource is considered non-renewable as the extraction of heat is invariably at a faster rate than replenishment. Currently, only the very highest-grade geothermal resources can be developed economically, and Scottish resources are not of this type. The primary barriers to rapid development of geothermal resources are costly or inadequate technology, and high drilling and exploration costs. The greatest geothermal potential appears to lie within the Midland Valley, where Upper Devonian sandstones may contain water with temperatures high enough to exploit. However, development is frustrated by the great difficulty in forecasting the location of extensive fracture systems at the depth necessary to give suitably high temperatures (Barker *et al.*, 2000).

20.2.4 Nuclear

About 40% of electricity in Scotland comes from nuclear power stations. Nuclear power has the advantage over fossil fuels of not contributing to carbon emissions, although other issues have constrained its wider development in the UK.

Within Scotland there are three nuclear power stations: Hunterston B, Torness and Chapelcross. Their dates of commissioning and proposed decommissioning are 1976/2011, 1988/2018 and 1959/2010, respectively. These dates suggest that the power stations could be decommissioned within the next 20 years or so, which may potentially bring about a significant energy shortfall. However, decommissioning dates are routinely reassessed and a station's life could be extended well beyond the dates given here, provided that safety is not compromised. Costs associated with station decommissioning and safe waste storage are significant factors in the economics of nuclear power generation.

20.3 Environmental impacts of existing energy use

Environmental concerns associated with current fuel use are raising questions about the sustainability of established patterns of energy consumption in developed countries. For example, a build-up of atmospheric CO_2 from fossil fuel combustion is implicated, along with other gases, in global climate change. While it is difficult to reach a balanced view on the overall environmental implications of climate change, statistical depiction of the Central England Temperature Record spanning from 1659 to 1998 does show a warming trend, especially after about 1900 (Benner, 1999). The Kyoto Protocol and Framework Convention on Climate Change are international frameworks for addressing these issues. The UK Government has adopted a domestic aim of 20% reduction in CO_2 emissions by 2010 (Department of Trade and Industry, 1999b), to be implemented through a broad programme of policies on transport, planning and energy efficiency, as well as energy supply.

The burning of fossil fuels affects the environment in other ways too. Oxides of sulphur and nitrogen can lead to acid precipitation, which can affect water bodies and native flora and fauna on unbuffered soils (Morrison, 1994).

20.4 A more sustainable energy future?

Bearing in mind uncertainties over the sustainability of current fuel use, a number of options exist for future energy supply. Improved efficiency of energy use is an important element of 'good housekeeping' to reduce environmental impacts of all forms of energy use. Steps to reduce future CO_2 emissions could involve more efficient energy conversion of fossil fuels, switching to low-carbon fuels such as natural gas, decarbonisation of flue gases and fuels and associated CO_2 storage, and switching to renewable sources of energy (Watson *et al.*, 1996). Both the EU and UK Government have established targets for electricity generation from renewable sources. The UK Government is working towards a target of renewable energy providing 10% of UK electricity supplies as soon as possible and hopes to achieve this by 2010 (Department of Trade and Industry, 1998). The Scottish Executive is likely to seek a higher target than this in Scotland, since about 9% of Scotland's electricity already comes from large hydro-power stations.

20.4.1 Renewable energy sources

Scotland has significant renewable energy resources, including some of the best wind resources in Europe (Figure 20.4), as well as excellent wave energy (Duckers, 1991; Office of Science and Technology, 1998). However, most renewable energy technologies bring about changes to the natural environment. For example, tidal barrages can threaten estuarine bird populations of international importance, and windfarms and hydro schemes can be visually intrusive and affect areas of sensitive landscape character. Scotland is renowned for its scenery, which is of major economic importance to the tourism industry. There is a need, therefore, to get the right kind of developments for renewable energy in the right place, and to ensure that the development of renewables in Scotland does not compromise the overall quality of the landscape. Bearing in mind the extent of renewables resources in Scotland, it should be possible to reduce CO_2 emissions while also safeguarding the natural heritage. A strategic approach is needed which integrates development of renewables with natural heritage interests.

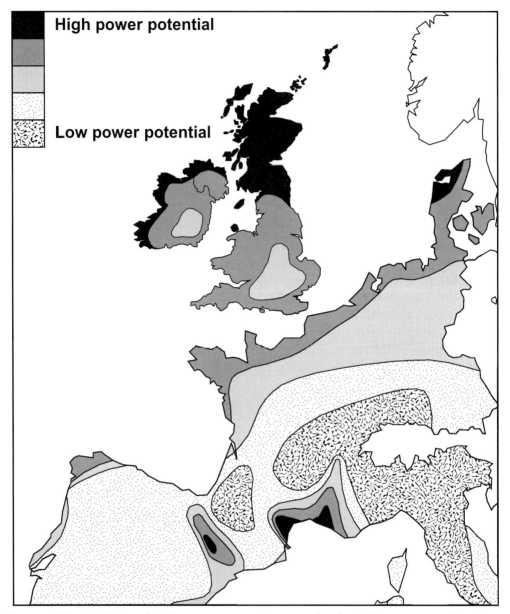

Figure 20.4 The distribution of wind resources at 50 m above ground surface in Western Europe (from Troen and Petersen, 1989).

SNH has recently undertaken a study to assess the sensitivity of landscape character to windfarm developments, from a search of descriptions on a landscape database (Plate 32). This study focused entirely on the sensitivity of landscape character; it does not address issues of visual amenity, and is non-judgemental about the acceptability of landscape change. This sort of approach, though still in its early days, may offer a way forward for securing appropriately located development. In the future, the exploration and exploitation of suitable sites for offshore wind energy may also be attractive, as many of the natural heritage problems associated with onshore sites are less severe offshore.

20.4.2 Oil and gas industry

The petroleum industry has taken some steps towards reducing its carbon emissions. For example, in the Sleipner Field (Norwegian sector), Statoil and partners are disposing of around 1 million tonnes of CO_2 per year into a sandstone reservoir beneath the North Sea. The basic requirement for underground storage of CO_2 is a geological structure with suitable reservoir and sealing rocks to contain the CO_2 and prevent its release to the atmosphere. Such conditions are relatively common within most oil and gas provinces. Within the Sleipner Field, the CO_2 occurs naturally mixed with methane and other hydrocarbon gases, and without re-injection it would otherwise be emitted to the atmosphere. The British Geological Survey (BGS) is part of a consortium that includes oil companies, the UK Department of Trade and Industry and the EU that is learning from this activity and is producing a best practice manual for the underground disposal of CO_2.

The removal and storage of CO_2 from power-station stack gases are also feasible, but significantly increase the production cost of electricity. For a conventional coal power plant, removing 87% of CO_2 emissions from flue gases would increase electricity costs by about 80% (Watson *et al.*, 1996). Another approach to decarbonisation uses fossil fuels as a feedstock to make hydrogen-rich fuels, such as hydrogen itself or methane converted from coal. Both approaches generate a stream of CO_2 that could be stored, for example, in depleted natural gas fields.

Using these technologies, it may not be long before electricity generation from fossil fuels with near zero emissions to the atmosphere could be achieved. The Norwegian company, Norsk Hydro, is considering bringing natural gas onshore from the North Sea and splitting the methane into hydrogen and carbon dioxide. The hydrogen would then be used as a clean fuel for electricity generation and the CO_2 would be sent to a North Sea oilfield for enhanced oil recovery.

20.4.3 Nuclear industry

Within the nuclear power industry, safety issues such as the disposal of hazardous wastes are politically significant. There is no 'best geological advice' for radioactive waste disposal; different countries have adopted different solutions. However, the basic geological criteria are commonly considered to include the selection of a site with physical stability and simple, low hydraulic gradient groundwater regimes that can be predicted and modelled into the far future with confidence. The search for an underground long-term disposal route for intermediate level radioactive waste within the UK is currently on hold. However, the recent Select Committee on the management of nuclear waste (Parliamentary Report, 1999) concluded that the construction of such a facility is both feasible and desirable. If this aim is to be achieved successfully, further research is required on the detailed geology of the potential sites that are identified.

20.5 Conclusions

Energy use is essential for Scotland's continued prosperity, yet all forms of energy use have some impact on the environment. The proportion of fossil fuel usage within Scotland's future energy mix depends to some extent on the level of success in finding new reserves, particularly on the Atlantic frontier. The proportion of nuclear energy in the mix will depend on political and public perception of safety regarding the disposal of waste and the operation of new power stations. Geoscience expertise is important in the search for oil and gas, coal and new sources of energy such as coalbed methane, gas hydrates and hot groundwater. This expertise is also contributing to solutions to some of the problems associated with the continued use of fossil and nuclear fuels. The rate of increase in the use of renewable energy resources will depend in part on public attitudes towards changes in landscape and visual amenity, as well as regulatory/incentive frameworks and technological advances. Future decisions on energy usage in Scotland, or on reducing energy needs, will have to be made in the context of this complex set of issues regarding resource availability, technology, our needs as a society and the costs and benefits of generation in both financial and environmental terms.

References

Barker, J.A., Downing, R.A., Gray, D.A., Findlay, J., Kellaway, G.A., Parker, R.H. and Rollin, K.E. 2000. Hydrothermal studies in the United Kingdom. *Quarterly Journal of Engineering Geology and Hydrogeology*, **33**, 41-58.

Benner, T.C. 1999. Central England temperatures: long-term variability and teleconnections. *International Journal of Climatology*, **19**, 391-403.

Blandford Associates in association with Tyldesley Associates 1999. *Capacity of Landscape Character Types to Accommodate Wind Energy Development*. Report to Scottish Natural Heritage.

British Geological Survey 1988. *Geothermal Energy in the United Kingdom: Review of the British Geological Survey's Programme 1984-1987. Investigation of the Geothermal Potential of the UK*. British Geological Survey, Nottingham.

British Geological Survey 1999. *Coal Resources Map of Britain*. Chapman, G.R. (Compiler). Geological map © NERC and The Coal Authority 1999. British Geological Survey, Keyworth, Nottingham.

Daly, M.C., Bell, M.S. and Smith, P.J. 1996. The remaining resource of the UK North Sea and its future development. *In* Glennie, K. and Hurst, A. (eds) *NW Europe's Hydrocarbon Industry*. The Geological Society, London, 187-193.

Department of Trade and Industry 1993. *An Assessment of the Potential Renewable Energy Resource in Scotland*. Report to Scottish Hydro Electric plc, Scottish Power plc, the Department of Trade and Industry, the Scottish Office, Scottish Enterprise, Highlands and Islands Enterprise and the Convention of Scottish Local Authorities.

Department of Trade and Industry 1998. *The Energy Report. Transforming Markets. Volume 1*. The Stationery Office, London.

Department of Trade and Industry 1999a. *Cleaner Coal Technologies: Future Plans for Research and Development, Technology Transfer and Exports*. The Stationery Office, London.

Department of Trade and Industry 1999b. *Development of the Oil and Gas Resources of the United Kingdom*. The Stationery Office, London.

Duckers, L.J. 1991. *Wave Energy Research and Development Around the World*. Papers presented at a Seminar organised by the Energy Committee of the Power/Process Industries Divisions of the Institution of Mechanical Engineers, held at the Institution of Mechanical Engineers on 28 November 1991.

Fellows, A. and Snodin, H. 1999. Generation overcapacity in Scotland - fact or fiction? *Wind Engineering*, **23**(1), 45-52.

Ferguson, M. and 17 others 1997. *The Atlantic Frontier Environment Network: a Case Study*. SPE 37837. Society of Petroleum Engineers, Richardson, Texas.

Friends of the Earth Scotland 1999. *Opencast Coal Mining in Scotland: the Hole Story*. Friends of the Earth Scotland, Edinburgh.

International Mining Consultants Limited 1999. *Prospects for Coal Production in England, Scotland and Wales.* Department of Trade and Industry, The Stationery Office, London.

Morrison, B.R.S. 1994. Acidification. *In* Maitland, P.S., Boon, P.J. and McLusky, D.S. (eds) *The Freshwaters of Scotland: a National Resource of International Significance.* Wiley, Chichester, 435-462.

Office of Science and Technology 1998. *Foresight: Report of the Working Group on Offshore Energies.* Department of Trade and Industry, Office of Science and Technology, London.

Parliamentary Report 1999. *Management of Nuclear Waste.* Select Committee on Science and Technology, Third Report. The Stationery Office, London.

Scottish Natural Heritage 2000. *Minerals and the Natural Heritage in Scotland's Midland Valley.* Scottish Natural Heritage, Perth.

Troen, I. and Petersen, E.L. 1989. *European Wind Atlas.* Riso National Laboratory, Roskilde.

United Kingdom Offshore Operators Association Limited 1996. *Towards 2020: a Study to Assess the Potential Oil and Gas Production from the UK Offshore.* United Kingdom Offshore Operators Association Limited, London.

Watson, R.T., Zinyowera, M.C. and Moss, R.H. (eds) 1996. *Technologies, Policies and Measures for Mitigating Climate Change.* Intergovernmental Panel on Climate Change Technical Paper 1. Intergovernmental Panel on Climate Change, Geneva, Switzerland.

21 NATURAL AREAS MAPPING: A TOOL FOR ENVIRONMENTAL IMPACT ASSESSMENT

Lars Erikstad and Odd Stabbetorp

Summary

1.   We have developed an interdisciplinary landscape analysis procedure for use in environmental impact assessment (EIA). This is designed to give ecological data with geographical coverage in an early stage of the planning process.

2.   Environmental interests are often introduced as obstacles at a late phase in the planning process when most technical and economical realities are fixed. In contrast, the approach described here has the advantage that natural heritage interests are taken into account at a very early stage of the planning process. Natural areas mapping, together with the other EIA themes and the technical engineering data, forms the platform for detailed planning of alternatives.

3.   The physical structure of the terrain and information on land use and vegetation cover are required to aid classification of the natural areas. For a large part, existing digital map data are used. The information is stored digitally in a GIS which is also used for analysis and presentation.

21.1 Introduction

Biodiversity is important for physical planning and management of the natural heritage. According to the Rio Convention, biodiversity should be addressed at the level of genes, species and ecosystems (Glowka *et al.*, 1994). Ecosystem diversity has strong links to the abiotic parts of nature, and in particular to geodiversity (Johansson *et al.*, 2001). A holistic approach is therefore fundamental in delivering practical and sound management of the natural heritage. An approach based on biogeographical regions (e.g. Natural Heritage Zones (Mitchell, this volume) and Natural Areas (English Nature, 1998)) at different scales offers important potential in this respect.

We have tested such an approach for the purpose of environmental impact assessments (EIA). The study includes two impact assessments for the road authority in Buskerud county, South Norway (Erikstad *et al.*, 1998; Stabbetorp and Erikstad, 1999). Here, the road authority has developed a new approach to the EIA process that involves investigations of the natural environment (as well as the other EIA themes) early in the process, before alternative routes for the new road are planned.

Environmental interests are often introduced as obstacles at a late phase in the planning process when most technical and economic realities are fixed. In contrast, the natural areas approach has the advantage that natural heritage interests are taken into account at a very early stage. The procedure we have developed for natural areas mapping gives the geographical coverage needed for this purpose. This approach also has the advantage that it produces a better understanding of the level of knowledge relevant to the EIA process, and hence identifies the need for, and assists in, the design of supplementary investigations.

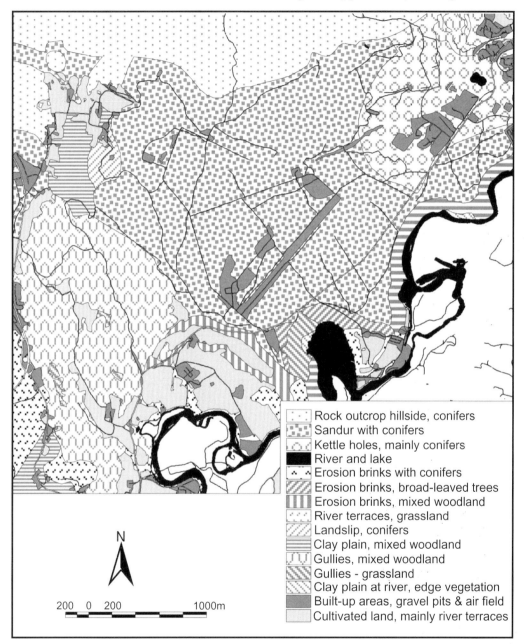

Figure 21.1 Map of natural areas at the glaciofluvial delta, Eggemoen, South Norway.

21.2 Natural areas mapping

The two areas tested were: 1) a cuesta/marine clay and lake landscape at Sundvollen; and 2) a landscape with a large, raised, marine glaciofluvial delta and marine clays with gullies at Eggemoen. The analysis was based on the mapping of natural areas at a detailed scale, mostly using existing data and data from aerial photographs and field survey. The information is stored digitally in a GIS which was also used for analysis and presentation using the software packages ArcView (ESRI, 1996) and MF Works (ThinkSpace, 1997).

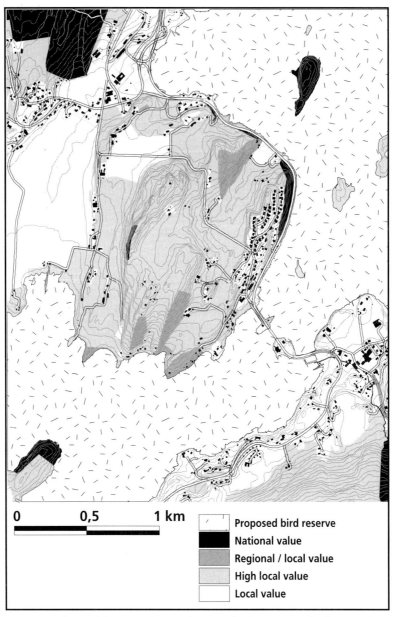

0 0,5 1 km	

▨	Proposed bird reserve
■	National value
▩	Regional / local value
▨	High local value
□	Local value

Figure 21.2 Assessment of natural heritage values in the cuesta landscape at Sundvollen, South Norway. Values are assessed by standard criteria used in Norwegian nature management for inventories for the different disciplines involved (e.g. see Erikstad, 1994).

The main input data were topographical maps at 1:5000 scale, with contour intervals of 5 m, including land use information on arable land and forest. Additional data layers were related to geology, wildlife and protected areas. The contour maps were used to construct a

10 x 10 m digital elevation model and to calculate slope and aspect. Together with geomorphological knowledge of the area, these features describe the physical structure of the terrain. Information on land use and vegetation cover was added and contributes to the classification of the natural areas (Figure 21.1). As an example, a profile from one of the areas shows how the classification is relevant for both Earth sciences and ecology. Going from a clay plain with agricultural fields over a cuesta limestone hill and down to the next clay plain, the following natural areas are represented: 1) edge vegetation of broadleaf forest on clay; 2) gentle sloping bedplane limestone with dry, rich pine forest; 3) cliffs and scree with patchy spruce forest; and 4) steep slopes with spruce forest. This classification also gives a basis for ecological and biodiversity modelling.

Existing database information on areas of special interest, as well as information obtained from field investigations, is included in the model. The approach does not suppress identified interests of any one specific field of science (e.g. geology), but it identifies a higher natural heritage value when a concentration of different interests occurs within the same area (Figure 21.2). Conservation value and vulnerability to specific aspects of the development project can be adapted from existing and accepted sets of criteria, and they are used transparently. This secures the possibility for open discussions, reproducibility (as far as possible in value judgements) and flexibility to change priorities and criteria in the light of new knowledge, priorities or changes in policy.

The results are documented in a GIS that is fully integrated in the road authority's planning system, and they are therefore available at all stages of the planning process. The road authority also presents the results of the EIA studies both as written reports and web documents on its internet site. This represents a valuable quality control. The tests show promising results both for the EIA process and as a general physical planning tool.

References

English Nature 1998. *Natural Areas. Nature Conservation in Context.* English Nature, Peterborough.

Erikstad, L. 1994. Quaternary geology conservation in Norway, inventory program, criteria and results. *Mémoires de la Société Géologique de France*, NS **165**, 213-215.

Erikstad, L., Reitan, O., Stabbetorp, O. and Sloreid, S.E. 1998. Mapping of natural types and assessment of nature value and vulnerability in the vicinity of Sundvollen, Hole municipality, Buskerud county. *NINA Oppdragsmelding*, 540, 1-40. (In Norwegian with English summary).

ESRI 1996. *ArcView GIS.* ESRI Inc., Redlands, California.

Glowka, L., Burhenne-Guilmin, F. and Synge, H. 1994. *A Guide to the Convention on Biological Diversity.* Environmental Policy and Law Paper, No. 30, 1-161. IUCN, Gland.

Johansson, C.E., Alapassi, M., Andersen, S., Erikstad, L. Geirsson, K., Jansson, A. and Suominen, V. 2001. *Geodiversity in Nordic Nature Conservation.* NORD 2000:8. Nordic Council of Ministers.

Stabbetorp, O. and Erikstad, L. 1999. Mapping of natural types and assessment of nature value and vulnerability in the vicinity of Eggemoen, Ringerike municipality, Buskerud county. *NINA Oppdragsmelding*, 577, 1-33. (In Norwegian with English summary).

ThinkSpace 1997. *Map Factory Module Reference.* ThinkSpace Inc. London, Ontario, Canada.

22 GEOLOGICAL CONSERVATION AND INTEGRATED MANAGEMENT IN ONTARIO, CANADA

Robert J. Davidson, Philip S.G. Kor, John Z. Fraser and George S. Cordiner

Summary

1.   Ontario is one of the few jurisdictions in North America that specifically recognises, identifies and protects geological features within a framework of protected areas. Protection on Crown land is afforded by National Parks, Provincial Parks and Conservation Reserves, and on other public and private land by Areas of Natural and Scientific Interest (ANSIs) and a variety of landowner agreements and private stewardship initiatives. The historical development of the site protection network is decribed.

2.   The geological features may be threatened by timber harvesting, mining exploration and development, aggregate extraction, hydroelectric development (dams and reservoirs), road construction, housing development and some farming practices. However, protected areas benefit from increased planning controls, and financial incentives may be available to private landowners who guarantee protection for geological sites.

3.   Implementing a recent Land Use Strategy for northern Ontario will require integrated management strategies and will be based on more local participatory planning, stewardship and education.

22.1 Introduction

Ontario is Canada's second largest province, covering some 110 M ha, approximately five times the size of Great Britain. More than 87% of the province, primarily the sparsely populated northern portion, is Crown land owned and administered by the Provincial Government. Much of the remainder, mainly in the densely populated south, is privately owned.

Geologically, Ontario is centered on the Canadian Precambrian Shield which consists primarily of metamorphosed sedimentary, volcanic and intrusive rocks. Palaeozoic carbonate and clastic rocks occur along the Hudson Bay/James Bay coast and underlie southern Ontario. The whole province was repeatedly glaciated during the Quaternary, and the sedimentary products of these glaciations mantle the bedrock to varying degrees.

Ontario is one of the few jurisdictions in North America that specifically recognises, identifies and protects geological features within a framework of protected areas (Davidson, 1981, 1982). Protection on Crown land is afforded by National Parks, Provincial Parks, and Conservation Reserves, and on other public and private land by Areas of Natural and

Scientific Interest (ANSIs) and a variety of landowner agreements and private stewardship initiatives.

On Crown lands, geological features may be at risk from timber harvesting, mining exploration and development, hydroelectric development (dams and reservoirs), and associated aggregate extraction and road construction. On private land, aggregate extraction, housing development and some farming practices pose the greatest risk to identified geological values.

22.2 Historical perspectives

Geological conservation has always been a fundamental (but silent) part of society's desire to protect Nature's wonders. Ontario's first park, Queen Victoria Niagara Falls Park, established in 1887, was set aside to guarantee the public's right to view a great natural spectacle. Similarly, Algonquin, Quetico, Sleeping Giant, Lake Superior and other large provincial parks, originally designated for their scenic and recreational values, protect spectacular landscapes of the Precambrian Shield. However, the protection of sites in Ontario specifically for their geological values was not common (Prest, 1974) until the late 1960s when Montreal River and Waubaushene Beaches Provincial Nature Reserves were created to protect proglacial and postglacial lake shorelines in the Great Lakes basin, and Ouimet Canyon Provincial Nature Reserve was established to protect a spectacular canyon in diabase bedrock (Kor and Teller, 1986).

Two significant events in the 1970s helped to forge a more comprehensive effort to protect Ontario's geological heritage. The first was a major revision of the provincial park policy by the Ontario Ministry of Natural Resources (OMNR). The second was a public outcry to protect the Niagara Escarpment from uncontrolled development.

22.2.1 Revision of Provincial Park policy

The new park policy openly embraced the concept that a system of protected areas should represent the diversity of landscapes and features found within Ontario. To implement this objective, science frameworks were developed to identify representative geological, biological and cultural features (e.g. Davidson, 1981), and inventories were completed to locate the best examples. This work culminated in 1983 with an expansion of the provincial park system.

This work also resulted in the creation of a provincial policy for Areas of Natural and Scientific Interest (ANSIs), and guidelines for the protection of sites on private land. This policy was inspired in part by the British model of Sites of Special Scientific Interest (SSSIs), and by the Ice Age National Scientific Reserve and Trail in Wisconsin, U.S.A.

One hundred and fifty-five new parks were established to protect, in part, a wide variety of Precambrian, Palaeozoic, Pleistocene and Recent features significant for their stratigraphy and geomorphology. At the same time, more than 300 Earth science ANSIs on privately-owned lands were identified. These new parks and ANSIs brought the representation of the features identified as being significant of Ontario's geological history and diversity to about 50%. The new sites included many key type sections, reference sections and type areas.

22.2.2 Protection of the Niagara Escarpment

The evolution of Ontario's park policy and efforts to protect the Niagara Escarpment converged in the mid-1970s (Killan, 1993). The Escarpment is one of Ontario's most spectacular, recognisable and famous Earth heritage features, and was at serious risk from aggregate production and uncontrolled housing development. The Niagara Escarpment Planning and Development Act of 1975 delineated a planning area incorporating the entire escarpment on the Ontario mainland, stretching 750 km from Niagara Falls to Tobermory. The Niagara Escarpment Commission (NEC) was established to oversee planning and development control within the plan area. The most significant features of the Escarpment, including many features representative of its rich geological heritage, were inventoried and protected in parks and special zones along its length. As a result, the overall character of the Escarpment, its associated geological features, and the lands in its vicinity have been afforded lasting protection.

22.2.3 Areas of Natural and Scientific Interest

Ontario's 1983 policy for ANSIs represented a significant step in protecting geological features. ANSIs complement Provincial Parks and Conservation Reserves by providing opportunities to protect and appreciate significant geological features on public and private lands. On public land, ANSIs are managed by the OMNR to ensure that land uses and activities within identified sites provide for the protection of geological values.

On private lands, OMNR ensures that local planning authorities and landowners are aware of the significant geological features on their properties and seeks their cooperation in protecting these features. Policies under the *Planning Act* also require planning authorities to demonstrate that there will be no negative impacts on the features identified in ANSIs when preparing official plans. At the same time, private landowners are eligible for property tax relief through the *Conservation Land Tax Incentive Program*, if they agree to protect geological values in ANSIs on their property.

Conservation easements established under the *Ontario Heritage Act* can also be used to provide added protection of geological features with landowner cooperation. The first conservation easement in Ontario, and to the best of our knowledge, in Canada, to protect a geological feature was established for part of an Ordovician type section and fossil locality near Owen Sound, Ontario. In return for the loss of certain development rights, the landowners were provided with an income tax rebate for the full value of this gift to the province.

22.2.4 Land Use Strategy

In 1996, Government reconfirmed its intention to complete a system of parks and protected areas that would be representative of the province's geological and biological diversity. An intensive period of inventory and public debate was followed by the release of a new Land Use Strategy for an area of land and water roughly corresponding to Ontario's portion of the Canadian Shield (Ontario Ministry of Natural Resources, 1999). This strategy recommends 61 new provincial parks, 45 park additions and 272 conservation reserves, ranging in size from 31 to 158,729 ha, and totalling some 2,386,679 ha. When added to the existing provincial park and conservation reserve system, Ontario's network of protected areas has grown to include 629 areas covering 9,424,068 ha, or close to 9% of the province's total area.

Many of the new areas were selected specifically to protect representative and significant geological features. The new Land Use Strategy has increased Earth science representation levels to over 80% of the protection targets identified in the *Earth Science Framework* (Davidson, 1981) used to identify such targets.

22.3 Current status of inventory and protection initiatives

Given the tight time frame and limited resources for the study leading up to the new Land Use Strategy, the selection of new protected areas focused on sites representing glacial landform features and associations, as these tend to be large, relatively fragile, and have more impacts on competing uses such as logging and mining exploration. The larger sites, representing glacial landscapes, tend to be in the northern parts of the province, where urban development is concentrated in small areas, and large tracts of relatively untouched lands are available for research. For instance, the Whitemud Conservation Reserve (over 17,000 ha), incorporates an untouched landscape of moraines, kames and eskers related to the extensive Lac Seul Moraine and the effects of erosion and deposition in glacial Lake Agassiz. At the other end of the spectrum, small protected areas represent discrete landform features; for example, the Cartier Moraine Conservation Reserve (c. 34 ha) was established to protect the type locality for the Cartier Moraine system of ice marginal positions north of Lake Huron.

Additions to existing Provincial Parks also incorporate significant geological features. For example, French River Provincial Park and Killarney Provincial Park, along the north shore of Lake Huron, contain spectacular exposures of bedrock with sculpted surface forms (s-forms) related to the flow of subglacial sheetfloods during deglaciation (Kor *et al.*, 1991). They also contain bedrock exposures showing the roots of mountains formed during the collision of two continental masses over a billion years ago.

Most bedrock outcrops with special values tend to occur predominantly as natural or man-made exposures along roads, where they are treated like Crown-land ANSIs. The geological information is made available to local highway authorities, who then consider the identified values during their planning process.

Other bedrock outcrops occur in natural settings such as cliffs and streambeds. Those that occur on private land are dealt with by local planning authorities through the ANSI process. Two widely divergent examples of Crown land exposures of this type include the cliffs of the Niagara Escarpment, which exhibit the most extensive Silurian stratigraphy in North America, and a tiny outcrop of Precambrian fossils on the north shore of Lake Superior. Here, some of the oldest life forms known on Earth are exposed (Davidson and Kor, 1980). This world-renowned site is still studied under strict controls within Schreiber Channel Provincial Nature Reserve.

The inventory of bedrock sites is not yet complete. This reflects the incomplete knowledge of Ontario's bedrock history and the traditional focus on areas of economic interest.

22.4 Integrated management, stewardship and education

The province has developed distinct planning approaches which recognise the unique resource management and natural heritage protection challenges in the sparsely populated, largely Crown-owned, northern areas of the province, as well as the significantly different management challenges in the more densely populated and predominantly privately-owned, southern portions of the province. The implementation of both approaches over the next

5-10 years will incorporate integrated management strategies and concepts of ecological sustainability, and will be based on more local, participatory planning, stewardship and education.

The new Land Use Strategy for northern Ontario reflects insights gained in a three-year consultative process involving all major resource management and natural heritage stakeholders. In addition to the new protected areas, it also provides an integrated and sustainable approach to the management of resources on an additional 39 M ha of Crown Lands. While Provincial Parks and Conservation Reserves will be regulated by the province under existing legislation, integrated management of most of the remaining area will be undertaken through Forest Management Planning. Guidelines for the protection of Earth science features are currently being developed to assist in the Forest Management Planning process.

Since most of the land in southern Ontario is in private ownership, it has been recognised that effective future management of resources and heritage protection will require consultation and consensus building among a large and diverse group of stakeholders and interest groups. OMNR has recently undertaken a comprehensive Natural Stewardship Program. The aim is to co-ordinate local, non-government agency and public participation in the development of specific resource stewardship and protection initiatives, undertaken at the local level and with local ownership and responsibility.

OMNR is also considering the development of integrated, consensus-based management approaches for specific, physiographically defined landscapes. The Oak Ridges Moraine, a complex Quaternary deposit north and east of Toronto, provides an example of this type of approach, and may serve as a model for future, long-term planning approaches. An integrated resource management and protection strategy was developed for the area. This recognises both the economic values of hydrogeological and mineral aggregate resources which are of strategic importance in the on-going urbanisation of one of Canada's largest, and fastest growing cities, Toronto, as well as the significant, but less quantified natural heritage and aesthetic values of the landforms associated with the moraine (Oak Ridges Moraine Technical Working Committee, 1994).

22.5 Conclusion

It is anticipated that in the future, integrated and ecologically sustainable planning and management strategies will focus on larger, geomorphologically defined spatial scales, and over longer periods of time. They will also reflect stakeholder values and awareness, and will require local commitments to stewardship and education. At the same time, the protection of significant, more discrete landform and geological features will continue to be pursued through protected areas and ANSIs.

References

Davidson, R.J. 1981. *A Framework for the Conservation of Ontario's Earth Science Features*. Ontario Ministry of Natural Resources, Open File Earth Science Report 8101.

Davidson, R.J. 1982. Protecting sites of Earth science significance in Ontario. Geological Association of Canada/Mineralogical Association of Canada, Joint Annual Meeting, Winnipeg, 17-19 May 1982. Program with Abstracts, **7**, 45.

Davidson, R.J. and Kor, P.S.G. 1980. Protecting Ontario's ancient fossil record: Schreiber Channel Provincial Nature Reserve and Kakabeka Falls Provincial Park. *Geoscience Canada*, **7**, 118-120.

Killan, G. 1993. *Protected Places: a History of Ontario's Provincial Parks System.* Dundurn Press, Toronto.

Kor, P.S.G., Shaw, J. and Sharpe, D.R. 1991. Erosion of bedrock by subglacial meltwater, Georgian Bay, Ontario: a regional view. *Canadian Journal of Earth Sciences,* **28,** 623-642.

Kor, P.S.G. and Teller, J.T. 1986. Ouimet Canyon, Ontario - deep erosion by glacial meltwater. Canadian Landform Examples – 1. *The Canadian Geographer,* **30**, 118-120.

Ontario Ministry of Natural Resources 1999. *Ontario's Living Legacy, Land Use Strategy, July 1999.* Ontario Ministry of Natural Resources, Toronto.

Oak Ridges Moraine Technical Working Committee 1994. *The Oak Ridges Moraine Area Strategy for the Greater Toronto Area. An Ecological Approach to the Protection and Management of the Oak Ridges Moraine.* Ontario Ministry of Natural Resources, Toronto.

Prest, V.K. 1974. Preservation of geological sites. *In: Conservation in Canada.* Canada Department of the Environment, Canadian Forestry Service, Publication 1340.

23 NATURAL HERITAGE ZONES: PLANNING THE SUSTAINABLE USE OF SCOTLAND'S NATURAL DIVERSITY

Clive Mitchell

Summary

1.   Scotland's diverse geology, soils, active processes and wildlife have combined with human activity over time to create a landscape which displays the cumulative impact of natural processes and people.

2.   Scottish Natural Heritage (SNH) recognises this diversity in determining a vision, objectives and action programmes for Scotland's natural heritage.

3.   Natural Heritage Zones are areas that share similar natural heritage characteristics and are defined on the basis of information on species and habitats, landscape character and other geographical factors.

4.   SNH has divided Scotland into 21 Natural Heritage Zones, and the information underpinning the definition of the Zones constitutes the most comprehensive baseline available from which to measure change in the future.

5.   Information on Natural Heritage Zones is being presented in three main ways: National Assessments, National Prospectuses and Local Prospectuses.   These documents and their uses are described.

23.1 Introduction

The wide variety of geology, soils, landscapes and wildlife, together with the effects of human endeavour over the last 5,000 years, makes Scotland one of the most diverse countries in the world. Scotland's landscapes can be viewed as sensitive indicators of the cumulative impact of natural processes and people.

Scottish Natural Heritage (SNH) recognises this diversity in determining a vision, objectives and action programmes for Scotland's natural heritage. Natural Heritage Zones are areas that share similar natural heritage characteristics and are defined on the basis of information on species and habitats, landscape character and geographical factors. SNH has identified a total of 21 such zones (Figure 23.1).

23.2 Aims and objectives

Through Natural Heritage Zones, SNH aims to provide a carefully argued presentation of the needs and opportunities facing the natural heritage in different parts of Scotland. Natural Heritage Zones provide a framework, referenced to the environment, in which to evaluate changes taking place. Changes result from natural processes and from human endeavour, including policies and financial incentives and the degree to which they encourage sound environmental stewardship. It should be possible to identify where

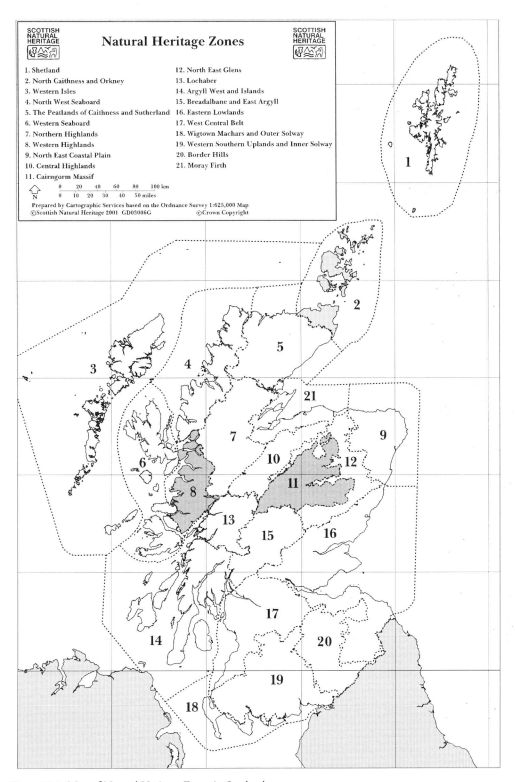

Natural Heritage Zones

1. Shetland
2. North Caithness and Orkney
3. Western Isles
4. North West Seaboard
5. The Peatlands of Caithness and Sutherland
6. Western Seaboard
7. Northern Highlands
8. Western Highlands
9. North East Coastal Plain
10. Central Highlands
11. Cairngorm Massif
12. North East Glens
13. Lochaber
14. Argyll West and Islands
15. Breadalbane and East Argyll
16. Eastern Lowlands
17. West Central Belt
18. Wigtown Machars and Outer Solway
19. Western Southern Uplands and Inner Solway
20. Border Hills
21. Moray Firth

Prepared by Cartographic Services based on the Ordnance Survey 1:625,000 Map
©Scottish Natural Heritage 2001 GD03006G   ©Crown Copyright

Figure 23.1 Map of Natural Heritage Zones in Scotland.

policies are working well, where they are working less well and where there are gaps relating to untapped potential that may yield environmental, social and economic benefit.

Natural Heritage Zone boundaries are referenced to the environment and so are likely to change only over long timescales. The framework is therefore more sensitive than administrative boundaries to variations in natural processes and can be used to evaluate the impact of both natural processes and human endeavour over the 20-25 year period of the vision. The information underpinning the definition of the Zones constitutes the most comprehensive baseline available from which to measure change in the future.

23.3 Information on Natural Heritage Zones

Information on Natural Heritage Zones is being presented in three main ways.

23.3.1 National Assessments

National Assessments comprise a series of documents and databases that provide the best available information on six themes: Recreation and Access, Landscape, Physical Characteristics, Earth Heritage, Biodiversity (Species and Habitats) and Freshwater. They are the foundation for the Local and National Prospectuses (see below).

These six themes underlie the definition of the Natural Heritage Zone boundaries, and they are the basis for describing the natural heritage and its changes. Although the information gathered in the National Assessments is the most comprehensive to date, there are gaps in our knowledge about the distribution and status of various resources linked to the natural heritage (e.g. variations in soil quality and erosion). An important role for the Natural Heritage Zones programme is to provide a context to evaluate the significance of those gaps and how best to fill them. The significance of the gaps can be assessed in terms of our ability to answer the question - 'is this development sustainable?' This question may be answered from a nature conservation standpoint, focusing on elements such as biodiversity, freshwater and Earth heritage. It can also be addressed at the landscape scale, for example in the diversity of landscapes and the extent to which the landscape can be 'read' as a historical record of environmental change or our cultural heritage. In addition, by collating data on recreation and access, SNH can comment on issues such as social inclusion and the important relationship between nature conservation and promoting enjoyment and awareness of the countryside.

23.3.2 Local Prospectuses

For each of the 21 Zones, SNH is preparing a Local Prospectus which:

- states SNH's vision for the natural heritage;
- describes the natural heritage, including the processes that have led to the current situation;
- discusses the changes taking place and the likely impact of current human activities on the natural heritage - a test of current sustainability;
- presents a series of key goals and specific actions which aim to close any gap between the vision and current trends over a 25 year period.

Each prospectus will attempt to clarify the links between the natural heritage and the social and economic aspirations of communities and will be the basis for extensive consultations seeking agreement on the vision and the means and objectives to work towards it. The objectives will result from an analysis of current policies and financial incentives, building on examples of good practice or indicating untapped potential and aiming to check unsustainable use of the natural heritage. For example, part of the vision for a zone might include a rich diversity of farmland habitats and farmed landscape, which could be achieved in part through objectives to increase the variety of stock and their management. Many objectives will require action at a national or international level, but the Local Prospectuses will focus on objectives that can be pursued locally. In the example given, the objective could be achieved through a local demonstration scheme, and the results could be used to inform the wider issues relating to the value placed on stewardship of the land *versus* its productivity, reflected in mechanisms such as the Common Agricultural Policy and its implementation in Scotland.

Much of the information available on the natural heritage refers to designated areas. However, an important aspect of the Natural Heritage Zones programme is to set these areas within a wider geographical context to ensure that they are no longer solely 'islands' for protection, but rather that they contribute to broader strategies for maintaining and enhancing the natural heritage of the zone.

23.3.3 *National Prospectuses*

Many of the human activities that drive changes within each zone are the result of national or international policy, and many zones share common themes (e.g. farmed landscapes, water courses and coastlines). The National Prospectuses cover a range of natural heritage settings: Mountain and Moorland, Coast and Sea, Forest and Woodland, Farmland, Freshwater, and Settlements. These documents will address nationally or internationally relevant issues (e.g. trends in landuse management and their interaction with the natural heritage, and management of shorelines as sea level rises), involving Scottish, UK and European policy, and will identify specific actions required to work towards sustainable development across Scotland.

23.4 Natural Heritage Zones, sustainable development and integrated planning

Sustainable development requires working towards a long-term goal, or vision, which brings together social well-being, economic prosperity, and environmental stewardship. Traditionally, planning has been carried out on a sectoral basis. In order to work towards sustainable development, various sectoral plans need to be considered over a geographical area in order to identify and resolve potential issues of conflict.

There is no one 'ideal' geographical area over which to carry out this integrated planning. There are many administrative boundaries that suit particular organisations. If spatial planning is carried out at a variety of scales, then issues common to neighbouring areas are more likely to be dealt with sensibly. Planning at more than one spatial scale can provide important checks and balances to ensure that, overall, development progresses in a sustainable way.

Natural Heritage Zones provide a framework in which to consider how best to work towards sustainable development in Scotland. It is important that this framework is referenced to the environment and is able to ensure that all three aspects of sustainable development - social, economic and environment - are addressed in an integrated way.

23.5 Working with others

The vision set out for each Natural Heritage Zone is intended to be challenging, but not one that SNH or any other organisation can achieve on its own. The vision must be a shared aspiration of all bodies working within a single zone, or across several zones.

The vision is not intended to be a 'blue-print', but a general statement about how SNH would like to see the natural heritage functioning 25 years from now. The vision refers to a rolling horizon, so that at any time SNH is looking 25 years ahead and considering how best to use and refine policy and legislation to work towards a more sustainable future. SNH therefore envisages that the objectives required to work towards the vision will be reviewed regularly, and the prospectuses underpinning the vision will need to be revised every 10-15 years to ensure they remain relevant.

The Local and National Prospectuses will be the basis for extensive consultations with key stakeholders to develop a shared vision and the actions required to achieve it. The key stakeholders are all those who are able to contribute to the objectives given in these prospectuses, including local and national government, housing associations, enterprise companies and the business community, conservation bodies, landowners and land managers, fishing and aquaculture representatives and tourism boards.

Plate 1

View across the city of Edinburgh to Arthur's Seat and Salisbury Crags, where James Hutton first demonstrated the existence of molten rocks and past volcanic activity. (Photo copyright: J.E. Gordon).

Plate 2

Hutton's section at Salisbury Crags shows the intrusion of molten lava within a sequence of Lower Carboniferous sedimentary rocks. (Photo copyright: C.C.J. MacFadyen).

Plate 3

The Tertiary volcanic rocks on the island of Rum have played an important role in understanding modern volcanic processes. (Photo copyright: P. and A. Macdonald).

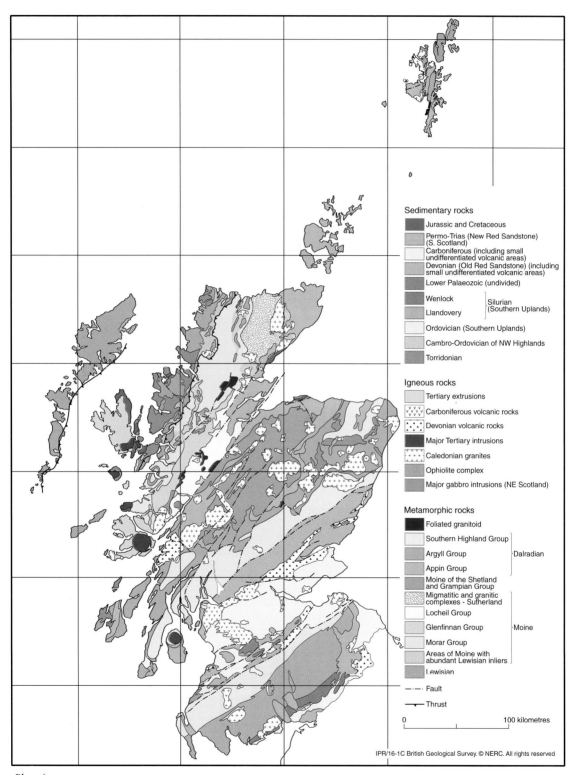

Sedimentary rocks

- Jurassic and Cretaceous
- Permo-Trias (New Red Sandstone) (S. Scotland)
- Carboniferous (including small undifferentiated volcanic areas)
- Devonian (Old Red Sandstone) (including small undifferentiated volcanic areas)
- Lower Palaeozoic (undivided)
- Wenlock ⎱ Silurian
- Llandovery ⎰ (Southern Uplands)
- Ordovician (Southern Uplands)
- Cambro-Ordovician of NW Highlands
- Torridonian

Igneous rocks

- Tertiary extrusions
- Carboniferous volcanic rocks
- Devonian volcanic rocks
- Major Tertiary intrusions
- Caledonian granites
- Ophiolite complex
- Major gabbro intrusions (NE Scotland)

Metamorphic rocks

- Foliated granitoid
- Southern Highland Group ⎫
- Argyll Group ⎬ Dalradian
- Appin Group ⎭
- Moine of the Shetland and Grampian Group
- Migmatitic and granitic complexes - Sutherland ⎫
- Locheil Group ⎪
- Glenfinnan Group ⎬ Moine
- Morar Group ⎪
- Areas of Moine with abundant Lewisian inliers ⎭
- Lewisian

- –·–·– Fault
- —▼— Thrust

0   100 kilometres

Plate 4

Geology of Scotland (Reproduced by permission of the British Geological Survey. ©NERC. All rights reserved. IPR/16-1C).

Plate 5
Satellite image of Scotland. (Copyright: Science Photo Library).

Plate 6

Knockan Crag (right of centre), in Assynt, is an area of outstanding historical importance for geology, showing Moine rocks thrust over younger Cambrian rocks along the line of the Moine Thrust. (Photo copyright: P. and A. Macdonald).

Plate 7

Devonian fossil fish, *Cheirocanthus*, from Tynet Burn, Banffshire. The length of the specimen is approximately 16 cm. (Photo copyright: National Museums of Scotland).

Plate 8

Carboniferous fossil plant, *Mariopteris*, from Whiterigg, Airdrie. The length of the specimen is approximately 12 cm. (Photo copyright: National Museums of Scotland).

Plate 9

Glen Roy is a classic site for glacial lake shorelines and played a part in the development of the glacial theory in the 19th century. (Photo copyright: P. and A. Macdonald).

Plate 10

Raised shorelines on the west coast of Jura are among the finest in Europe and provide an exceptional record of land- and sea-level changes during the ice age. (Photo copyright: J.E. Gordon).

Plate 11

The braided, gravel-bed reach of the upper River Feshie is a near-natural river system and displays some of the highest rates of channel change in Britain. (Photo copyright: P. and A. Macdonald).

Plate 12

Key exposures at Banniskirk Quarry, a Middle Devonian fossil fish site in Caithness, have been obscured through tipping of agricultural waste. (Photo copyright: C.C.J. MacFadyen).

Plate 13

Stromatolite beds at Yesnaby, Orkney, have been damaged by fossil collectors using crowbars and sledgehammers. (Photo copyright: C.C.J. MacFadyen).

Plate 14

Exposures at Birk Knowes, Lanarkshire, have been damaged by unauthorised collecting of Silurian fossils, with large amounts of spoil produced in the pursuit of rare and complete specimens. (Photo copyright: C.C.J. MacFadyen).

Plate 15
The machair land of Hougharry, North Uist. (Photo copyright: P. and A. Macdonald/SNH).

Plate 16
Ad hoc protection of small sections of machair coastline is unsustainable, leading to accelerated erosion elsewhere and arrest of the sand-feed to machair grassland inland. (Photo copyright: S. Angus).

Plate 17

The reed beds of the River Tay create a rich, silt-dependent habitat in a depositional environment. The reeds were previously exploited for thatch. (Photo copyright: P. and A. Macdonald/SNH).

Plate 19

The Torridonian sandstone cliffs of Handa provide important breeding sites for seabirds and habitats for salt-tolerant plants and lichens. (Photo copyright: L. Campbell).

Plate 18

The freshwater pearl mussel sits in a coarse sand or fine gravel bed and filters its food from the flowing river. (Photo copyright: S. Scott/SNH).

Plate 20

Urban flooding on the River Eden at Cupar, Fife. (Photo copyright: A. Black).

Plate 21

Coastal erosion at Montrose. (Photo copyright: J.E. Gordon).

Plate 22

The lower reaches of the River Spey are braided right down to the river mouth. The high rates of lateral movement, frequent flooding and abandonment of palaeochannels create the closest approximation in the UK to a high-energy, sandur environment. (Photo copyright: P. and A. Macdonald/SNH).

Plate 23

The claimed land of Alloa Inch, in the Forth Estuary, is reverting to saltmarsh, following natural breakdown and breaching of the flood embankments in the early 1980s. (Photo copyright: P. and A. Macdonald/SNH).

Plate 24

Skinflats (centre right), an area of claimed land near Grangemouth, is potentially well-suited to managed realignment. (Photo copyright: P. and A. Macdonald/SNH).

Plate 25

Bank erosion on the River Spey due to animal trampling and poaching. (Photo copyright: K.F. Leys).

Plate 26

Bank management on the River Spey: stable vegetated banks resist erosion and provide some buffering capacity. (Photo copyright: K.F. Leys).

Plate 27

Self burying croys on the Moffat Water. These flow-deflection structures are formed from rock matress and have been designed to slump, over time, into the pools they create. (Photo copyright: K.F. Leys).

Plate 28

Peat erosion at Cunningsburgh, Shetland. (Photo copyright: J.E. Gordon).

Plate 29

Soil erosion on exposed parts of Cul Mor, in Assynt, has led to loss of the montane grassland habitat and its replacement by a stony lag surface. (Photo copyright: J.E. Gordon).

Plate 30

Erosion is a natural process in the uplands but is also accelerated by human activities. In the Cairngorms, fragile vegetation is sensitive to disturbance by geomorphological processes and human activity. (Photo copyright: J.E. Gordon).

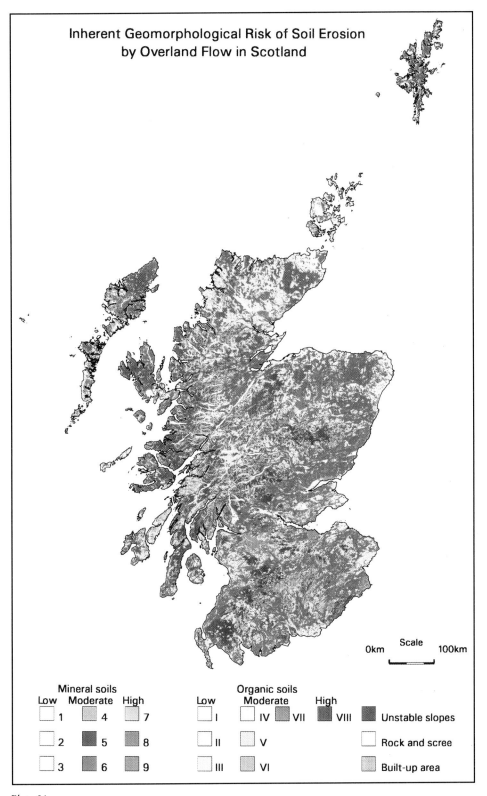

Inherent Geomorphological Risk of Soil Erosion by Overland Flow in Scotland

Scale
0km   100km

Mineral soils
Low   Moderate   High
□ 1   ▨ 4   ▨ 7
□ 2   ▨ 5   ▨ 8
□ 3   ▨ 6   ▨ 9

Organic soils
Low   Moderate   High
□ I   □ IV   ▨ VII   ▨ VIII   ▨ Unstable slopes
□ II   ▨ V   □ Rock and scree
▨ III   ▨ VI   ▨ Built-up area

Plate 31

Inherent geomorphological risk of soil erosion by overland flow in Scotland. (See Chapter 18).
(Source: Lilly *et al.*, 1999). (Copyright: MLURI/SNH).

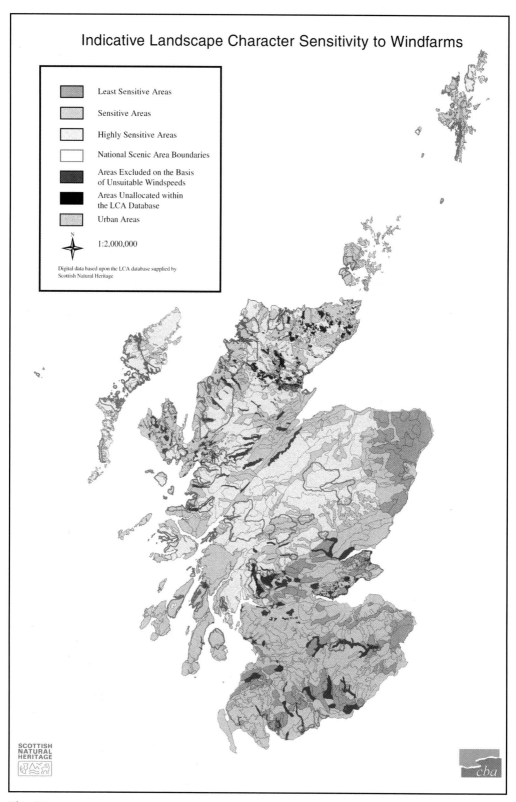

Indicative Landscape Character Sensitivity to Windfarms

Least Sensitive Areas

Sensitive Areas

Highly Sensitive Areas

National Scenic Area Boundaries

Areas Excluded on the Basis
of Unsuitable Windspeeds

Areas Unallocated within
the LCA Database

Urban Areas

N

1:2,000,000

Digital data based upon the LCA database supplied by
Scottish Natural Heritage

SCOTTISH
NATURAL
HERITAGE

cba

Plate 32

Indicative landscape character sensitivity to windfarms. (See Chapter 20). (Source: Blandford Associates, 1999). (Copyright: SNH).

Plate 33

Large-scale audio-visual show, 'Shaping the Surface', at Our Dynamic Earth. (Photo copyright: Our Dynamic Earth).

Plate 34

Children at work in one of the Discovery Rooms at Our Dynamic Earth. (Photo copyright: Our Dynamic Earth).

Plate 35

Interpretation site at Clashach Quarry, near Elgin, showing blocks of sandstone with fossil trackways on their surfaces (bottom right). (Photo copyright: S. Miller).

Plate 36

Interpretation panel at Clashach Quarry, near Elgin. (Photo copyright: C.C.J. MacFadyen).

PART FOUR

Earth Heritage Awareness, Involvement and Education

Earth Heritage Awareness, Involvement and Education

A central theme in the presentations and subsequent discussions at the Conference was that support for Earth heritage conservation will only thrive if Earth scientists can interest and enthuse others in the subject. Raising public awareness is important, and many Earth heritage practitioners recognise that their subject starts from a lower level of public awareness and general interest than there is for the biological sciences (Gordon and Leys, this volume). The chapters in Part 3, on the sustainable management of the natural heritage and use of Earth resources, demonstrate that the relevance of Earth heritage to everyday life is not a matter of dispute and that a crucial challenge is to promote the applications of Earth science knowledge within different frameworks of integrated management. The chapters in Part 4 deal with the parallel challenge for practitioners to become more effective advocates in the public arena.

The chapters in Part 4 demonstrate that raising Earth heritage awareness and education can be undertaken both formally and informally. They report work being undertaken in schools (Milross and Lipkewich, Chapter 25), museums (Miller and Hopkins, Chapter 29), visitor attractions (Monro and Davison, Chapter 24), voluntary groups (Leys, Chapter 30) and through partnerships (Miller and Hopkins; McKirdy *et al.*, Chapter 26; and McKeever and Gallagher, Chapter 27). The potential for progressing this work through a co-ordinated approach to interpretation and geotourism in Scotland is discussed (Brown, Chapter 28; McKirdy *et al.*), with recent successful work in Ireland being a clear example of good practice (McKeever and Gallagher).

The tenet underlying all the chapters in this section is that relevant, interesting and accessible themes and language should be used to involve and enthuse others in Earth heritage matters. This approach is valid both for interpretation aimed at the general public (Brown; McKeever and Gallagher) and for education (Milross and Lipkewich). Milross and Lipkewich stress the need to maintain the viability, relevance and practicality of education. Their chapter describes a unique partnership in British Columbia, between the mining industry and teachers, to develop up-to-date material on the industry, geological resources and environmental issues. The programme involves industry sponsored curriculum material written by teachers for teachers. It includes supplying resources for all age ranges, provision of expertise, field visits, workshops, placement for pupils and career links for students. A similar approach has not been tried in Scotland, but this model offers significant opportunities to improve wider awareness not only of the minerals industry, but also of associated Earth heritage and environmental issues.

McKeever and Gallagher note that scientists have a duty to bring their work to the public. They report cross-border collaboration to develop and popularise the rocks and landscapes of the twelve northern counties of Ireland. Geotourism, targeting the discerning visitor, is helping the economic regeneration of the entire region. The integration of geology into the tourism infrastructure has led to the development of walking, driving and cycling trails and accompanying literature. McKirdy *et al.* examine the potential for geotourism in Scotland. Partnerships with the tourist industry, the promotion of quality and the generation of added value are all based on opportunities for developing the tourist potential of the Earth heritage resource.

Brown examines the interpretation currently available in the Loch Lomond and Campsie Fells area of Scotland. Part of this area falls within the provisional boundaries of the first National Park in Scotland. Brown argues that a full inventory of existing landscape interpretation, provided by a range of agencies, is a necessary first step in developing a co-ordinated approach to future interpretative planning. The need for a co-ordinated, strategic, inter-disciplinary approach on a national scale has helped drive the establishment of 'Interpret Scotland', a collaborative venture involving many of the major agencies in Scotland such as Forest Enterprise, The National Trust for Scotland, Historic Scotland and SNH. Recently, interpretation practitioners have developed a network (Scottish Interpretors Network) and web site to share knowledge and experience on a county-wide basis. The development of both these initiatives is ongoing.

Some members of the general public have an active rather than passive interest in Earth heritage matters. This is demonstrated by Miller and Hopkins who report that more than 270 new fossil trackways were found at Clashach Quarry, near Elgin, through a partnership between a local geologist and enthusiastic quarrymen. The trackways of greatest scientific importance were removed to the National Museum of Scotland, but others were left for local educational purposes. This approach clearly demonstrates the benefits that can be obtained by working in partnership. Leys reports on the development of the Regionally Important Geological and Geomorphological Sites (RIGS) movement in Scotland. This is a voluntary network of people interested in Earth heritage. Membership is varied and the future for RIGS in Scotland looks positive, with opportunities for members to become involved in issues such as Local Agenda 21, Local Biodiversity Action Plans, access and lifelong learning, which are much wider than the historical RIGS focus on site selection.

Monro and Davison describe the educational programme at Our Dynamic Earth, a visitor attraction and educational resource in Edinburgh highlighting Earth heritage issues. Their educational task is aided by state-of-the-art interpretative techniques (including smell, audio-visuals and sets) which provide an holistic view of planet Earth. The emphasis on Earth 'processes' rather than 'products' means that there are few artifacts, and the attraction does not seek to duplicate the activities of a museum. The opening of Our Dynamic Earth, dubbed 'Scotland's successful Millennium Dome' by the press, and an extensive advertising programme at the time of its launch, has helped raise the profile of Earth heritage issues with its many visitors.

The chapters in this part of the book clearly demonstrate what has been achieved, as well as the potential for new ideas and opportunities. In taking the latter forward, it will be crucial to maintain existing partnerships and to develop new ones as appropriate. It will be equally important to ensure that new initiatives are properly integrated and networked with existing developments and facilities.

24 DEVELOPMENT OF INTEGRATED EDUCATIONAL RESOURCES: THE DYNAMIC EARTH EXPERIENCE

Stuart K. Monro and Dee Davison

Summary

1.   Our Dynamic Earth is a visitor attraction that is also an important educational resource. The blending of education with entertainment is one of the hallmarks of Our Dynamic Earth.
2.   The main scientific messages are carried within the exhibition, but the subject matter integrates well with the educational curriculum in Scotland and throughout the United Kingdom.
3.   The Dynamic Earth Education Service is providing an education programme targeted to the 5 to 14 Environmental Studies curriculum, with the exhibition providing the focus for the development of the programme of activities.
4.   The development of Our Dynamic Earth and the integration of the exhibition content, the interpretative methods and the education service provide a model for other initiatives.
5.   The experience in developing Our Dynamic Earth visitor attraction also highlights principles which have a wider application to the public understanding of science, particularly in delivering coherent messages to a mass audience.

24.1 Introduction

James Hutton, in his 1785 abstract of the 'Theory of the Earth', concluded:

"In this manner, there is opened to our view a subject interesting to man who thinks; a subject on which to reason with relation to the system of nature; and one which may afford the human mind both information and entertainment."

Our Dynamic Earth aims to open windows on science to people of all ages and abilities. It stretches the mind while, at the same time, is engaging, accessible, fun and relevant to the people of the 21st century (Monro and Crosbie, 1999). In these days of life-long learning, Hutton's concept of education through entertainment is still very relevant. The educational aspects of Our Dynamic Earth embrace not just children of school age, but all visitors to this attraction. For this reason, Our Dynamic Earth is an educational resource that extends beyond more formal teaching to all parts of the attraction, and therefore an integrated approach is necessary.

24.2 Conceptual overview

Our Dynamic Earth presents a holistic view of planet Earth. It demonstrates the natural forces, whose interaction through time has created and shaped the Earth as we know it today. It explores the environments which have resulted from these processes, taking the visitor into the depths of the oceans and on a journey from the polar regions to the tropics. It is more concerned with 'process' than 'product', and therefore artifacts are few. However, audio-visuals, which re-create and transport the visitor into the heart of a process or environment, are used extensively.

Our Dynamic Earth impinges on many areas of science, including geography, geology, astronomy, biology, ecology and oceanography. It focuses on the interaction between these disciplines and presents the important concept that the boundaries between disciplines reveal some fascinating principles relevant to the past and future development of the planet. Hutton's ideas, summarised in the two phrases, *"the present is the key to the past"*, and *"the past is the key to the future"*, encompass the science presented in Our Dynamic Earth. Similarly, the relevance of these ideas to people is critical in establishing the coherence of the experience.

Today, most people have an opinion on a wide variety of environmental issues. However, many of those opinions are based on scant knowledge and are often strongly influenced by the hype of the popular press and media. Providing some underpinning science to these issues in a way that is accessible yet allows an informed judgement to emerge, is part of what has been attempted in Our Dynamic Earth.

24.3 Breaking the mould – an innovative presentational style

Our Dynamic Earth is trying to be different in its presentational style. It is charged with delivering big messages to large numbers of people. The challenge in designing the exhibition has been to tell a story, which was millions of years in the making, to visitors with widely differing expectations, while dealing with the logistical problems of high visitor throughput. The story is communicated as an immersive experience, taking people on a trip through the Universe, to the edge of a volcano, across glaciers, and into the oceans, polar areas and the tropical forest. It is a story which is gradually built up, first exploring the physical formation of the planet and its landscape, then the evolution of its life and diverse environments.

It is important to convey the relevance of the subject matter to each and every visitor, and so we begin and end with people. *The State of the Earth* is the first part of the exhibition and it looks at the ways in which the Earth is being continually investigated and monitored and how, largely through the advent of satellite technology, we have built up a comprehensive picture of this dynamic planet. It raises many questions about the processes that cause this dynamism, questions which will be addressed later in the exhibition. Here, links with Reuters and NASA, and satellite images from the Meteorological Office, keep the visitor's finger on the pulse of the planet.

The concepts of geological time and the enormous periods involved in the formation of the Universe are difficult to convey. *The Time Machine* takes the visitor from the present, familiar images back through the World Wars, the Roman Invasion, the Stone Age, human origins, the age of dinosaurs, early life forms and finally, with the Big Bang, to the beginnings of the universe where the story begins.

In *How it all Started*, a starship allows the visitor to witness the Big Bang and the beginnings of the physical universe, and transports them through the universe to a planet capable of sustaining life. It demonstrates the position of the Earth within the Universe and the vast distances involved. Images from the Hubble telescope allow the visitor to look back in time towards those moments soon after the formation of the Universe. *The Restless Earth* is concerned with the internal processes of the planet. It explains what causes volcanoes and earthquakes, how mountains are built up and why continents move. *Shaping the Surface* examines the surface processes that sculpt the landscape, specifically glaciation which has been an important agent in moulding the scenery of Scotland. *Casualties and Survivors* looks at the biological processes that have transformed the planet, creating the environments and habitats we know today. It is a feature of the evolutionary record that mass extinctions have taken place in the past for various reasons. This will undoubtedly be a feature of the future. Will *Homo sapiens, The Human Animal,* who is now a 'shaper of the landscape' and a major cause of change in the environment, be a casualty or a survivor?

The exploration of *The Oceans* has been advanced immeasurably by remote sensing techniques, greatly increasing our understanding of the interactions between the oceans and the atmosphere. Within the oceans, a range of environments from the tropical coral reefs to the ocean depths and the cold polar waters is revealed within the setting of a submersible. In *The Polar Regions,* the similarities between the Arctic and the Antarctic are found to be superficial as one is oceanic, the other continental. They are, however, united in their cold, icy climate, and the large (real) ice feature, central to this gallery, gives a tactile expression to these polar environments. In *The Journey of Contrasts,* the visitor travels from the tundra to the tropical regions, exploring the contrasting environments, how they change between day and night and through the seasons. Here, too, the resources which are needed to support life are identified. Food, water, energy and shelter are the fundamental human requirements but these are also vital to the survival of other organisms. In *The Tropical Regions* the visitor experiences the hot, wet environment of the tropical rainforest where the Sun's energy encourages an abundant diversity of plant and animal life and twice daily the thunderstorm breaks.

The Showdome is a conclusion to the exhibition, highlighting the dramatic processes that have shaped planet Earth. Many of these processes may be regarded as destructive 'hazards', but, many are also processes of renewal, rejuvenating the planet. The analogy is drawn between the dynamic nature of the planet and a living entity, 'Gaia', a concept developed by James Lovelock, which considers the planet as a self-sustaining organism. This is closely related to Hutton's idea of 'geophysiology', drawn from his medical training, where he makes the comparison between the way the planet operates and the physiology of an organism. It is also a planet inhabited by human beings who respond to the drama and dynamism of the planet and have some power in controlling its future shape and destiny. *The Showdome* explores the relationship between the dynamic planet and the people who live on it.

Throughout the exhibition, there has been a conscious decision to use a variety of presentational styles. Large-scale audio-visual shows are used extensively in *How it all Started, Restless Earth* and *Shaping the Surface* (Plate 33). Elsewhere, audio-visuals on a smaller scale are used together with accurate setwork, lighting, colour and smell, which creates an atmosphere of realism. Special effects, such as the ice feature in the *The Polar Regions* and the rainstorm in the *The Tropical Regions,* add to the 'total experience'. This approach has been very successful, in that a visit to Our Dynamic Earth becomes a shared experience for the family or group, or for the individual visitor who is seeing Our Dynamic Earth in the company of other visitors. Computer interactives have been used less extensively than was initially envisaged. They are very much one-to-one activities and consequently are less effective in a facility which has a high throughput of visitors. However, they are proving to be very effective in communicating some particularly difficult concepts in an accessible way to younger visitors.

24.4 Responding to feedback

The process of creating Our Dynamic Earth continues to be dynamic. It is important that feedback mechanisms are in place to maintain the exhibition's high quality. Input from both the scientific community and the general public is required. Preliminary work indicates a very encouraging response from both. However, surveys of the general public (Table 24.1) are indicating that some of the messages inherent in the story line are not being conveyed as effectively as they could be. One of the aspects highlighted has been the complexity of some galleries and the subtle nature some of the messages. Occasionally, the success of one particular element, for example, the ice feature in *The Polar Regions*, overpowers the message being conveyed in the audio-visual presentation in the same gallery. An analysis of visitor responses to the exhibition will more clearly highlight the successful and less successful galleries.

Table 24.1. Visitor responses to galleries.

Gallery	Excellent (%)	Good (%)	OK (%)	Poor (%)	Very Poor (%)	Unable to Say (%)
State of the Earth	18	52	18	3	1	9
Time Machine	46	45	7	2	0	n/a
How it all Started	31	60	8	1	0	n/a
Restless Earth	55	42	2	1	0	n/a
Shaping the Surface	66	32	2	1	0	n/a
Casualties and Survivors	25	58	15	3	0	n/a
Oceans I	26	55	16	2	0	n/a
Oceans II (yellow submarine)	24	60	13	2	1	n/a
Polar Regions	54	41	5	1	<0.5	n/a
Journey of Contrasts	1	16	53	25	7	n/a
Tropical Rainforest	59	36	5	<0.5	0	n/a
Showdome	30	51	14	4	1	1%

N = 397 in all cases

There is also the need to be responsive to the scientific community and to refine continually the content as scientific ideas change. In order to achieve this, Our Dynamic Earth is in the process of establishing a Scientific Advisory Board which will advise on the scientific programme, and an Education Advisory Board which will be concerned with the educational programme offered.

24.5 Addressing issues – providing the underpinning science

Our Dynamic Earth raises a large number of questions which are at the forefront of public awareness of science at this time. It raises the issue of global warming, but set against a backdrop of natural climate change which is continuing and outwith any anthropogenic influence. It looks at the changing landscape and how the human species has become 'a shaper of the surface'. It emphasises the importance of the currents circulating within the ocean in maintaining the pattern of world climate and the record of climate change that is contained in the ice of the polar regions. Sustainability issues underpin many aspects of the Dynamic Earth story but our aim is to provide the science behind sustainability, while encouraging the public to make up their own minds about where to go from here. As time moves on, these issues will change. The challenge for Our Dynamic Earth is to be up-to-the-minute in terms of the relevant phenomena which capture the public interest. For example, a period of more intense sunspot activity after 2000 will result in the Aurora Borealis being seen more frequently, and so this phenomenon may need to be explained as part of Our Dynamic Earth's continuing programme. Many of these issues are cross-curricular within the formal educational programme and are a vehicle for teaching a wide range of subjects. These will be addressed as the educational programme develops.

24.6 Delivering to pupils – supporting the curriculum

The educational potential of Our Dynamic Earth is enormous. As with the exhibition, the main aim is to present a holistic view of our planet and to allow pupils to explore and experience for themselves the physical and biological processes that have created and shaped the Earth. The educational programme is provided by the Education Service which builds upon the curricular aspects of Our Dynamic Earth. Within the 11 galleries of the exhibition, many disciplines are brought to life, introducing astronomy, geology, geomorphology, evolutionary biology, oceanography and marine and terrestrial ecology. As a result, Our Dynamic Earth is unique in terms of its breadth and in communicating the complex relationships between these subjects.

The Education Programme will grow and develop with time. Initially it is focusing on the Environmental Studies component of the 5-14 National Guidelines, but this is already expanding to encompass Standard and Higher Grades as well as pre-school learning and adult education. The element of 'entertainment' extends to the formal educational programme as well. A visit to Our Dynamic Earth will give pupils a fun-filled, exciting adventure which at the same time delivers different elements of the curriculum. Pupils of all ages and abilities will be inspired to ask questions and, with the help of the education staff, to discover answers for themselves.

Two themed *Dynamic Discovery Rooms*, providing an innovative and exciting educational environment, are the focus for educational activities (Plate 34). One is decorated to illustrate a selection of the world's different environments, inspired by *The Oceans, Journey of Contrasts* and *Tropical Rainforest* galleries. The other reflects the Earth's physical processes, based on the *How it all Started, Restless Earth* and *Shaping the Surface* galleries. They are equipped with slide projectors, overhead projectors, video monitors, visualisers and video microscopes for examining geological and biological samples. Computers, sponsored by Hewlett-Packard, are also available for hands-on multimedia activities.

In response to suggestions from teachers throughout Scotland, in the first year of operation, the Education Service is providing *Discovery Activities* that relate to: *The Restless Earth* – investigating plate tectonics, volcanoes and earthquakes; *Shaping the Surface* – focusing on glaciers and rivers as agents of erosion and deposition; *Casualties and Survivors* – covering extinction and evolution; and *Tropical Rainforest* – focusing on the rainforests of south-east Asia. These will be available at different levels to suit P1-P3, P4-P6 and P7-S2 pupils. The number of Discovery Activities will be expanded each year, eventually to cover all the topics within Our Dynamic Earth, as well as other multidisciplinary (cross-curricular) topics such as water and weather. Discovery Activities are also being developed for Standard and Higher grade pupils. To accompany and support the Discovery Activities, education packs are being prepared for teachers and pupils. These packs introduce the relevant subject matter, illustrate the various curricular links and outline the activities undertaken by pupils during the Discovery Activity, as well as providing preparatory and follow-up materials for both teachers and pupils. Teacher placement teams, within the Industry and Enterprise Awareness for Teachers and Schools (IEATS) scheme, are being used to develop materials in support of Standard Grade activities. This is proving to be an excellent vehicle for involving teachers and for ensuring that Our Dynamic Earth activities are directly related to the curriculum.

A limited number of subject and age-specific *Discovery Chests*, sponsored by Dorling Kindersley, National Geographic and Scottish Natural Heritage, will be available for loan to schools who have booked a Discovery Activity. These will complement the Discovery Activities and will contain a variety of resource materials to facilitate schools' preparation and/or follow-up work in the classroom, including reference books, fiction books, slide/photo packs, posters, maps, video and audio tapes, CD-ROMs, games, models and specimens.

At least one week per term will be dedicated to providing ten half-day *Exploratory Workshops*. Education Service staff and external experts, including scientists, artists, musicians and theatre groups, will lead these workshops which will focus on specific themes related to the Environmental Studies curriculum or cross-curricular topics and targeted at specific age groups. Workshops offered during 1999 – 2000 involved:

1. producing a giant map for Scottish Geology Week, to illustrate Scotland's major geological features;
2. creating ten mini-dramas with supporting costumes, masks and props, to reflect the themes of the galleries;
3. exploring the Big Bang and our Solar System; and
4. exploring the topic of weather and weather forecasting.

The evidence from bookings so far suggests that Our Dynamic Earth is being successful in attracting a higher proportion of the secondary end of the educational spectrum than would be anticipated. Normally, visitor attractions have a primary-secondary split of around 70-30. In Our Dynamic Earth, the split is nearer 50-50. This is very encouraging.

The *Dino's Dynamos Children's Club* is sponsored by Atlantic Telecom and was launched on Saturday, 30 October, 1999. The club runs annually between Halloween and the end of June and is open to children aged between 6 and 12. Demand for membership and places on the Saturday morning workshops is very high.

Future developments will respond to the evolving syllabus of schools, in particular the development of the Scottish Higher Still and other initiatives. These provide opportunities for further collaboration with teachers as part of placement schemes. With the increasingly proactive approach to public awareness of science and the development of university post-graduate courses around this topic, there is the potential for Our Dynamic Earth to be involved in Higher Education.

24.7 Supporting the teachers – continuing professional development

There are a number of areas within the curriculum, particularly Earth sciences and Astronomy, where teachers may require additional support to help deliver specific topics in the classroom. Our Dynamic Earth is building partnerships with education authorities, schools and individual teachers to develop programmes and support materials that will help teachers to deliver these parts of the curriculum. As a start, the Education Service has offered free familiarisation visits and charged in-service sessions for teachers. Teams of secondary teachers on Industry and Enterprise Awareness for Teachers and Schools (IEATS) placements can discover how education is delivered within the commercial framework of a visitor attraction and the consequent operational implications.

The development of the educational programme will be guided by feedback from focus groups for nursery teachers, primary teachers, secondary teachers and special needs teachers, along with primary, secondary and special needs pupils. These groups will assist the Educational Service in establishing how well the existing galleries and education programmes meet the needs of the educational community and identify how future requirements can be fulfilled.

24.8 Our Dynamic Earth – part of a science network

Our Dynamic Earth also has an external dimension. It is part of a network of sites within the Edinburgh area and elsewhere which explore different aspects of the planet. Following the opening of Our Dynamic Earth, all of the science-based attractions in the Edinburgh area have come together to promote each other and encourage visitors to 'Explore Edinburgh'. The Explore Edinburgh Group, involving Our Dynamic Earth, the Royal Zoological Society of Scotland, the Royal Botanic Garden, the National Museums of Scotland, Deep Sea World, Camera Obscura, the Royal Observatory, Butterfly and Insect World and the Scottish Mining Museum, hopes to extend the reasons why visitors come to the city. Edinburgh is generally perceived to be a centre for cultural and heritage attractions, but is now increasingly seen as a place to come to explore science. In this context, visitors to Our Dynamic Earth are encouraged to continue their voyage of exploration by looking at Edinburgh's volcanic features or by visiting the other science-based attractions within the area.

The networking concept extends beyond the city of Edinburgh and to aspects other than marketing the facility. Embedded within the thinking behind Our Dynamic Earth is the concept that it is the start of a voyage of exploration. As a result of that, 'Where next?' is an important question to ask our visitors. As other science-based visitor attractions open throughout the United Kingdom, it is important that there should be effective signposts to places where the aspects of the Dynamic Earth story can be explored in more detail. Networking also gives the opportunity to share experience and good practice and to provide a common platform for the broader public awareness of science issues. The development of the Scottish Science Trust provides the potential for many of these concepts to become reality.

24.9 Our Dynamic Earth – its place beyond 2000

Our Dynamic Earth is a project for beyond the year 2000. As such, it must continue to develop and evolve. This presents particular challenges given the linear nature of the Dynamic Earth exhibition. There are changes that can be made in video footage throughout the exhibition to keep it up-to-date. This is a maintenance function. There is the opportunity to use new and exciting developments in dome technology to re-tell the story of how humanity copes with living on a dynamic planet. There may also be scope for a completely new gallery which looks to the future.

Our Dynamic Earth is one of five major science-based visitor attractions, each focusing on a different aspect of science, that has received financial support from the Millennium Commission. It has been recognised that in the present millennium there is a fundamental need to encourage an understanding and appreciation of science among the public, not least the science of the planet we live on. It is one of the objectives of the Dynamic Earth Charitable Trust "to encourage and support the dissemination of knowledge on the Dynamic Earth." This broadly based educational goal is a keystone of Our Dynamic Earth; the task is to continue to cultivate the integrated educational objective.

Reference

Hutton, J. 1785. Abstract of a Dissertation read in the Royal Society of Edinburgh upon the seventh of March, and fourth of April, MDCCLXXXV, concerning the System of the Earth, its Duration and Stability.

Monro, S.K. and Crosbie, A.J. 1999. The Dynamic Earth project and the next millennium. *In* Craig, G.Y. and Hull, J.H. (eds) *James Hutton - Present and Future*. Geological Society of London, Special Publication, **150**, 157-167.

25 MILLENNIUM CONNECTIONS: FOSTERING HEALTHY EARTH SCIENCE EDUCATION AND INDUSTRY LINKS

James Milross and Maureen Lipkewich

Summary

1.   The only constant in education is constant change. Funding for new programmes always lags behind the demand for up-to-date and relevant material.

2.   The Mining Association of British Columbia (MABC) recognised a need to get the facts about mining out to the public. Information on resource-based industry in the public schools was archaic and misleading.

3.   Working with teachers, MABC provided funding, resources and expertise in a collaboration designed to upgrade material being presented to school children. The result was a number of resource packages that give factual mineral-relevant information which is all curriculum-based, and delivered in a variety of innovative lesson plans.

4.   The industry-education relationship is a partnership that can, and does, work as long as the respect is mutual, and the trust unconditional.

25.1 Introduction

Few would argue that the 'industry' of education is dynamic; practice and techniques that were valid even a few short years ago may now be considered archaic by the standards of today. It can be argued (and most often *is* in the hallowed halls of those bastions of pedagogical debate we call universities) that even ideologies fall out of favour. It would seem that the singular constant in education is change, and this, more often than not, means a change in the nature and makeup of the clientele - namely the students. Ironically, in a profession that touts its 'free-spirited free-thinkers', change in teaching styles and practice typically comes about with rapidity that can only be described as glacial. Nothing is more sacrosanct to a teacher than the comfort ceded by the prepared lesson plan - even if the lesson plan's validity is in question because the material has not kept pace with the constantly evolving needs of the students. The imminent need in education is to retain its viability, relevance and practicality.

25.2 The rationale

In 1990, the Mining Association of British Columbia (MABC) recognised that the vast majority of information on mining which was available in the classrooms around the province was twenty to thirty years out-of-date. This was also during a period where public scrutiny of resource-based industry was never more diligent or merciless. Mining, fishing, and forestry practices, both historical and current, were being chastised (often without challenge) by the media, and by the public as a whole. MABC understood that changes needed to be made in the delivery of information about their industry. It chose to address the quandary: what is the most effective method of getting the facts about the industry out to the public? The answer was as simple as it was sublime: develop a partnership between MABC and the classroom teachers of British Columbia, and work together to research and develop teaching units supported by practical, relevant teaching resources. The industry has seized the opportunity to help teachers get factual and current information on modern mining, allowing teachers to present well-balanced lessons and activities about the practical and responsible use of land and resources in their classrooms. The goal remains to protect and enhance an insightful partnership between education and industry.

25.3 The history

Simply put, the relationship between MABC and teachers is a partnership - in the purest sense of the word: two colleagues forming an association towards a mutually-beneficial endeavour. In this case, the common endeavour is Earth science education in public schools. The partnership exists between industry and teachers, with the goal of bringing British Columbia's mineral industry into the classroom. The support from the Mining Association comes in a variety of forms, from supplying physical resources and expertise, to funding field experiences for the practising teacher, to sponsoring workshops that guide teachers through the delivery of the many programs offered. The reason the MABC - education connection has worked where many other industry - education collaborations have failed is the construction: each program, or resource package, has been written *by* teachers *for* teachers, which ensures that it is practical, relevant and workable. In the past, industry-driven resources have had a number of deficiencies: they are usually written by someone within industry (usually associated with public relations) who typically does not understand the workings of the classroom - this affects the viability of the material; if written by an industry person, the material undoubtedly has a bias. Teachers (and students) are too discerning to tolerate propaganda, even if it is cleverly disguised in full-colour glossy presentations that are provided free of charge. In addition, industry may not understand what is curricular - therefore, even excellent material may be irrelevant. When a teacher already has to deal with a curriculum that is incredibly rich and full, new material that does not fit the core tends to get ignored. In British Columbia, each grade level has an Integrated Resource Package (IRP) which specifies Prescribed Learning Outcomes for each subject taught. Because the IRPs are extremely comprehensive, a teacher has little opportunity to digress from the set curriculum. One of the principal reasons that the MABC products are so successful is the fact that they are designed to be integrated into existing the curriculum.

25.4 What the Mining Association provides

The principal products are the resource units on minerals, mining and geoscience, written and delivered by teachers. In addition, MABC provides funding and resources for teacher and student fieldtrips, class visits by professionals, one- to four-day courses on mining, work experience placements for high school students, collaboration with interested groups and post-secondary institutions, and linkages for students interested in the mineral industry as a career.

25.5 Teacher-written resource units

All of the following resource units were written by teachers for the practising teacher. Each package was designed with a particular student level in mind, and all conform to the Provincial curriculum for the specific target level. The programme's resources are matched to the core curriculum (80%) and to locally developed programs (20%). The packages are designed to be versatile enough to be taught as complete units, or broken into smaller segments. In addition, the units are cross-curricular and can be easily adapted in a variety of different subjects.

25.5.1 K - 3 Rocks and Minerals - Integrated Science Kit

This kit was developed for use at the kindergarten to grade 3 levels with the intention of offering a thematically integrated study of rocks and minerals. The youngest learners can begin to appreciate the complex study of geology and the Earth's structure. Additionally, the integration of this unit spans language arts, science, social studies, geography, mathematics and careers.

25.5.2 Grade 5 Integrated Resource Unit on Mining

This unit is written with a thematic approach to mining, integrating learning across the curriculum. The lessons were developed around the past, present and future of mining. The unit can be used in whole or part, as the individual teacher sees fit. This particular unit may be taught in the classroom for up to two months. It is integrated into language arts, science, social studies, the environment, art and careers, and has many extended activities.

25.5.3 Social Studies Grade 10/11 Resource Unit On Mining

This package is intended to increase the basic knowledge of students on the mineral industry, as well as review the overall process of mine development   The heart of the unit is a case study of a mine proceeding through the Environment Assessment Act (EAA), legislated in British Columbia.   Once students have gained a basic overview and understanding of a party involved in the development of a proposed mine, the goal of the case study is to create real classroom discussion and decision making.   Additionally, environment issues and careers are integrated into the unit.

25.5.4 Science of Mining Resource Unit

This kit can be utilised to fulfill resources topics in the Junior High School Science Curriculum. Individual laboratory activities in the unit can easily be used independently as application examples of mining processes and also as other components of the Science curriculum and the Earth Science and Environment curriculum. Experiment materials are included in the kit, which mimic mining from process to environment issues. No background in mining is required.

25.5.5 Earth Science 11 Geology 12 'Resources and Ideas'

This resource package represents a compilation of lesson plans, activities and projects. It offers something for teachers experienced in these courses as well as for teachers with little or no background in these subjects. Optional teacher-selected materials such as slide sets and hand samples are available to enhance this unit. Teachers of Geography find this unit valuable too.

25.5.6 'Careers In The Minerals Industry'

This resource is a teacher-student developed video which addresses career potential within the industry, and follows the stages of the life of a mine: Exploration, Extraction, Processing and Reclamation. Additionally, information relating to corporate head office activities, as well as the service and supply sectors, is included. Supplementary information and activities accompany the video, which fits well with other classroom resources.

25.5.7 'Digging For Answers'

This material comes in the form of an environmental video produced by teachers. Students play key roles in the video, investigating environmental issues facing mining (filmed in British Columbia). Their travels take them to five British Columbia mine sites where they explore the issues of water quality, air quality, acid rock drainage, reclamation and wildlife habitat. This video is integrated with the other classroom resources.

25.6 The record

The MABC Education Program is unique in Canada, and we are quickly finding - through communication with colleagues around the world - that the program has no contemporary anywhere else. It is without exception the most successful resource industry and teacher-developed programme in the country. The demand for the resource has become overwhelming. Teachers are quick to recognise the winning, workable formula that makes the resource packages so successful: all materials are written by teachers, and the packages are factual, credible resources. The MABC Education programme has assisted more than 4000 teachers working in 1350 different schools in 57 out of the 59 school districts in British Columbia. As a result, over 420,000 students, from kindergarten to grade 12, have been reached. The program is designed to evolve continually, changing with the demand of any or all of the stakeholders - the students, teachers and industry. Thus, there is no reason to believe the momentum will decrease. The new millennium only brings new opportunity.

25.7 The risk to the program

There are problems for the program, but they are the problems any business would be more than happy to face: the program is being smothered by its own popularity. We currently cannot meet the teacher demand for the resources. It is essential that industry realises that although fiercely loyal, teachers will choose and use resources they have available. These resources may not be particularly relevant to the mineral industry. By not meeting the demand, it is possible that industry may interpret this as a lack of interest. Once lost, the opportunity of collaborating with teachers at this level, and with this degree of exposure will be lost.

The teacher-written resources are matched to the curriculum from Kindergarten to Grade 12. Along with the classroom resources, the MABC Education Program includes teachers and student field trips, classroom visits from industry and courses and seminars for teachers. Also, by assisting with work-experience placements for high school students, and collaborating with other interest groups and post-secondary institutions, effective academic and social links are developed for students interested in the minerals industry as a career.

25.8 Conclusion: 'why should resource-based industry and education collaborate?'

Industry must recognise that education is the only way to build long-term awareness, acceptance, and support for responsible mineral resource development. Both parties realise that factual, mineral-relevant information must be available for the classrooms. The only hope for present and future generations to understand resource-based industry is through classroom activities designed by professional teachers. Essentially, industry is investing in 'good', sound education, which promotes understanding. Funding an education program is not an altruistic endeavour - the benefits can be numerous as well as mutual: i) impact - over 4000 teachers have been reached, with over 420,000 students exposed to the materials; ii) credibility - all materials are developed by teachers for teachers; iii) cost effectiveness - it costs the equivalent of approximately £100 per teacher (and materials will tend to be used consistently and constantly by participants); iv) time effectiveness - programmes can go from concept to development to delivered product in under six months.

The final say comes in the form of a quote from a 13 year old participant in one of the MABC Education Programs:

" I want [industry] to understand that we, the young people, represent a large part of the population and we need to be able to talk to them and learn from them as we are the future and must be informed. We also have the responsibility of passing information on to future generations and we must know the facts."

26 GEOTOURISM: AN EMERGING RURAL DEVELOPMENT OPPORTUNITY

Alan P. McKirdy, Robert Threadgould and John Finlay

Summary

1.   Scotland is now at the top of the league for visitor destinations in Europe. Research by the Scottish Tourist Board has recently confirmed that most visitors come to Scotland for its combination of landscape and history. For Scotland to maintain this position, it must look to new attractions, promoting quality. One of its most closely kept secrets lies right beneath our feet.

2.   For its size, Scotland represents perhaps the most fascinating collection of rocks and landforms in the world, which combine to reveal a remarkable story of landscape evolution. With the current upsurge in public interest in different aspects of Earth heritage, geotourism now offers a timely opportunity to promote a greater understanding of why and how Scotland looks the way it does.

3.   Geotourism is, however, a relatively new concept and existing facilities that promote public understanding and appreciation of rocks, fossils and landforms are rare. In addition, the perceived technical nature of the science has proved a barrier to the wider appreciation of our geological heritage.

4.   This paper outlines some new approaches to the interpretation of geology for non-specialist audiences, using landscape and scenery as the theme.

26.1 Introduction

Scottish Tourist Board research indicates that the majority of visitors come to Scotland for its combination of landscape and history (Scottish Tourism Co-ordinating Group, 1992). In 1998, tourism (by visitors from home and abroad) was worth some £2.5 billion to the Scottish economy, making it one of the country's most important industries. Moreover, tourism-related activity accounts, both directly and indirectly, for around 180,000 jobs, ranging from catering to visitor management.

Scotland is high on the list of visitor destinations - eighth in the world by tourism receipts per head of population. Some two million overseas visitors spend around £940 million in Scotland each year. In a survey undertaken in 1999, 90% of all visitors cited 'beautiful scenery' as something they associate with Scotland, before they ever come to the country, while 30% of visitors highlighted the landscape/countryside and rugged scenery as the main reason for visiting (System 3, 2000). A recent study in the Highlands and Islands indicated that marine wildlife tourism alone generates almost £10 million directly and a further £35 million on associated spend (Masters, 1998). Nationally, wildlife tourism generates £57 million directly and supports an estimated 2000 jobs (A & M Training and Development, 1997). This level of activity is particularly significant in the remote and sparsely populated areas of Scotland; for example, in Shetland around 26% of all tourist expenditure is generated through the visits of birdwatchers. Wildlife tourism generates £4.4 million per annum on Islay and Jura, and visitors to nature reserves in Highland Perthshire spend almost £3 million annually (Crabtree *et al.*, 1994). The results from a detailed survey undertaken on the Rothiemurchus and Glenmore Estates, near Aviemore, indicated that almost 500,000 people visited the area during the period April 1998 to March 1999. The study, involving interviews with 2000 people and the completion of 600 questionnaires, showed how the scenery, natural heritage and recreation opportunities formed the primary reason for visitors spending time and money in the area (Scottish Natural Heritage, 2000).

In order to maintain and develop its marketability, Scotland must look to new attractions that promote quality and generate added value to what it already offers. There is considerable potential to give the natural heritage in general, and specific aspects in particular, such as rocks and landforms, an even higher profile.

The geological and landform resource – Scotland's geological heritage - lies all around us and beneath our feet, yet to many it is one of our best-kept secrets. Realising its full potential requires the promotion of the geological heritage as an integral part of the tourism resource. Geotourism already operates *de facto* in some parts of the world, where it makes a significant contribution to the tourism industry. Many natural wonders, such as Old Faithful in Yellowstone Park, the Grand Canyon and Stromboli, represent long-established visitor attractions that confirm a public appreciation of, or fascination with, natural phenomena. Scotland may lack the dramatic scale of these features, yet nevertheless is well endowed with places 'with a story to tell', each within relatively easy travelling time.

However, facilities to promote public understanding and appreciation of rocks and landforms in Britain are limited. Moreover, there is a general perception that, with the exception of dinosaurs, volcanoes and earthquakes, geology is a dull and rather opaque subject. This perception often stems from the innate inability of the 'expert' to communicate their subject effectively to the wider public. The potential to develop a greater understanding of Scotland's rocks and landforms, through a co-ordinated approach between Earth scientists and professional interpreters, is therefore considerable.

26.2 The resource

For three billion years, Scotland has wandered the globe collecting souvenirs of its journey in the form of its rocks and landforms. These provide clues to an incredible story - one which reveals that Scotland, for most of its past, formed a little piece of North America; was once separated from England by an ocean the size of the Atlantic; and, early in its history, brushed past Peru! The journey brought with it a cargo of plants and animals, including Scotland's own Jurassic Park, the Earth's first reptile, the most complete ancient wetland ecosystem, and some of the world's earliest fish. In its time, Scotland has seen mountains rise and fall, oceans come and go, volcanoes erupt and fizzle-out. The final chapter, the Ice Age, unfolded during the last two million years, as carpets of ice and snow ebbed and flowed across the country, in common with much of Northern Europe. All these processes left an indelible imprint on the landscape, and their story is told in the rocks and landforms throughout Scotland.

This geological heritage provides the foundation for Scotland's habitats and species. It dictates, amongst other factors, altitude, aspect, and the availability of minerals and water. Scotland's changing landscapes, from the rolling, rounded hills of the Southern Uplands in the south, through the low-lying, fertile lands of the Midland Valley, to the craggy mountains of the north, owe all to millions of years of geological history that saw Scotland's fragments of crust come together.

Scotland's geological heritage guided the country's industrial development and built heritage. The equatorial swamps of the Carboniferous became the coalfields of the Midland Valley, whilst, in many places, local stone defines the character of buildings and settlements – the slate roofs of Glasgow, the sandstone buildings of Edinburgh and the granite city of Aberdeen.

Geological heritage also provides an historical human interest. As the birthplace of modern geology, Scotland has many sites that played a fundamental role in our current understanding of the subject. Important historical localities studied by the early pioneers remain today as they were when first described. Siccar Point (Hutton's unconformity) on the Berwickshire coast is often referred to as 'the most important geological site in the world'. It is where Dr James Hutton, widely acknowledged as the founder of modern geology, made one of the most fundamental observations in the development of the geological sciences, the enormity of geological time, questioning at once the age of the Earth laid down by the scriptures.

Hutton co-founded the Royal Society of Edinburgh. He was also a leading figure in the Edinburgh Enlightenment movement that flourished in the latter part of the 18th century, an environment where he rubbed shoulders with other eminent individuals of the Scottish intelligentsia, such as Joseph Black and Adam Smith. His writings also provide an important social archive.

Hutton was followed by Hugh Miller, a stonemason from Cromarty, and later by the pioneers of the Geological Survey, Benjamin Peach and John Horne, who all made significant contributions to the development of geology. Hugh Miller's cottage, now managed by The National Trust for Scotland, attracts many visitors each year. Geology appeals not only to those interested in understanding the landscapes of today and their geological past, but also to those interested in a human dimension. There is no reason why the work of other significant historical figures, could not be celebrated in a similar fashion.

26.3 The challenge

Using Scotland's rocky past to enhance visitor enjoyment of the landscape is not entirely new. Scottish Natural Heritage (SNH) has been one of the leading proponents through its series of booklets, *Landscape Fashioned by Geology*, and other initiatives (Scottish Natural Heritage, 1993-2001; Threadgould and McKirdy, 1999). Many geologists now consider the need for greater public awareness of the subject as being of the utmost importance. In his closing remarks, in 1998, to the Hutton Symposium at the Royal Society of Edinburgh, Professor R.H. Dott Jr. (University of Wisconsin) thought that there were few activities more important to the survival of our many geological institutions than explaining to the general public the need for, and value of, geological information (Dott, 1999). He contended that without broad-based support, public funding for national museums, geological surveys and university departments in many countries throughout the world, is unlikely to be sustained at present levels. Professor Dott commended the publications produced by SNH as "examples for our profession to emulate everywhere."

It is true to say that, apart from limited interpretive provision, geology has yet to reach the mainstream tourist market. The success of scientific experts in effectively communicating the subject may have been limited historically. However, recent television successes, such as *Earth Story, The Essential Guide to Rocks* and *Walking with Dinosaurs,* have shown how skilled communicators, in conjunction with 'experts', can bring the subject to life.

26.4 Developing new approaches

26.4.1 Use of doorways

Much of the geological interpretation available fails to engage the public. Often, this is due to the use of technical language, making invalid assumptions about the level of prior knowledge, or the failure to use tried and tested interpretive techniques. It is not the message that is dull, but the way it is told. Engaging the public requires the use of the familiar or 'doorways', to relate geology to people's everyday lives. Doorways can include the use of popular culture to present information in cartoon form, for example casting historical geologists as heroes. Not only will this engage younger visitors, but also remain relevant to older age groups, who may find a light-hearted approach preferable to conventional, instructional methods. People discover more when the learning experience is fun. It is important to recognise that, for many, experiencing the natural heritage is a leisure activity; it is unrealistic to expect to achieve anything more than a superficial understanding of the subject. Even so, for the geological heritage, this would represent a significant improvement on the current position.

26.4.2 New technology

Where appropriate, new technology can engage the user in a learning-through-discovery experience. Interactive devices and computer-based CD-ROMS now form an integral part of many interpretive displays. These media have particular application in understanding the evolution of the landscape, since the story is incredibly dynamic. Images of colliding continents, changing environments, erupting volcanoes and evolving plants and animals are ideally suited to this type of interactive process.

26.4.3 Sculpture and poetry

Art provides a powerful medium through which to engage public understanding and curiosity. By its nature, messages through the use of art are often subliminal and thought provoking. Although presently limited, art is increasingly being used to connect people with geology and the landscape. One such example, in Dorset, uses sculptures of ammonites and snail-like shells to link geology and the landscape on the approach to Lulworth Cove, in what is described as "a powerful exposition of cultural intimacy with the land" (Clifford, 1994).

SNH, the Heritage Lottery Fund, the European Union and Ross and Cromarty Enterprise are all involved in a project at Knockan Crag, Sutherland (Plate 6), which includes the development of a rather literal rock installation: a rock wall. The 'wall', representing the contorted, concertinaed rock layers of the area, is aesthetically pleasing and helps visitors visualise the rock structures, their geometry and relative simplicity. The wall is part of a project to interpret the area which includes plans for other rock installations and carvings, and a major cliff-top sculpture intended to draw visitors from the car park and main interpretation area below, up a path to the summit of the crag. Interpretation at Knockan will include the use of poetry and historical quotations. Pride of place on Knockan's geological trail will be, perhaps, one of the most famous quotations in the history of science - Hutton's enunciation that he could find "no vestige of a beginning and no prospect of an end".

The site was important in the development of our understanding of geology. Here, Sir Roderick Impey Murchison, the first director of the Geological Survey in Scotland and Professor James Nicol from Aberdeen University, advanced competing theories on how the rocks of Assynt formed. It took the painstaking work of Benjamin Peach and John Horne, from the Geological Survey, to unravel the complexities of the rock structures, work celebrated in a series of new interpretative displays to be unveiled at Knockan Crag early in 2001.

26.4.4 Geological hubs
Scotland contains a number of major 'hubs', or concentrations, of geological interest. Edinburgh, Skye and Arran are just three examples that represent popular destinations with an existing reputation for the provision of high quality cultural and aesthetic facilities. Beyond these hubs lie many smaller areas of local interest, or nodes, where imaginative interpretation and well-planned visitor management could effectively contribute to the wider economy. For example, ten satellite sites are planned for the vicinity of Knockan Crag. Combining these hubs into a network provides a real prospect of revealing Scotland's geological history to the public. Plans are already in hand to give a greater degree of coherence to existing provision, so that visitors can navigate between areas of interest, deriving maximum appreciation and enjoyment from what is on offer.

The Millennium project, Our Dynamic Earth (Monro and Davison, this volume), potentially provides a major gateway into the network of geological hubs. This visitor attraction, housed in its futuristic building, is a world-class facility that will contribute a great deal to the public understanding of science over the coming years. An estimated 500,000 people will visit Our Dynamic Earth every year, each exposed to a series of shows, displays and interactives that seek to explain the processes of formation, evolution and renewal influencing Planet Earth. Many will emerge from that experience, and wonder "where next? - where can I see some of these wonders for myself?" No 'signposting' currently exists; only prior knowledge or good fortune would guide anyone from Edinburgh's Holyrood Park, the site of Our Dynamic Earth, to other locations.

There are many other geological gems throughout Scotland - Beinn Eighe National Nature Reserve in Ross and Cromarty, Fossil Grove in Victoria Park, Glasgow, the Cairngorms and Loch Ness 2000 to name but a few. The Cairngorms, already a National Nature Reserve and a future National Park, is a candidate World Heritage Site because of its unique landforms. SNH, in association with the British Geological Survey, is producing four self-guided walks ('Journeys Through Time') which describe the geological and landform development of the area. Publication is due in 2001, and it is hoped that further collaborative work of this nature will encourage visitors to make the added journeys to Scotland's prime Earth heritage sites. However, intuition alone cannot guide visitors there - they must be informed and encouraged to go those extra miles.

26.4.5 Partnership working with the tourist industry
The key to the development of geotourism is effective partnership with the tourism industry. The Scottish Tourist Board is keen to exploit niche markets and is now aware of

the potential of geotourism. Nevertheless, many key players remain unaware - local tourist boards, tour operators and those offering accommodation, for example, many of whom live and work in prime territory and would benefit from tapping into this potentially lucrative market. Such awareness will, hopefully, develop over time. Scottish Geology Week, instigated in 1997, has already helped in this respect. It involves a combination of illustrated talks, walks and exhibitions to raise awareness of rocks, fossils and landforms amongst the public - visitors and residents alike. Organised by SNH, in conjunction with the British Geological Survey, the National Museums of Scotland, the Hunterian Museum, Our Dynamic Earth and the Edinburgh Geological Society, the programme involves the staging of events across the country, with over 100 planned for 2001. Now a permanent fixture, Scottish Geology Week takes place in September, every second year.

26.5 Conclusions

Wildlife tourism, alternatively described as ecotourism, already represents a significant slice of the Scottish tourist market. Geotourism, essentially an extension of this activity, can represent a significant growth area if developed enthusiastically and creatively. In some places, it may be more appropriate to combine geology with the broader canvas of wildlife, cultural and historical interest, and to present the subject matter holistically. It is perhaps no surprise that some of Scotland's most spectacular landscapes and geology coincide with relatively remote and sparsely populated areas, so there is no doubt that geotourism can contribute significantly to the rural economy.

Geology, for many, is a closed book, but this need not be the case. Imaginative and innovative interpretation provides the means to open-up the subject up to a new audience.

Surely it is time for geologists, the tourism industry, interpreters and local authorities to come together to map out a more co-ordinated approach to promote the understanding of Scotland's landscapes and geology.

References

A & M Training and Development 1997. *Review of Wildlife Tourism in Scotland. A Report for the Scottish Tourism and Environment Initiative.* Tourism and Environment Task Force, Inverness.

Clifford S. 1994. Sculpture, community and the land. *In* O'Halloran, D., Green, C., Harley, M., Stanley, M. and Knill, J. (eds) *Geological and Landscape Conservation.* The Geological Society, London, 487 - 491.

Crabtree, J.R., Leat, P.M.K., Sartarossa, J. and Thompson, K. 1994. The economic impact of wildlife sites in Scotland. *Journal of Rural Studies*, **10**, 61-72

Dott, R.H. Jr. 1999. Closing remarks for the Hutton Bicentenary, Edinburgh. *In* Craig G.Y. and Hull J.H. (eds) *James Hutton - Present and Future.* Geological Society of London, Special Publications, **150**, 169 – 173.

Masters, D. 1998. *Marine Wildlife Tourism: Developing a Quality Approach in the Highlands and Islands.* Unpublished report prepared for the Tourism and Environment Initiative and Scottish Natural Heritage, Edinburgh.

Scottish Natural Heritage/British Geological Survey 1993 – 2001. *Edinburgh, Skye, Cairngorms, Loch Lomond to Stirling, Orkney and Shetland, East Lothian & the Borders, Arran & the Clyde Islands Scotland, Fife and Tayside and North-West Highlands – A Landscape Fashioned by Geology.* Scottish Natural Heritage, Perth.

Scottish Natural Heritage 2000. Rothiemurchus and Glenmore recreation survey summary. *Scottish Natural Heritage Research, Survey and Monitoring Report*, No. 166.

Scottish Tourism Co-ordinating Group 1992. *Tourism and the Scottish Environment - A Sustainable Partnership.* Scottish Tourist Board, Edinburgh.

System 3 2000. *Tourism Attitudes Survey 1999.* Report to Scottish Tourist Board and Scottish Natural Heritage. System 3, Edinburgh.

Threadgould, R. and McKirdy, A.P. 1999. Earth heritage interpretation in Scotland: the role of Scottish Natural Heritage. *In* Barettino, D., Vallejo, M. and Gallego, E. (eds) *Towards the Balanced Management and Conservation of the Geological Heritage in the New Millennium.* Sociedad Geológica de España, Madrid, 330-334.

27 LANDSCAPES FROM STONE

Patrick J. McKeever and Enda Gallagher

Summary

1.   The relationship between the scientist and the general public has changed in recent years, with scientists increasingly recognising that they have a duty to inform non-specialists about their research.

2.   In Ireland, geology has been part of this debate and the collaborative work reported here is an example of bringing geology to the public.

3.   In 1997, the Geological Survey of Northern Ireland (GSNI) and the Geological Survey of Ireland (GSI) began a cross-border initiative, *Landscapes from Stone*. Its aim was to develop and popularise the landscapes and rocks of the twelve northern counties of Ireland.

4.   Literature for the mainstream tourism industry is being produced, with walking, driving and cycle trails used to link sites of geological interest with sites of archaeological, cultural and mythological interest. A parallel effort has also been made to promote the area as a field study destination, particularly within the higher education community.

5.   Marketing the geology of northern Ireland has helped encourage visitor stays in the area. It has helped increase the public profile of both Geological Surveys, and demonstrated the appetite of the wider public for accessible scientific material.

27.1 Introduction

In late 1994, the Geological Survey of Ireland (GSI) and the Geological Survey of Northern Ireland (GSNI) were successful in attracting funding from the International Fund for Ireland to engage in a joint project covering Counties Cavan and Fermanagh. The parent bodies of both organisations agreed to supply additional funding, and both Cavan County Council and Fermanagh District Council agreed to contribute some local-based resources. The project, *The Mineral Market and Geotourism Development Assessment of County Cavan and County Fermanagh*, had a duration of 18 months. The chief aim was to use these two specific topics to develop a new level of co-operation between both Geological

Figure 27.1 Map of Ireland showing the location of Counties Cavan and Fermanagh.

Surveys in subject areas where neither had operated widely before. Cavan and Fermanagh were chosen as the geographical area as they form two so-called border counties, both belonging to the province of Ulster, but Cavan lying within the Republic of Ireland and Fermanagh forming part of Northern Ireland (Figure 27.1). Economically, both counties have suffered a great deal as a result of the political unrest in Northern Ireland and it was felt that an assessment of the mineral development potential of the counties might help expand existing, and create new, employment opportunities within this field. Similarly, both counties had a well-established tourism industry but it was widely recognised that the full scale of the tourism potential in the area had yet to be realised.

27.2 Geotourism in Cavan and Fermanagh

The two strands of the project were closely integrated. Geological, engineering and environmental data were collated as part of the minerals market assessment. Extensive contacts were made with the local extractive industry, which varies in scale from major international-scale operations such as the Séan Quinn Group based at Derrylin, to the small-scale operator who extracts for his own immediate use. A GIS-based CD-ROM was developed that allows developers and locals alike to find out quickly where the best rocks, for example for roadstone, are found and also to see if there is any conflict with the interests of the environment and the region's tourism industry.

The tourism strand also initiated extensive contacts with the local community, ranging from individuals and local community groups up to the county council level. The rationale behind this was to ensure that the local tourism industry and the local community were not only fully aware of the project, but would also become supporters and, just as importantly, advisors to the project. As a result of these contacts, it quickly became apparent that geology needed to be marketed in an indirect way. The term 'geotourism' was quickly dropped as it was seen as being 'jingoistic' and rather esoteric. The local tourism industry recommended the integration of geology with the existing tourism infrastructure of both counties, rather than the development of products without regard to what was already in place. Tourism officials also expressed a wish to see an expansion of opportunities for walking, to encourage more overnight stays in the region.

As a direct result of these concerns, it was decided to adopt what is now called 'the holistic approach'. This involves integrating geology not only with the existing tourism infrastructure, but also with as many other aspects of the natural environment as possible.

Limited funding for product development restricted the focus to one particular part of the area: the Cuilcagh Mountains. These cover a very small area of southern Fermanagh and west Cavan, but include the Marble Arch Showcaves, the National Trust owned Florencecourt House and the Shannon Pot, the mythological source of the River Shannon. This small upland area also has a very rich archaeological heritage, and the limestone pavements flanking Cuilcagh play host to a specialised flora that forms the foundation of several nature reserves.

Two products were developed. First, the Cuilcagh Scenic Drive card links the main visitor attractions of the area with sites of geological, archaeological, environmental and mythological interest (McKeever, 1997a). Second, the Cuilcagh Mountain Walks package (McKeever, 1997b) is a set of ten circular walks, providing a greater level of detail about the area's natural heritage. It was devised to bring walkers into the more remote communities of west Cavan and south Fermanagh. The locations of the walks were also indicated on the scenic drive card, thus forming a link between the two products. The products were loosely branded as belonging to a series entitled *The Scenic Landscapes and Rocks of Counties Cavan and Fermanagh*, but no new logo was devised. An additional, related product, a card entitled *The Upper Erne Scenic Drive*, was also produced, and the routes of a further four drives were identified (McKeever, 1997c).

27.3 Landscapes from Stone

Feedback obtained from council and tourism officials and community groups in both counties led the Geological Surveys to conclude that this type of 'landscape tourism' could be expanded right across the north of Ireland. This region, representing the counties of Antrim, Armagh, Cavan, Derry, Donegal, Down, Fermanagh, Leitrim, Louth, Monaghan, Sligo and Tyrone, qualifies for several special funding sources, comprising as it does the six counties of Northern Ireland and the six neighbouring counties of the Republic of Ireland (Figure 27.2). With strong backing and advice from both the Northern Ireland Tourist Board and Bord Fáilte (Irish Tourist Board), the Geological Surveys secured major new funding from the EU Special Support Programme for Peace and Reconciliation to develop innovative, popular, geological products covering the twelve county region. The adoption of

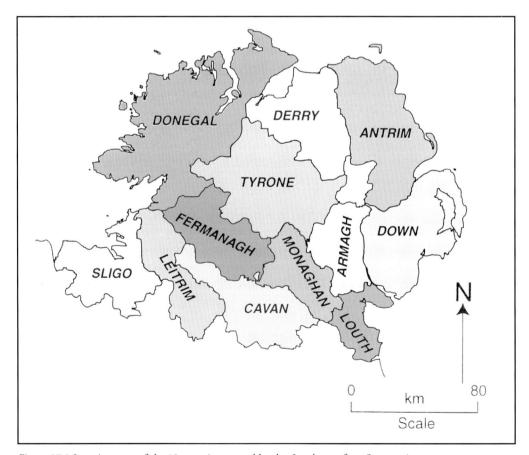

Figure 27.2 Location map of the 12 counties covered by the *Landscapes from Stone* project.

the holistic approach was instrumental in obtaining funding for the work and was also a recognition by the Geological Surveys of the very limited market for solely geological products. Additional funding from local government councils also meant that the council-operated Tourist Information Centres across the region would act as a ready-made retail network for the products. The project also included a major marketing initiative that was funded separately by the EU Interreg programme.

27.3.1 Product development

A new brand name and logo were devised, *Landscapes from Stone* (Figure 27.3). As with the Cavan – Fermanagh project, several linked product tiers were devised. The first involved two products designed to provide an overview of the region's geological heritage. A map, simply entitled *Landscapes from Stone*, uses the holistic approach but divides the region into geographical areas, based on the landscape rather than counties or districts (McKeever *et al.*, 1999). It is an outdoor resource map and includes forest parks, waymarked walking routes, archaeological sites and EU-designated blue-flag beaches, as well as sites of geological interest. The geological sites selected have interests that are visually obvious to the lay person even if, to the geologist, they may not be especially significant scientifically. Accompanying the map is a book entitled *A Story through Time* (McKeever, 1999). Written strictly for the non-geologist, it links chronologically the different landscapes of the region to its geological history, opening up a new view of familiar landmarks such as the Mourne Mountains, Lough Neagh and the Donegal Highlands. It must be stressed that no pretence has been made that these products are for the geologist, either professional or amateur. They are intended to bring geology to a whole new market, to those people who have no prior knowledge of the subject, but who have an interest in the scenery and

Figure 27.3 The *Landscapes from Stone* logo.

landscape of the region. The tourism industry refers to the 'discerning visitor' when categorising this sector of the market.

While the first tier of products provides a regional overview, the second and third target much smaller areas, essentially the landscape areas defined in the *Landscapes from Stone* map and the *Story through Time* book. As with the Cavan – Fermanagh products, these new products are touring cards and walking sets. The touring cards, entitled the *Explore* series, integrate geology with the existing tourism infrastructure of each specific area, as well as other aspects of the outdoor environment. The walking sets, developed as the *Walk* series, explore in greater detail the geological heritage of each area, but are still aimed at the non-geologist market. To ensure that the stated aim of integrating geology into the mainstream tourism industry of the region is met, all products are checked by industry officials, both at the national and county/district level. As part of this process, elected county/district councillors also receive an opportunity to provide an input.

27.4 Marketing

The research, preparation and publication of the landscape tourism products is funded largely by the Special Support Programme for Peace and Reconciliation. Separate funding, from the EU Interreg Programme, supports the promotion of these products, the marketing of the region as a destination for the field study of geology, and the achievement of the objectives of the project as a whole. A marketing strategy has been essential for the success of the project, as it encourages focus and direction, initiates the setting of objectives and provides a timetable for the completion of specific activities. It was necessary to decide who the customers are, what products to offer and how best to communicate their existence. Research, which is the key ingredient underpinning all marketing strategy, was crucial to the execution of the project and largely guided its overall direction.

27.4.1 Aim

The aim of the *Landscapes from Stone* project is to develop and promote landscape tourism within the twelve northern counties of Ireland, thereby adding geology to the existing tourism product for the area. There are two aspects to this:

1. to market the region to the educational community as a field study destination; and
2. to promote the popular publications to the wider general public.

The marketing strategy was comprehensively defined at the outset and was supported by both Bord Fáilte and the Northern Ireland Tourist Board. One of the main features of the strategy was the decision to concentrate marketing activities primarily on the educational market, specifically the university geology department sector. This is where the Surveys' natural expertise lies, where a target market can be most easily identified and where initial success would most likely be achieved.

27.4.2 The product

After deciding that the target market was the university sector, it was necessary to decide what product was appropriate. However, it is the *concept* of field study that is being promoted, rather than a product that can be priced and sold. Furthermore, whilst the geology of the region is of crucial importance in the decision-making process, so too are factors such as cost, accessibility and local facilities. Both tourist boards emphasised the need to make access to the region as easy as possible for potential visitors, but advised the Surveys not to be responsible for the actual organisation of specific travel itineraries for visiting groups. This would be more the role of a tour operator. Two options were researched:

1. development of linkages with Incoming Tour Operators and Overseas Tour Operators who will quote for a travel/accommodation package; and
2. preparation of listings of travel/accommodation options that could be sent to interested groups who can then make their own arrangements independently.

Apart from travel itineraries, one of the most interesting issues to arise from the primary research was the perceived need for assistance with geological itinerary preparation. The extent of the need varied from simply some advice about certain geological localities, to the more extreme case of the minority who were of the opinion that a professional guide would be desirable. Overall, however, the majority of field leaders were of the view that a field guide to some of the main localities of the region would be very useful as a reference for possible trip preparation. This need was addressed through the publication of a field guide for a familiarisation trip, which was in effect a summary geological tour of the region. The guide has proved to be a very rewarding product in promotional terms, forming the centrepiece of discussions with interested parties at conferences and is distributed free of charge to field trip leaders who express an interest.

27.4.3 Communication
Following the decision on what 'products' to offer, it was then necessary to raise awareness of them among the target market. This involved addressing the potential customer directly through branding (as discussed earlier), conference participation, a familiarisation visit and publicity.

27.4.3.1 Conferences
Academic geological conferences represent the best possible way to reach large numbers of the educational target audience. They are ideal for promotional purposes since they enable the Surveys to:

- reach large numbers of our target audience;
- create awareness of our initiative and opportunities;
- encourage interest in the concept of field study in Ireland;
- research reaction to our concept and current practice;
- generate contacts amongst the academic community;
- facilitate and assist those who may already be thinking of the concept;
- overcome (via the provision of information) any existing prejudices (e.g. too costly); and
- obtain publicity.

Those conferences at which the Surveys chose to exhibit were selected to cover as wide an area of the Earth sciences as possible and to represent each of the three main geographical markets - Britain (Geoscience '98 in Keele, England), North America (Geological Society of America's Annual Meetings for 1998 in Toronto and 1999 in Denver) and mainland Europe (European Union of Geosciences 1999 meeting in Strasbourg, France).

Both questionnaire and verbal feedback were actively canvassed. It was quickly realised at all four conferences that knowledge of the excellence and diversity of Irish geology was high. Thus it was unnecessary to concentrate on promoting the geology itself, but rather on emphasising to potential visitors the added convenience benefits, should they decide to proceed. As such, the main talking points became the summary field guide to the region and the information brief (which includes guideline prices). Reactions to both were emphatic - the twelve-county region has a very strong geological appeal and is also financially competitive relative to other field study destinations, such as the Isle of Arran in Scotland.

27.4.3.2 Familiarisation trip
Familiarisation trips, where a group of decision-makers is invited on a pre-paid promotional trip, are standard practice within the tourism industry. Experience at the Geoscience

conference in Keele suggested that this concept could also work well for the academic market. A familiarisation trip was therefore arranged in October 1998. A total of 14 universities sent representatives, and the editor of a leading UK-based geoscience journal, *Down to Earth*, also attended.

The six-day trip covered a largely coastal route from Dublin, north through Louth, Armagh, Down and Antrim, then across Derry to Donegal, and finishing off with visits to sites in Sligo, Fermanagh and Cavan, before returning to Dublin. It was prepared and led by staff from both Surveys and became a classic example of a fact-finding mission that allowed the participants to see at first hand the geological wealth of the region. The obvious primary benefit of the trip was that it allowed a demonstration of the quality of the region's geology to key opinion leaders. Furthermore, mindful of the other variables in the decision-making process, the trip also included visits to at least one accommodation centre each day, to highlight the excellent facilities on the ground. Armed with this scientific and practical knowledge, it is hoped that the participants will bring the region to the attention of their respective universities.

The trip was also an ideal opportunity to research in closer detail the needs of the British university geology sector, through the use of questionnaires and focus groups. The responses, coupled with the conference feedback, have been hugely influential in defining later activities.

27.4.3.3 Publicity

Publicity is, in effect, a free form of advertising and was an area of particular focus for the *Landscapes from Stone* project. Both geological and mainstream media were targeted successfully. For the marketing side of the project, the familiarisation trip produced the first television and radio coverage, together with articles in leading geoscience journals and in the local press across the region. For the popular market, the Surveys have acquired reviews of their publications, publicised the launch of their regional guides and promoted their existence in the local press via a separate media campaign.

Another means of publicity for *Landscapes from Stone* has been through oral and poster presentations to various audiences and interest groups, including geological conferences, and individual university tourism or geology classes, Landscape Forums and local community groups.

27.5 Conclusion

The production of popular publications by geological surveys across the world is seen as one way of raising public awareness of the Earth sciences and also of the existence of the surveys themselves. This has been the case with *Landscapes from Stone*. During the life of the project and its immediate predecessor, there has been a significant rise in media interest in Irish geology and increased public awareness of the work of both Geological Surveys. Local newspapers and radio stations are now more willing to view local geology as a 'good-news' story, of interest to their readership or listening public. Within the GSNI, increasing the accessibility of geological information to a wider market has now progressed from the area of popular publications into core products such as the 1:50,000 solid series geological maps. The publication in 1998 of a new style geological map for the Causeway Coast marked an innovative departure for either Survey. In addition to retaining as much scientific information as is normally expected on a 1:50,000 scale geological map, the mapface includes further information for the layperson, including, photographs of obvious geological features, a layperson's guide to reading a geological map and an excursion guide. The second map in this new series is now in preparation.

Throughout the duration of the project, much groundwork has been completed in building all the essential elements of a marketing strategy. Contact has been firmly established with local tourism organisations, leading to co-operation on various fronts (e.g. financial support for the familiarisation trip). Links have been forged with tour operators who are now actively quoting for business opportunities referred by the Surveys. Contacts have been made with local accommodation providers, coach companies and carriers into the region, and information sheets on best options have been prepared and distributed.

Visits by geological field parties are now increasing as a result of these efforts. The University of Maine and the University of Ontario at Waterloo in Canada were the first North American successes, and the State University of New York at Brockport and the University of Alabama visited in 2000. British universities are now returning, with the Universities of Liverpool, Manchester, Birmingham and Southampton leading the way. The first UK A-level school success was Cowbridge Comprehensive from Wales. The University of Mainz in Germany has also visited, and although there is further potential in mainland Europe, an increased marketing effort will be required. Some effort has also been directed towards the popular market, with the publication of a walks flier in German for a joint mailshot with Kleemann Irlande Reisen, an Irish based German tour operator.

The Surveys' popular products, pitched as they are at the enquiring tourist, represent a significant addition to the overall tourism product of Northern Ireland and the six border counties of the Republic of Ireland. This region has significant potential for further tourism development, when compared to other tourism hotspots such as Killarney and south-west Ireland. The industry in Ireland is now increasingly aware that geology is something that should be included in the tourism portfolio. Roadside panels and signs are now incorporating geology as well as other aspects of the natural environment, such as flora, fauna and archaeology. The economic benefit that can be obtained by attracting shoulder-season geological field parties to the region is likewise being recognised. Moreover, by inviting people (both visitors and locals alike) to explore the landscape, they are helping in the economic regeneration of the entire region.

Acknowledgements

The Geological Surveys wish to acknowledge the Special Support Programme for Peace and Reconciliation and the EU Interreg programme as the primary sources of funding for the *Landscapes from Stone* project. We also wish to acknowledge financial support from local authorities across the region and support and advice from Bord Fáilte, the Northern Ireland Tourist Board and numerous individuals from the tourism industry throughout Ireland.

References

McKeever, P.J. 1997a. *Cuilcagh Scenic Drive.* Geological Survey of Northern Ireland – Geological Survey of Ireland, Belfast and Dublin.

McKeever, P.J. 1997b. *Cuilcagh Mountain Walks.* Geological Survey of Northern Ireland – Geological Survey of Ireland, Belfast and Dublin.

McKeever, P.J. 1997c. *Upper Erne Scenic Drive.* Geological Survey of Northern Ireland – Geological Survey of Ireland, Belfast and Dublin.

McKeever, P.J., Kearns-Mills, N. and Gallagher, E. 1999. *Landscapes From Stone.* Geological Survey of Northern Ireland – Geological Survey of Ireland, Belfast and Dublin.

McKeever, P.J. 1999. *A Story Through Time.* Geological Survey of Northern Ireland – Geological Survey of Ireland, Belfast and Dublin.

28 INTERPRETING QUATERNARY LANDSCAPE EVOLUTION: LOCH LOMOND AND THE CAMPSIE FELLS

Eleanor J. Brown

Summary

1.   Quaternary landscape interpretation presents existing information on the rapid climate, geomorphological and environmental changes experienced during the last 2.5 million years of Earth history, in an accessible and interesting form.
2.   The Loch Lomond and Campsie Fells areas have a diversity of excellent landforms and Quaternary deposits produced by processes including glaciation, sea-level change and mass movement, and so provide an excellent opportunity to promote wider public awareness of Quaternary landscape change.
3.   Diverse approaches to landscape interpretation can be adopted to interest and enthuse visitors to the area.

28.1 Introduction

The Quaternary period, the last 2.5 million years of Earth history, is characterised by rapid climate, geomorphological and environmental changes. These changes had a fundamental impact on Scotland's landscapes, flora and fauna and are recorded in a variety of landform and sediment records (Gordon and Sutherland, 1993). The aim of Quaternary landscape interpretation is to present this information in an accessible and interesting form for a variety of audiences, including the wider public and schools.

The interpretation of Quaternary landscape evolution is important in several respects. First, geomorphology, together with the underlying geology, forms the very basis of the landscape and scenery that visitors to our countryside recognise and enjoy. Second, the influence of geomorphology and soils is reflected closely in the variations in habitats and in human activities such as agriculture. Third, palaeoenvironmental records hold the key to reconstructing past changes in climate, flora and fauna. Together with landform and sedimentary records, they allow unique insights into the processes and forces that have shaped the present landscape and the role of human activities, such as woodland clearance. Fourth, many Scottish landscapes are the product of processes that are no longer operating in this region (e.g. glaciation), so that relict landforms such as drumlins and moraines are non-renewable once destroyed (Gordon et al., 1994). Raising public awareness of our Earth heritage and promoting greater understanding of its relevance to our lives should help to increase concern for its conservation (McKirdy and Threadgould, 1994).

This paper examines the potential for Quaternary landscape interpretation in the Loch Lomond and Campsie Fells area (Figure 28.1), part of which will lie within Scotland's first national park, Loch Lomond and the Trossachs. The existing Quaternary landscape interpretation provided by several different agencies is outlined, and some principles are proposed as a basis for development.

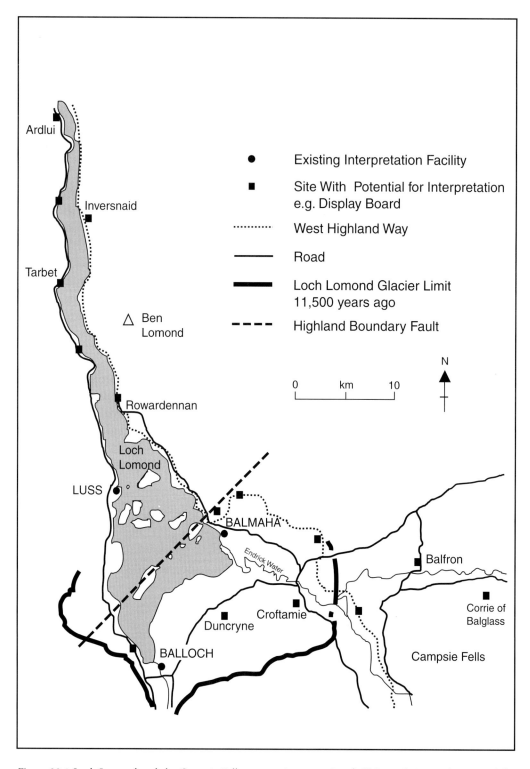

Figure 28.1 Loch Lomond and the Campsie Fells: current interpretation facilities and sites with potential for additional interpretation based on the existing infrastructure.

28.2 Potential of the area for Earth heritage interpretation

The Loch Lomond and Campsie Fells area provides an excellent opportunity to promote wider public awareness of Quaternary landscape change. Loch Lomond is also the type-area (Rose, 1989) for the Loch Lomond Readvance (12,900 – 11,400 years ago), when glaciers were last present in Scotland (Figure 28.1). This means that it is internationally important for Quaternary studies. The area has a diversity of excellent landforms and Quaternary deposits produced by many processes, including glaciation, sea-level change and mass movements (Rose, 1981; Gordon and Sutherland, 1993; Pierce, 1999). These include landforms of glacial erosion, such as the glacial trough of northern Loch Lomond. This contrasts sharply with the landscape to the south of the loch, which is characterised by glacial deposition and ice-marginal landforms. The sediments between Loch Lomond and the Campsie Fells contain evidence of former ice-dammed lakes and at least two separate periods of glaciation. Several spectacular landslips are visible along the margins of the Campsie Fells. There are also rare and unique sites with organic sediments that record former vegetated land surfaces, which experienced very different climatic conditions to the present day. These have all been well researched and there is detailed scientific understanding of the landscape forming processes, which is an essential foundation for interpretation.

The landscape also has a high scenic, aesthetic and recreational value founded on its geology and Quaternary landforms. It received over 4 million visitors in 1991, with the major reason for visits being the scenery (Centre for Leisure Research, 1992). The high visitor numbers, the proximity to large population centres and good transport links therefore maximise the potential for developing innovative interpretation facilities based on an outstanding natural resource. The imminent national park designation will provide an infrastructure and an opportunity for the co-ordination of interpretation throughout the area and help to focus resources appropriately.

28.3 Current interpretation facilities

Current facilities include visitor centre displays by the Loch Lomond Park Authority at Balmaha and Luss (Figure 28.1), which incorporate aspects of Quaternary landscape interpretation such as glaciation, sea-level change and vegetation change. Publications, such as *Loch Lomond to Stirling: a Landscape Fashioned by Geology* (Brown and Mendum, 1995) produced by Scottish Natural Heritage and the British Geological Survey, and *The HMSO West Highland Way Official Guide* (Aitken and Smith, 1995), also discuss the evolution of the area. The landscape of the Trossachs is interpreted at Tourist Information Centres in Aberfoyle and Callander. The car parks in Arrochar have eye-catching woodcarvings with panels which interpret topics from geology and glaciation to cultural and military history. However, a full inventory of the existing landscape interpretation provided by the various agencies is needed as a basis for a co-ordinated approach to future interpretive planning (Aldridge, 1974).

28.4 Recommendations for future developments

The selection of appropriate themes is a key element of future interpretive planning (Veverka, 1994). It is important to make landscape interpretation relevant, interesting and accessible to the visitor. McKirdy and Threadgould (1994) advocate linking interpretation facilities into an overall framework for the area to reduce duplication, especially where several agencies provide interpretation, as this can be off-putting to visitors (Aldridge, 1974). There is scope for increasing interpretation provision by maximising the existing tourist and transport infrastructure. For example, the new National Cycle Network passes through the area to the south of Loch Lomond and into the Trossachs. This opens up additional sites for interpretation, including the important Quaternary site at Croftamie, where sediments record two glacial events, an ice-dammed lake and a former treeless tundra environment. However, some landscapes have sufficient aesthetic appeal to be special to visitors without interpretation. Therefore, planning should include 'interpretive blanks' where interpretation may be intrusive (Jones, 2000). In some cases, the interpretation of landscapes within the proposed national park may rely on the interpretation of features outwith the boundary. When other topics are the primary focus, such as cultural history or industry, often the landscape has a place in the interpretation; for example, the use of glacial outwash for gravel extraction.

The choice of interpretive media should be made with respect to the target audience and theme. For example, since visitors to car parks may only stay briefly, displays should interpret visible landforms. Visitor centres are better placed for dealing with less obvious or tangible processes, such as sea-level change. Modern analogues are also a powerful tool to illustrate former landscape processes, such as glaciation, along with interactive displays or simulations; for example, a computer reconstruction of glacier growth and decay in the Loch Lomond basin. The use of art as an interpretive medium and eye-catching links to celebrities or television programmes such as *Essential Guide to Rocks, Tracks* and *Earth Story* may also help to popularise landscape interpretation.

The provision of curriculum material to facilitate fieldwork for formal education and increasing the availability of landscape products in visitor centres should be seen as a priority. Sales of products can also help to measure the effectiveness of landscape interpretation (Aldridge, 1974).

Finally, is important to keep in touch with visitors by asking them what interpretation they would like to see. Successful interpretation relies on evaluation and feedback from visitors to inform future strategies and generate repeat visits. Collaboration between interpreters and landscape researchers is also important to ensure that the interpretation and scientific expertise and knowledge keep pace with each other.

28.5 Conclusion

Appropriate conservation strategies, combined with facilities to raise public awareness, are vital to sustain and manage our natural heritage effectively. Loch Lomond and the Campsie Fells have significant potential for interpreting Quaternary landscapes to the public. There is an excellent range of interests in an area of great scenic and recreational value, and with a high level of visitor numbers. The designation of Scotland's first national park will provide an outstanding opportunity to develop innovative interpretation and to integrate the Earth heritage fully into the story of this unique area.

Acknowledgements

This work is funded by Royal Holloway University of London, Scottish Natural Heritage and the Bill Bishop Memorial Trust. Thanks go to Dr John Gordon, Professor Jim Rose and Professor John Lowe for their constructive criticism and advice.

References

Aitken, R. and Smith, R. 1995. *The HMSO West Highland Way Official Guide.* 4th edition. HMSO, Edinburgh.

Aldridge, D. 1974. Upgrading park interpretation and communication with the public. *In* Elliott, H. (ed.) *Second World Conference on National Parks. Proceedings.* IUCN, Morges, 300-311.

Brown, M.A.E. and Mendum, J. 1995. *Loch Lomond to Stirling. A Landscape Fashioned by Geology.* Scottish Natural Heritage, Perth.

Centre for Leisure Research 1992. *Loch Lomond and Dumbarton Area Visitor Survey.* Centre for Leisure Research, Edinburgh.

Gordon, J.E. and Sutherland, D.G. (eds) 1993. *Quaternary of Scotland.* Geological Conservation Review Series, No. 6. Chapman & Hall, London.

Gordon, J.E., Brazier, V. and Lees, R.G. 1994. Geomorphological systems: developing fundamental principles for sustainable landscape management. *In* O'Halloran, D., Green, C.P., Harley, M., Stanley, M. and Knill, J. (eds) *Geological and Landscape Conservation.* Geological Society, London, 185-189.

Jones, R. 2000. In defence of place. *Interpret Scotland,* **1**, 9.

McKirdy, A. and Threadgould, R. 1994. Reading the landscape. *In* O'Halloran, D., Green, C.P., Harley, M., Stanley, M. and Knill, J. (eds) *Geological and Landscape Conservation.* Geological Society, London, 459-462.

Pierce, L. 1999. Loch Lomond: an example of Quaternary megageomorphology. *Scottish Geographical Journal,* **115**, 71-80.

Rose, J. 1981. Field guide to the Quaternary geology of the south eastern part of the Loch Lomond basin. *Proceedings of the Geological Society of Glasgow,* 1980-81, 1-19.

Rose, J. 1989. Stadial type sections in the British Quaternary. *In* Rose, J. and Schlüchter, Ch. (eds) *Quaternary Type Sections: Imagination or Reality?* Balkema, Rotterdam, 45-67.

Veverka, J. 1994. *Interpretive Master Planning.* Acorn Naturalists, Tustin, California.

29 THE CLASHACH FOSSIL FOOTPRINT INTERPRETATION SITE: A JOINT VENTURE

Suzanne Miller and Carol Hopkins

Summary

1.   The Permian Hopeman sandstone at Clashach Quarry has provided a rich source of fossil trackways formed by mammal-like reptiles.

2.   An outdoor interpretation display has been created near to the quarry entrance through partnership between various organisations. This provides an important opportunity for local people to learn more about their geological heritage.

29.1 Introduction

"You're in an arid desert, surrounded by massive dunes up to 90 m high.   The prevailing northerly wind occasionally brings rain, causing flash flooding.   There is very little vegetation, mainly ferns and horsetails, and animals whose like you've never seen before; long-legged reptiles with incisor-like tusks. So where are you?"

These were the opening remarks to a group of children and adults who had assembled at the entrance to Clashach Quarry, near Elgin, where a new Fossil Footprint Interpretation Site was officially opened in April 1999.

To the bemusement of the audience, the answer to the question was: "Right here, 250 million years ago, when the sandstone beneath your feet was those very dunes."

29.2 Geological setting

The Permian Hopeman sandstone outcrops north of Elgin for 10 km along the southern shore of the Moray Firth. It comprises large-scale aeolian dune deposits, with corridors containing fields of smaller dunes or interdune flats (Clemmensen, 1987).   In some areas there are thin beds of pebbly, water-lain sediments. The sandstone is mostly exposed as sea cliffs, in a number of small disused quarries and in the working quarry at Clashach.

29.3 The Trackway Project

Clashach Quarry lies within a geological Site of Special Scientific Interest (SSSI). It had long been known to yield fossil trackways, although it was believed that these were very rare. Fossil bone material was unknown. During the 1990s, working at Clashach Quarry was stepped up to provide facing stone for the Museum of Scotland that was being constructed in Edinburgh. In 1997, after finding trackways at the quarry, Carol Hopkins approached Moray Stone Cutters and, together with the quarrymen, instigated a programme of checking all blocks removed from the quarry.   Within a very short time, several new trackways had been uncovered – some on loose blocks, some *in situ*. As a result of the enthusiasm and diligence of the quarrymen, over 270 new fossil trackways were discovered during the following two years. Each trackway was measured, photographed and recorded, the information being included in a new register of fossil trackways from the Elgin area. The research carried out (Hopkins, 1999) has shown that the trackways (most of which are 1-4 m in length) were produced by a variety of animals of differing sizes and morphologies. The footprints range in size from 0.5 – 24 cm wide, mostly preserved as digitigrade prints of five toes or claws. Many of the tracks display pairing of the front and back feet and show characteristic features consistent with the trackmaker moving across a dune slope. An additional unusual feature of the specimens at Clashach is the number of tail drags associated with the trackways. The discovery of the tail drags was significant, as few (4%) of the Scottish Permian trackways were previously associated with tail drags (McKeever, 1994). There are now 105 tail drags from Clashach, some 42% of current trackway finds at this locality.

29.4 The interpretation site

Following the new discoveries, Scottish Natural Heritage (SNH) asked the National Museums of Scotland (NMS) to report on the conservation of the trackways. It was not possible for Elgin Museum to house these specimens, some of which are up to 4 m in length. In discussions with Moray Stone Cutters, SNH, the NMS, Elgin Museum and the Hunterian Museum, Glasgow, it was agreed that the more scientifically important specimens would be removed to the NMS collections in Edinburgh. It was, however, very important that some of the material was left in the Clashach area, where it could be used for local educational purposes. It was decided that the most appropriate method of display for the robust specimens would be to create a new outdoor interpretation site near the entrance to the quarry. The site chosen is beside the coastal footpath, easily and safely accessible by members of the public and school and university groups alike. The positioning of the site was agreed by the landowners and SNH. Moray Stone Cutters donated the trackways, landscaped the site and, under the direction of the NMS and Carol Hopkins, moved and installed all the designated trackways from the quarry (Plate 35). In a collaborative project involving SNH, NMS and the Elgin Museum, interpretation panels were designed for the site (Plate 36). The *in situ* conservation of the trackways was carried out by NMS geology conservators, with funding from the NMS Charitable Trust.

29.5 Fossil skull discovery

In August 1997, a block of sandstone some 3 m long was excavated from the quarry. On splitting the block, the quarrymen noticed a cavity in the rock, quite unlike anything they had encountered before. They contacted Carol Hopkins who realised the great significance of the find – the first fossil mould from the Hopeman Formation. The mould was taken to Glasgow University where CT and MRI scanners were used to investigate the fossil, revealing the mould of a complete skull (Clark, 1999). This work has resulted in the identification of the animal as a species of *Dicynodon*, a mammal-like reptile, and has enabled the more accurate dating of the Hopeman Formation (previously dated as Permo-Triassic) as upper Permian. The fossil skull has now been returned to Elgin Museum and a cast will be made from the scanned images.

29.6 Conclusion

Clashach Quarry is an important trackway locality for several reasons: the range of footprint types, the number of trackways on different horizons, the length of the trackways and the large number of associated tail drags.

The Clashach Interpretation Site has provided a very successful opportunity for the local people to learn something of the geological heritage of the area and of the positive impact that quarrying has had on their environment. The discovery and preservation of the trackways has been a true partnership between Moray Stone Cutters, the National Museums of Scotland, Scottish Natural Heritage, the Hunterian Museum, The Elgin Museum and local geologist Carol Hopkins. The project was the recipient of the 1999 LASMO Geological Challenge Award.

References

Clark, N.D.L. 1999. The Elgin Marvel. *Open University Geological Society Journal*, **20**(2), 16-18.

Clemmensen, L.B. 1987. Complex star dunes and associated aeolian bed-forms, Hopeman Sandstone (Permo-Triassic), Moray Firth Basin, Scotland. *In* Frostick, L. and Reid, I. (eds) *Desert Sediments: Ancient and Modern*. Geological Society of London, Special Publications, **35**, 213-231.

Hopkins, C. 1999. New finds in the Hopeman sandstone. *Open University Geological Society Journal*, **20**(2), 10-15.

McKeever, P.J. 1994. The behavioural and biostratigraphical significance and origin of vertebrate trackways from the Permian of Scotland. *Palaios*, **9**, 477-487.

30 VOLUNTARY EARTH HERITAGE CONSERVATION IN SCOTLAND: DEVELOPING THE RIGS MOVEMENT

Katherine F. Leys

Summary

1.   Regionally Important Geological and Geomorphological Sites, or RIGS, are selected by local volunteer groups by reference to set national criteria. There are currently four RIGS groups in Scotland.
2.   There are significant challenges and opportunities for the RIGS movement in Scotland. These include the need for a more strategic approach and involvement in wider initiatives such as Local Agenda 21, biodiversity, public access to the outdoors and lifelong learning.

30.1 Introduction

The concept of voluntary Earth heritage conservation was introduced to the Earth science community in 1990 (Nature Conservancy Council, 1990). The underlying premise, that local groups would identify a number of Regionally Important Geological and Geomorphological Sites, or RIGS, by reference to set national criteria, has not changed in the last decade (Green, 1994; Harley, 1994). However, despite the number of potential sites, the RIGS initiative has historically been less widely developed in Scotland than elsewhere in the UK (Leys, 2000). There are currently four RIGS groups in Scotland, in Lothians and Borders, Fife, Tayside and Highland, and there are enthusiastic and hard working members in all these groups.

In contrast to the sedate pace of historical developments and the rather narrow focus on the selection of potential sites, there are significant challenges and opportunities ahead for the RIGS movement in Scotland. The need for a more strategic approach, and the involvement of RIGS in wider initiatives such as Local Agenda 21, biodiversity, public access to the outdoors and lifelong learning (Royal Society for Nature Conservation, 2000), are becoming increasingly recognised and understood.

30.2 RIGS development in Scotland

The RIGS network in Scotland has traditionally operated independently, with bodies such as Scottish Natural Heritage (SNH) and the British Geological Survey (BGS) providing support through the activities of individual staff members at both a local and national level. Funding for some RIGS work, including site development, education and interpretation, has been eligible for environmental grants from SNH at a local level, but competition for finite funds and the need for matching funding from other sources has prevented RIGS groups from making great use of these grants. In 1999, SNH gave a grant to the Royal Society for Nature Conservation (RSNC) to fund a part-time RIGS

Development Officer for Scotland. The purpose of the grant was to support RIGS groups to allow the preparation of a development strategy/business plan for RIGS in Scotland (Leys, 2000).

30.3 A development strategy for RIGS in Scotland

In 1997, RSNC published a three-year National Strategy for RIGS (Royal Society for Nature Conservation, 1997). The strategy focused primarily on the future development of RIGS in England and Wales, since issues such as (then) proposed devolution and the different historical development of RIGS groups in Scotland made the situation sufficiently different to warrant a separate Scottish strategy.

From discussion with RIGS groups in Scotland, the following key issues were identified: the integration of geological, geomorphological and biological conservation; the encouragement of an equal weighting of geomorphology and soils with geology; ways of attracting members and funding for RIGS; and ways of supporting the RIGS volunteers long-term. The strategy addresses these issues.

30.4 Scottish Association of RIGS Groups

At the first national meeting of RIGS members in Scotland, a need was identified for a Scottish Association of RIGS Groups. It was proposed that this body should work to provide a forum for networking and sharing experiences and to provide a coherent national voice for RIGS and voluntary Earth heritage conservation. It was envisaged that this national body would then help to steer the development and implementation of a Scottish strategy for RIGS. A steering group of six members has worked to develop a constitution for the proposed association.

30.5 RIGS and current issues in Scotland

The protection of a RIGS site is dependent upon it being recognised by the Local Authority planning process. In 1999, The Scottish Office published National Planning Policy Guideline (NPPG) 14, *Natural Heritage*. The NPPG series provides statements of Government policy on planning and landuse matters and are important for development control and development plan preparation. NPPG 14 specifically mentions RIGS and places them within the statutory framework as a local or regional designation comparable with Local Nature Reserves or Areas of Great Landscape Value. As a result, many Local Authorities are now considering the inclusion of conservation policies for the protection of RIGS in their Strategic and Local Plans. This provides a great opportunity to ensure existing sites are protected and to encourage expansion of site networks.

Local Authorities are also working at present to produce their Local Biodiversity Action Plans (LBAPs). The representation of Earth heritage issues within these plans has, to date, been mixed, and in some cases, excluded. This means that fundamental relationships between Earth heritage and biodiversity, which are seen most clearly through the medium of the soil, have, in some instances, been ignored. RIGS groups have worked with Scottish Natural Heritage, the British Geological Survey and local authority representatives to develop a guidance note for LBAP staff which highlights the role of geology and geomorphology in creating and maintaining habitats for biodiversity. This note provides a basis for increased RIGS involvement in the LBAP process.

Devolution of environmental issues to the Scottish Parliament is viewed by many as being a great opportunity for development, progress and change. The presence of a Minister at the conference is indicative of this new approach. The proximity of the Parliament and the Scottish Executive provides an opportunity to tackle environmental issues in a new way, as well as opportunities for RIGS groups to raise awareness of Earth heritage issues with policy makers and decision makers.

30.6 The potential for progress with RIGS in Scotland

In order to be a successful national voluntary body, the network of RIGS groups needs to expand in Scotland. The current distribution of Scottish groups is skewed to the east coast, with large areas of the country, particularly around the population centres of Glasgow and Stirling, un-represented. In more remote areas such as Skye, there are excellent sites for Earth heritage conservation, but development of the RIGS network is hampered because of the absence of a focal centre of professional Earth scientists that can be found in cities or centres of learning such as Edinburgh and St Andrews.

Several initiatives by existing RIGS groups provide a blueprint for the development of education and awareness-raising activities elsewhere. For example, Fife RIGS group have recently published a geological trail leaflet for a coastal walk at St Andrews (Batchelor and Browne, 1999), which is intended to be one of a series. It was published with the help of local business and will be promoted by the local Tourist Office. Lothians and Borders RIGS group have developed a successful partnership with Sainsbury's supermarket to provide geological interpretation at the site of the former Craigleith Quarry.

Involvement with the LBAP initiative also potentially offers an excellent opportunity to demonstrate the relevance of RIGS to wider conservation and biodiversity initiatives. However, as involvement depends upon being invited to participate in individual local plans, RIGS members must learn to be more vocal advocates for their subject at a local and national level.

30.7 Conclusion

The RIGS groups that exist in Scotland are currently at varying stages of development, but are generally less advanced than those in England and Wales. Further development of the network in Scotland is a priority, and ongoing initiatives such as the formation of the Scottish Association of RIGS and the implementation of a Scottish strategy will provide an impetus and a focus for further action. Significantly, such action will not be limited to site selection but will seek to demonstrate the wider interest and value of RIGS as a local resource and to integrate RIGS more closely with initiatives such as LBAPs and Local Agenda 21.

Acknowledgements

The author is grateful to the members of the RIGS groups in Scotland for their input and support. The views in this chapter are the author's own.

References

Batchelor, R.A. and Browne, M.A.E. 1999. *St Andrews' Geological Trail*. Fife RIGS Group, St Andrews.

Green, C.P. 1994. The role of voluntary organisations in Earth science conservation in the UK. *In* O'Halloran, D., Green, C., Harley, M., Stanley, M. and Knill, J. (eds) *Geological and Landscape Conservation*. The Geological Society, London, 309-312.

Harley, M. 1994. The RIGS (Regionally Important Geological/ Geomorphological Sites) challenge – involving local volunteers in conserving England's geological heritage. *In* O'Halloran, D., Green, C., Harley, M., Stanley, M. and Knill, J. (eds) *Geological and Landscape Conservation*. The Geological Society, London, 313-317.

Leys, K.F. 2000. RIGS in Scotland – a progress report. *In* Oliver, P.G. (ed.) *Proceedings of the Second UK RIGS Conference, Worcester, 1999*. Herefordshire and Worcestershire RIGS Group, Worcester, 137-140.

Nature Conservancy Council 1990. *Earth Science Conservation in Great Britain – A Strategy*. Nature Conservancy Council, Peterborough.

Royal Society for Nature Conservation 1997. *RIGS National Strategy*. Royal Society for Nature Conservation, Newark.

Royal Society for Nature Conservation 2000. *RIGS Handbook*. Royal Society for Nature Conservation, Newark.

The Scottish Office 1999. *Natural Heritage. National Planning Policy Guideline 14*. The Scottish Office Development Department, Edinburgh.

PART FIVE
KEY ISSUES FOR A SUSTAINABLE FUTURE

KEY ISSUES FOR A SUSTAINABLE FUTURE

Part 5 identifies challenges for the future. It retains elements of the three themes of the Conference identified in Chapter 1 - the integrity of Earth science and the natural heritage, sustainability, and raising public awareness and involvement - but concentrates on sustainability issues. Whilst the discussions move more towards the inclusive agenda of sustainability, the underlying messages remain the same, namely the importance of Earth science in shaping human activities and the need to spread understanding more widely.

Crofts (Chapter 31) identifies some popular Earth science myths and contrasts them with the understanding of Earth science practitioners. He suggests that these myths could be undermining our message of conservation and sustainability, and that they could be preventing the real message from being understood by the public and by decision makers. Crofts suggests that the 'true Earth science message' is so significant that an agenda for action is needed for influencing key partners and bridging the gap in understanding. He identifies a series of guiding principles and operating principles for sustainable development based on existing knowledge of Earth systems. These principles are clear and are well supported by the extensive evidence and arguments presented in the other chapters of this book.

Climate is a key driver of many Earth system processes, and understanding change and coping with its effects is a significant challenge for the future. Harrison and Kirkpatrick (Chapter 32) examine the evidence for recent and future climate change in Scotland. They identify the complexity of the climate system and the difficulties of separating natural and human-induced climate change. The uncertainty associated with the climate system and climate models means that the only certainty is that change is inevitable. The implications of identified climate trends on the natural heritage are equally complex. Changes in habitat and species distributions seem likely, but current models do not offer sufficient precision to be able to make predictions at this time. The precautionary principle obviously has application in situations of such uncertainty.

Brazier (Chapter 33) summarises the results of the Conference workshop sessions. These addressed sustainable mineral exploitation, river and catchment management, coastal management, soil protection and Earth science education. Each group was asked to identify the main issues, potential actions, partners and timescales for change. The groups consistently concluded that practitioners are failing to spread information on current knowledge and recent developments in accessible forms outside their subject areas. The key message, again, is the need for clearer information dissemination.

Usher (Chapter 34) concluded the Conference with the message that the interactions between the geosphere, biosphere and anthroposphere (physical, biological and human worlds) are the basis of life. Soils are the meeting point between physical processes and biological processes, and geology and climate determine the nature of the soil, the local biodiversity and the opportunities for land use and land cover. Viewed in this context, the relevance of Earth science to modern society is obvious.

Usher concludes with a quotation from Martin Holdgate, which echoes the aspiration expressed by Aubrey Manning (Chapter 2) at the start of the Conference that "our task, as informed people with a concern for the natural world, is to help others to understand the way the Earth works and thus to adopt policies which will enable humanity to get through the next 50 years or so." The Conference demonstrated that there are two issues of over-riding importance in meeting this aspiration: that all practitioners understand and appreciate the major contribution Earth science can make; and that they expend more effort on the wider dissemination of Earth science knowledge and understanding for the benefit of society as a whole.

31 SUSTAINABLE USE OF THE EARTH'S RESOURCES

Roger Crofts

Summary

1. The natural resources of the Earth are many and varied. They provide an essential basis for the survival of civil society.
2. This chapter examines some widely-held popular myths, and contrasts these with our present state of knowledge.
3. Building on our present knowledge, and within the context of the concept of sustainable development, 6 guiding principles and 6 operating principles for the sustainable use of the Earth's resources are proposed.
4. Proposals are made for improved communication about Earth resources to decision-makers and influencers.

31.1 Introduction

The media, newsletters of environmental and resource-using organisations, the web, academic literature and other sources illustrate that the debate about the availability of the Earth's natural resources is far from resolution. Perceptions that non-renewable resources are plentiful in quantity, and that renewable resources are available without restraint of use are still widely held by many decision-makers and within society as a whole. Even amongst the academic community, there are those who consider that the careful management of resource use demanded by environmentalists is unnecessary. However, observation and analysis do show a somewhat different picture, as seen for example in the problems of global water supply and the desiccation and salination of soils in some parts of the world. All is not gloomy, as the discussion at Scottish Natural Heritage's (SNH) Conference on 'Earth Science and the Natural Heritage' demonstrated. Increasingly, there is a greater meeting of minds on key issues, and recognition that new principles, founded on the pillars of sustainable development and environmental sustainability, are vital. New policies and decision-support systems to take into account such variables as natural processes in coastal, mountain and catchment systems, climate change and tectonic activity will all improve the quality of decision-making from an environmental perspective.

31.2 Popular myths

There are many views about the Earth's resources. I contend that some key ones are popular myths based perhaps on ignorance of our present state of knowledge or perhaps on dogged adherence to outmoded views. I have developed these personal views over many years as a practitioner. Two good general sources on Earth resources are Goudie and Viles (1997) and Holdgate (1996).

The first of these popular myths is that **the Earth's resources are plentiful**. If true, it follows that it is perfectly legitimate to remove large quantities of non-renewable resources through quarrying operations for minerals and fossil fuels on land, or extraction of various forms of hydrocarbon from below the surface. Recent examples are proposals for coastal superquarries in Scotland, such as at Lingarabay in Harris, despite their potential impact on landscape and the operation of natural systems, particularly in the sea. Other examples are the removal of coal seams below coastal areas without due consideration to effects on ground level, water circulation and the inter-tidal mud flats on which important bird species depend.

Second, it is sometimes claimed that **nature is resilient to human intervention**. There are examples where nature can and does adapt, but often to a different state and rhythm than previously. If the popular myth is true, it follows that it is perfectly legitimate to interfere with the operation of natural systems. Classic examples include major river systems, such as the Danube, Columbia, Colorado and the Nile, where the creation of dams has interrupted sediment movement, destroyed ecosystems downstream and had a detrimental effect on biological and soil productivity (Boulton, this volume). Closer to home, engineering structures, such as groyne systems and coastal edge walls, have been placed on sandy beaches to maintain the beach, and croys have been constructed in rivers to improve fisheries. Such installations not only disrupt the local natural processes and habitats, but, by reducing sediment supply to the coast or changing river flow, may cause greater problems through erosion downdrift or flooding downstream.

Third, it is claimed that **natural hazards can be mitigated by human activity**. This is demonstrated, for example, in the case of the 1973 volcanic eruption on Heimey, off the south coast of Iceland. The local community, with the aid of bulldozers and water jets, managed to stop an advancing lava flow from cutting off the harbour, with the result that a much more sheltered harbour was created for the fishing fleet. Often, however, human intervention can increase hazard risk. For example, removal of the toe of a landslide and its replacement with a retaining wall, seen in many parts of Britain following road widening and new road development, does not solve the problem. Indeed, partly as a result of this attempted mitigation activity, the instability remains and can be increased. Similarly, construction of floodbanks and the isolation of a river from its floodplain, can increase flood discharges and exacerbate flooding downstream, as happened in the case of the Perth floods on the River Tay in 1993.

Fourth, it is claimed that **natural resources are infinitely renewable**. It follows that it is perfectly legitimate to continue to utilise soil for food and timber production. While that may be the case, account must be taken of a number of additional factors. The rate of formation of the soil is slow, and the rate of erosion from agricultural land can exceed this in some areas of central and eastern Scotland. It is true that production is maintained and in some places increased, but only by substituting artificial inputs to compensate for the loss of nutrient-rich topsoil. However, excess inputs can lead to leaching of nitrogen and phosphorous, eutrophication of surrounding water bodies and decline in biodiversity, such as nitrogen-fixing bacteria. Similarly, compaction and damage to soil structure and hydrology have been linked to inappropriate cultivation.

31.3 Knowledge-based statements

By contrast, our current state of knowledge allows us to make a series of statements. The first of these is that **the rate of depletion of natural resources is greater than the rate of**

accumulation. This is a self-evident truth to experts but may not be to people in the wider world. For example, the use of sand, gravel and crushed rock in Europe continues to increase (Cook and Plant, 1994), whereas the rate of production of this material is extremely slow. Similarly, the rate of use of hydrocarbons is increasing, whereas there is a progressive decline in the level of proven resources in the UK sector.

The second knowledge-based statement is that **critical natural resources, such as soils, pristine water sources and native woodlands, are being lost through misuse by human activity**. There are many examples of this close to home. For instance, on intensively cultivated soils in eastern Scotland, there have been localised soil erosion incidents during the winter period of the year (Davidson and Harrison, 1995). This has been exacerbated by the Common Agricultural Policy which, through its Arable Aid measures, stimulates farmers to remove the stubble and therefore disturb the soil in order to plant crops in the autumn, so leaving the ground bare at the time of the year when it is most vulnerable. The effects of longer-term misuse are strikingly demonstrated in the severe soil erosion found in many parts of Iceland (Arnalds, 2000). This accelerated greatly following the Viking settlement in AD 874 through a powerful combination of natural factors and human activity - fragile soils and vegetation, climate change, effects of dust from deposition of tephra from a succession of volcanic eruptions, the removal of trees and over-grazing by sheep - and has produced a succession of very extensive erosion fronts which are very difficult to stabilise without great expense and ingenuity.

The third knowledge-based statement is that **rates of natural change are variable and unpredictable**. An obvious example is the fluctuation of climate during the Quaternary period. For decades many were taught that the Quaternary period comprised five cold periods and some intervening warm periods. We know now from cores drilled in the floors of the world's oceans and the Greenland and Antarctic ice sheets that this is not the case. The frequency, rate and scale of climate change are much more significant than previously understood (Boulton, this volume). Similarly, large-scale events have shaped our landscape in relatively recent geological time; an excellent example is the submarine slides on the continental slope off the coast of Norway, which triggered tidal waves with substantial consequential effects on our coasts about 8000 years ago (Dawson *et al.*, 1988). Slightly more prosaically, perhaps, there are many cases where significant changes in our natural systems occur over short periods of time in a manner which remains difficult to predict. For instance, at river mouths, like the River Spey in Scotland, there has been considerable variability in the channel position and beach configuration over the last century in response to flood events and sediment movements of different magnitudes and frequencies (Gemmell *et al.*, 2000), and accurate predictive modelling of river behaviour remains some way off (Parker, 1996).

Finally, **landscapes and landforms are highly sensitive to change**. Over the last 20 years geomorphologists (e.g. Brunsden and Thornes, 1979) have been developing the concept of landscape sensitivity, essentially a methodology for analysing the likelihood of change to the landscape from natural and human agents. We are now aware that, for example, very delicate hydromorphological systems like the Flow Country in Caithness and Sutherland can be destroyed by drainage works and the planting of trees (Lindsay *et al.*, 1988). Furthermore, the disturbance of these delicate systems has also released carbon and methane into the atmosphere to a much greater extent than ever the trees at their maximum growth could capture (Pearce, 1994). There are also very sensitive geomorphological systems on some of our slopes. For example, for the Trotternish Ridge in north-east Skye, one of the most active series of slopes in the whole of Scotland, there is a documented record of inherently unstable slopes going back over at least the last 6000 years (Hinchliffe, 1999). There are a number of reasons for this: the friability of the rock in the cliffs, the high slope angle of the cliffs, apparent increases in extreme precipitation events, and over-grazing by sheep and rabbits. The combination of these factors results in periodic failures that are not easy to predict in terms of their scale, timing or location. The landscape is susceptible in geomorphological terms in a situation where grazing pressure represents an additional stress contributing to accelerated soil erosion.

There is a clear difference between those statements that I regard as popular myths and those that I consider to be based on knowledge which is familiar to Earth scientists. Maybe the contrast has been heightened by the examples chosen, but it is borne out of many other examples given in the literature and in the other chapters in this volume. The conclusion I draw is a very simple and very obvious one. We need to get over the messages about our knowledge of the importance of natural systems and the processes and functions which they perform. The key targets for this information are decision-makers and their advisers. I conclude that we should use our scientific knowledge more effectively to inform decision-making.

31.4 Sustainable development

Before considering further how the four knowledge-based statements can be applied, they need to be placed into the broader context of the philosophy of sustainable development. Reference is made in other chapters to sustaining resources and to sustainable natural systems, but these concepts need to connect with the other two legs of the sustainable development trilogy: economic prosperity and social well-being. Unfortunately, there are many misnomers which have crept into the common parlance of sustainable development since it became current in the 1980s. For example, we often hear claims of sustainable tourism, as opposed to economically viable and environmentally sustainable tourism. We need to make sure that environmental sustainability is included and, by this, I mean sustaining environmental systems and functions as well as the natural resources themselves.

As the foundation of the sustainable use of the Earth's natural resources, I propose that there should be a shared societal vision for the future, which comprises three components. First, it is important to develop a world where human society and its natural environment are accepted to be inter-dependent and that people are an intrinsic part of the environment. If we feel that we can consider natural systems alone and ignore the human element, then we do not live in the real world. Second, and related to this, the environment represents a capital asset for society: the capital elements are water, air, soil, rocks, minerals, the climate regime, native plants and animals, and the natural processes which sustain them. Third, and crucially in the context of Earth science and the natural heritage, we can use the environment for human benefit. We must, however, apply a number of provisos borne out of our scientific knowledge and understanding in order to achieve this. The first proviso is that natural resources should be used within their carrying capacity; by this I mean that if use goes beyond a certain threshold, then the resource itself and the way it functions will be reduced. The second is that undue risks should not be taken. This is, in effect, the precautionary principle (Scottish National Heritage, 1999a). The precautionary principle recognises that we cannot predict the effect of all of our activities on the environment, so if there is not enough information to allow us to take decisions, we must pause to re-think before going ahead with care in those situations where we believe that the activity will not damage the environment. The third proviso is that the functioning of natural systems, including the flows of air, water and materials, should not be significantly impaired.

If we seek to put this shared vision over to decision-makers who are not Earth scientists, they may struggle to understand it unless we put it over in non-technical language and use easily understood concepts. Bringing together our current knowledge and recognising the importance of practical and understandable messages, I propose six guiding principles and six operating principles for the sustainable use of the Earth's resources. These are in part derived from the literature - Brunsden's 'Ten Commandments of Geomorphology' (Brunsden, 1990), from the framework for the Convention on Biological Diversity: the ten principles of ecosystem management (Maltby *et al.*, 1999) and the 12 principles of the ecosystem approach (UNEP, 2000), together with work which has been done by Scottish Natural Heritage: our Five Principles of Sustainable Development (Scottish Natural Heritage, 1993) together with some work of my own (Crofts, 1994 and 2000).

31.5 Guiding principles for sustaining the Earth's resources

The guiding principles are not Earth shattering. There is strength in them both being acceptable to the Earth science community, and at that same time being simple and obvious to those whom we seek to influence.

The first principle is that **natural change is inevitable**. The most obvious manifestations of this principle in Scotland are on rivers and on soft sediment coastal systems. Nature is not static and there are major drivers of change such as tectonic movements and climate, which have consequences, for instance, for sea-level change and for the operation of hydrological systems. Put simply, over short time-scales, slopes move, rivers flood, their channels shift position and coastal edges retreat or prograde. Over longer time-scales, there are significant re-distributions of land and sea, some relatively rapid and others more gradual. The rate, scale and timing of change is not necessarily predictable. We now know from the many observations, some reported in other chapters of this volume, that it is not easy to predict an end state and certainly not a stable state, and that it is usually impossible to turn the clock back when seeking to devise any strategies of intervention in the use of the Earth's resources.

The second principle is to **work with natural functions and processes**. This is another self-evident truth. However, all too often there are examples of working against nature, particularly by engineers, with consequences unforeseen to them but quite foreseeable to Earth scientists. Classic examples include engineering slopes beyond their natural angle of repose, removing the toes of landslides and halting the natural flow of water and sediment in rivers and on coasts (Goudie and Viles, 1997). Experience shows that interventions which seek to work with natural systems are likely to be more durable, predictable and, therefore, effective. This is best exemplified, for instance, in the application of coastal sedimentary cells as a basis for shoreline management planning (Brampton *et al.*, 1999), in implementing managed realignment of the coast (e.g. Pethick, 1999; Hansom *et al.*, this volume), and in river basins by de-engineering flood banks and so allowing rivers to encroach on to their flood plains (Gilvear *et al.*, 1995). If we fail to learn from this experience, then there will be unpredicted consequences and very substantial costs to society, for example in shifting the locus of coastal erosion or increased risk of flood damage downstream.

The third principle is to **manage natural systems within the limits of their capacity**. Although natural systems are dynamic, human intervention can create such perturbations that the natural system is, to all intents and purposes, destroyed, as, for example, in the damming of major rivers. We now know that there are situations where natural systems respond repeatedly to change but within limiting thresholds, so that the overall response is stable within these thresholds (Schumm, 1977; Werritty and Brazier, 1994). However, natural systems can, in response to major external factors (either natural or human induced), totally change their pattern and rhythm by crossing extrinsic thresholds into new process regimes (Schumm, 1977), seen, for example, in the change from a stable coastline to an eroding one where sediment supply to the beach is interrupted (e.g. Bray and Hooke, 1998). It is clear, therefore, that we should seek to determine those thresholds and what causes them to be breached, in order to improve the basis of our advice. In the case of a river valley, this is important in relation to roads, railways and to settlements. Thresholds are important in other concepts in Earth sciences, such as carrying capacity, where, for example, the quantity of effluent poured into a river system is beyond its capacity, with consequent nutrient enrichment, or where, for example, soils are cultivated in such a way that their natural fertility and other biological and physical functions are impaired irretrievably.

Fourth, we should **manage natural systems in a spatially integrated manner**. Too often, for example, river systems are considered in isolation from slope systems, and mountain systems are considered as if they are separate from watersheds in the upper parts of river basins. We need to examine our approach within a spatial framework at the appropriate geographical scale. A coastal cell, a hydromorphological system, a drainage basin and a mountain system are all obvious spatial units. They can be considered at scales from major river and mountain systems through to tributary basins and small massifs, respectively. Integrated planning approaches can help to make sure that the connections between different natural elements and natural processes are addressed. It also provides the basis for considering the impacts of actual and potential human activity. SNH is developing an integrated approach at geographical scales appropriate to its work in Scotland through Natural Heritage Zones (Scottish Natural Heritage, 1999b; Crofts *et al.*, 2000, Mitchell, this volume). The development of integrated catchment management in response to the EU Water Framework Directive and the development of shoreline management plans are other cases in point.

Fifth, we should **use non-renewable Earth resources wisely and sparingly at a rate which does nor restrict future options**. Non-renewable Earth resources are critical natural capital for the future. Depleting a particular resource within a generation removes the options for future generations to have access to that resource. This guideline is not a counsel for stopping the use of non-renewable resources: that is quite out of the question in our society, whether we, as conservationists, like it or not. The essential point is to seek to influence the rate of resource depletion and at the same time to stimulate the use of secondary, non-pristine resources (such as waste materials rather than new rock) and to stimulate research and development into substitutes which have a less significant environmental impact than the use of primary materials. The progressive switch from non-renewable resources, such as coal and other hydrocarbons, for the production of electricity, to renewable resources, such as wind, wave and water, is an obvious example. The recent report by the Royal Commission on Environmental Pollution (Royal Commission on Environmental Pollution, 2000) makes clear the environmental imperatives, particularly from the perspective of climate change, of the need to switch from non-renewable to renewable resources.

Sixth, we should **use renewable resources within their regeneration capacity**. In recognition that renewable resources, such as sand and gravel, soil and peat and in a different way, water, are renewable, we should also recognise that the rates of production and renewal are usually much less than the rate of use. If society is to maintain the critical renewable natural assets for its future use, then it needs to have a clear understanding of the renewal rates and the activities which impair their natural regeneration. It follows that as a society we must be cautious in the rate at which we use renewable resources and the type of use to which they are put.

31.6 Operating principles

The guiding principles will be more applicable if they are supported by a series of operating principles.

If Earth scientists are going to help decision-makers and their advisers, then they should seek ways of improving the understanding of decision-makers and improving the decision-making process itself. The first operating principle is, therefore, that we should **use our scientific knowledge to inform decision-making,** much more than we do at present. Conferences of like-minded individuals with similar training are fine to a degree in order to exchange knowledge and develop new thinking, but participants all talk to each other and in language they understand. The crucial question is - how many people who are really the decision-makers and their key advisers are engaged in the process? The answer is likely to be relatively few with the present way of doing things. Therefore, as well as the publication of the proceedings of this Conference, we should also be looking for different outputs from such events, ones much more accessible to decision-makers and their advisers. There are a number of approaches which should be considered. A short, layman's summary could be produced, on a similar basis to the ones now produced for all SNH Research Review and Research, Survey and Monitoring Reports. An action-orientated document could be produced. This was done recently, for example, as one of the outcomes from the joint Royal Society of Edinburgh/SNH Conference, 'The Future for the Environment in Scotland: Resetting the Agenda?'. A short paper styled 'an agenda for action' was produced (Royal Society of Edinburgh and Scottish Natural Heritage, 2000), and mailed to all Members of the Scottish Parliament and their researchers. As a matter of course, these types of outputs must be available on websites. Media briefings for the popular and the more specialist press should also be undertaken.

Second, Earth scientists need to recognise that they operate within a civil society and, therefore, should **recognise human needs and aspirations**. This does not mean being slaves to them, but rather working to develop solutions which seek to meet those needs and aspirations, and at the same time ensuring rigour in the application of the six guiding principles. This is a significant challenge to the Earth science community in a number of respects: working collaboratively with other disciplines especially in the social and economic fields, translating the results of research into practical propositions and actions, and maybe involving interest groups in the interpretation of the research and the definition of conclusions and recommendations.

Third, we should **adopt the precautionary principle**. This is not, as some claim, the "do not do anything" approach; rather it is what I call judicious risk taking. SNH (Scottish Natural Heritage, 1999a) has developed a step-by-step approach to the precautionary principle, basically a decision tree which enables one to determine an outcome of 'yes' or 'no' or 'yes, with adaptations'. Development of these broad principles and process issues is worthy of consideration.

Fourth, we should ourselves, and seek to persuade others to, design intervention to **work with rather than against natural systems and processes**. There are now many good expositions of how this can be done: for example, the development of low-impact engineering methods for Scottish gravel-bed rivers (Hoey *et al.*, 1998), lowland rivers (Royal Society for the Protection of Birds *et al.*, 1994) and soft coasts (HR Wallingford, 2000).

Fifth, we should **recognise the link between Earth processes and biodiversity**. Biological systems and the distribution of species and habitats are not static and there is a close interaction between them and the distribution of substrate and Earth surface processes. Getting ecologists and geomorphologists to work more closely together is a critical step, as demonstrated by the chapter by Soulsby and Boon in this volume.

Finally, we should make sure that we have **indicators to measure natural systems and processes** in a way which allows the material to be used to inform better future decisions. The development of indicators for assessing the achievement of sustainable development is a growth area. But much of the work fails to recognise the importance of natural resources and natural Earth processes on which there is a fair deal of information gathered by Earth scientists. Neither the Government's review (Department of the Environment, Transport and the Regions, 1999), nor the review by environmental bodies (MacGillivray and Kayes, 1999) adequately cover these issues.

31.7 Conclusion

The state of our knowledge of the processes and functions of the Earth has increased enormously. However, there is still a major gap in the understanding of natural systems by decision-makers and their advisers. It is vitally important, therefore, for such scientific knowledge to be translated and interpreted to improve the decision-making process. As a result, we should be in a better position to safeguard natural functions and processes and, therefore, the Earth's resources as a whole. The outputs from the 'Earth Science and the Natural Heritage' Conference should, therefore, in addition to this book, be in a variety of forms accessible to a wider audience, as is suggested in my discussion of the first Operating Principle.

References

Arnalds, O. 2000. The Icelandic 'rofabard' soil erosion features. *Earth Surface Processes and Landforms*, **25**, 17-28.

Brampton, A.H., Lees, R.G. and Ramsay, D.L. 1999. The coastal cells of Scotland and their application. *In* Baxter, J.M., Duncan, K., Atkins, S.M. and Lees, R.G. (eds) *Scotland's Living Coastline*. The Stationery Office, London, 69-78.

Bray, M.J. and Hooke, J.M. 1998. Geomorphology and management of sites in Poole and Christchurch Bays. *In* Hooke, J. (ed.) *Coastal Defence and Earth Science Conservation.* The Geological Society, London, 232-266.

Brunsden, D. 1990. Tablets of Stone: towards the ten commandments of geomorphology. *Zeitschrift für Geomorphologie,* NF **79**, 1-37.

Brunsden, D. and Thornes, J.B. 1979. Landscape sensitivity and change. *Transactions of the Institute of British Geographers,* NS **4**, 463-484.

Cook, P.J. and Plant, J.A. 1994. Industrial and construction mineral resources in Europe. In '*Mineral Resources and Sustainable Development: a Workshop*'. British Geological Survey, Technical Report WG/94/12, 22-26.

Crofts, R. 1994. Sustaining the Earth's resources. *In* O'Halloran, D., Green, C., Harley, M., Stanley, M. and Knill, J. (eds) *Geological and Landscape Conservation.* Geological Society, London, 7-10.

Crofts, R. 2000. *Sustainable Development and the Environment: Delivering Benefits Globally, Nationally and Locally.* Scottish Natural Heritage, Edinburgh, Occasional Paper, No. 8.

Crofts, R., Maltby, E., Smith, R.D. and Maclean, L. (eds) 2000. *Integrated Planning: International Perspectives.* Scottish Natural Heritage and IUCN, Edinburgh.

Davidson, D.A. and Harrison, D.J. 1995. The nature, causes and implications of water erosion on arable land in Scotland. *Soil Use and Management,* **11**, 63-68.

Dawson, A.G., Long, D. and Smith, D.E. 1988. The Storegga Slides: evidence from eastern Scotland for a possible tsunami. *Marine Geology,* **82**, 271-276.

Department of the Environment, Transport and the Regions 1999. *A Better Quality of Life.* The Stationery Office, London.

Gemmell, S.L.G., Hansom, J.D. and Hoey, T.B. 2000. The geomorphology, conservation and management of the River Spey and Spey Bay SSSIs, Moray. *Scottish Natural Heritage Research, Survey and Monitoring Report,* No. **57**.

Gilvear, D., Hanley, N., Maitland, P. and Peterkin, G. 1995. *Wild Rivers Phase 1: technical paper.* WWF Scotland, Aberfeldy.

Goudie, A. and Viles H. 1997. *The Earth Transformed.* Blackwells, Oxford.

Hinchliffe, S. 1999. Timing and significance of talus slope reworking, Trotternish, Skye, northwest Scotland. *The Holocene,* **9**, 483-494.

Hoey, T.B., Smart, D.W.J., Pender, G. and Metcalfe, N. 1998. Engineering methods for Scottish gravel bed rivers. *Scottish Natural Heritage Research, Survey and Monitoring Report,* No. **47**.

Holdgate, M. 1996. *From Care to Action.* Earthscan, London.

HR Wallingford 2000. *A Guide to Managing Coastal Erosion in Beach/Dune Systems.* Scottish Natural Heritage, Perth.

Lindsay, R.A., Charman, D.J., Everingham, F., O'Reilly, R.M., Palmer, M.A., Powell, T.A. and Stroud, D.A. 1998. *The Flow Country.* Nature Conservancy Council, Peterborough.

MacGillivray, A. and Kayes, R. 1999. *Environmental Measures: Indicators for the UK Environment.* New Economics Foundation, London.

Maltby, E., Holdgate, M., Acreman, M. and Weir, A. 1999. *Ecosystem Management: Questions for Science and Society.* Royal Holloway, Institute for Environmental Research, University of London, Egham.

Parker, G. 1996. Some speculations on the relation between channel morphology and channel scale flow structures. *In* Ashworth, P.J., Bennet, S.J., Best, J.L. and McLelland, S.J. (eds) *Coherent Flow Structures in Open Channels.* John Wiley, Chichester, 423-457.

Pearce, F. 1994. Peat bogs hold bulk of Britain's carbon. *New Scientist,* **144** (1952), 6.

Pethick, J. 1999. Future sea-level changes in Scotland: options for coastal management. *In* Baxter, J.M., Duncan, K., Atkins, S.M. and Lees, R.G. (eds) *Scotland's Living Coastline.* The Stationery Office, Edinburgh, 45-62.

Royal Commission on Environmental Pollution 2000. *Energy - the Changing Climate.* Royal Commission on Environmental Pollution, 22nd Report. The Stationery Office, London.

Royal Society of Edinburgh and Scottish Natural Heritage 2000. *The Future of the Environment in Scotland: an Agenda for Action.* Royal Society of Edinburgh and Scottish Natural Heritage, Edinburgh.

Royal Society for the Protection of Birds, National Rivers Authority and Royal Society for Nature Conservation 1994. *The New Rivers and Wildlife Handbook.* Royal Society for the Protection of Birds, Sandy, Beds.

Schumm, S.A. 1977. *The Fluvial System.* John Wiley, New York.

Scottish Natural Heritage 1993. *Sustainable Development and the Natural Heritage: the SNH Approach.* Scottish Natural Heritage, Edinburgh.

Scottish Natural Heritage 1999a. *The Precautionary Principle: a Step-by-Step Approach.* Scottish Natural Heritage, Edinburgh.

Scottish Natural Heritage 1999b. *Natural Heritage Zones.* Scottish Natural Heritage, Edinburgh.

UNEP 2000. The ecosystem approach. *Convention on Biological Diversity, Fifth Conference of the Parties,* Paper **23**, 103-109.

Werritty, A. and Brazier, V. 1994. Geomorphic sensitivity and the conservation of fluvial geomorphology SSSIs. *In* Stevens, C., Gordon, J.E., Green, C.P. and Macklin, M. (eds) *Conserving our Landscape.* Proceedings of the Conference, Conserving Our Landscape: Evolving Landforms and Ice-Age Heritage, Crewe, 1992. Peterborough, 100-109.

32 Climatic Change and its Potential Implications for Environments in Scotland

S. John Harrison and A. Hilary Kirkpatrick

Summary

1.   The variable nature of the Scottish climate makes it difficult to isolate long-term trends, although increases in temperature, rainfall and the frequency and strength of westerly winds have been identified.

2.   These trends have had a measurable impact on the Scottish environment, through increases in the incidence of soil erosion and severe floods, in addition to changes in the biosphere.

3.   Many changes in the Scottish climate are associated with changes in the mid-latitude westerly winds, but prediction of future climatic conditions is based on models assuming enhancement of the greenhouse effect. These models predict raised sea levels, higher temperatures and higher precipitation totals over Scotland.

4.   Isolating climatic change from anthropogenic changes is difficult, except perhaps in coastal or upland areas.

5.   The variable nature of the Scottish climate and the uncertainties inherent in predictive models mean that it is naïve to assume that a particular pathway of change will be followed. It will be safer to base policy on a range of different climatic scenarios.

32.1 Introduction

A mid-latitude location on the western approaches to the world's largest land mass ensures that Scotland has a climate which is characterised by variability over a range of temporal scales. The use of climatic normals under such circumstances is not meaningful, but long-term averages of the principal climatic variables define a regime which is equable and moist, lacking the severe extremes which are characteristic of more continental climatic regimes. Seasonal variation in precipitation, solar heating, and consequently in air and surface temperature, results in a climate characterised by winters which are cool and wet with a lengthy period of snow-lie on the highest mountains, and summers which are of variable quality but are occasionally warm and dry, particularly along the coast of the North Sea. There is a well-developed, and frequently under-estimated, eastwards gradient in rainfall.

With more than 4,500 km² of its land surface being more than 600 m above sea level, altitudinal gradients of change in climatic variables are a dominant controlling factor in the spatial pattern of climate across Scotland. Such gradients are particularly steep, resulting in cool, wet and windy climatic conditions at relatively modest elevations, and rough moorland grazing dominates much of the Scottish landscape above 300 m. The large extent of wet heath in the Scottish uplands is of international importance.

A succession of published reports from, for example, the Intergovernmental Panel on Climate Change (IPCC) and the UK Hadley Centre, has established that, within the limitations imposed by the quality of the available climatic data, it is now possible to affirm with some confidence that the global near-surface temperature has increased since the middle of the 19th century (Houghton *et al.*, 1996; Hulme and Jenkins, 1998). This has been particularly marked over the last twenty years of the 20th century and has been accompanied by, for example, changes in rainfall regimes, global ocean and atmospheric circulation patterns, sea level, and in the spatial extent of ice and snow.

32.2 Climatic changes in Scotland

There have been a number of studies of recent climatic changes in Scotland. The indices of winter severity and summer quality developed by Harrison *et al.* (1999), based on deviations of key climatic variables from long-term means (Figure 32.1), reveal an oscillating pattern, with winters becoming milder over the last fifteen years, and summers becoming steadily warmer and drier over the last thirty years. The recently developed Scottish Mainland Index and Scottish Islands Index both indicate marked upward trends in mean air temperatures (Purves *et al.*, 1999). An analysis of rainfall by Mayes (1996) has indicated that while winter rainfall has been increasing in western and north-western Scotland, there has been very little change in the east. Summer rainfalls appear to suggest a general decrease which has been most marked over the eastern half of the country. Smith (1995) analysed a long rainfall series (1757-1992) for Scotland and concluded that rainfalls in the 1980s and 1990s represented the longest sustained positive anomaly in the record. Earlier work by Smith and Bennett (1994) linked such changes in rainfall to changes in the flow regimes of Scottish rivers, which showed statistically significant increases in mean flows over the period 1970 to 1989. Observations of the location and persistence of snow patches in the Scottish Highlands (Watson *et al.*,1994, 1997) indicate earlier melting dates and a reduced likelihood of patches surviving through the summer. It is difficult to establish long-term trends in wind speed, but the indications are that there has been an increase in the frequency of severe gales in recent years. A summary of the changes which have been identified is presented in Table 32.1.

The impacts of such changes on physical systems have yet to be fully established, but Davidson and Harrison (1995), for example, have related increased rainfall to increases in soil erosion, while Steele *et al.* (1999) concluded that flood frequencies in the west of Scotland have reached unprecedented levels in recent years, with events clustered during the winter months. It is worth noting that the ratio between rainfall in Scotland and that in south-east England has been selected as one of the primary indicators of climatic change (Cannell *et al.* 1999).

There have been a number of attempts in recent years to relate observed changes in climate to changes in the biosphere at a range of spatial and temporal scales. Myneni *et al.* (1997) used satellite data to show that, between 45°N and 70°N, there was a marked increase in the photosynthetic activity of terrestrial vegetation between 1981 and 1991. This was associated with the earlier disappearance of snow cover in the spring. In the UK, Crick *et al.* (1997) have identified a trend towards earlier laying dates for 20 out 65 species (using data from the British Trust for Ornithology's nest record scheme), and Beebee (1995) has suggested that the reproductive cycles of amphibians are responsive to climatic change.

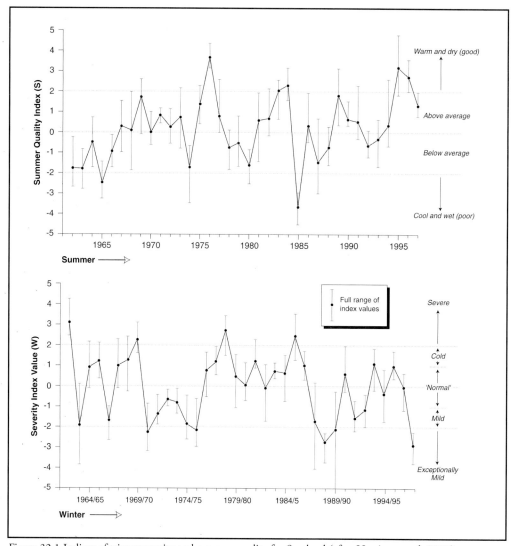

Figure 32.1 Indices of winter severity and summer quality for Scotland (after Harrison *et al.*, 1999).

The fundamental questions which arise from such documented changes are whether they can be projected forward and, if so, what impact these may have on the Scottish environment. While much of the scientific literature and governmental reporting has attributed global warming and associated climatic changes to anthropogenic enhancement of the greenhouse effect, it would be wholly inappropriate to neglect the important contributions made by other natural climate-changing agencies such as solar radiation receipt and the concentrations of volcanic dust in the atmosphere. Analysis of the climatic record, which incorporates meteorological observations such as the Central England Temperature series and indicators derived from other sources such as dendrochronology, has led to the conclusions that the most recent changes in climate have fallen outside the likely range of natural variability, and that these are attributable directly to human influences on the gaseous composition of the troposphere. The collective view is thus that "… global

Table 32.1 Recent changes in the Scottish climate (From Mayes, 1996; Harrison, 1997; Hill *et al.*, 1999).

Hours of Bright Sunshine

- Imperfect measure of insolation but indications are of a significant decrease during the winter months, particularly in the west.

- Some evidence (weak) of an increase in the east during winter and over the whole of Scotland in the summer and autumn.

Air temperature

- *Maximum temperatures*: changes are relatively small but some evidence of increases up to 0.3°C in recent decades when comparing long-term means. The most significant long-term upward trend is in spring.

- *Minimum temperatures*: evidence of considerable increases >0.5°C during the winter months when comparing long-term means. The most significant long-term upward trend is in spring and summer.

- Significant decrease in annual frequency of *air frosts* in many locations.

Precipitation

- *Rainfall:* increased totals noted in all seasons but only significant during the winter months, most particularly in the north and west.

- *Snowfall:* little evidence of a long-term downward trend except in the east.

Airflow

- Very difficult to identify long-term trends in wind speed due to the nature of the available data. Indications are that *gales* (westerly) have increased in frequency and severity since the early 1970s. Decade 1988-1997 has recorded the highest frequency of gales since 1881.

---

warming ...is due, at least in part, to the increased concentrations of greenhouse gases in the atmosphere" (Cannell *et al.* 1999). Explanation of ongoing global climatic change, and as a corollary the future course of climatic change, has thus been based primarily on forcing by greenhouse mechanisms.

The observed changes in the Scottish climate can be most directly attributed to the characteristics of the mid-latitude westerly winds. Winter and spring warmth, reduced lowland snow cover and frost occurrence, greater cloud cover and rainfall in the west of Scotland, and a strengthening of the west-east climatic gradients across Scotland have all been attributed to more dominant, and more vigorous, maritime westerly airflows (Mayes, 1996; Harrison, 1997). However, as a first approximation to the future course of climatic change, given the overwhelming consensus of scientific opinion expressed in two IPCC reports (Houghton *et al.*, 1990, 1996), it may be assumed that enhancement of the greenhouse effect will be the major driving force for change.

32.3 Future changes in climate

Models of climatic changes are usually based on global circulation models (GCM) in which assumptions are made regarding the future course of greenhouse gas concentrations in the atmosphere, principal amongst which is carbon dioxide. These are based on a range of incremented increases in radiative warming potential in the troposphere, which provide a number of future climatic scenarios. Modelling is, in itself, an imperfect exercise, given that human understanding of atmospheric systems, and capacity to represent fluxes of energy, moisture and momentum, are limited, and that spatial and temporal resolutions are relatively coarse. The adoption of a single predicted pathway of change for planning purposes is thus to deny the fallibility of models and the inherent errors and uncertainties in model outputs.

The projection of the Scottish climate forward in time using Hadley Centre models suggests a general upward trend in temperature and precipitation, predicting mean annual temperatures between 0.9°C and 2.6°C higher than present and rainfalls between 3 and 17% higher by the 2080s (Hulme and Jenkins, 1998). Sea-level changes are more difficult to predict, given that they are a result of a dynamic balance between eustatic and isostatic changes, but the predictions are for sea levels to be relatively higher than at present, with rises being greatest on the west coast of Scotland. It is entirely reasonable to suppose that Scotland is facing changes in many of its habitats, although in the Scottish lowlands it may prove difficult to isolate directly climatic and anthropogenic habitat changing mechanisms.

32.4 Climatic changes and upland environments

Most analyses of the potential impacts of climatic change have drawn particular attention to upland areas, and arguments having been based on the marginality of these environments from both agricultural and ecological viewpoints. Of concern here is a tendency to over-simplify and to neglect the complex nature of the relationship between altitude and climate. It has been common practice to take climatic predictions for lowland sites and to extrapolate these to higher elevations using crude altitudinal gradients based on long-term averages and a limited number of case studies. A typical line of argument has been, for example, to assume that a 2.0°C change in the lowlands will be matched by a change of similar magnitude in the Scottish mountains, which is then translated into a lowering of effective elevation of the order of 300 m. Further translated into area, this then leads to dubious predictions relating to the loss of snow patch communities and the disappearance of upland plant and animal species which are already at the 'warm' end of their range.

While it is clear that changes have been taking place in the uplands, chief amongst which have been a reduction in the duration of snow cover and increase in wind strength, there is a need to look more closely at the assumptions that have been made about future climatic changes in the uplands. Parry (1976) drew attention to the non-linearity of the relationship between heat availability, expressed in terms of day-degrees, and altitude, which implies that relatively small changes in temperature may have proportionally greater effect on growth conditions at higher altitudes. Pepin (1995, 1997) has highlighted the fact that lapse-rates in temperature are, to a large extent, influenced by those in the free atmosphere, which will be influenced by changes in the North Atlantic atmospheric or oceanic circulation. This makes prediction of, for example, changes in growing season or frost occurrence very difficult. On the other hand, Garnett *et al.* (1997) have analysed a long temperature record for Moor House in the Northern Pennines and have found no evidence of significant long-term changes over the latter half of the 20th century. It is also unfortunate that many assessments of the potential effect of climatic changes in the uplands have not considered the very important seasonal changes in the differentiation between lowland and upland, which are often most strongly marked in spring when snow lingers, or soils remain relatively wetter, on higher ground (Harrison, 1975).

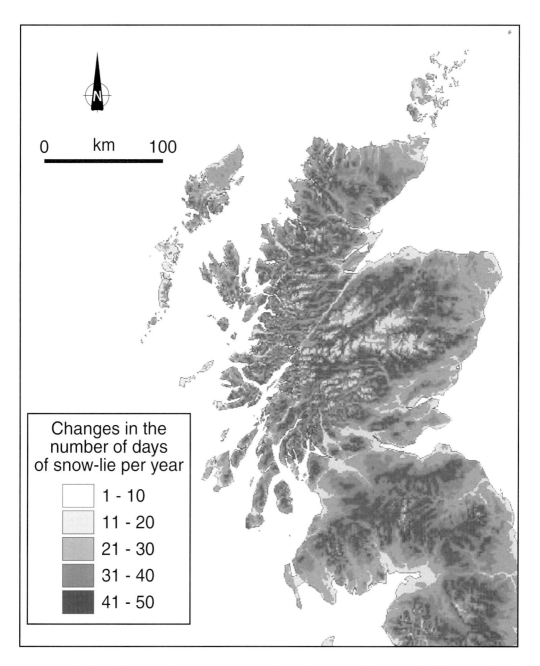

Figure 32.2 Predicted changes in the winter snow cover (November to March) over Scotland between cold and warm winters.

These problems can be illustrated with reference to the duration of snow cover in the Scottish uplands, as both contiguous cover and snow patches (Sant, 1994), which may be the single most important driving force for habitat changes. Early assumptions that a warmer climate would lead to a greatly reduced duration of snow cover in the uplands neglected to consider attendant changes in precipitation, particularly during the winter months. Increased winter precipitation in maritime airstreams is likely to fall as snow at those elevations which lie above the freezing level for much of the winter. An analysis has been undertaken of the record of 'days with snow lying', which is a standard observation at most climatological stations. A fundamental problem in this regard is that such data are limited to relatively modest elevations, which it is necessary to extrapolate to higher elevations. A revised model of the snow-cover elevation relationship has been combined with latitude and longitude to produce spatial models of snow-lie duration for the core winter months, November through to March, using more than 40 Scottish climatological stations (Harrison *et al.*, 1999). These were then used in a GIS to produce maps of changes in snow-lie duration (Figure 32.2). In order to estimate the potential impact of continued global warming, historical analogues were used. The winters 1978/79, 1981/82 and 1985/86 were adopted as analogues of traditionally cold winters with relatively high frequencies of easterly winds, while the winters 1987/88, 1988/89 and 1989/90 were adopted as analogues of 'globally warmed' winters. The difference between the two sets of winters reveals that the most marked changes occur within the altitude range 500-700 m but that changes above this become progressively smaller (Figure 32.2).

However, an analysis of days with snow lying at different altitudes on Creag Meagaidh (Figure 32.3) clearly shows that, over the course of a year, there has been a steady decrease in snow lie at 1,100 m. The reason for the difference between the two analyses is that, although there is only a small decrease in the duration of snow cover during the core winter months, there has been a very marked reduction in autumn and spring snow cover. The conclusions with regard to upland snow cover are, therefore, that the greatest changes will occur during the winter at intermediate altitudes, and in spring and autumn at higher altitudes. With regard to the latter, melt dates will occur progressively earlier during the spring. It is also increasingly likely that snow patches will not survive over the summer months. There may also be an increased risk of avalanches.

Alongside such changes in snow cover, it is likely that at intermediate altitudes, fluctuation in snowlines implies a greater freeze-thaw frequency and more frequent exposure of the ground surface to strong winds and driving rain. The implication is that such surfaces may become more susceptible to erosion by wind and driving rain, a conclusion reached by Haynes *et al.* (1998). Other important changes which may well affect the uplands include a longer thermal growing season but probably reduced solar radiation.

Interactions between climate and biological processes in the uplands are relatively complex, but Coulson (1988) and Coulson and Butterfield (1985), for example, have shown that there is a spring peak of emergence of terrestrial insects on blanket peat at higher altitudes, which seems to be driven, in part, by temperature changes in spring. On the other hand, Bardgett *et al.* (1995) have examined heather-dominated ecosystems in England and Wales and have found that the extent of open moorland is not sensitive to substantial increases in temperature, but that changes in species composition are, nevertheless, likely to occur due to changes in surface water balance.

32.5 Limitations in greenhouse-based predictions

Greenhouse predictions based on models are subject to limitation and error but represent a best estimate of the course of change. It would be unwise to adopt an uncritical approach to the interpretation of model outputs, and the fact remains that there is considerably more

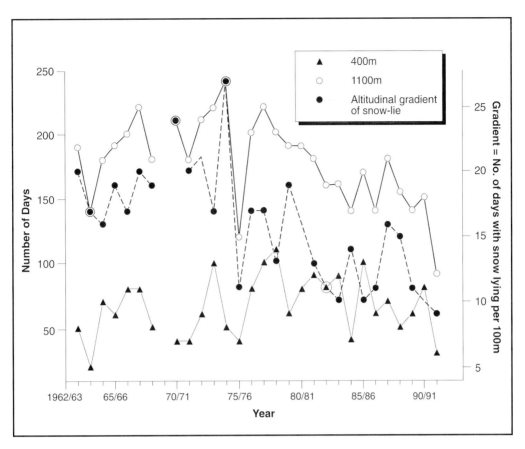

Figure 32.3 Changes in the number of days with snow lying at two altitudes on Creag Meagaidh (after Mordaunt, 1997).

uncertainty than certainty in the whole exercise. Reference has been made to the important influence of the mid-latitude westerlies blowing from the North Atlantic, variation in the strength and persistence of which are quantified in the North Atlantic Index (NAI) and the North Atlantic Oscillation (Wilby *et al.*, 1997). In recent years, the NAI has been increasing in value but its future course of change is by no means certain. Any decrease in the NAI would indicate a reduction in the strength of the westerly influence in the Scottish climate and a possible increase in continental influence from the east. The result for Scottish winters could be a relatively rapid return to longer cold spells and deeper frosts.

The North Atlantic Drift exerts a considerable influence on the Scottish climate, particularly during the winter months when its warm waters reduce the risk of severe frost in western Scotland. Increased volumes of freshwater melting from the Arctic Ocean, resulting from a general global warming of the troposphere, taken together with increased rainfall over the North Atlantic, may well disrupt what Broecker (1997) has referred to as the 'Atlantic Conveyor Belt', which brings warmer waters north towards Scotland. Current models suggest that such a disruption is unlikely to occur with the next 100 years, but should the warmer waters disappear from the Scottish coast, winters would remain wet but much colder.

32.6 Conclusions

The main points of this chapter are as follows:

1. Climatic conditions in Scotland have been changing quite markedly through the latter part of the 20th century, which has been reflected in measurable changes in the biosphere.
2. Confidence in the prediction of the future course of climatic changes in Scotland is limited by the capacity of models to represent adequately the principal climatic processes, and by uncertainties regarding possible changes in the atmospheric pressure patterns and ocean currents in the North Atlantic.
3. Some uncertainty also remains as to how predicted changes in climate will impact upon biological aspects of the environment, but it is suggested that their effect upon upland environments in Scotland may be considerable.
4. Composite management strategies linked to a range of possible climatic change scenarios would appear to offer the best way forward.

References

Bardgett, R.D., Marsden, J.H., Howard, D.C., and Hossell, J.E. 1995. The extent and condition of heather in moorland, and the potential impact of climate change. *In* Thompson D.B.A., Hester A.J. and Usher M.B. (eds) *Heaths and Moorland: Cultural Landscapes*. Edinburgh, HMSO, 43-50.

Beebee, T.J.C. 1995. Amphibian breeding and climate. *Nature*, **374**, 219-220.

Broecker, W.S. 1997. Thermohaline circulation, the Achilles heel of our climate system: will man-made CO_2 upset the current balance? *Science*, **278**, 1582-1588.

Cannell, M.G.R., Palutikof, J.P. and Sparks, T.H. (eds) 1999. *Indicators of Climate Change in the UK*. Department of the Environment, Transport and the Regions, London.

Coulson, J.C. 1988. The structure and importance of invertebrate communities on peatlands and moorlands, and effects of environmental and management changes. *In* Usher, M.B. and Thompson, D.B.A. (eds) *Ecological Change in the Uplands*. Special Publication of the British Ecological Society, No. 7. Blackwell Scientific Publications, Oxford, 365-380.

Coulson, J.C. and Butterfield, J.E.L. 1985. The invertebrate communities of peatlands and upland grasslands in the north of England and some conservation implications. *Biological Conservation*, **34**, 197-225.

Crick, H.Q., Dudley, C., Glue, D.E. and Thompson, D.L. 1997. UK birds are laying earlier. *Nature*, **388**, 526.

Davidson, D.A. and Harrison, D.J. 1995. Water erosion on arable land in Scotland: results of an erosion survey. *Soil Use and Management*, **11**, 63-68.

Garnett, M.H., Ineson, P. and Adamson, J.K. 1997. A long-term upland temperature record: no evidence for recent warming. *Weather*, **52**, 342-351.

Harrison, S.J. 1975. The elevation component of soil temperature variation. *Weather*, **30**, 397-409.

Harrison, S.J. 1997. Changes in the Scottish climate. *Botanical Journal of Scotland*, **49**, 287-300.

Harrison, S.J., Winterbottom, S. and Sheppard, C. 1999. Potential effects of climate change on the Scottish tourist industry. *Tourism Management*, **20**, 203-211.

Haynes, V.M., Grieve, I.C., Price-Thomas, P. and Salt, K. 1998. The geomorphological sensitivity of the Cairngorm high plateaux. *Scottish Natural Heritage Research Survey and Monitoring Report*, No. 66.

Hill, M.O., Downing, T.E., Berry, P.M., Coppins, B.J., Hammond, P.S., Marquiss, M., Roy, D.B., Telfer, M.G. and Welch, D. 1999. Climate changes and Scotland's natural heritage: an environmental audit. *Scottish Natural Heritage Research Survey and Monitoring Report*, No. 132.

Houghton, J.T., Jenkins, G.J. and Ephraums, J.J. 1990. *Climate Change: the IPCC Scientific Assessment* Cambridge, Cambridge University Press.

Houghton, J.T., Meira Filho, L.G., Callander, B.A., Harris, N., Kattenberg, A. and Maskell, K. 1996. *Climate Change 1995: the Science of Climate Change.* Cambridge University Press, Cambridge.

Hulme, M. and Jenkins, G.J. 1998. *Climate Change Scenarios for the UK: Scientific Report.* UK Climate Impacts Programme, Technical Report No.1. UK Climatic Research Unit, Norwich.

Mayes, J. 1996. Spatial and temporal fluctuations of monthly rainfall in the British Isles and variation in the mid-latitude westerly circulation. *International Journal of Climatology,* **16**, 585-596.

Mordaunt, C.H. 1997. Association between weather conditions, snow lie and snowbed vegetation. Unpublished PhD thesis, University of Stirling.

Myneni, R.B., Keeling, C.D., Tucker, C.J., Asrar, G. and Nemani, R.R. 1997. Increased plant growth in the northern high latitudes from 1981 to 1991. *Nature,* **386**, 698-701.

Parry, M.L. 1976. The significance of the variability of summer warmth in upland Britain. *Weather,* **31**, 212-217.

Pepin, N.C. 1995. The use of GCM scenario input to model effects of future climate change on the thermal climate of marginal maritime uplands. *Geografiska Annaler,* **77A**, 167-185.

Pepin, N.C. 1997. Scenarios of future climate change effects on frost occurrence and severity in the maritime uplands of northern England. *Geografiska Annaler,* **79A**, 121-137.

Purves, R.S., Harrison, S.J., Tabony, R.C. and Turrell, W. 1999. *Development of Temperature Indices for Scotland and Northern Ireland.* Unpublished Report SR(99)07F to Scotland and Northern Ireland Forum For Environmental Research.

Sant, R. 1994. An investigation into the location of persistent snow patches in a limited area of the Scottish Highlands. Unpublished undergraduate honours dissertion, University of Stirling.

Smith, K. 1995. Precipitation over Scotland, 1757-1992; Some aspects of temporal variability. *International Journal of Climatology,* **15**, 543-556.

Smith, K. and Bennett, A.M. 1994. Recently increased river discharge in Scotland: effects on flow hydrology and some implications for water management. *Applied Geography,* **14**, 123-133.

Steele, M.E., Black, A.R., Werritty, A. and Littlewood, I.G. 1999. Reassessment of flood risk for Scottish rivers using synthetic runoff data. *In Hydrological Extremes: Understanding, Predicting, Mitigating.* Proceedings of IUGG '99 Symposium HS1, Birmingham 1999. *IAHS Publication,* No. 255, 209-215.

Watson, A., Davison, R.W. and French, D.D. 1994. Summer snow patches and climate in north-east Scotland *Arctic and Alpine Research,* **26**, 141-151.

Watson, A., Pottie, J., Rae, S. and Duncan, D. 1997. Melting of all snow patches in the UK by late October 1996. *Weather,* **52**, 161.

Wilby, R.L., O'Hare, G. and Barnsley, N. 1997. The North Atlantic Oscillation and British Isles climate variability. *Weather,* **52**, 266-276.

33 Earth Science and the Natural Heritage: Developing an Agenda for Scotland

Vanessa Brazier

Summary

1. This chapter summarises some of the conclusions from the Conference workshops.

2. The main themes that emerged provide the starting point for developing a future agenda for Earth science and the natural heritage in Scotland. These are to:

*   promote understanding and awareness of how Earth systems work, targeting key decision makers, policy makers and their advisors, and land and water managers;
*   initiate a campaign to raise the level of understanding and awareness of our Earth heritage and Earth systems, targeting three groups of audience: 1) land and water managers, decision makers, the minerals industry and conservation practitioners; 2) all levels of formal education; and 3) local people, tourists, the voluntary Earth science movement (RIGS groups) and ranger services (Scottish Countryside Rangers Association).
*   co-ordinate evaluation of the state of Scotland's Earth heritage and development of a soil strategy; and
*   develop working partnerships to share resources and influence other.

33.1 Introduction

The Scottish Natural Heritage (SNH) Conference reported in this book and a Conference on 'Landscape Sensitivity' held at Stirling University in September 1999 (see Thomas and Simpson, 2001) provided an opportunity to assess future directions for Earth heritage conservation in Scotland and the potential for furthering the understanding and appreciation of Earth sciences in many aspects of Scottish life. The purpose of this chapter is to explore these issues. A review of the discussions of the workshops held during the SNH Conference, together with the key messages from the Landscape Sensitivity Conference, provide a starting point for developing an agenda for the future.

33.2 Conference workshops

The purpose of the workshops was to provide a forum for discussion where different perspectives could be explored for a selection of the issues facing Earth heritage conservation. The topics of the workshops were:

1. sustainability and minerals development;
2. river and catchment management;
3. coastal management: defend or abandon?;
4. soil protection strategy: Scottish perspectives; and
5. Earth Science education and awareness: resources and needs.

Each workshop was asked to consider what the main issues are in the subject area; what needs to be done in respect of each; what the priorities are for action, now and in the next five years; and who should be leading the action. The workshops were all well attended and discussions lively, but some had difficulty in defining responses to each of these questions. The following sections summarise the main conclusions of each workshop, but do not report unresolved differences of opinion expressed during the discussions.

33.2.1 Sustainability and minerals development
This workshop focused on onshore industrial minerals. The main need identified was for a strategic overview of mineral resources, together with a strategy for restoration and conservation of quarries and mineral workings. An overview of this type needs to address issues at local, national and European scales. It should include:

- an inventory of mineral resources, including quantity, quality and location;
- an assessment of the demand for resources; and
- a strategy for development and restoration of mineral workings, which balances environmental and local sensitivities.

It was further recognised that there should be local area and site-specific mineral plans which cover both development and restoration, and which involve the local communities. Such plans should be prepared for areas where mineral working is taking place, or planned to take place in the future. They should include detailed plans for site working and restoration, as well as plans for educational use (both during working and after restoration). Crucially, local people should be involved in the development of these plans.

The need for a partnership approach between industry, local communities, planners, SNH and other conservation organisations was also highlighted. Other points raised at the workshop included: the need to maximise recycling of industrial waste in order to minimise the need for mineral extraction, and the need for a code of good practice for mineral developers with reference to education and conservation.

33.2.2 Rivers and their catchments
This workshop concluded that there is fragmentary and piecemeal management of Scottish rivers, invariably addressing only a single issue at a reach scale, and that there is a lack of understanding by decision makers of river processes and landscape sensitivity. Flooding was identified as being the most widespread environmental concern from a public and administrative viewpoint.

It was acknowledged that simply providing information on matters such as river processes and alternative methods of river management is unlikely to influence key decision makers in river and catchment management, or influence a landowner with a rapidly eroding bank. However, one approach that could help to promote more sympathetic ways of living with rivers (rather than working against them), would be through a partnership approach. This could be formalised as a 'Scottish Rivers Forum', with representation from key partners including, SNH, the Scottish Environment Protection Agency (SEPA), the Scottish Executive, the Convention of Scottish Local Authorities (COSLA), the Scottish Landowners Federation (SLF) and representatives from local communities, the insurance industry, freshwater-related businesses and fisheries management groups.

There are two incentives for such a forum. First, Scotland has a history of costly expenditure on locally based flood alleviation and *ad hoc* river management intervention, often carried out in response to one or more damaging flood events, with little understanding of the nature of flooding within the catchment as a whole. Second, the forthcoming EU Water Framework Directive will require Scotland to adopt integrated catchment management. The main objective of the forum would be to address the fundamental problem of lack of appreciation of how, and over what timescales, river and catchment processes work. Getting the message across effectively requires several different approaches that target both professionals and the public alike. The activities of the forum could include:

- initiation of a demonstration project, such as managed retreat and re-location of development away from the floodplain;
- co-ordination of shared responsibilities between partners within the forum for developing the management of rivers at a catchment scale;
- delivery of information to key target audiences to raise awareness of how rivers work; and
- agreement on common standards for good environmental practice in planning and implementing river engineering.

33.2.3 *Coastal management: defend or abandon?*
This workshop identified several coastal issues which required action. The priorities are:

- preparation of a high-profile strategy for sustainable and effective management of Scotland's shorelines;
- assessment of the implications of climate change and sea-level rise for the coastal zone;
- increased awareness of natural shoreline dynamics and the need for these to be the basis for shoreline management; and
- establishment of a 'Coastal Environmental Change Network' (in liaison with external partners), for example to co-ordinate long-term monitoring of shoreline change.

It was suggested that the formation of a partnership with the key players in coastal management, including SEPA, SNH, the Scottish Wildlife Trust (SWT), the Scottish Coastal Forum (SCF), the Scottish Executive, COSLA, Historic Scotland, other non-governmental organisations (NGOs), academics and others, would be an appropriate action to take forward work on these issues. Partnership would enable a wider sense of ownership and could promote a desire to implement new approaches. Different partners would take a leading role in each area of the programme. Potential projects for partnership working include the development of a coherent strategy for coastal management based on the understanding of how coastal systems work; identification and development of demonstration sites for coastal defence (dune management and managed retreat); a flagship campaign to raise awareness of both the issue of coastal management and the demonstration projects (cf. *Campaign for a Living Coastline*); and development of a site monitoring network across Scotland.

33.2.4 Soil protection strategy: Scottish perspectives

There was general agreement that Scotland needs a strategy for sustainable soil management, particularly given that separate soil strategies are now being developed for England and Wales. A strategy for Scotland should take into consideration the nature of the resource and landuse patterns, in the context of the pressures upon the resource. Soils are a finite resource and at present are not adequately protected by legislation relating to air and water quality, which only indirectly protect certain aspects of the soil. A particular concern is that some Scottish soils contain a very large reserve of terrestrial carbon which, if liberated by inappropriate use, could increase the quantity of greenhouse gases released into the atmosphere.

It was proposed that SNH and SEPA should jointly promote the development of a soil strategy for Scotland with the Scottish Executive. It was envisaged that such a strategy would combine into a single document current codes of good practice and existing indirect legislation designed to protect other environmental media. The main focus would be on the sustainable use of soils. An important requirement would be to gain information about the soils resource and to develop methods and indicators for monitoring its state and condition for a multitude of functions.

33.2.5 Earth science education and awareness

The wide-ranging discussions in this workshop identified three fundamental themes that need to be addressed to ensure wider appreciation of our Earth heritage: the need for Earth heritage interpretation to become more holistic, and to develop links with allied interests such as archaeology, industrial archaeology, architecture, local history, biodiversity and sustainable development; the need for partnership with bodies such as the Scottish Tourist Board, British Geological Survey (BGS), Scottish Countryside Rangers Association (SCRA), The National Trust for Scotland (NTS), the Regionally Important Geological and Geomorphological Sites (RIGS) initiative and representatives in Earth science research and education; and the benefits of increased liaison of Earth heritage practitioners with Scottish education. The last is especially important at school level through liaison with the Scottish Association of Geography Teachers (SAGT) and the Earth Science Teachers Association (ESTA), because changes in the national curriculum could further reduce access to Earth sciences at secondary school level, and consequently threaten the take-up of Earth science in tertiary education.

33.3 Themes for a future agenda

The history of Earth heritage conservation (Gordon and Leys, this volume) is one of evolution, with perceptible progress from an *exclusive* academic approach based on designated sites (Ellis, 1996) toward a more *inclusive* approach which promotes appreciation of Earth heritage as both an interesting and vital part of our natural heritage. Through the adoption of biodiversity and sustainability initiatives, the perception of the immense practical problems associated in delivering conservation objectives for non-renewable resources, and for habitats and species dependent on dynamic environments, is slowly being realised. This was certainly demonstrated during the wide-ranging discussions within the SNH conference workshop sessions. Several common themes emerged, in particular from the workshops on sustainable minerals exploitation and coastal and river management, and from the Landscape Sensitivity Conference as a whole. These are the need to:

1. promote understanding and awareness of how Earth systems work, among key decision makers, policy makers and their advisors, and land and water managers;
2. initiate a campaign to raise the level of understanding and awareness of our Earth heritage, targeting conservation practitioners; the formal and informal education sectors; and local people, tourists, the voluntary Earth science movement (RIGS groups) and ranger services (SCRA).
3. co-ordinate evaluation of the state of Scotland's Earth heritage and develop a soil strategy; and
4. develop working partnerships to share resources and influence.

33.4 Application of understanding of Earth systems and their dynamics

Many of the presentations at the Conference and the papers in this book argue cogently the value of understanding Earth systems and their dynamics as part of an integrated approach to environmental management, a message that also emerged strongly from the Landscape Sensitivity Conference. However, there is a general lack of awareness that landscapes change over time (principally because most landforming events occur only occasionally, and sometimes as a result of rare and extreme weather events) and what landscape change itself may indicate about the changing state of health of the natural environment. The Landscape Sensitivity Conference closed with a call for positive action in this area. The key target audiences are decision makers, policy makers and their advisors, and land and water managers.

It would, however, be short sighted only to recognise an 'applied' role for Earth science in response to immediate pressing needs, such as coastal erosion. To deliver better understanding of Earth systems and processes amongst decision makers and others, requires continued support for 'pure' research and there must also be a general raising of awareness of the intrinsic value and role of Earth sciences. Scotland's landscapes comprise an extraordinary geological, geomorphological and soils heritage, but this is rarely noticed by the general public and conservationists alike, and this will continue to be the case for as long as Earth science is marginalised throughout our education system.

33.5 Earth heritage interpretation

A fundamental theme for Earth heritage conservation must be getting the message across that Scotland's Earth heritage is of great interest, a national treasure, that forms the foundations of all life. The growth in tourism, recreation and the sustained interest in our environment from the public and all sectors of education provide real opportunities for raising awareness and enjoyment of our Earth heritage. The target audiences identified in the workshop sessions and in conference discussions are: conservation practitioners; all levels of formal education; and local people, tourists, amateur Earth scientists (RIGS groups) and ranger services (SCRA). Each will need a different approach in attracting and sustaining interest in the message.

The starting point could be the preparation of an Earth heritage awareness plan, which explores the potential for a co-ordinated network of interpretative experiences and events across Scotland, identifies priorities for each target audience, and also identifies all potential partnerships to ensure the success of such a campaign. This would encompass existing, but so far unlinked, educational and interpretative initiatives and activities including: Dynamic Earth; the new Knockan Interpretation Centre; the *Landscape Fashioned by Geology* series; publication of the biannual magazine *Earth Heritage*; the British Geological Survey 'Open Day'; field guides published by, amongst others, the Edinburgh and Glasgow Geological Societies and the Quaternary Research Association; initiatives such as Scottish Geology Week; and 'Selling Geology to the Public' and 'Understanding Landscapes' events. It would also identify and develop new partnership initiatives.

33.6 The state of Scotland's Earth heritage

The pool of information on the current state of all aspects of Earth heritage interests is selective and in most cases limited to protected sites. Although geology, soils and drift geology maps exist for most of Scotland, these alone do not provide sufficient baseline inventory information on the state and composition of the Earth heritage resource and its changes and trends. With some exceptions, such as the beaches reports of the 1970s, there is a significant absence of systematic data on geomorphological heritage and change and soil quality changes. Furthermore, there is great potential for misinterpretation of the meaning of landscape changes, given the complexity of geomorphological responses that result in landscape change. Critical to the reliability of any assessment of Earth heritage changes is the timescale and spatial scale of monitoring landsystems.

There are various needs and possibilities for researching basic state of the Earth heritage monitoring and assessment. One approach would be to establish a landscape change network, to act as a forum for exchange of up-to-date information about modern and Holocene landscape change studies. Alternatively, a working group on landscape change, comprising a small number of key researchers and conservationists, could be established. Their brief could include: developing a monitoring methodology for state of the Earth heritage reporting; identifying Earth science indicators for monitoring and assessment of change; identifying benchmark areas for monitoring changes in the nature and rate of exploitation of non-renewable resources (e.g. aggregate, coal, and other mineral resources); and identifying key partner organisations to share research on state of the Earth heritage reporting. SNH recently undertook a baseline geomorphological inventory of the North West Seaboard Natural Heritage Zone (Kirkbride *et al.*, 2001). This could form a template for a baseline geomorphological inventory of Scotland.

One specific requirement recognised in the Conference discussions was for a strategy for sustainable use of soils in Scotland. Such a strategy would co-ordinate measures and guidelines for soil protection and the setting of standards for monitoring the condition of the resource.

33.7 Earth heritage partnerships

During the conference, the audience agreed that effective promotion and appreciation of Earth sciences and Scotland's Earth heritage must be undertaken through shared, partnership action. Key potential 'universal' or 'Scotland-wide' partners might include BGS, SEPA, NTS, SCRA, SAGT, ESTA, local authorities, the water authorities, the minerals industry (Quarry Products Association) and representative bodies from land owning or land and water managing groups. One current example is a partnership between SNH and BGS that was initially set up to share information and expertise on the Cairngorm Mountains. This is now formalised in a joint project that will deliver materials to support interpretation of how the landscape of the Cairngorms has evolved, some of which will developed into co-produced interpretative products for both the National Park and wider education. Not all forms of interpretation are to be delivered in material form. In October 2000 the SNH Sharing Good Practice programme event 'Journeys Through Time', based in the Cairngorm Mountains, provided practical training for rangers who are interested in setting up their own Earth heritage guided walks. A follow-up event will be held in central Scotland in 2001.

33.8 Conclusion

One of the most striking aspects of the both SNH and Landscape Sensitivity conferences was the universal call for wider understanding and appreciation of what Earth sciences tell us about how our landscape has been formed, and how Earth system processes work and change over time. Getting the message across effectively is a key theme for the future agenda. Each target audience will need a different approach in attracting and sustaining interest in the message.

The priorities within Earth heritage conservation are changing, and now the need to join forces with other interested groups, agencies and industry to form focused partnerships appears to be the logical next step in developing the future agenda and its core themes, as discussed in outline in this chapter. Deciding a workable balance between pursuing issues such as coastal and river flooding, that already have high public and political interest, and lower profile but fundamentally important schemes to raise understanding of how our world works, will be an interesting challenge.

Acknowledgements
The author thanks the following people for co-ordinating the responses form the workshops: Dr. J. E. Gordon, Dr. K. Goodenough, Dr. R.G. Lees, Dr. K. F. Leys, Dr. C. MacFadyen and Dr. G. Puri.

References
Ellis, N.V., Bowen, D.Q., Campbell, S., Knill, J.L., McKirdy, A.P., Prosser, C.D., Vincent, M.A. and Wilson, R.C.L. 1996. *An Introduction to the Geological Conservation Review*. GCR Series No.1. Joint Nature Conservation Committee, Peterborough.

Kirkbride, M.P., Duck, R.W., Dunlop, A., Drummond, J., Mason, M., Rowan, J.S. and Taylor, D. 2001. Geomorphological database and geographical information system (GIS) for the North West Seaboard Natural Heritage Zone. *Scottish Natural Heritage Commissioned Report*, F99AC102.

Thomas, M.F. and Simpson, I.A. 2001. *Landscape Sensitivity: Principles and Applications in Northern Cool Temperate Environments. Catena*, **42**(2-4), 81-383.

34 EARTH SCIENCE AND THE NATURAL HERITAGE: A SYNTHESIS

Michael B. Usher

Summary

1. In this synthesis, there are seen to be three spheres of activity, termed the 'geosphere', the 'biosphere' and the 'anthroposphere'. The overlapping nature of these spheres emphasises the fact that so many facets of the world are, or should be, working together.
2. It is where these three spheres intersect that there is the greatest integration - the pair-wise intersections are discussed by the use of examples relating to the soil, mineral use and land use. Each of these three topics is dealt with individually.
3. The intersection of all three spheres is characterised by the term 'sustainable use'. The chapter concludes with both a discussion of this term and a brief review of the 'ecosystem services' which are enjoyed free by the human population of the planet. It is these services that provide the foundation for the future human economy in Scotland.

34.1 Introduction

In opening the conference, Aubrey Manning (this volume) said "The Earth supports life: life supports the Earth". This is very much a key message of the conference; the world abounds in interactions, implying that so many facets of the world are more or less working together. It is these interactions and their integration that form the focus for this synthesis.

The focus of the conference was on the Earth sciences — the rocks and landforms, waters and soils — and the processes that determine the quantity and quality of each. It is the nature of these rocks that has shaped Scotland's landscape today, and provides the basis for so much of our natural heritage. There is a close correspondence between the rocks and the type of vegetation community, the 'green veneer', that develops on top. Table 34.1 gives a brief analysis of the first of the volumes of the *National Vegetation Classification* (Rodwell, 1991), indicating how the 25 woodland and scrub communities relate to the local conditions of soil and geology. There is a close correspondence, and it extends from the plant community to the animal community because of the feeding relationships of the invertebrate species (e.g. Southwood, 1961). And there is an obvious feed-back loop as the dominant plants in the community also influence the development of the soil. For instance, the moving sand dunes of Culbin Forest were stabilised by the planting of pine trees, and the acid litter from these has contributed to the development of the podzolic soils that are found at Culbin today.

In this synthesis of the conference, it is useful to focus on three spheres of influence, shown in Figure 34.1. The 'geosphere' includes the subjects of geology and geomorphology, but it also includes the water and air. The 'biosphere' incorporates all living species of

Table 34.1 A brief analysis of the relationships between National Vegetation Classification (NVC) communities and the soils and rocks that support them. The analysis is based on the first published volume of the NVC (Rodwell, 1991), which deals with the 25 communities of woodland (w), scrub (s) and underscrub (u). Communities mapped by Rodwell (1991) as occurring in Scotland, or inferred from the distributional notes to occur in Scotland, are indicated by an asterisk (*). The habitat notes are extracted from the extensive habitat notes given by Rodwell (1991).

NVC number	NVC name	Notes on habitat of major occurrence
W1*	*Salix cinerea - Galium palustre* w	Wet mineral soils on the margins of standing or slow-moving open waters and in moist hollows
W2	*Salix cinerea - Betula pubescens - Phragmites australis* w	Topogenous fen peats, especially flood-plain mires
W3*	*Salix pentandra - Carex rostrata* w	Peat soils kept moist by moderately base-rich and calcareous groundwater
W4*	*Betula pubescens - Molinia caerulea* w	Moist, moderately acid, though not highly oligotrophic, peaty soils
W5	*Alnus glutinosa - Carex paniculata* w	Wet or waterlogged organic soils, base-rich and moderately eutrophic
W6*	*Alnus glutinosa - Urtica dioica* w	Eutrophic moist soils
W7*	*Alnus glutinosa - Fraxinus excelsior - Lysimachia nemorum* w	Moist to very wet mineral soils, only moderately base-rich and usually only mesotrophic
W8*	*Fraxinus excelsior - Acer campestre - Mercurialis perennis* w	Calcareous soils with mull humus
W9*	*Fraxinus excelsior - Sorbus aucuparia - Mercurialis perennis* w	Permanently moist brown soils derived from calcareous bedrock and superficial deposits
W10*	*Quercus robur - Pteridium aquilinum - Rubus fruticosus* w	Base-poor, brown soils
W11*	*Quercus petraea - Betula pubescens - Oxalis acetosella* w	Moist, but free-draining, and quite base-poor soils
W12	*Fagus sylvatica - Mercurialis perennis* w	Free-draining, base-rich and calcareous soils
W13	*Taxus buccata* w	Moderate to steep limestone slopes with shallow, dry rendzina soils
W14	*Fagus sylvatica - Rubus fruticosus* w	Brown earths, with low base status and slightly impeded drainage
W15*	*Fagus sylvatica - Deschampsia flexuosa* w	Base-poor, infertile soils
W16	*Quercus* spp. *- Deschampsia flexuosa* w	Very acid and oligotrophic soils, with pH£4 and mor humus
W17*	*Quercus petraea - Betula pubescens - Dicranum majus* w	Very acid and often shallow and fragmentary soils, usually where precipitation exceeds 1,600 mm a^{-1}
W18*	*Pinus sylvestris - Hylocomium spendens* w	Strongly leached, podsolic soils
W19*	*Juniperus communis* spp. *communis - Oxalis acetosella* w	High altitude, with colder climate, but on a wide variety of soils
W20*	*Salix lapponum - Luzula sylvatica* s	High altitude rocky slopes and ledges with wet, mesotrophic and base-rich soils
W21*	*Crataegus monogyna - Hedera helix* s	Circumneutral to base-rich soils, often a seral community on abandoned/neglected ground
W22*	*Prunus spinosa - Rubus fruticosus* s	Mesotrophic soils of moderate base status and mull humus
W23*	*Ulex europaeus - Rubus fruticosus* s	Moderately to strongly acid brown earths; freely draining
W24*	*Rubus fruticosus - Holcus lanatus* u	Abandoned and neglected ground on a range of circumneutral and oligotrophic soils
W25*	*Pteridium aquilinum - Rubus fruticosus* u	Deeper, free-draining, circumneutral to moderately acid soils

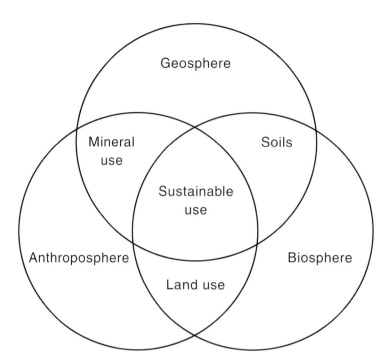

Figure 34.1. A diagrammatic representation of the three spheres of influence discussed at the conference: the geosphere (essentially the earth science component of the natural heritage), the biosphere (the biological science component) and the 'anthroposphere' (representing the human-centred activities associated with the socio-economic context of human society). This chapter is structured on the four zones of interaction between these spheres.

microbes, plants and animals, and their interactions. The 'anthroposphere' includes the human population with its social and economic aspirations and constraints. In terms of the theme of the conference, it is the interactions between these three spheres that are of especial interest. As indicated in Figure 34.1, the three two-way interactions have been exemplified in terms of 'soils', 'land use' and 'mineral use'. These examples form the subject matter for the following three sections. The interaction between the three spheres has been characterised as 'sustainable use', and that forms the subject of the concluding two sections.

34.2 Soils: the basis for most terrestrial life

The example chosen to demonstrate the intersections between the 'geosphere' and the 'biosphere' is soil. Throughout the world, soils develop even in the most unlikely of places, such as near cliff-nesting bird colonies in Antarctica. However, there are many other more specific interactions between the two spheres. Geomorphological processes frequently relate to habitat types; the machair system of the west of Scotland and Ireland is one example of blown coastal sand, and many of the coastal habitats, such as saltmarshes and mudflats, are also related to geomorphological processes. None of these is entirely separate from the 'anthroposphere' because there are links between all of these processes and land use and the value of the land for nature conservation. However, a frequently recurring theme is that of the soil that develops, particularly both its fertility and its stability over time.

Jacks (1954) defined soils as "what plants grow in". This brief description encapsulates a number of concepts. Soils provide the mechanical support for plants to grow upwards and not to be moved from place to place by the wind or water. Soils provide the chemical environment which nourishes the growth of the plant. Soils provide the water that all plants, and animals, require for their respiration and growth. But to set against these three positive roles of soil, there is also the possibility of erosion, whereby the mechanical support is reduced or lost, and the possibility of pollution, whereby the soil poisons rather than nourishes the plants and animals which depend on it, or pollutes habitats elsewhere if transported by erosion.

Soils are at the meeting point between the physical processes and the biological processes. Whereas they provide the mechanical support for plants, the roots of those plants ramify through the soil and are in turn connected to an immense network of mycorrhizal fungi. Large quantities of non-living organic matter fall on to the soil surface, be it parts of dead plants, dead animals or faecal material, and enter deeper into the soil via dead plant roots, dead fungi and bacteria, and dead animals. All of this organic material provides a wealth of food, and energy resources, for the large number of organisms that inhabit the soil. Indeed, a square metre of grassland in the temperate parts of the world may have 2,000 or more species of microbe, fungi and animals inhabiting it (Usher, 1996). It is truly the 'poor man's tropical rain forest' because of its species richness compared to most terrestrial and marine ecosystems.

Albeit briefly outlined, this important role for soil has a number of implications. It is essential in maintaining Scotland's biodiversity. Without soil, few of the characteristic habitats and their range of species would persist. The diversity of soil organisms is responsible for the decomposition of dead organic matter, releasing nutrients and making them available for uptake by the plants. Yet, despite the importance of soil, there is no conservation strategy for soils in Scotland (see Brazier, this volume, for a summary of the workshop discussion). Aspects of the soil system itself have started to malfunction when the soil is acidified (Anon., 1990) or when nitrogen deposition becomes too great (Anon., 1994a). Soil erosion can be severe (Anon., 1997), but yet the need for a national soil conservation strategy (Taylor *et al.*, 1996), also advocated by the Royal Commission on Environmental Pollution (Houghton, 1996), is a goal that still has to be realised. Scotland's soils are too important to Scotland's land-based industries and to Scotland's natural heritage to continue to be ignored.

34.3 Land use: changing the nature of the land cover

Any parcel of land can be conceived as being described by a number of variables. There is a physical set, including the nature of the parent material of the soil and its chemical composition, and a climatic set relating to precipitation, temperature, wind and so on. Interacting with these sets are aspect, drainage and position in relation to frost. Given the complete set of variables for any location, there is a number of options for how the land can be used, as well as a list of uses to which the land definitely cannot be put. There is therefore a range of possibilities, and the decisions as to which form of land use to opt for is often based on economic and political considerations rather than environmental considerations. If there is grant support for one option and no support for the others, then the decision is usually very simple!

In very broad terms, rocks which are acidic in nature give rise to soils that are low in nutrient status, support a relatively poor above-ground biodiversity, and can be used primarily for coniferous forests, extensive grazing land, grouse moor and deer forest. On the other hand, rocks that are basic in nature, such as limestones and andesite, give rise to much more fertile soils, support a much richer above-ground biodiversity, and are frequently used for arable agriculture or grassland for intensive livestock production. The geology and climate determine both the nature of the soil, the local biodiversity and the opportunities for land use.

Land use is, however, ever-changing, largely being driven within its environmental constraints by social and economic considerations. Mackey *et al.* (1998) have demonstrated how political activities in the 40 years following the Second World War have influenced land use, and hence the observed land cover of Scotland. There has been a gradual loss of the semi-natural ecosystems, with an emphasis on land management practices such as drainage of moorland and mires, coniferous afforestation of land which has more acidic soils, improvement of grasslands on the more basic soils, and changes in arable crops. These changes in land cover, which reflect the changing patterns of land use, are shown in Figure 34.2.

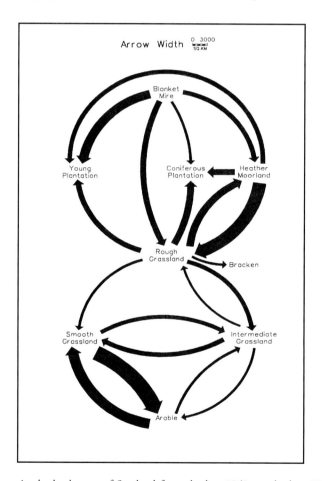

Figure 34.2. Changes in the land cover of Scotland from the late 1940s to the late 1980s. Only changes involving more than 0.5 per cent of the total land area are shown (from Mackey *et al.*, 1998).

The changing patterns of land use can have major effects on all three spheres in Figure 34.1. As well as impacting directly on the ecosystem, they can also influence geomorphological processes, especially by flooding, soil erosion and sediment movement. Land use describes the way that the human population is using the land resource available to it; land cover describes what is actually covering the land. For example, within an agricultural land use there may be many land cover types, varying from the long-term cover of a grass ley to the short-term cover of most arable crops (where the soil may be exposed to wind and precipitation for many months, thus enhancing the possibility of erosion and sediment movement). It is thus usually better to study land cover rather than land use.

Changing land cover has a number of effects. It has a very long-term effect on hydrology and hence on the whole of a drainage basin. Harding *et al.* (1998) have shown how the land management of a catchment of the 1950s is a better indicator of river invertebrates and fish than the contemporary land cover. This is a 40-year delay in effects. Hence, there is a need to consider how land use impacts on the whole spectrum of natural resources, including the natural heritage and on both geomorphological and ecological processes. This has implications for sustainable management of resources, and hence for assessing risks to habitats and species of conservation importance (Dale *et al.*, 1998).

34.4 Mineral use: shaping the land and seabed

The interaction between the 'geosphere' and the 'anthroposphere' could be exemplified in many ways. One might be the human modifications to many natural systems, such as through coastal protection or river engineering. Although meant to alleviate problems, often with short-term success, many such modifications have been much less successful in the long-term. Coastal protection often moves the problem elsewhere, whilst the loss of floodplains due to river canalisation has led to serious flooding at times of abnormally intense precipitation (or of massive snow melt). An example of the problems of the human propensity to undertake massive engineering works is in the Everglades National Park, Florida, USA. Now, as a result of the loss of biodiversity and habitat, further engineering works are required to restore the natural water flows from much of inland Florida, especially in the vicinity of Lake Okeechobee, down the Shark River Slough (and some other smaller sloughs) and thence into Florida Bay. An account of the management of the Everglades is given by DeAngelis (1999). However, rather than focusing on human modification of geomorphological systems, the example is drawn from the human use of minerals.

Deep mining can have an effect on the natural heritage, but perhaps only minimal (unless, as has happened at one site in Scotland, the mine workings drained an area of active raised mire). It is shallow mines, open cast workings and dredging in the coastal environment that could have major impacts on the natural heritage.

Scottish Natural Heritage's position on mineral working is set out in a policy statement (Anon. 2000). The over-riding principle for society should be based on sustainable development - bring into use a minimum of 'new' minerals and recycle a maximum of 'old' minerals. The extent of all mineral sources is finite (except, perhaps, for another glaciation affecting Scotland and hence new deposits of sand and gravel being laid down as the ice retreats!). Peat forms only very slowly, with a few millennia being required to form exploitable depths. Maerl, a calcified alga, grows only very slowly in the coastal waters, and although a living resource it is treated as if it were a mineral. Peat and maerl, albeit capable of regenerating after exploitation, regenerate so slowly that they cannot be considered as renewable resources in the usual sense of this expression. At best, they are only slightly renewable, taking centuries or millennia to regenerate their volume again.

Recycling is therefore likely to be increasingly important, and there are many opportunities to explore possibilities (Pieda, 1995). These range from the use of construction and demolition wastes (conventional recycling) to the use of new forms of waste such as spent oil shale or power station ash. If the wastes cannot be reused, then they will be dumped, exacerbating the effects on the natural heritage and leading to further re-shaping of the land surface or sea bed, and possibly also causing pollution problems.

Extractive industries have effects on shaping the land. Open cast workings create great and generally relatively shallow (perhaps not more than 50 m deep) holes. Although these may expose geological sequences of interest, they totally destroy the biological interest of the area. Quarries can often be deeper, especially the large coastal quarries, such as at Glen Sanda which is more than 2 km in diameter and ultimately up to 600 m in depth. Coastal dredging for aggregates or maerl re-shapes the sea bed, resulting in highly modified communities of marine plants and animals, and maybe the loss of larval feeding areas for some fish species. These major effects on the land surface or the sea bed have to be minimised; society will continue to want minerals, but the guiding principle should be to use only newly extracted minerals if recycled minerals are unavailable or unsuitable.

Thought also should be given to the restoration of sites from which minerals have been extracted. In the coastal situation this may be difficult or impossible. However, on land, there is a variety of restoration possibilities. Restoration to agricultural land or as a recreational facility may have the smallest gains for wildlife; restoration of wetlands or as woodland of native tree species may have much greater wildlife gains. An important principle might be to seek to restore habitat types that would have greater natural heritage value than the habitat types prior to the mineral extraction. Whilst this might not always be possible, it is an important ambition if, as will often be the case, the original habitat types cannot be recreated. However, natural processes of ecological succession can yield important habitats and species, as for example the occurrence of Young's helleborine (*Epipactis youngiana*) on a few bings in the Central Belt of Scotland (Usher, 2000).

34.5 Sustainable use: thinking of the future

The problem with the concept of sustainability is that it is impossible to know if an activity is completely sustainable or not. It is simple to know if an activity is not sustainable; the activity will have to stop at some stage in the future because a resource essential to it will be totally used up. In contrast, it is very difficult to know if an activity is sustainable; it requires a prediction that the activity can continue in perpetuity. The longer that the prediction indicates that the activity can continue, then the more sustainable it is. Thus, sustainability is probably best judged on a comparative basis; for example, activity A is more sustainable than activity B because we predict that A can continue further into the future than B. Sustainability is therefore certainly concerned with balancing the volume and regeneration (or discovery) capacity of resources with the aspiration of humankind to use those resources. Guidelines (Anon., 1993) have therefore been developed to indicate how sustainable activities actually are (see Table 34.2).

Table 34.2 The five guidelines for sustainable development advocated by Scottish Natural Heritage (Anon., 1993).

Number	*Guideline*	*Notes*
1	Non-renewable resources should be used wisely and sparingly, at a rate which does not restrict the options of future generations.	This guideline is discussed in section 34.4.
2	Renewable resources should be used within the limits of their capacity for regeneration.	Applicable to all biological resources, but note some, such as maerl, are extremely slow at regenerating.
3	The quality of the natural heritage as a whole should be maintained and improved.	'Quality' is more subjective, and relates as much to aesthetic (landscape) and moral concepts as to the more measurable biological or geological resources.
4	In situations of great complexity or uncertainty we should act in a precautionary manner.	The so-called 'Precautionary Principle', but is it a principle?
5	There should be an equitable distribution of the costs and benefits (material and non-material) of any development.	Essentially part of the 'anthroposphere'.

Sustainability is concerned with the total resources of the planet, and especially with the ecological and geomorphological processes that are the basis for so much of the regeneration of natural resources (be those processes the growth of animals or plants, the de-toxification of pollutants by microbes, the water storage and buffering capacity of soil, the role of beaches and saltmarshes to protect against coastal erosion, or the value of floodplains in floodwater storage at times of peak discharges). It is exceedingly difficult to value these ecosystem functions, and it is a challenge that is currently being faced by many environmental economists (e.g. Alexander *et al.*, 1998; Schaberg *et al.*, 1999). Whereas societies have developed methods of assessing anthropocentric economic activity, via the gross domestic product (GDP), virtually no attention has been paid to the biological or geological aspects of economic activity. However, Alexander *et al.* (1998) explored the possibilities of 'green GDP' accounts, including the value of the services provided by the environment.

Whilst such economic analyses form one line of enquiry, and others are exploring how much more is spent on harming biodiversity than conserving it (James *et al.*, 1999), demonstrations of sustainability form a more pragmatic way forward. Four case studies - the Scottish uplands, lowland ecosystems, Scotland's freshwater resource, and creating indicators of sustainable development - provided some interesting pointers (Anon., 1994b). These were put into practice in the study of Ettrick and Lauderdale (Anon., 1994c), which aimed to provide guidance and encouragement for bottom-up initiatives by local authorities, local communities, landowners and businesses. Each of these studies contributes to the development of the concept of sustainability in a Scottish context, generally demonstrating, as discussed at the conference, that developments should work with natural processes rather than trying to oppose these processes.

This, however, demonstrates one of the themes of the conference - that the issue of communication and education is a key one. First, there needs to be an understanding of why human development needs to be more sustainable; then there needs to be a knowledge of how to make developments (and, indeed, all everyday activities) more sustainable; and then this needs to be personalised so that 'I can make a difference'. Has the study of sustainability been too academic; and is now the time to popularise it so that far more people are aware of its importance in the nation's life, and in their life? What can demonstrate to Government, to a local authority, to a community or to a person, that Scotland is becoming more sustainable? In most forms of life, indicators are used so as to avoid the complexities and intricacies of natural or anthropogenic systems. What then are the indicators of sustainability? This is clearly where there is a gap in our knowledge.

It is important that work continues on the development of indicators of greater or lesser degrees of sustainability. The need for indicators was outlined by Selborne (1997) and has been taken up with 'headline' indicators (Anon., 1998) and with indicators of climate change (Cannell *et al.*, 1999). In a complex situation where we wish to make the operation of our society more sustainable, indicators of the 'holy grail of sustainability' are about the only way forward. Let us hope that the indicators are founded on good scientific principles, can be measured with a known degree of accuracy, and do help us to make our society, and indeed all societies on this planet, more sustainable.

34.6 Dynamics: reflections on our changing environment

The Earth sciences remind us that the planet is continually changing. Over tens to hundreds of millions of years, the plates of solid rock are drifting very, very slowly across the surface of the globe. In Antarctica, a continent with only two contemporary native species of vascular plant, *Deschampsia antarctica* and *Colobanthus quitensis*, there are rocks with a rich assemblage of fossil plants. The rocks that now form the frozen continent were not always frozen! On the shorter timescale of tens to hundreds of thousands of years, Scotland has experienced a series of 'ice ages', with interglacial periods that have supported rich biological communities, often of species that currently occur geographically in areas far removed from the present-day Scotland. Over still shorter periods, geomorphological processes are occurring; weathering of rocks is producing soils, and the coastline is changing. Natural systems are dynamic, ever-changing, yielding interesting patterns in the landscape that influence the development of plant, microbial and animal communities and the location of human societies (see, for example, Robertson and Angspurger, 1999).

In viewing the relationship between the Earth sciences and the rest of the natural heritage, change will be the norm; a stable or static relationship is unlikely ever to exist, other than for extremely short periods of time. Just as the environment has changed in the past, natural processes will result in changes in the future. But added to this are the changes being introduced anthropogenically. There is a scientific consensus that the increasing amount of carbon dioxide in the thin layer of air that surrounds the planet is leading to a changed climate. Predictions abound, but it looks as if Scotland could warm by up to 2°C in the next century, with an increased rainfall averaging 14 per cent (more than this in the west, less in the east; see Harrison and Kirkpatrick, this volume). This will undoubtedly have both Earth science and biological science implications, though both will clearly interact. The sea level is predicted to rise, which means that we shall have to rethink coastline management. How does one retain the machair habitat of the west with a sea level of 30 cm or more higher than now and with a predicted increase in the frequency of storm surges? How does one manage estuaries other than by working with the natural processes (i.e. using the strategy of managed realignment)? What will happen to Scotland's biodiversity, especially in the coastal zone and in the uplands? There are clearly going to be major implications for many species and habitats (Hill *et al.*, 1999) and we may have to think radically about different ways of managing our land area, especially near the coast (French, 1999). Already the indicators of climate change (Cannell *et al.*, 1999) are pointing to the fact that spring is getting earlier and the growing season longer.

This conference has taken a holistic view of the natural heritage of Scotland. It has attempted to incorporate concepts of the 'geosphere', the 'biosphere' and the 'anthroposphere' as outlined in Fig. 34.1. At the end of the conference I was left with a strong feeling that the conference's theme had really been that of a 'sustainable Scotland'. Words such as 'interactions', 'integration' and 'holism' had been used frequently. Perhaps this can best be summed up with a few words from Holdgate (1997) that "what [we] are seeking to do is safeguard the foundations of the human future".

Acknowledgements

I should like to thank Dr. John Gordon for his comments on a draft of this concluding chapter.

References

Alexander, A.M., List, J.A., Margolis, M. and d'Arge R.C. 1998. A method for valuing global ecosystem services. *Ecological Economics*, **27**, 161-170.

Anonymous, 1990. *Acid Deposition in the United Kingdom, 1986-1988: Third Report of the United Kingdom Review Group on Acid Rain*. Department of the Environment, Middlesex.

Anonymous, 1993. *Sustainable Development and the Natural Heritage: the SNH Approach*. Scottish Natural Heritage, Perth.

Anonymous, 1994a. *Impacts of Nitrogen Deposition in Terrestrial Ecosystems*. Department of the Environment, London.

Anonymous, 1994b. *Sustainable Systems of Land and Water Use in Scotland: Four Case Studies*. Scottish Office Agriculture and Fisheries Department, Edinburgh.

Anonymous, 1994c. *An Area Sustainability Study for Ettrick and Lauderdale: Summary Report*. Scottish Natural Heritage, Perth.

Anonymous, 1997. *Controlling Soil Erosion: an Advisory Booklet for the Management of Agricultural Land*. Ministry of Agriculture, Fisheries and Food, London.

Anonymous, 1998. *Sustainability Counts: Consultation Paper on a Set of 'Headline' Indicators of Sustainable Development*. Department of the Environment, Transport and the Regions, London.

Anonymous, 2000. *Minerals and the Natural Heritage in Scotland's Midland Valley*. Scottish Natural Heritage, Perth.

Cannell, M.G.R., Palutikof, J.P. and Sparks, T.H. (eds) 1999. *Indicators of Climate Change in the UK*. Department of the Environment, Transport and the Regions, London.

Dale, V.H., King, A.W., Mann, L.K., Washington-Allen, R.A. and McCord, R.A. 1998. Assessing land-use impacts on natural resources. *Environmental Management*, **22**, 203-211.

DeAngelis, D.L. 1999. The use of modelling in restoration ecology: the Everglades Case. *In* Farina, A. (ed.) *Perspectives in Ecology: a Glance from the VII International Congress of Ecology (Florence 19-25 July 1998)*. Backhuys Publishers, Leiden, 41-50.

French, P.W. 1999. Managed retreat: a natural analogue from the Medway estuary, UK. *Ocean and Coastal Management*, **42**, 49-62.

Harding, J.S., Benfield, E.F., Bolstad, P.V., Helfman, G.S. and Jones, E.B.D. 1998. Stream biodiversity: the ghost of land use past. *Proceedings of the National Academy of Sciences of the USA*, **95**, 14843-14847.

Hill, M.O., Downing, T.E., Berry, P.M., Coppins, B.J., Hammond, P.S., Marquiss, M., Roy, D.B., Telfer, M.G. and Welch, D. 1999. Climate changes and Scotland's natural heritage: an environmental audit. *Scottish Natural Heritage Research, Survey and Monitoring Report*, No. 132.

Holdgate, M. 1997. *What Future for Nature?* Scottish Natural Heritage, Perth.

Houghton, J. (chairman) 1996. *Sustainable Use of Soils: 19th Report to the Royal Commission on Environmental Pollution*. Cm 3165. HMSO, London.

Jacks, G.V. 1954. *Soil*. Thomas Nelson, London.

James, A.N., Gaston, K.J. and Balmford, A. 1999. Balancing the Earth's accounts. *Nature*, **401**, 323-324.

Mackey, E.C., Shewry, M.C. and Tudor, G.J. 1998. *Land Cover Change: Scotland from the 1940s to the 1980s*. The Stationery Office, Edinburgh.

Pieda plc 1995. *Scottish minerals recycling*. Scottish Natural Heritage Review, No. 36.

Robertson, K.M. and Angspurger, C.K. 1999. Geomorphic processes and spatial patterns of primary forest succession on the Bogne Chitto River, USA. *Journal of Ecology*, **87**, 1052-1063.

Rodwell, J.S. (ed.) 1991. *British Plant Communities, volume 1: Woodlands and Scrub*. Cambridge University Press, Cambridge.

Schaberg R.H., Holmes, T.P., Lee, K.J. and Abt, R.C. 1999. Ascribing value to ecological processes: an economic view of environmental change. *Forest Ecology and Management*, **114**, 329-338.

Selborne, The Earl of, 1997. *From Selborne to Summit*. Scottish Natural Heritage, Perth.

Southwood, T.R.E. 1961. The number of species of insect associated with various trees. *Journal of Animal Ecology*, **30**, 1-8.

Taylor, A.G., Gordon, J.E. and Usher, M.B. (eds) 1996. *Soils, Sustainability and the Natural Heritage*. HMSO, Edinburgh.

Usher, M.B. 1996. The soil ecosystem and sustainability. *In* Taylor, A.G., Gordon, J.E. and Usher, M.B. (eds) *Soils, Sustainability and the Natural Heritage*. HMSO, Edinburgh, 22-43.

Usher, M.B. (ed.) 2000. *Action for Scotland's Biodiversity*. Scottish Executive, Edinburgh.

INDEX

Note: Page references for papers are **emboldened**. Most entries refer to *Scotland* unless otherwise indicated.

Printed by The Stationery Office, 6/01 c5